HANDBOOKS

MICHIGAN'S UPPER PENINSULA

PAUL VACHON

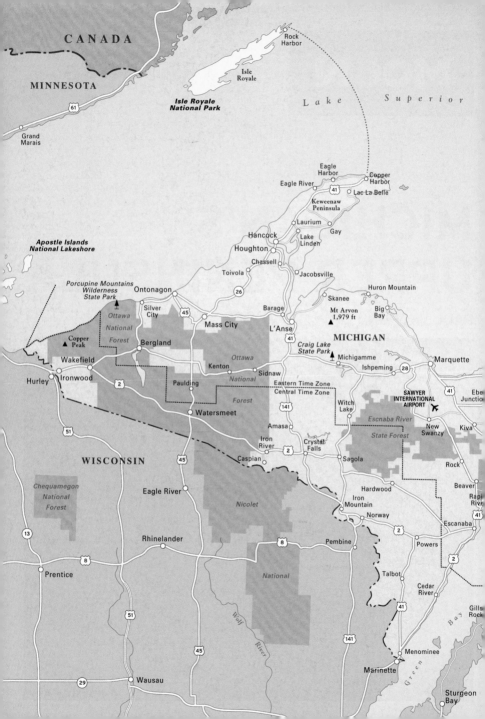

Contents

Discover Michigan's Upper Peninsula

Welcome to the other Michigan.

While Lower Michigan is a blend of urban and rural, superhighways and rolling hills, the landscape of the Upper Peninsula contrasts starkly. Flat farmland gives way to ancient boreal forests, hundreds of waterfalls, and thousands of miles of shoreline – all waiting to be explored by travelers hungry for adventure. The U.P. is sequestered on three sides by a crystal blue waterscape: Lakes Superior, Michigan, and Huron offer countless opportunities for boating, fishing, and even scuba diving to mysterious shipwrecks. (Yes, scuba diving in Michigan!) You'll stumble on an extensive chain of rustic campgrounds and lush green parks, transformed in winter by virgin white snow and seemingly endless ski and snowmobile trails.

Many come to the U.P. seeking solitude – with a population density of only nineteen people per square mile, Michigan's extreme north has plenty of it. The dense urban centers of Lower Michigan are replaced with tiny communities proudly sporting their unique traditions. Pockets of the U.P. hold strong ties to the mining and auto industries, with the historical impact still visible today. The diverse ethnic culture can be absorbed through the art, music, and the food: Enjoy meatballs at a Swedish café, homemade raviolis at an Italian eatery, or try a Cornish pasty

(a bread turnover filled with pork, chicken, or venison), a regional favorite. The blend of heritage and warm hospitality makes stops in small towns — of which there is no shortage — a mind-expanding experience.

U.P. residents also reflect a diversity of regional identifications, with those in the eastern half relating more to the Lower Peninsula (think the Detroit Tigers and Lions) and "uplanders," natives of the western half, being partial to Wisconsin (the Milwaukee Brewers and Green Bay Packers). Beyond sports loyalties, regional differences can be heard in the speech patterns of the locals — the "Yooper dialect" of the western U.P. is hard to miss, featuring heavy Scandinavian and German influences.

The Upper Peninsula is for a different type of traveler: One who is looking for something out of the ordinary; one who appreciates nature at its most pristine, but also one who values adventure — found in the thrill of a waterfall hike or the mystery of a secluded ghost town.

If you're up for it, the other Michigan may be just what you're looking for.

Planning Your Trip

► WHERE TO GO

The Straits of Mackinac

As the only physical connection between the two peninsulas, all the traffic from the Lower Peninsula funnels into the five-mile-long Mackinac Bridge and into the great north. It's here where many travelers decide to stop. Picturesque Mackinac Island is one of America's more perfect getaways, while historic sites and state parks both on and off the island bring the region's long history to life. For some unforgettable exposure to this, visit Colonial Michilimackinac in Mackinaw City and Fort Mackinac on the island.

Escanaba and the Lake Michigan Shore

The Lake Michigan shoreline makes for a pleasant drive with many worthy stops along the way. Sandy beaches off U.S. 2 invite travelers to pull over and wade into the water. Head south into the Garden Peninsula, where Fayette Historic State Park memorializes the region's mining history. Detour south into Escanaba and Menominee, two of the Upper Peninsula's largest cities—each filled with its own unique charm. An old mining town, Escanaba has seen better days, but don't let that keep you from the city's pleasant waterfront; tour the Sand Point Lighthouse and spend time in Ludington Park.

The Superior Upland

The western U.P. is best known for downhill skiing and Porcupine Mountain National Park (aka "the Porkies"). The area's relatively mountainous terrain and extreme levels of snowfall combine to make Ironwood and its environs the top downhill ski destination

IF YOU HAVE . . .

- **THREE DAYS:** Visit Mackinac Island, Whitefish Bay, and the Soo Locks.
- **FIVE DAYS:** Add the historic Fayette Townsite and Big and Little Bays de Noc.
- **ONE WEEK:** Add a few nights of camping in the Hiawatha National Forest.
- **TWO WEEKS:** Continue your local adventures in nature by camping and hiking on Grand Island and taking in Pictured Rocks National Lakeshore. Get a taste of U.P. city life by stopping in Marquette.
- **THREE WEEKS:** Head up the Keweenaw to see the old mining towns. Leave Copper Harbor for Isle Royale for an unforgettable wilderness experience. Top it off with a scenic drive through the Porcupine Mountains and iron country.

beautiful rapids on the Presque Isle River at Porcupine Mountains State Park

Houghton

in the Midwest. Hit up Ski Brule, Big Powderhorn Mountain, or Blackjack Ski Resort. There's downhill skiing in the Porkies as well, but the real draw are the miles and miles of hiking trails that wind through the pristine wilderness. When it comes to outdoor pursuits, only Isle Royale National Park surpasses the Porkies.

Keeweenaw Peninsula and Isle Royale

Copper Harbor, at the top of the Keeweenaw Peninsula, has a well deserved reputation as the end of the road in Michigan. Stop in the twin cities of Houghton and Hancock on your way through. Enjoy a beer at The Library pub or tour the Quincy Mine. You

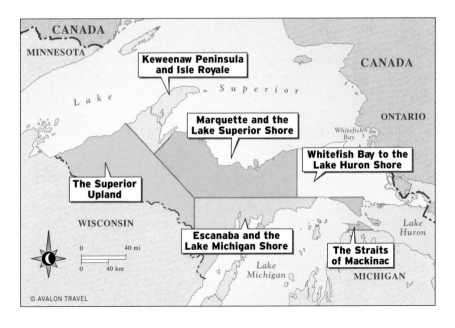

may also want to stop at the quaint, historic town of Calumet.

The island of Isle Royale would be Michigan's true end of the road if it were part of the mainland. The rugged Isle Royale National Park can be reached only by boat or plane. While there, hike or paddle and watch for reclusive moose and wolves.

Marquette and the Lake Superior Shore

Lake Superior provides some of the nation's most beautiful scenery: tough pine, stony beaches, and craggy rocks carved into a dramatic panorama by relentless waves. Rent a sea kayak to get a proper look at the unique natural formations of the famous Pictured Rocks National Lakeshore. Spend time in Marquette, checking out the city's vibrant arts scene, historic downtown, and Presque Isle Park. Visit Munising, a darling town located on a picturesque bay. Take the ferry to Grand Island or reserve a spot on a Pictured Rocks boat cruise.

Whitefish Bay to the Lake Huron Shore

Whitefish Bay offers natural protection from Lake Superior's wildly inclement weather. The bay drains south into the St. Mary's River like

view of Lake Superior from Pictured Rocks National Lakeshore

a giant funnel, guiding ships through the Soo Locks that connect Lakes Superior and Huron, providing the Great Lakes with an essential shipping lane. A visit to the Soo Locks is a must while visiting Sault Ste. Marie, a dynamic city, second only to Marquette in population and perhaps in popularity. On the shore of Lake Huron, Les Cheneaux and Drummond Island are remote, quiet destinations forgotten by tourists and perfect for secluded relaxation.

▶ WHEN TO GO

Summers can get exceedingly hot and humid—although this is when nature is at its most vibrant. Backwoods campers, hikers, mountain bikers, sea kayakers, and fishermen descend on the Upper Peninsula during June, July, and August. Hotel rates generally are highest on the weekends of July 4 and Labor Day, and moderately lower outside the traditional tourist season.

In autumn, the Upper Peninsula is at its most beautiful. Nights cool down to a pleasant chill and the turning leaves color the forests in brilliant combinations of reds and yellows. Days become less humid, less hot, and less crowded than during the peak summer season. Many customary summertime pursuits are more appealing after the heat leaves and before the long winter arrives. You can hike the same trails, fish the same streams, and camp at the same sites,

FALL COLORS

Fall brings a stunning canopy of color to the U.P.

Planning a fall color tour of Michigan's Upper Peninsula can be tricky, as the timing of peak colors is often unpredictable. Often one of two things will happen: you'll arrive a week early and be met with a landscape of midsummer green, or you'll come too late and be greeted by a sea of bare trees. But the fortunate (and perhaps the well-organized) traveler is in for a real treat. If your timing's right, all you need to enjoy the glory of countless trees in their peak color is the will to get outside, whether it's on a hiking trail, in a kayak along the shoreline, or in a car on one of the main highways.

One of the finest routes in the U.P. is the circle formed between **Eagle River** and **Copper Harbor** by U.S. 41 and M-26, an hour-long 45-mile loop. It may be the most beautiful hour of your life, especially the section along U.S. 41/Copper Country Trail Scenic Byway. Visit the Keweenaw from mid-September to early October to see the best colors. The **Marquette-Negaunee-Au Train tour** will take you into the Huron Mountains on the way to Big Bay and back, as well as on a wider loop south and east of the city along M-35, U.S. 41, M-94, and M-28. There is a trail that follows Lake Michigan from Menominee through Escanaba and on toward Manistique, and another that includes Sault Ste. Marie, Drummond Island, and Hessel. **Pure Michigan** (www.michigan.org) lists eight Upper Peninsula color trails on their website, including stops along the way and detailed maps for each tour.

but they're now tinted by the changing deciduous colors.

In winter, much of the U.P. is covered in snow, making it an ideal destination for downhill and cross-country skiing, snowshoeing, and snowmobiling. The western U.P. is well suited for winter recreation, with a handful of ski resorts and miles of cross-country ski and snowmobile trails. Double-check with your host while planning a winter trip since some accommodations and restaurants do close down for the winter.

Spring days tend to be overcast or rainy. Snow often lingers until April, while the trails

Tunnel Road above Houghton

get soggy and muddy, and the temperature can be chilly. On the other hand, it can be particularly impressive to watch the magnificent transition of seasons. Snowmelt overfills the rivers and streams, making this season especially attractive to waterfall watchers.

▶ BEFORE YOU GO

Transportation

The Upper Peninsula is accessible by any manner of transportation: plane, boat, bus, bike, snowmobile, and foot. Once there, however, a car is a virtual necessity. Public transportation is scarce, and is mostly limited to occasional stops between the bigger cities. The U.P. is much larger than most people assume. It can take several hours to drive from one city to the next. If you have any intention of getting off the major roads, a four-wheel drive vehicle with a high clearance is *highly* recommended.

What to Take

The best way to see the U.P. is to pack a tent and other necessities and travel from campsite to campsite across the peninsula. Be sure to get the outdoors staples: bug spray, sturdy shoes, and clothing for inclement weather. Take a small backpack for day trips or short hikes. You won't need dress clothes unless you're planning on dining at one of Marquette's finer restaurants or enjoying a formal dinner at the Grand Hotel (*several* places on the island have dress codes).

It is a good idea to get a Michigan State Park sticker ahead of time. This annual pass will allow you easy access to even the most popular sites. If you plan to cross the International Bridge into Canada, be sure to pack your passport.

Explore Michigan's Upper Peninsula

▶ BEST OF MICHIGAN'S UPPER PENINSULA

When looked at on a map, the enormity of the Upper Peninsula can be deceptive. The unique qualities that give the U.P. its appeal are scattered over 30,000 square miles, 14 counties, and two times zones. Rustic hiking trails, breathtaking lake views, and charming small towns are interspersed between miles of two-lane highways and scores of abandoned iron and copper mines. But hours spent behind the wheel will pay off handsomely. The route on the map shown here will offer the most efficient way of limiting your driving time to segments of just a few hours while allowing you to take in as many attractions as possible.

The Evening Before

Chances are you'll be arriving in Mackinaw City, the gateway to the U.P., after a very long drive from home. Check into a comfortable hotel room; enjoy a meal at one of the local restaurants, and take a bit of time to explore downtown. A respite like this is the perfect tonic for early vacation fatigue—one you'll thank yourself for later on.

Day 1

Catch an early ferry to Mackinac Island (7:30 is the earliest). If you plan on spending just one day on the island, it's best to be a "commuter visitor" and return to your Mackinaw City lodgings at day's end. Visit Fort Mackinac, take a captivating carriage ride past the lovely Victorian cottages, and visit the Governor's Residence and the magnificent veranda at

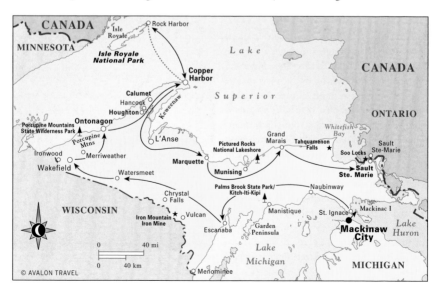

the Grand Hotel as seen from the veranda of the Governor's Residence

the Grand Hotel. Yes, they charge $15 for the veranda privilege but the experience is truly unforgettable. After lunch, take in a relaxing round of golf at Jewel or spend some time at Mackinac Island Butterfly House. If you have a sweet tooth, and few people don't, pick up a wedge or two of world-famous Mackinac Island fudge at either Murdick's or Ryba's—but don't overdo it!

Day 2

Set out early—you have a bit of a drive ahead of you. Cross the bridge, turn right and make a brief stop at Straits State Park. Here you can enjoy a breathtaking bridge view for the Upper Peninsula side and indulge your desire for scenic photographs. Begin heading west along U.S. 2. As you begin your trip from St. Ignace to Naubinway you'll be treated with a pleasing panorama of the Lake Michigan Shore, with St. Helena Island in the distance. There are many turnouts along this route, and with a good zoom lens and clear weather you can get a shot of the island's lighthouse. Continue on towards Manistique and stop for lunch at Clyde's Drive in No. 2 for a great burger and malt. After lunch, turn off

onto M-149 and head to Palms Brook State Park to see Kitch-Iti-Kipi, better known as "Big Spring." Continue on U.S. 2, ending your day's sojourn in Escanaba. Have dinner and stay the night at the historic House of Ludington.

Day 3

Continue west on U.S. 2 towards Iron River. Along the way you'll cross into the Central Time Zone and begin to see some of the rough terrain the U.P. is known for. This area was the heart of iron country during the heyday of mining. To learn about this historic period, visit the Iron Mountain Iron Mine near Vulcan. Afterwards get back on U.S. 2 and stop in Iron Mountain for lunch; either Romagnoli's Restaurant on North Stephenson if you appreciate good Italian fare (owing to the area's Italian heritage), or Famers on Pine Mountain Road if you'd prefer a sports bar atmosphere. Continue

aerial view of historic Mackinac Island during spring time

U.S. 45 runs from Ontonagon all the way to Mobile, Alabama.

west on U.S. 2, taking a brief detour into a corner of Wisconsin on the way to Crystal Falls. You're entering the Superior Uplands, the area of rough beauty known as iron country. Stop in Crystal Falls just long enough to admire the spectacular view looking down Main Street and take a picture of the highlands in the distance. Continue west along U.S. 2 until you come to Watersmeet. Book a room at the Lac Vieux Desert Resort Casino for a well deserved rest. After dinner at the Thunderbird Sports Lounge, make the short trek up U.S. 45 to view the baffling Paulding Mystery Light.

Day 4

Continue west on U.S. 2 stopping in Ironwood, a hardscrabble but friendly town that bills itself as "Michigan's Western Gateway." After lunch at the Hoop 'N' Holler Tavern in Merriweather which, believe it or not, is located on a road of the same name, take some time to tour the Old Depot Historical Museum on Lowell Street. The

lovely building is a Romanesque-style train station turned museum, featuring exhibits about the era of iron mining and the golden age of the railroads. As evening approaches, take M-505 into Wisconsin to get to Superior Falls, the terminus of the Montreal River and Michigan's most western point. From there, head just a bit east to Little Girl's Point on Lake Superior and take time to admire the dramatic sunset over Lake Superior. Priceless. Finally, head down to Wakefield along M-519, and check in at the Victorian-style Regal Country Inn.

Day 5

The most picturesque wilderness of the Upper Peninsula awaits you. After breakfast at the Regal Country Inn, pick up what you'll need for a picnic lunch and take M-519 north towards the Lake Superior shore. There you'll find the western end of Porcupine Mountains State Wilderness Park and the Presque Isle waterfalls. Head east and take M-107 up the large hill to Lake of the

Lake of the Clouds

Clouds Overlook. Park your car and take the very short hike up to the top of the cliff to take in the breathtaking view. Follow M-107 through the park, being careful of the frequent turns in the road. After exiting the park near Union Bay you'll find a series of scenic turnouts along the Lake Superior shore. Most have tables, so stop here to enjoy your picnic lunch and chat with some of your fellow travelers. After lunch, head to Ontonagon to take in the Ontonagon County Historical Museum, which offers a fascinating look at the community's past, with an emphasis on the logging and mining industries. The historical society also offers tours of the Ontonagon Lighthouse, an 1853 structure being gradually restored. Grab dinner at Syl's and get a cabin for the night at the Mountain View Lodges on M-64, featuring a waterfront view and a sandy beach.

Day 6

Adventure beckons! You'll be heading into the Keweenaw, as north as you can go and still be in mainland Michigan. From Ontonagon take U.S. 45 to M-26 and head north. As you

progress you'll see more pine and spruce trees mixed in with maples and elms. When you come to Houghton, a college town playing host to Michigan Technological University, stop and take a leisurely break, possibly at Cyberia Café, 800 Sharon Avenue, a internet café offering terrific java and the best cinnamon rolls you've ever tasted. Stop to view the unusual "lift bridge" linking the city to Hancock across the Keweenaw Waterway. The bridge functions much the same as a drawbridge, but instead of two sections of roadway elevating 90 degrees, the entire driving surface simply raises upward, allowing ships to pass. Continue north on U.S. 41 until you come to Calumet. Considered by some to be the capital of the once-dominant copper industry, Calumet is a city of magnificent, if somewhat neglected architecture flanked by abandoned mines. Take some time to breathe in the atmosphere. Looking around, you can almost see and hear the tireless workers of the past. Continue until you get to Copper Harbor, and the end of U.S. 41. Take a tour of the Copper Harbor Lighthouse, which involves a fun fifteen-minute boat ride from

the marina. Book a room at the Keweenaw Mountain Lodge.

Day 7

Take a well deserved break from all that driving. Shift into nautical mode and board the *Isle Royale Queen IV* for the three-hour tip to its namesake park, the least visited property in the National Park system. Although the park is very rugged and most visitors choose to camp, indoor accommodations are available at the Rock Harbor lodge at Rock Harbor at the far eastern tip. Either way, you'll have virtually unlimited opportunities to commune with nature.

Hiking, fishing, observing wildlife, and kayaking are some of the activities you can enjoy. Spend two to three days exploring Isle Royale—a truly unforgettable experience.

Days 8-9

You've got a couple of days on the island. If you stayed at the Rock Harbor Lodge, you won't want for things to do. Take a few more

Chippewa Harbor in Isle Royale National Park

day hikes along some of the shorter trails into the island—Scoville Point and Lookout Louise are good choices, and the view from Ojibway Tower is phenomenal. Look into a Park Service boat tour or rent a sea kayak and explore the shoreline yourself. Pack your lunches and take them with you, but note that dinners at the lodge are satisfying.

Backwoods campers and hikers will have 165 miles of trail to explore. There's no way to hike it all in a few days, but a well planned trip will have you walking from campsite to campsite while you keep a lookout for moose.

Day 10

Regardless of where you stayed last night, make sure you're back at the ferry dock by 2:45 P.M. for the ride back to Copper Harbor. You'll get into town a little before 6 P.M., just in time for dinner at the Harbor Haus, or start out for Marquette, which is about a three-hour drive. Complete your journey to Marquette, where you'll find numerous lodging choices along U.S. 41.

Day 11

Spend the morning in the Upper Peninsula's largest, most cosmopolitan city. An early morning stroll along the waterfront will be invigorating after plenty of time behind the wheel. Bring your camera so you can get some great shots of Marquette Harbor Lighthouse, a photogenic lighthouse on rocks and located a bit offshore. Children will have a blast at the U. P. Children's Museum where they can dig up some ore at the Wonderground exhibit or learn about nutrition at the Incredible Journey display. After lunch, set course on M-28 for Munising and Pictured Rocks National Lakeshore. Since they can only be seen from the water, either book a boat tour or kayak to gain an appreciation of these colorful cliffs. Stay the

Spray Falls plunges into Lake Superior at Pictured Rocks National Lakeshore.

night in Grand Marais. Renting one of the Hilltop Cabins will offer a great waterfront view.

Day 12

Get an early start and hit the road for Tahquamenon Falls, without a doubt the most magnanimous waterfall in the U.P. You can observe the upper falls from the observation deck, which is only a short trail walk from parking facilities. Four miles downstream, the lower falls produce a similar spectacle. The awe-inspiring power of the falls is hard to overstate. As much as 50,000 gallons of water per second cascade over upper Tahquamenon, the second most powerful waterfall in the eastern U.S., exceeded only by Niagara. Enjoy lunch at the Tahquamenon Falls Brewery and Pub before setting out for Sault Ste. Marie. Take a boat tour through the always fascinating Soo Locks and marvel at how the gargantuan ships can transit though the locks with just inches to spare. Cap off your adventure with a special dinner at Freighters. Check in at the Ojibwa Hotel for the night before departing for home.

tugboats leaving the Locks

► ECHOES OF THE *EDMUND FITZGERALD*

Without a doubt, one of the most popular highlights of the Upper Peninsula is history, both military and maritime, especially as it relates to the tragic story of the *Edmund Fitzgerald*, the mighty ore freighter that succumbed to Lake Superior in 1975. Devoting your time to exploring these places can be a great deal of fun and intellectually stimulating at the same time. Don't forget your camera!

Day 1

Begin by checking into Mackinaw City's Parkside Inn Bridgeview just across from Fort Michilimackinac (doing so the evening before would be best). Take your time exploring the fort, which portrays as accurately as possible how the British military lived and worked during the 1770s, complete with costumed interpreters. Be sure to stay long enough to see the musket and/or cannon firings. Stop for lunch at Darrow's Family Restaurant and then head over to Old Mackinac Point Lighthouse to see how this beautifully restored facility operated during the late 19th century. Next is the Icebreaker Mackinaw Maritime Museum, housed aboard the *Mackinaw,* the behemoth of an ice breaker that spent over six decades clearing paths for Great Lakes freighters. Finish with dinner at the Dixie Saloon. If you have time afterward, drive over to McGulpin's Point Lighthouse, recently opened to the public.

Day 2

Grab an early ferry to Mackinac Island for a day of unique sightseeing. First stop (and a must on any sojourn to the island) is Fort Mackinac, the successor to its counterpart on the mainland. Here you'll find a meticulously restored 19th century fort demonstrating how both officers and enlisted men lived

McGulpin's Point Lighthouse

MUSH! DOGSLEDDING IN THE U.P.

The U.P. 200

The art and sport of mushing has become a growing pastime in places like Colorado's Rocky Mountains. In Alaska, it's been a wintertime favorite for decades. And in recent years, the sport has arrived in the U.P. Thanks in part to the popularity of the **U.P. 200,** a mid-February sled dog race that begins and ends in Marquette, sled dog excursions have become a midwinter tradition. Watching the race is fun, but taking the leap from spectator to participant is truly a unique experience. Contact one of the Upper Peninsula's kennels to see about taking a full-, half-, or multi-day trip. Contact **Triple Creek Sled Dog Kennels** (E5372 M-94, Munising, 877/275-7533) to arrange for a guided trip across the winter landscape.

during the period. Musket firings are done with actual Civil War era rifles. The cannon demonstrations produce an echo that can be heard for miles! After the excitement, enjoy lunch at the Tea Room, located in what was once the officer's quarters. After lunch, take in an informative carriage ride provided by Arrowhead Carriages. The trip give you a great overview of the island's history, including stories about the palatial "cottages" along the East Bluff, Ste. Anne's Church, and John Jacob Astor's fur trading empire. After having such a full day, treat yourself to night at the Grand Hotel. If you travel in the spring or fall, try to get in on their Bed-and-Breakfast Special—offering a considerable discount off the regular rates.

Day 3

After enjoying a very sumptuous breakfast at

Fort Mackinac maintains a towering presence over the village below.

the Grand, take in a tour of the Governor's Residence just down the way. After it served as a private home, the State of Michigan purchased the house during the 1940s to make it the governor's summer residence. It continues to do so today, along with the tradition of each governor adding his or her own personal touch to the home's decor. After your tour, rent either a bike or (if you really want to honor history) a horse and follow Lakeshore Drive around the perimeter of the island. You'll love the feeling of the wind in your hair and the calming view of the straits. Stop at the historical marker for the British Landing, the spot where the enemy came ashore during the War of 1812 and retook Fort Mackinac, only because the Americans didn't yet know there was a war on. Afterward, have a quick lunch, grab your luggage, and catch a ferry for the mainland. Find your car, cross the Mighty Mac bridge and head for Whitefish Point, a short ride up M-123. Book a room at the aptly named Paradise Inn, located in its namesake town.

Day 4

Take a brief break from all that history and make a detour to Tahquamenon Falls, the

Tahquamenon Falls in autumn

grandest waterfall in the Upper Peninsula. Both the Upper and Lower falls are spellbinding sights—with the Upper ranking second only to Niagara Falls in water volume. Note the unusual bronze like color of the water—caused by the decomposition of fallen hemlock and cedar trees. After lunch at the Tahquamenon Falls Brewery and Pub, make the short trip up to Whitefish Point to visit the Great Lakes Shipwreck Museum.

The informative yet somber museum tells the story of some of the most infamous maritime disasters on the Great Lakes. Most noteworthy is the space devoted to the *Edmund Fitzgerald,* an ore carrier that met its demise during a violent storm on Lake Superior in 1975. The exhibit includes a scale model of the ship, a life preserver, and the ship's bell, recovered during a salvage expedition. A film about the dive is also offered, along with an enjoyable gift shop. After dinner, spend another night in Paradise.

Day 5

After breakfast, set out for Sault Ste. Marie, which plays host to the Soo Locks and Michigan's oldest city. The massive locks allow ships to traverse between Lakes Superior and Huron. The best way to appreciate these marvels of engineering is by taking the ever popular Soo Lock Boat Tour, which will raise and lower your tour boat some twenty feet in a matter of minutes. You might just share space with an aging Great Lakes freighter or an oceangoing "salty." Have a good budget-style lunch at Antler's Family Restaurant and follow up your locks tour by visiting the River of History Museum. The museum is devoted to area's heritage going back to the Ojibwa, through the period of the French fur trappers and the era of the American Revolution through the prism of the St. Mary's River. Cap off your day

with a delicious meal at Freighters, located in the Ojibwa Hotel with a splendid view of the locks. Since you're dining there anyway, spend the night at the Ojibwa.

Day 6

Top off your adventure with some excitement across the border. Get in your car and cross the International Bridge, gateway to Canada and to Sault Ste. Marie, Ontario. You'll find plenty to do over here; the Bushplane Heritage Centre, plus the *Norgoma,* the last passenger ship to be constructed for cruise on the Great Lakes. Built to transport up to 100 passengers, the vessel is now a museum to a bygone maritime era. Ticket proceeds fund further restoration of the ship.

Time to plot a course for home, but after this tour you're sure to look at this slice of northern Michigan with a newfound curiosity!

Watch the massive ships go by in Sault Ste. Marie.

▶ WEEKEND GETAWAY: MACKINAC ISLAND AND BEYOND

To the uninitiated, the Upper Peninsula's deceptively large size can come as a shock. Visiting the U.P. with too little time can be a real disappointment. The solution? A well-planned weekend getaway! If you have only a few days and are arriving from the Lower Peninsula, follow this plan to take in the highlights of the eastern U.P. And don't look at the odometer!

Horses are the only form of transportation allowed on Mackinac Island.

Day 1

Arrive at night and stay at the Boardwalk Inn in St. Ignace. Start your first day with the complementary breakfast, then take Shepler's ferry to Mackinac Island to visit Fort Mackinac and the Governor's Residence. Get a lay of the land with a leisurely carriage tour past the Grand Hotel, St. Anne's Cemetery, and Skull Cave. If you're more athletically inclined, rent bicycles from Ryba's and go on a power ride along Lakeshore Drive, which rings the island's perimeter. Grab a quick dinner on Main Street, catch the ferry back to St. Ignace and top it off by taking in a sunset cruise on the Star Line, which offers a narrated tour of the lighthouses at Mackinaw Point and on Round Island, and culminates with a view of the Lake Michigan sunset.

Day 2

After breakfast, head out early, heading north on I-75 until coming to U.S. 134. Continue on to DeTour Village—as far east as you can go on the mainland peninsula. After strolling through the frozen in time hamlet, catch the ferry to Drummond Island for a relaxing 18 holes at The Rock on South Maxon Road. Head back to DeTour for a sumptuous meal at the Port of Call restaurant. Book a night's stay at the Spring Lodge Cottages

Sherman Park, Sault Ste. Marie

SHIPWRECK DIVES

When the weather is warmer, you can spend some time beneath the surface of the Great Lakes, diving among its numerous shipwrecks. Lake Superior is home to scores of wrecks, as it is known to harbor a menacing anger against the ships that have plied its waters. Today, many of these wrecks are waiting beneath the surface at five underwater diving preserves.

Dive with scuba gear and full wetsuits (these waters are cold, especially well below the surface) at preserves in Alger, Whitefish Point, Marquette, Keweenaw, and the Straits of Mackinac. One of the finest is **Alger Underwater Preserve,** which features the wreckage of seven ships at depths ranging from 12 to 105 feet. The Straits of Mackinac Shipwreck Preserve has 15 wrecks, but they're spread farther apart than in Alger, and they tend to be deeper – with some in excess of 200 feet below the surface.

Exploring Lake Superior shipwrecks is a great activity for the more courageous tourist.

in Les Cheneaux, which offer a tranquil view of the water.

Day 3

After breakfast at Fisher's Restaurant in DeTour, continue on I-75 to Sault Ste. Marie, Michigan's oldest city. Although there's plenty to do here, you'll certainly be able to satisfy your curiosity—and spend a whole day—taking in the majestic locks. Begin at the visitors center to learn about this marvel of engineering before boarding one of the new luncheon cruises offered through Soo Lock Boat Tours, where you can enjoy a buffet lunch while experiencing the transition between Lakes Superior and Huron. After the cruise, cross over the International Bridge to Sault Ste. Marie, Ontario, and visit the interesting Bushplane Heritage Centre. After an exciting afternoon, return to the American side for dinner at Freighters, and enjoy the panoramic view

of the locks. Check into the storied Ojibway Hotel for a good night's rest.

Day 4

Begin your day, appropriately, at the Cup of the Day on Ashmun Street for a good strong shot of caffeine along with a hearty breakfast. Take M-28 west to M-123 north before reaching Tahquamenon Falls State Park, home to what is arguably one of the most beautiful waterfalls in North America. Plan on experiencing the falls up close and personal—either by hiking the nearby trails or by canoeing the Tahquamenon River. It's an experience you won't soon forget. From the park, check into the Paradise Inn, located in its namesake town. Spend an afternoon unwinding, have a delightful meal at the Tahquamenon Falls Brewery and Pub before retiring for the evening. And don't forget to make plans for next year.

THE STRAITS OF MACKINAC

The Straits of Mackinac have long separated the "Yoopers" from the "Trolls." Yoopers get their nickname from the U.P. (as in, "U.P.-ers"), while "Trolls" is their good-natured name for Michiganians who live to the south, "under the bridge."

Five miles wide at their narrowest point, the Straits are largely responsible for the Upper Peninsula's profound isolation. Before the completion of the Mackinac Bridge in 1957, passenger cars waited in miles-long lines for a spot on one of the ferries that crossed the Straits each day. Now, thanks to the bridge, the only ferries are headed for Mackinac Island, occasionally offering a side trip to the bridge for tourists to catch a glimpse of its underside.

If the Mackinac Bridge is how tourists bypass the Straits, then Mackinac Island is why they come. Resting strategically in the middle of the Straits, between Lake Michigan and Lake Huron, between the Upper and Lower Peninsulas, the island has been a favorite destination since it became Mackinac National Park in 1875—the United States's second national park, after Yellowstone. The park, which has since been transferred to state control, covers some 80 percent of the island.

Visitors to the island will notice a conspicuous lack of automobiles; they've been banned since the 1920s. As a result, Mackinac Island really does seem frozen *Somewhere in Time,* which just happens to be the name of a semi-famous movie, starring Christopher Reeve and Jane Seymour, that was filmed on the island. The Victorian atmosphere draws families, romantics, history buffs and anyone

© PAUL VACHON

HIGHLIGHTS

◖ Mackinac Island Butterfly House: A delightful place where you can be entertained by hundreds of butterflies amidst a wide variety of geraniums (page 31).

◖ Fudge: Fudge wasn't invented on the island, but it has since become its most popular confection. But is it really all that good? Yoobetcha (page 31).

◖ Grand Hotel: The 1887 hotel is the most famous in all of Michigan, with 385 guest rooms and the world's longest front porch. Jane Seymour circa 1980 didn't hurt, either (page 32).

◖ Fort Mackinac: British and American troops fought over the fort during the War of 1812. Today, Fort Mackinac's costumed interpreters bring its glory days to life (page 33).

◖ Lilac Festival: Of all the times to visit Mackinac Island, this 10-day festival in early June is the best (page 36).

◖ Mackinac Bridge: Drive across Michigan's pride and joy, the five-mile long "Mighty Mac" suspension bridge or stop at Mackinac Bridge View Park to take pictures of this amazing feat of engineering (page 42).

◖ Colonial Michilimackinac State Park: The site of the original fort, built in 1715, is the location of a 50-year-long archaeological dig, summertime reenactments, and a big, wooden, stockade replica fort (page 54).

◖ McGulpin's Point Lighthouse: A lighthouse reopened to the public after decades as a private residence. Still a work in progress, but the restoration efforts completed so far are first rate (page 55).

LOOK FOR **◖** TO FIND RECOMMENDED SIGHTS, ACTIVITIES, DINING, AND LODGING.

looking for a good old-fashioned horse-and-buggy taxi ride.

Oh, and try not to be offended when you hear locals refer to you as a "Fudgie," probably under their breath, but usually in good humor. While fudge wasn't invented on Mackinac, the island has since become famous for it—and then some. Odds are you'll be buying at least one sliver of fudge while you're here, which is why residents have dubbed you and

the millions of other visitors with the endearing nickname. Get used to it, it comes with the territory.

St. Ignace in the U.P. and Mackinaw City in the Lower Peninsula bookend the bridge and have carved out reputations worthy of the high traffic passing through. Stop in Mackinaw for the fudge, St. Ignace for the auto shows, and both for the history. Museums in each city interpret the region's distinct history, ranging from

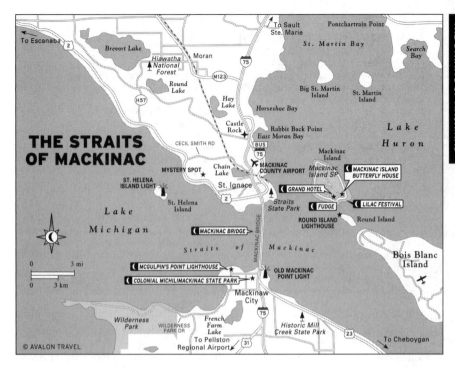

the era of native peoples to today. Noteworthy too is the cultural juxtaposition. Despite being small, Mackinaw City gives off a slightly urban, if still northerly feel. In St. Ignace a more rural texture becomes dominate.

Travelers looking for a good base for hub-and-spoke day trips to other U.P. locations can take advantage of the area's copious lodging and restaurants. Of course, if you're coming to the Straits, a word to the wise: Regardless of how it's spelled, it's pronounced "MACK-i-*naw*," never "MACK-i-*nack*."

PLANNING YOUR TIME

Travelers coming north across the bridge have no choice but to pass through the cities on either end of the five-mile stretch. Sure, you may be on the way to Copper Harbor for some kayaking or driving west for Ironwood's downhill skiing, but it's worth your time to get off the

highway and spend some time in the Straits, perhaps the most picturesque location in all of Michigan.

Although two days will be enough time to see the best of the Straits, the region's natural beauty and Mackinac Island's unique atmosphere often entice people to stay longer. Plan on spending a full day on the island. Lodging tends to be cheaper on the mainland, but if you don't mind digging a little deeper into the pocketbook, a stay on Mackinac (particularly at the costly Grand Hotel) is worth it. Mackinaw City and St. Ignace can both be tackled in a single day.

Summers are the busiest (and the best) season for visiting, and Mackinac Island draws the largest crowd, while St. Ignace tends to be best for outdoor activities. If you're interested in the area's history, you'll want to make an afternoon of Mackinaw City's historical sites.

THE FRENCH FUR TRADE

In the beginning, the economy of New France was driven in large part by the fur trade. European demand for animal pelts combined with the abundance of New World animal life – particularly the beaver – created a nearly perfect arrangement of supply and demand. But the fur trade didn't just open up the cash flow – it helped spur Canada's westward expansion.

The fur trade was a highly regulated business at first, but before too long, illegal traders, known as *coureurs de bois* or "runners of the woods," traveled away from the settlements and deep into Native American territory, where they traded European goods like rifles, blankets, and fishing gear for canoe-loads of fur. The *coureurs* traded, worked, and lived among the native peoples, often marrying native women and integrat-ing into their communities. They learned the skills necessary to survive in the wilderness and they adopted native clothing, food, and transportation.

Not much time passed before the French government realized that the unchecked illegal fur trade was bad for business, so they created a system of permits to separate legal *coureurs*, called *voyageurs*, from illegal ones. The *voyageurs* worked as laborers, interpreters, and guides, pushing deeper and deeper into the continent, taking New France with them.

It was the push by these fur traders that, along with Jesuit missionaries, greatly accelerated the expansion of France's territory; they've since become legendary folk heroes, particularly in French Canada.

HISTORY

Native Americans knew of the abundant hunting and fishing resources in the Straits area long before the French or British arrived. Originally called Michilimackinac (Land of the Great Turtle), the island was considered sacred by the Anishinaabe-Ojibwe, who thought it was populated by Earth's first people and was the home of the Great Spirit Gitchie Manitou. In addition to using the island as a tribal gathering place, Ojibwa, Ottawa, and other tribes hunted on Mackinac Island and neighboring Bois Blanc Island. They did a good job of it, too, trading some of their catch to tribes farther south in exchange for vegetables and grain.

The French soon entered the picture. The first Europeans to visit the area were French Jesuits who arrived in the 1670s to both take advantage of the fur trade and convert the Native Americans to Christianity. Jacques Marquette, a priest and an explorer, founded a town and mission at St. Ignace in 1671, naming it after the founder of the Society of Jesus, Saint Ignatius of Loyola. It was quickly followed by a trading post and later Fort Michilimackinac. The British and French skirmished over the land, with the fort periodically changing hands between them until the Treaty of Paris gave it—and all French land east of the Mississippi—to the British in 1763. Seven years later, the British commander abandoned the fort for a more easily defendable position on Mackinac Island, where the British would overstay their welcome even after the land was given to the United States after the American Revolution.

American soldiers took over Fort Mackinac in 1796 and managed to hang on to it for almost twenty years. Enter the War of 1812. The British retook the fort by sneaking onto the island at night and surprising the American soldiers, who turned over the fort without a fight. The British ran the fortification for two years, despite repeated American assaults aimed at retaking the fort; in 1814 the Treaty of Ghent returned the island to the United States.

Throughout it all, the fur trade formed the foundation of the area's economy. Europeans traded canoe-loads of goods for pelts from beaver and other animals that had been trapped by the Native Americans. Mackinac Island became one of the country's most valuable trading posts during the 1820s, making way for

America's first millionaire, John Jacob Astor. His American Fur Company was the leader in Mackinac's thriving fur trade. Eventually, the trade in overhunted furs gave way to commercial fishing.

After the military skirmishes ended, the island began earning a reputation as one of the Victorian era's most popular and fashionable resort areas. An American soldier wrote, "The air up here is so healthy, you have to go somewhere else to die." The vacation spot grew more and more famous, drawing vacationers from the Midwest and beyond. A growing interest during the second half of the 19th century culminated in the 1890s as lumber barons, railroad magnates, and other wealthy Americans began building large, sumptuous cottages on the island, many of which still stand today and can be viewed on one of the many carriage tours offered to visitors.

Cars were banned on the island in the 1920s, and things have more or less stayed the same ever since. Around 600 horses serve visitors in the summertime, though that number dwindles to just a few dozen in the winter, when most stay on the mainland. The horses, carriages, carts, and well-kept Victorian homes and hotels combine to give Mackinac its timeless charm, and have made it one of the most popular vacation destinations in the Midwest.

Mackinac Island

During its peak tourism season, Mackinac Island draws some 15,000 people each day, and you'll want to prioritize it as one of the Upper Peninsula's quintessential destinations. There's plenty of history on this little island: Native Americans, French traders, and British soldiers eventually gave way to Victorian resorts. By design, the island today displays little evidence of the contemporary world. Fort Mackinac stands above a town that really does seem frozen in time.

Much of the downtown area can feel overly touristy —and a little kitschy and crowded, but there are plenty of treasures here for those willing to spend some time looking. Most of the island—80 percent of it—is undeveloped state land, much of which adjoins commercial areas within just a block or two of downtown. Getting away from showy commercialism is easy.

SIGHTS
Downtown
Your ferry trip across the Straits ends at the docks. If you decide to linger a while, you can get a taste of the necessary "heavy lifting" that keeps of Mackinac Island running. At the Arnold Line Dock, you can sneak a peek at workers unloading cartons of vegetables from the ferry and reloading them by hand onto drays (wagons) for delivery to local restaurants. A horsedrawn wagon pulls huge bales of hay to feed the island's numerous equines. Even the UPS carriers do their routes on bicycle, pulling carts loaded with packages.

After spending a little time at the four blocks of shops and restaurants on Main Street, make the most of your visit by getting off the main drag. For an overview of what the island has to offer, take a carriage tour with **Mackinac Island Carriage Tours** (906/847-3307, www.mict.com, $23.50 adults, $9 children), located across from the Arnold Line ferry dock next to the chamber of commerce. The pleasant narrated tour takes about 1.75 hours, rambling along at a relaxing pace past the Grand Hotel, Arch Rock, Skull Cave, Fort Mackinac, and most of the island's other key sites. This locally owned business is the world's largest horse-and-buggy livery, with more than 300 horses, mostly crosses of beefy Percherons, Belgians, and Clydesdales. Seasonal peak hours (mid-June through Labor Day) are from 9 A.M.–5 P.M., with slightly shorter hours from early May to mid-June and after Labor Day through the end of October, weather permitting.

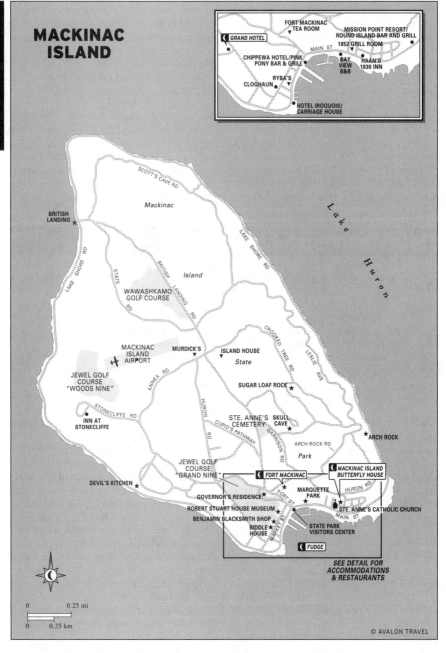

MACKINAC ISLAND

FORT MACKINAC
TEA ROOM

GRAND HOTEL

MISSION POINT RESORT/
ROUND ISLAND BAR AND GRILL
1852 GRILL ROOM

MAIN ST

CHIPPEWA HOTEL/PINK
PONY BAR & GRILL

BAY
VIEW
B&B

HAAN'S
1830 INN

RYBA'S
CLOGHAUN

HOTEL IROQUOIS/
CARRIAGE HOUSE

SCOTT'S CAVE RD

Mackinac

BRITISH
LANDING

Lake

LAKE SHORE RD

Huron

STATE RD

BRITISH LANDING RD

LAKE SHORE RD

Island

WAWASHKAMO
GOLF COURSE

CROOKED TREE RD

MACKINAC
ISLAND
AIRPORT

MURDICK'S

ISLAND HOUSE

LESLIE AVE

State

JEWEL GOLF
COURSE
"WOODS NINE"

ANNEX RD

SUGAR LOAF ROCK

STONECLIFFE RD

INN AT
STONECLIFFE

HURON RD

CUPID'S PATHWAY

STE. ANNE'S
CEMETERY

SKULL
CAVE

GARRISON RD

ARCH ROCK RD

ARCH ROCK

Park

JEWEL GOLF
COURSE
"GRAND NINE"

FORT MACKINAC

MACKINAC ISLAND
BUTTERFLY HOUSE

DEVIL'S KITCHEN

GOVERNOR'S RESIDENCE

FORT ST

MARQUETTE
PARK

HURON RD

ROBERT STUART HOUSE MUSEUM
BENJAMIN BLACKSMITH SHOP

STE. ANNE'S CATHOLIC CHURCH

MAIN ST

BIDDLE
HOUSE

MARKET ST

STATE PARK
VISITORS CENTER

FUDGE

SEE DETAIL FOR
ACCOMMODATIONS
& RESTAURANTS

0   0.25 mi

0   0.25 km

© AVALON TRAVEL

One block inland from Main, some of Mackinac's original residences line up on **Market Street.** Much quieter than frenetic Main, Market has several interesting stops for visitors. The headquarters of the American Fur Company, John Jacob Astor's empire, is now the **Robert Stuart House Museum** (906/847-3307, May–Oct., donations appreciated). The 1817 building retains many of its original furnishings, including fur company ledgers, fur weighing scales, and other artifacts.

A block west, knowledgeable interpreters demonstrate spinning at **Biddle House** and smithing at the **Benjamin Blacksmith Shop.** These and other historic buildings are part of the state park, and are included with the admission ticket to Fort Mackinac. They have shorter hours than the fort, though, open from 11 A.M.–6 P.M. For current information, stop by the park visitors center across from Marquette Park on Huron Street, or contact Mackinac State Historic Parks (231/436-4100, www.mackinacparks.com).

Work your way down one of the sets of public steps to the lakefront, where Main Street becomes Huron Street. Continue your walk east, passing smaller but no less appealing cottages and homes. Many are skirted with geraniums and lilacs, the island's signature flowers, and boast a stunning view of the Straits.

(MACKINAC ISLAND BUTTERFLY HOUSE

Tucked away on McGulpin Street, the Mackinac Island Butterfly House (906/847-3972, www.originalbutterflyhouse.com, 10 A.M.–7 P.M. during the summer months and 10 A.M.–6 P.M. Labor Day–Memorial Day, though hours of operation may vary from year to year; $8.50 adults, $4 children) is a true delight. Owner Doug Beardsley used to use his greenhouses to grow thousands of geraniums for the Grand Hotel and other clients. He relied on biodynamic growing methods, releasing beneficial insects to care for his plants instead of using chemical sprays. When economics made his small greenhouse less viable,

he stuck with his insects. After hearing about a butterfly house in Europe, Beardsley added some different plants and began ordering pupae from around the world. Now hundreds of butterflies flutter freely in his greenhouse/atrium, some nearly six inches long. You can observe them up close on walls and plants, or sit still long enough and they'll land on your knee—both an unusual and delightful experience.

(FUDGE

You knew it was coming. Sooner or later you'll succumb to Mackinac Island's famous fudge. A visitor treat since Victorian tourism days, the confection can be found in shops lining Main Street. Two of the oldest, **Murdick's** (906/847-3530, http://mackinac.murdicks.comm, 9 A.M.–10 P.M.) and **Ryba's** (906/847-4065, www.ryba.com, 9 A.M.–10 P.M.) have multiple island locations. You can buy a sizeable slab to take or mail home, or just a small sliver to nibble. Both stores also accept phone orders and will ship virtually anywhere. A little goes a long way—it's very rich stuff, and you'll regret it later if you overdo it.

GOVERNOR'S RESIDENCE

From Marquette Park, follow Fort Street up the hill to the Governor's Residence at the corner of Fort and East Bluff Road. The state purchased the "cottage" in the 1940s. It's the official summer residence of Michigan's chief executive, though different governors spend varying amounts of time here. The house is open for tours on Wednesday mornings until mid-August, except when the governor is in residence. Photography is not permitted inside the house.

Some of the island's more impressive "cottages" line up along **East Bluff.** Wander east from the governor's mansion to see some of these Victorian marvels. Fortunately, most survived the Depression era—when they could be purchased for pennies on the dollar, of course. Today, they're well cared for and worth more than $1 million. And remember, most are only summer homes as they lack central heat!

MACKINAC ISLAND FUDGE

Mackinac's most famous sweet wasn't invented on the island at all. No one is really sure exactly how it happened, but it's commonly accepted that the sugary goodness was the result of a screwed up, or "fudged," batch of caramels.

Fudge was first made on the island in the late 1800s by Newton Jerome "Rome" Murdick, who began selling the candy to resorters who came to the island and the just-opened Grand Hotel. Now in the fifth generation of the family, Murdick's Fudge is still selling the stuff on the island, in Mackinaw City, and at a few other locations. Rome Murdick began making his fudge on a marble slab, which gave summer tourists incredible fudge, and a show to boot.

Of course, Murdick's isn't the only place that sells fudge. It isn't even the only place that sells *great* fudge. There are currently 15 fudge shops on Mackinac Island, and each one is worth a visit (though if you visit all of them, you'll end up with the stomachache of a lifetime).

Before long, Mackinac earned a reputation. It wouldn't be fair to say that people come for the fudge, but while they're here they buy it by the pound – no, by the *ton*. The tourists' relentless appetite for fudge has earned them the nickname "Fudgies."

Ste. Anne's Catholic Church

You'll find the oldest church on Mackinac Island near the butterfly house. It's worth a visit, even if it is a quick one, for its architecture and history. Ste. Anne's is a testimony to the island's long history of Roman Catholicism; Jesuits were the first non-natives to set foot here. The parish has served the community since the 1740s.

In addition to daily mass, you'll find a community square dance on the spacious front porch once a week. The basement hosts a small museum that preserves and interprets the religious history of Mackinac Island. A number of religious articles and church documents (baptismal, marriage, and burial records) date as far back as 1695.

Ste. Anne's gift shop has a number of souvenirs and collectibles, plus standard religious items. If you're interested in old cemeteries you'll want to check out Ste. Anne's Cemetery, up the hill behind Fort Mackinac and on the way to Fort Holmes.

The museum and gift shop are open Monday–Friday 10 A.M.–4 P.M., Saturday until 5:30 P.M., and Sunday 9 A.M.–3 P.M. Call 906/847-3507 or visit www.steanneschurch.org for more information.

◖ Grand Hotel

The iconic Grand Hotel, a gracious edifice built on a scale appropriate to its name, has become practically synonymous with Mackinac Island. It is one of the largest summer resorts in the world, operating from early April through late October. Its famous 660-foot-long covered front porch gets decked out each spring with 2,500 geraniums planted in seven tons of potting soil. Its 12 restaurants and bars serve as many as 4,000 meals a day. The resort's impeccable grounds offer guests every amenity, from saddle horses to designer golf to bocce ball to swimming in the outdoor pool made famous by 1940s actress Esther Williams, who filmed *This Time for Keeps* here.

But opulence was the goal of the railroads and steamships companies when they formed a consortium and built the Grand Hotel in 1887, dragging construction materials across the frozen waters by horse and mule. The wealthiest of all Mackinac Island visitors stayed here, on a hill with a commanding view of the Straits.

Yet unlike other resorts from the Gilded Age that burned to the ground or grew dog-eared and faded, the Grand Hotel has managed to maintain its grace and dignity over the years. It still hosts all manner of celebrities and politicians—five U.S. presidents to date—and still offers a sip of a truly bygone era with high tea in the parlor each afternoon and demitasse

served after dinner each evening. Room rates still include a five-course dinner in the soaring main dining room. For gentlemen, the evening (6 P.M.) dress code calls for jackets and ties, and for ladies skirts, dresses, or formal pant suits.

The Grand Hotel's time-capsule setting prompted director Jeannot Szwarc to choose it as the location for the 1980 film *Somewhere in Time,* starring Christopher Reeve, Jane Seymour, and Christopher Plummer. For whatever reason, the movie has developed a huge following; its fan club reunites at the hotel each year in late October.

While room rates can get outright absurd ($675 and up per night, with doubles starting at $450), they do include breakfast and dinner, and perhaps can be considered a worthwhile splurge if you like this kind of thing. A more affordable option is to stay just one night for the experience and then book a room at a cheaper on- or off-island lodging for the rest of your visit.

Enjoy this moment in time! Take tea, loll in the beautifully landscaped pool, or dance to the swing orchestra in the Terrace Room. Nonguests can sneak a peek at the hotel's public areas and grounds for a mildly unreasonable $15 ($7.50 for children, free for those younger than five). It's needed to thin the sightseers more than anything. Highly recommended are a stroll through the grounds, filled with Victorian gardens—25,000 tulips in spring!—and a visit to the snazzy Cupola Bar, with views halfway to Wisconsin.

Each of the 385 rooms is decorated differently, and, as of 2007 (and for the first time in more than 120 years), the entire hotel is air-conditioned. For availability and rates, contact the **Grand Hotel** (800/334-7263, www.grand-hotel.com).

Fort Mackinac

Located at the crest of the bluff, whitewashed Fort Mackinac is worth a visit for the views alone, presiding over—as forts often do—the downtown, the marina, and Lake Huron. But there's also plenty to see at this military outpost, which the British and Americans haggled over for nearly 40 years.

Along with peering over the parapets, you can wander in and out of 14 buildings within the fort. The barracks, officers' quarters, post hospital, and other buildings are filled with interpretive displays and feature period decor. Costumed guides lead all sorts of reenactments, including musket firing and cannon salutes. A short audiovisual presentation, "The Heritage of Mackinac," does a good job of presenting basic history.

Admission to the fort is $10.50 adults, $6.50 children 5–17, and also includes admission to several other historic buildings on the island. If you're planning on visiting Colonial Michilimackinac, Old Mackinac Point Lighthouse, or Historic Mill Creek State Park on the mainland, the combination ticket is your best deal, giving you seven-day admission to three of the four parks for $23 adults, $14 children 5–17. The park is open early May–mid-October, with different times for each season: 9 A.M.–4:30 P.M. May 6–June 6, 9:30 A.M.–6 P.M. June 7–August 23, and 9:30 A.M.–4:30 P.M. August 24–October 12.

For information, stop by the park visitors center across from Marquette Park on Huron Street, or contact **Mackinac State Historic Parks** (231/436-4100, www.mackinacparks.com).

The Park

Too often overshadowed by other visitor attractions, Mackinac Island's natural history has drawn scientific interest for nearly 200 years. In the early 19th century, botanists discovered several species completely new to science, including the dwarf lake iris, still found only in the Straits of Mackinac region.

The island's landscape is made up of fields, meadows, marshes, coastline, swamps, bogs, and a boreal forest. Early scientists marveled at the island's unusual topography, especially the brecciated limestone that has been sculpted by millennia of wind and waves. The result is some dramatic rock formations, like the giant inland slab of limestone called **Sugar Loaf**

SOMEWHERE IN TIME

Beyond fantasy. Beyond obsession.
Beyond time itself...he will find her.

Somewhere in Time

Your reaction to the tagline for *Somewhere in Time*, a 1980 movie starring Christopher Reeve and Jane Seymour and filmed at the Grand Hotel, is a pretty good indication of whether you'll love or hate the movie. If you find it hopelessly romantic, a bit old-fashioned, and somewhat endearing – go rent the movie now. But if you thought it was too sweet and you shuddered a little, it isn't worth your time.

The film tells the story of Richard Collier, a writer who, after a strange encounter with an old woman who pleads, "Come back to me," tries to figure out who she was. While staying at the Grand Hotel, he learns she was a turn-of-the-century actress named Elise McKenna,

and he becomes infatuated with her. He manages to travel back in time to meet her and the two fall in love. But will Richard be able to stay in 1912?

Mackinac Island's Victorian setting, and in particular the Grand Hotel, made it a natural location for the film. Unfortunately, when the movie was released it was maligned by film critics, and its only Oscar nod was for Best Costume Design. Still, it's found a passionate following among people who are enthralled by its story of timeless love and old-fashioned values. In fact, the *Somewhere in Time* fan club has met at the Grand Hotel for a weekend each October since 1991.

It really is a decent, if affected, movie that's perfect for Valentine's Day or a first date, and it's a great way to relive your Grand Hotel stay – or to peek inside if you never make it there in person.

© PAUL VACHON

the Grand Hotel on Mackinac Island

© PAUL VACHON

The island's East Bluff is home to many elegant cottages.

Rock, the lakeside caves of **Devil's Kitchen,** and impressive **Arch Rock,** which rises nearly 150 feet above the eastern shore and spans some 50 feet.

In recognition of the park's distinctive "natural curiosities" and growing tourism, the U.S. government created Mackinac National Park in 1875—following Yellowstone as only the country's second national park. Twenty years later, it was returned to Michigan and became Mackinac Island State Park, Michigan's first state park.

Walk, run, or bike, but make sure you get out of downtown to really see Mackinac Island. You'll be surprised how quickly you can leave any crowds behind as you set out on the paved eight-mile path that circles the island. The trail never wanders far from the pleasant shoreline and passes many of the island's natural features, which are well marked. Traveling clockwise, the first you'll reach is Devil's Kitchen; heading in the opposite direction you'll arrive first at Arch Rock, the most dramatic of all Mackinac limestone oddities.

About halfway around, on the island's northwestern side, lies **British Landing,** where British soldiers sneaked onto the island during the War of 1812. They hiked across Mackinac's interior, totally surprising the American garrison stationed at the fort (who were apparently looking the other way), and recaptured the island. There's a small **nature center** here, staffed in summer months by a helpful naturalist. Hike the short **nature trail,** which has several interpretive signs as it weaves up a bluff.

British Landing is also a good spot from which to head inland and explore the island's interior. British Landing Road bisects the island and links up with Garrison Road near **Skull Cave,** leading to the fort. It's a hilly, three-mile trip from shore to shore. British Landing Road is considered a major thoroughfare by Mackinac standards, meaning you'll have to share it with carriages.

Lighthouses

The **Round Island Lighthouse** was built in 1895 to guide ships among the shoals and

channels between Mackinac Island and uninhabited Round Island, where it was built. Though unmanned, the Round Island light still guides ships through the Straits today. Your best bet to see it is by way of the eastbound lighthouse cruise offered out of Mackinaw City by Shepler's Ferry.

ENTERTAINMENT

For the best of the island's **live music,** you'll want to check out the Grand Hotel, which offers plenty of live entertainment nightly. Catch live music at the Jockey Club at the Grand Strand, listen to the Grand Hotel Orchestra in the Terrace Room, or hear live bands at the Gate House. You can also find live entertainment at the Cupola Bar and at Woods. You'll find acoustic music at Mission Point Resort's Round Island Bar and Grill. Downtown, Patrick Sinclair's Irish Pub entertains crowds with live Irish music, DJs, karaoke, and '70s night.

It's easy to understand why **pub crawls** are so popular on the island—it's hard to get a drunk driving infraction if no one can drive! Free from having to give up their keys, visitors participate in designated pub crawls. Local retailers join in the game, too, selling t-shirts commemorating the experience (you might not remember it otherwise). Don't overdo it! Finish your crawl over the course of a few nights.

FESTIVALS AND EVENTS
◖ Lilac Festival

For 10 days in early June, Mackinac Island celebrates the Mackinac Island Lilac Festival. During the festival, visitors can enjoy live music; A Taste of Mackinac, which showcases the talents of local chefs; and the Feast of Epona, the Celtic goddess of horses. These events culminate with the Grand Parade, one of North America's only all–hitch horse parades. Other events include a dog and pony show, the Blessing of the Animals, and a 10K run. It's not exactly Labor Day weekend, but the 10 days get pretty busy. Celebrations on this order represent Mackinac at its best.

Other Festivals

August is also a big month for Mackinac Island. Early in the month, the **Mackinac Island Horse Show** celebrates the island's love of all things equestrian with events like showmanship and grooming, English and Western equestrian, and barrel racing. The **Mackinac Island Music Festival** is held annually toward the end of August, featuring a wide variety of live musical performances. During the **Mackinac Island Fudge Festival,** late in the month, the Fudgies get their due as the entire island turns out to celebrate the estimated 10,000 pounds of fudge made each season.

SUMMER SPORTS AND RECREATION
Trails

At last count, Mackinac Island State Park had more than 2,250 acres with over 70 miles of trails and footpaths, suitable for exploration on bike or foot. Pick up a free *Mackinac Island Map,* available all over town, and venture off. The map marks the location of old cemeteries, rock formations, and such, but it's even more appealing to just explore the smaller trails on your own and discover the pristine and tranquil side of Mackinac Island. Everything's well marked, and getting lost is rather difficult—you're on a small island, after all.

For walking or biking tours, join **Doc Crain** as he shares local legends on the way through the island's boreal forest trails. Hiking tours meet Monday–Saturday at 2 P.M. at the Father Marquette Statue, while biking tours meet at Mackinac Wheels Monday–Saturday at 10 A.M. Friday and Saturday sunset bike tours depart at 7 P.M. Doc's tours can be described as "infotainment"—he fascinates his guests with a wide array of facts about the island's plants and flowers, the glaciers that shaped its cliffs, and its long military history. Doc won't charge you a fee for the tours, but be generous and leave him a good-sized tip; he will have certainly earned it.

Runners can participate in the **Lilac Festival 10K** in early June, the **Mackinac Island Eight**

Mile in September, or October's **Great Turtle Half Marathon.**

There are plenty of shops that offer hourly **bicycle rentals** on any variety of bike: single speeds, mountain bikes, bikes for children, tagalongs, buggies, or tandems for the hopeless romantic in all of us. Most rentals run about $6 per hour or $30 per day. Equipment varies, so look before you pay. Check out **Ryba's Bicycle Rentals** (906/847-3208, www.rybabikes.com) on Market Street—it's a great resource.

If you plan to do much cycling, you'll be happier bringing your own bike, since you can transport it on the ferry for about $7.50 roundtrip. You'll want a hybrid or mountain bike to negotiate most interior trails.

In order to accommodate visitors with disabilities, Mackinac Island has relaxed its ban on motorized transportation, albeit slightly. For those in need, motorized scooters can now be rented from vendors on Market Street, right near the embarkation point of the ferries. This accommodation makes it possible for those physically challenged to enjoy Mackinac Island.

On the Water

Open-water sailing excursions are available on the **Mackinaw Breeze** (906/847-8669, www.mackinawbreeze.com, $30 adults, $15 children eight and younger), a custom-built catamaran that can accommodate up to 26 passengers. The most typical (and affordable) trips last about an hour and a half and feature as many views—including lighthouses, surrounding islands, and Arch Rock—as wind conditions allow. Contact Mackinaw Breeze for information about chartering half- and full-day cruises.

Mackinac Island's beautiful coastline is perfect for relaxation and picnicking, and often irresistibly tempting for those looking to take a dip, especially children. The east side of the island is best for the little ones, but be warned: The rocky shores require swimming shoes or sandals and there are no lifeguards, so swim at your own risk. The water of the straits can also be rather chilly—even late in the season.

Of course, you can always bring a rod and reel and fish off the rocks on Mackinac Island's shore, but the lure of the Great Lakes makes deep-water **fishing** one of the island's most popular summer activities. There are no charter services based on the island itself, but, as with **parasailing,** a few boats (mostly private vessels from Mackinaw City or St. Ignace) dock here.

Horses

With more than 600 horses calling the island their summertime home, you won't be able to turn a corner without bumping noses with these beautiful animals. But to be honest, who would want it otherwise? It isn't every day you get the chance to ride a carriage down Main Street or take a buggy on an island circuit.

Carriage tours can be had with the island's largest livery, **Mackinac Island Carriage Tours** (906/847-3307, www.mict.com) which has been operating since 1869. Also, **Arrowhead Carriages** (906/847-6112) offer personalized tours of the island in relatively small carriages. The guides are very knowledgeable and the tours have a bit of an unusual fee structure. The hourly rate for the tour runs $100–175, depending on the specific route requested. If two families book the tour jointly, they can split the fee between them, allowing for a more cost-efficient hour. Both companies begin their tours on Market Street near the Father Marquette statue.

You'll be able to take the reins during a drive-it-yourself buggy tour from **Jack's Livery Stable** (906/847-3391, www.jacksliverystable.com, $54/hour for two passengers, $66/hour for four passengers, May–Oct.). After gauging your skill with horses, one of the livery's professionals will give you driving instructions before setting you loose on the town with a free map. At their sister company, **Cindy's Riding Stable** (906/847-3572, www.cindysridingstable.com, $40/hour per person, May–Oct.), you can take one of their 30-plus saddle horses into the island on your own.

Golf

In addition to a pleasant afternoon on the links, golfing Mackinac brings with it a cheap thrill: Golf carts are among the very few powered vehicles allowed on the island. So while other visitors are struggling to rein in an unruly horse or hoofing it across the island, you'll be smoking a cigar as you drive something that has a gas pedal.

Mackinac is the proud home of the oldest continuously played golf course in Michigan, **Wawashkamo** (906/847-3871, www.wawashkamo.com). Vacationers have been golfing the course's nine holes since 1898, and the second set of tee placements makes it possible to play a full 18 holes on rough natural terrain, which includes traditionally Scottish thistle and heather. Wawashkamo, which means "walk a crooked trail," is built on a former War of 1812 battlefield, adding to its historic appeal. Plan on paying $70 for 18 holes and a cart, $58 if you leave the wheels behind. Nine holes are $49 with cart, $37 without.

The Grand Hotel's 18 holes, known as **The Jewel** (906/847-3331, www.grandhotel.com), consists of two nine-hole courses—the Grand Nine, across the street from the hotel, and the Woods Nine in the island's interior. Horse-drawn transportation is provided between the two courses. Eighteen holes cost hotel guests $89 ($118 for nonguests) and nine holes will run guests $49 (nonguests pay $59). Golf carts run $30 for 18 holes and $15 for 9 holes, per person.

Mission Point Resort presents **The Greens at Mackinac** (906/847-3312, www.missionpoint.com), the executive putting greens where even the most experienced putters can hone their skills or try out the merchandise from the pro shop's selection of putters. Eighteen holes of fun cost $10 for adults and $5 for children under 18.

Other Activities

Three sets of **tennis courts** are available on Mackinac Island—there are public courts behind Fort Mackinac, and courts are available to guests at both the Grand Hotel and Mission Point Resort. The Grand offers its guests organized matches and equipment rental, as well as private or semi-private lessons. Reservations can be arranged by contacting Tennis Pro Razvan (Raz) Mag at 1-800/33-GRAND (1-800/334-7263).

WINTER SPORTS AND RECREATION

Ski and Snowshoe Trails

The island is a bit trickier to get to once the Straits freeze over, but for those willing to go through the extra effort, a winter paradise awaits. The 70-plus miles of trails that bring out the hikers, bikers, and runners in summertime are converted to cross-country ski and snowshoe trails for winter. Mackinac Island Ski Club volunteers team up with the state park to maintain a series of groomed winter trails. As an added bonus, the island is considerably less crowded. A calming solace grips the island in winter, so it'll feel like you have the place all to yourself.

The Balsam Shop (906/847-3591, www.balsamshop.com) is open winter weekends and holidays for cross-country ski and snowshoe rentals. Since most of the island shuts down well before the snows come, winter lodging is limited. Check out **Bogan Lane Inn** (906/847-3439, www.boganlaneinn.com, $85–120), **Pontiac Lodge** (906/847-3364, www.pontiaclodge.com, $85–350), or **Harbor Place Studio Suites** (800/626-6304, www.harborplacestudiosuites.com, $75–200) for rooms.

Horse-drawn taxis (bundle up!) are available from **Mackinac Island Carriage Tours** (906/847-3323, www.mict.com) with reservations. Mackinac Island Airport is the only way on and off the island after the ferries stop running in late November. Ferry service resumes in early April.

ACCOMMODATIONS

Along with the **Grand Hotel,** there are many other places to stay on Mackinac Island that still manage to offer the true Mackinac, Victorian-style experience. Yes, rates can be high, but as you'll see, prices can range considerably even within one particular property,

with water views commanding a considerable premium. But don't dismiss staying on Mackinac Island; you can find reasonable rates at smaller B&Bs and apartments, the latter of which often have good deals for weeklong stays. The options listed here tip both ends of the scale. For information on more island accommodations, including rates and photos, visit www.mackinacisland.org.

Unfortunately, camping is not permitted on Mackinac Island.

Hotels and Motels

The **Chippewa Hotel** (800/241-3341, www.chippewahotel.com, $95–565) is a venerable old Mackinac hotel that had a $3 million renovation several years back. The result is a classy and comfortable place to stay, with a location at the heart of the island, on Main Street, overlooking the marina. The 24-person lakeside hot tub alone may be worth the stay. If you enjoy being pampered, check out the relaxing Lilac Tree Spa.

Two separate buildings—Cudahy Manor and the Summer House—make up the **Inn at Stonecliffe** (906/847-3355, www.theinnatstonecliffe.com, May–Oct., $99–284 Cudahy Manor, $204–504 Summer House). More than 100 years old, the inn has been completely remodeled and restored. The Cudahy Manor is more B&B than hotel, a turn-of-the-century Tudor manor with 16 rooms, the more expensive of which have views of the Straits of Mackinac and the bridge. The Summer House has 33 studio suites.

One of the island's most striking buildings, the **Hotel Iroquois** (906/847-3321, www.iroquoishotel.com, $290–495 rooms, $590–1075 suites), was built in 1900 as a home for the island blacksmith. It's since been converted into a 46-room hotel with a fine dining restaurant ($28–60 entrées) and a private sunbathing deck. Hotel Iroquois is a Condé Nast Traveler Gold List hotel and earned a perfect score for its stunning location. Still, with suite rates on par with the Grand Hotel's luxury rooms, you'll be better off sticking with Hotel Iroquois's competitively priced regular rooms.

Bed-and-Breakfasts

Cloghaun (906/847-3885, www.cloghaun.com, May–Oct., $175–195 high season, $80–160 off season, including breakfast) was built in 1884 by Thomas and Bridgette Donnelly, who left their homeland during the Irish Potato Famine and followed a relative to Mackinac Island. Today, this grand Victorian (it's pronounced CLA-hahn) with extensive grounds is still owned by their descendents. It's located on Market Street, next to some of the island's historic attractions and just one block from Main. Eight rooms have private baths; two others share.

Below East Bluff near Ste. Anne's Church, **Haan's 1830 Inn** (906/847-6244, www.mackinac.com/haans, May 15–Oct. 11, $90–195) is a Greek Revival built by Colonel Preston, one of the last officers to preside over Fort Mackinac. Just try to drag yourself out of the wicker chairs on the big front porch. Four of the seven rooms have private baths.

Only a five- or ten-minute walk from the ferry docks, **Bay View Bed & Breakfast** (906/847-3295, www.mackinacbayview.com, May–Oct., $95–425) has exactly that: a great view of the bay. If you spend a little extra cash for a room with a view, you'll find yourself overlooking the yacht harbor. Breakfast is served on the veranda; make sure you try the custom Bay View Blend Coffee.

Other Lodging

◖ **Mission Point Resort** (6633 Main St., 906/847-3312, www.missionpoint.com) may have the island's very best location, spread across 18 acres at the island's southeastern tip. Though not Victorian era—it was built in the 1950s by the Moral Re-Armament movement, a post–World War II patriotic group—the sprawling, bright-white resort is attractive and well kept, with beautiful lawns lined with Adirondack chairs. Amenities include an outdoor pool, tennis and volleyball courts, and loads of kids' activities.

In addition to the professional putting green, bicycle rentals, lawn bowling, croquet, tennis, and professional spa, Mission Point

Resort offers hayrides around Mackinac Island. The resort's Tower Museum, eight stories up, provides a striking panoramic view of the island and the Straits. Interpretive displays on each floor present fascinating looks at topics such as maritime shipping history, Native American heritage, and building the Mackinac Bridge.

You'll have your choice of four restaurants while at the resort. Lakeside Marketplace can provide you with a picnic lunch on your way out to explore the island, while the Epicurean is the place for elegant dining and an impressive selection of wines. Rooms start at $149–309, but you can expect them to skyrocket at the height of summer. With all it has to offer, Mission Point is a quintessential self-contained summer resort.

FOOD

One of the finest dining deals on the island is the **Fort Mackinac Tea Room** (906/847-3331, www.grandhotel.com), located in the lower level of the Officer's Stone Quarters within the fort itself. Surrounded by thick masonry walls, the tearoom serves up both a great atmosphere and great food prepared by Grand Hotel chefs. Moderately priced entrées run up to $15; good soups, salads, and sandwiches can be had for around $10. Opt for a spot on the terrace since the high setting offers a dramatic panorama, and forts weren't exactly designed for expansive views.

Everyone has to hit the ◖ **Pink Pony Bar & Grill** (906/847-3341, www.chippewahotel. com) at least once during a Mackinac visit. Located in the Chippewa Hotel, overlooking the marina, this is *the* party place following the famed Chicago-to-Mackinac yacht race. The food's great, too, with good burgers, whitefish sandwiches, and other goodies on the lunch menu, and steaks, seafood, and ribs for dinner. Appetizers are especially popular in the dining room, where you'll find pan-fried calamari ($12) and wild mushroom bruschetta ($11)—choices a bit atypical for Mackinac Island. Dinner entrées average around $23. Outdoor patio dining is available in season.

© GRAND HOTEL

the elegant Main Dining Room at the Grand Hotel

The **Round Island Bar and Grill** (906/847-3312, www.missionpoint.com, 7 A.M.–midnight, with only light snacks and libations served after 9 P.M.) at Mission Point Resort, has sandwiches and salads in a casual setting overlooking the Straits and neighboring Round Island. Sample some of Michigan's best regional beers and wines.

The island's best fine dining is found at the high-end hotels and resorts. Try the **1852 Grill Room** at the Island House Hotel (906/847-3347, www.theislandhouse.com), the Hotel Iroquois's **Carriage House Dining Room** (906/847-3321, www.iroquoishotel.com), and the Grand Hotel's **Main Dining Room** and **Woods Restaurant** (906/847-3331, www. grandhotel.com). For the treat of a lifetime, choose the Main Dining Room at the Grand. For nonguests, an exquisite five-course meal is $75 per person and features choices from three rotating menus. You will not be disappointed.

INFORMATION

For help with accommodations and other information ahead of time, contact the **Mackinac**

Island Chamber of Commerce & Tourism Bureau (877/847-0086, www.mackinacisland.org). You can also get a visitors guide with maps of the state park at the **Mackinac Island State Park Visitor Center,** located on Main Street across from the island's Marquette Park and open from early May to mid-October.

GETTING THERE AND AROUND

Don't even think about bringing a car. The only motorized transportation allowed on the island are golf carts, scooters for the handicapped, and a few public service vehicles—a fire truck, an ambulance, and the like. Of course, you're welcome to drive to Mackinaw City or St. Ignace and catch a ferry to the island, but you'll have to leave your car behind.

Boat

Three ferry lines offer service to Mackinac Island: **Arnold Transit Company** (906/847-3351, www.arnoldline.com, $22 adults, $11 children 5–12), **Shepler's Mackinac Island Ferry** (231/436-5023, www.sheplersferry.com, $19 adults, $10 children 5–12), and the **Star**

Line (800/638-9892, www.mackinawferry.com, $22 adults, $11 children; orders through Star's website: $19 adults, $10 children 5–12). Ferries run, in general, from Mackinaw City between May and October, and from St. Ignace April through November. Free parking is available for day-trippers; overnight guests will have to pay.

If you're sailing your own boat, you can contact the **Mackinac Island State Harbor** (906/847-3561, www.michigan.gov/dnr) for reservations up to six months in advance of your stay. The marina's 76 slips are available from late May to mid-September. You can contact the marina on radio channel 9. It's located at 45° 50.40 N, 84° 36.42 W.

Air

Mackinac Island Airport (MCD) is the only way to get to the island in the winter, and it's always an option in the summer, too. Year-round flights are available from St. Ignace and Pellston through **Great Lakes Air** (906/643-7165, www.greatlakesair.net, $27 adults, $13.50 children under 12) by reservation only. Horse-drawn taxi service is available from

© RAYMOND MALACE, TRAVEL MICHIGAN

The island has a small number of permanent residents who brave the winter.

the airport to your hotel; contact **Mackinac Island Carriage Tours** (906/847-3323, www.mict.com).

Getting Around

While on the island, horses are certainly the most unique means of getting around. Taxis can be hired at **Mackinac Island Carriage Tours** (906/847-3323, www.mict.com). If you enjoy walking and hiking, you can get around Mackinac Island on foot; the island is about eight miles in circumference. Mackinac is a wonderful place for casual strolls and all-day hikes.

The island is also a great place to cycle. **Mackinac Island Bike Shop** (906/847-6337, www.mackinacislandbikes.com) at the Lake View Hotel has a wide array of choices, including mountain bikes for kids and adults, plus tag-alongs and bike trailers for babies. They also offer equipment for use by the handicapped, including electric wheelchairs and motorized scooters. At **Ryba's Bicycle Rentals** (906/847-3208, www.rybabikes.com) you'll find a similar selection. There are a number of other bicycle rentals on the island, most of which offer competitive prices, or you can bring your own on the ferry for about $7.50.

St. Ignace

St. Ignace is directly at the north end of the Mackinac Bridge, and is worthwhile for both its history and its off-island lodging. It's made a reputation of its own: with an annual auto show and plenty of tourist draws, this city (the first off the bridge) is often a traveler's introduction to the Upper Peninsula. It doesn't have the splendor of Mackinac Island's resorts, and it also lacks the touristy feel of Mackinaw City. Good news for campers, hikers, and the like: Its access to the eastern branch of the Hiawatha National Forest makes St. Ignace the Strait's best area for out-of-doors activity.

SIGHTS
◖ Mackinac Bridge

You can't miss it: it's that massive bridge. Its total length is 26,372 feet. At midspan, the roadway is 200 feet above water. It has 42,000 miles of wire in the main cables. Its size and grandeur stand as a testimony to 20th-century engineering and the determination of the iron workers who built it.

Known as "Mighty Mac" or simply "The Bridge," this is Michigan's pride and joy. Stretching across nearly five miles of open water, Mighty Mac has the third longest total suspension of any bridge in the world, and ranks as number one in the Western

Hemisphere. There are other ways of measuring suspension, such as the length of the main span between towers. Some of these methods put the Bridge farther down on the list, but try telling that to a Michiganian—of either the Upper or Lower Peninsula.

There are good photo spots on both ends of the bridge; just poke around St. Ignace's southern shore and perhaps try Straits State Park or Mackinac Bridge View Park just west of the toll plaza. Driving the bridge is different than looking at it, and if you can manage the approximately 10-minute-long and oddly exciting drive you should do it. If you can't bring yourself to stay behind the wheel—and many can't—bridge personnel will drive your car across at no additional charge. Pedestrians, bicyclists, and snowmobilers aren't permitted to cross, although transportation is provided for a fee of $2/person, including a bike, and $10 for a snowmobile and driver.

Father Marquette National Memorial and New France Discovery Center

High above the open Straits of Mackinac, this largely open-air site commemorates French explorer and Jesuit missionary Jacques Marquette. In the 1660s and 1670s, Marquette paddled

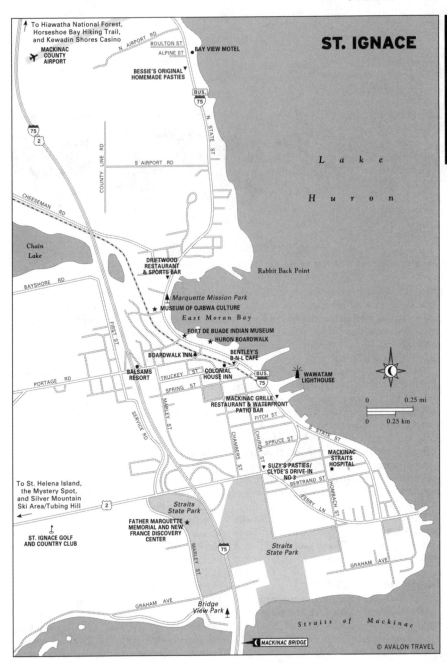

ST. IGNACE

To Hiawatha National Forest,
Horseshoe Bay Hiking Trail,
and Kewadin Shores Casino

MACKINAC
COUNTY
AIRPORT

N AIRPORT RD
BOULTON ST
ALPINE ST
BAY VIEW MOTEL

BESSIE'S ORIGINAL
HOMEMADE PASTIES

BUS. 75

N STATE ST

S AIRPORT RD

COUNTY LINE RD

L a k e

H u r o n

CHEESEMAN RD

*Chain
Lake*

BAYSHORE RD

FIRST ST

DRIFTWOOD
RESTAURANT
& SPORTS BAR

Rabbit Back Point

Marquette Mission Park
MUSEUM OF OJIBWA CULTURE

East Moran Bay

FORT DE BUADE INDIAN MUSEUM
HURON BOARDWALK

BOARDWALK INN
BENTLEY'S
B-N-L CAFE
BALSAMS
RESORT
COLONIAL
HOUSE INN

BUS. 75

WAWATAM
LIGHTHOUSE

PORTAGE RD

TRUCKEY ST

SPRING ST

SERVICE RD

MARLEY ST

MACKINAC GRILLE
RESTAURANT & WATERFRONT
PATIO BAR

FITCH ST

0   0.25 mi

0   0.25 km

CHAMBERS ST

CHURCH ST

SPRUCE ST

S STATE ST

To St. Helena Island,
the Mystery Spot,
and Silver Mountain
Ski Area/Tubing Hill

2

SUZY'S PASTIES/
CLYDE'S DRIVE-IN
NO 3

MACKINAC
STRAITS
HOSPITAL

BERTRAND ST

FERRY LN

HOMBACH ST

ST. IGNACE GOLF
AND COUNTRY CLUB

*Straits
State Park*

FATHER MARQUETTE
MEMORIAL AND NEW
FRANCE DISCOVERY
CENTER

75

*Straits
State Park*

GRAHAM AVE

GRAHAM AVE

*Bridge
View Park*

Straits   of   Mackinac

MACKINAC BRIDGE

© AVALON TRAVEL

© GARY PLATTE, TRAVEL MICHIGAN

The annual Bridge Walk has become a Labor Day tradition.

through the Great Lakes, founding dozens of cities along the way, including Sault Ste. Marie and St. Ignace. Marquette then linked up with Louis Jolliet and paddled another several thousand miles to become the first European explorer of the Mississippi.

Walking trails feature interpretive signs that discuss Marquette's Great Lakes travels and the impact the area's geography had on settlement. Little emphasis is given to the effect Marquette's missionary work had on Native Americans, thousands of whom Marquette converted to Christianity. A small museum on site burned down in recent years, but it's still worth a visit for the National Memorial, the outdoor trail, and the panoramic view of the Mackinac Bridge.

The Memorial is on the grounds of **Straits State Park** (906/643-8620, Memorial Day–mid-Sept.), west of I-75 and south of U.S. 2. A park sticker is required for entry.

Downtown St. Ignace

In contrast to the Father Marquette memorial, the **Marquette Mission Park and Museum of Ojibwa Culture** (500 N. State St., 906/643-9161, www.stignace.com/attractions/ojibwa, $2 adults, $1 children, $5 families) tells the story

of the Ojibwa and the effect the European explorers had on their culture. The museum is also the presumed site of Father Marquette's grave and the site of his Jesuit mission.

Displays housed in a former Catholic church include artifacts from archaeological digs on the grounds (some dating to 6000 B.C.), explanations of how the Ojibwa adapted and survived in the area's often harsh climate, and a discussion of how they allied with the French fur traders, despite how it greatly diminished their traditional way of life. Don't miss the museum's adjacent gift shop, featuring authentic, locally made crafts such as ash baskets, quill jewelry, and more. It also offers an excellent selection of books on both Native American and French history in the area of the Straits. During peak season (late June–Labor Day), the museum is open 9 A.M.–6 P.M. Early and late season hours are shorter (daily 9 A.M.–5 P.M. Memorial Day–June and 10 A.M.–3 P.M. Labor Day–early Oct.).

Fort deBaude Indian Museum (334 N. State St., 906/643-6622) interprets pre-contact Native, French, English, and American periods. With more than 6,700 square feet, the museum has one of the city's largest collections, including historical Native American

BUILDING THE BRIDGE

It was an impossible dream, but one that had been kept alive since 1884, when a story in the *Grand Traverse Herald* reported that ferry service had failed as a means of traversing the Straits. The only way, it said, was by a tunnel or a bridge.

Since the beginning, Michigan had been cut in two by the Straits of Mackinac – one third, isolated and rugged, to the north; two thirds below. As early as 1897 and as late as the 1970s, there was talk – serious talk – of the Upper Peninsula seceding from Michigan and forming its own state: The Superior State. It seems that the physical separation led to an ideological separation; even today, many Yoopers are Yoopers first and Michiganders second. The Straits were more than a pain to get across, with ferry lines stretching for miles. Getting across the Straits was an undeniable problem.

After years of planning and failure to get financial backing, bridge construction officially began in May 1954. At the time, it was the biggest bridge construction fleet ever assembled, and when the bridge was finally finished and opened to traffic in 1957, designer David B. Steinman wrote that "the people of Michigan built the world's greatest bridge."

"They built it in the face of discouragement," he wrote, "of faintheartedness on the part of many of their leaders, of warnings that the rocks in the Straits were too soft, the ice too thick, the winds too strong, the rates of interest on the bonds too high, and the whole concept too big." It wasn't too big, but it wasn't easy either. It took three years of construction and $99 million, and it regrettably cost five men their lives: Frank Pepper, James R. LeSarge, Albert Abbot, Jack C. Baker, and Robert Koppen. It's a steep cost for one of the world's finest engineering marvels.

"Mighty Mac" is five miles long, with a center span between the main towers of 3,800 feet. The main towers stand 552 feet above the water; the roadway itself is some 200 feet up. It weighs 1,024,500 tons, has 4,851,700 steel rivets and 1,016,600 steel bolts, and can withstand winds up to an amazing 600 miles per hour. The suspended bridge is capable of moving as much as 35 feet east-to-west in high winds, but the roadways are shut down long before the swaying reaches that point.

The cost of operating and maintaining the bridge is taken from the few bucks you'll pay as a crossing toll; the maintenance it takes to keep an over-50-year-old bridge safe for traffic is a staggering and unending job. But it's worth it – as frightening as it can be to drive across the bridge (it bows visibly in the wind, and you're 200 feet high), it's safe.

Michiganders are proud of their bridge, and they should be. On the down side, it does mean that you'll be shelling out obscene amounts of money for a room with a bridge view, but on the up side – look at the thing. It's gorgeous. And it's convenient, too. Without it, travelers from the south would be waiting in an hours-long queue for the ferries; with it, access to the entire Upper Peninsula is as easy as keeping your eyes on the road and your hands on the wheel.

---

and military weapons. Unfortunately, it's also one of St. Ignace's least visited museums. Summer hours are noon–8 P.M. Admission is free, but donations are requested.

The **Huron Boardwalk** follows the shoreline for a mile, with interpretive signs explaining the role of the bay in the area's settlement. Outdoor displays explore the Straits of Mackinac history and include a rudder from a wooden steamer sunk in 1894 and the windlass from an 1891 shipwreck.

Castle Rock

Three miles north of St. Ignace, you'll come across one of those tourist spots that is hopelessly, almost embarrassingly irresistible. Castle Rock (Castle Rock Rd., 906/643-8268, www.stignace.com, $0.50 admission, daily early May–mid-Oct.) is a vertical tower that rises nearly 200 feet and provides unparalleled views of Mackinac Island, the Straits, and Lake Huron. The oversized Paul Bunyan and Babe, his blue ox, is an exciting photo opportunity

for children or adults with a certain sense of humor. Most visitors just head up the 170-step climb without looking twice. Nearby is a very touristy gift shop.

The Mystery Spot

This would hardly bear mentioning if it wasn't for the billboards peaking curiosity around town. According to the story, in the early 1950s, some surveyors apparently stumbled across an area where their equipment stopped working correctly. Hence this tourist attraction constructed to show ways that the laws of physics don't seem to apply here: tall people seem smaller, chairs balance with two legs in the air, and you'll be able to walk up a wall without falling. Some find it corny, others find it ridiculously fun; most can agree that it's the kind of classic "tourist trap" that's just too difficult to pass up.

An attraction just added at the Mystery Spot are zip lines. A rider gets strapped into a harness attached to a pulley and allows gravity to propel her along a cable strung about twenty feet high between two towers—for a distance of about 200 yards. Don't do it on a full stomach. **The Mystery Spot** (150 Martin Lake Rd., 906/643-8322, http://mysteryspot-stignace.com) is open 9 A.M.–8 P.M. May 10–June 15, and 8 A.M.–9 P.M. June 16–Labor Day. Late-season hours are the most limited: 9 A.M.–7 P.M. Labor Day–October 19. Prices are listed online, and there is a discount for those wanting to take in both attractions.

Lighthouses

As far as historic lighthouses go, there aren't many to be had in St. Ignace. The closest historic lighthouse is on **St. Helena Island,** a few miles west of the city in the Straits of Mackinac. Built in 1873, the 71-foot tower and attached keeper's quarters fell into disrepair after the lighthouse was automated in the 1920s. It's gotten quite a bit of restoration during the past several years, and it's open to the public by appointment (313/436-9150). The island is accessible by boat, but landlubbers can get a decent view from a U.S. 2 pull-off in Gros Cap, six miles west of St. Ignace. Downtown's **Wawatam Lighthouse,** just off the Huron Boardwalk, looks handsome enough, but it's only a few years old.

ENTERTAINMENT

The Upper Peninsula isn't much for metropolitan entertainment—nightclubs and lounges are almost nonexistent—but it does manage to get gaming right, though the local casinos tend to lack Las Vegas–style flash and glitter. **Kewadin Shores Casino** (3039 Mackinac Trail, 800/539-2346, www.kewadin.com, open year-round), more commonly called "The Shores," has 25,000 square feet of space for games such as blackjack, poker, and roulette and more than 900 slot machines. The Northern Pines lounge features live entertainment every Friday and Saturday, and Wednesday night is comedy night every week.

Eighty-one rooms are available at the hotel, which is located on the shores of Lake Huron. Visitors can also enjoy the pool, fitness center, and game room. Dining options include **Horseshoe Bay Restaurant** (7 A.M.–9 P.M. Sun.–Thurs., 7 A.M.–11 P.M. Fri.–Sat.) and the **Whitetail Bar and Grill** (11 A.M.–10 P.M. daily).

FESTIVALS AND EVENTS

One of the best ways to learn about the Upper Peninsula's Native Americans is to attend a powwow. **Powwows** celebrate a tribe's heritage through colorful dancing, feasting, ancient stories, and ceremonies. Many are open to the public and can be wonderful learning experiences. Understand that powwows and many other Native American cultural events have a spiritual element to them. Revealing clothing, pets, drinking, smoking, and certain other behavior is considered inappropriate. Keep this in mind before attending, or ask questions of tribal representatives.

On Labor Day, the Mackinac Bridge Authority throws its no-pedestrian policy out the window for the **Annual Mackinac Bridge Walk.** The walk begins in St. Ignace and ends in Mackinaw City, with the Governor

of Michigan traditionally leading the crowd. To accommodate walkers, the bridge's two northbound lanes are closed to traffic. Walking begins at 7 A.M., and no walkers are allowed to start after 11 A.M., so make sure you get there on time or early, if possible. It takes about two hours to make the five-mile walk. Please note that there are no restrooms on the bridge. Transportation is provided from Mackinaw City back to St. Ignace for $5. Infants are free.

Auto Shows

Perhaps St. Ignace's biggest claims to fame are its summer and fall auto shows. These include the Antique on the Bay Vintage Car and Truck Show and the St. Ignace Car Show and Swap Meet, both held in June. In September you'll find On the Waterfront Car/Small Truck Show/Pedal Cars & Swap Meet, the Richard Crane Memorial Truck Show, and the Owosso Tractor Parts and Equipment Antique Tractor Parade and Show. For details, visit http://stignace.com.

SUMMER SPORTS AND RECREATION
Hiawatha National Forest

Named after "The Song of Hiawatha," a poem by Henry Wadsworth Longfellow that tells the story of the 16th-century Iroquois chief, the Hiawatha National Forest is a swath of protected land stretching all the way from St. Ignace north to the Lake Superior shore. Many of the forest's 860,000 acres are found in the central U.P., but the separate eastern district is where you'll find many of St. Ignace's summer recreation opportunities.

Trails

Thirty-five miles of the **North Country National Scenic Trail** lie in the St. Ignace District of Hiawatha National Forest, which stretches from New York state to North Dakota. Off-limits to horses and motor vehicles, the trail is perfect for hikers, who will pass through cedar, aspen, pine, and northern hardwood. The flat to rolling trail is fully marked,

but not all sections have been brought to trail standards. The **Horseshoe Bay Hiking Trail** is a short, two-mile (round-trip) trail that leads from Foley Creek Campground to a secluded, sandy Lake Huron beach and back. Only three miles from St. Ignace, the trail takes you through northern white cedar lowlands, where you're likely to spot ducks and great blue herons in the numerous ponds.

Hiawatha National Forest has more than 2,000 miles of forest road available for motor vehicle use, plenty of which is within easy reach of St. Ignace. Detailed maps of **ATV/ORV** trails are available. Rules are strictly enforced, so make sure you're thoroughly familiar with them before setting out.

You'll want to contact Hiawatha National Forest's **St. Ignace Ranger District office** (1900 W. U.S. 2, 906/643-7900, 8 A.M.–4:30 P.M. Mon.–Fri., www.fs.usda.gov/hiawatha) for detailed information, trail maps, and information on other recreation opportunities.

Fishing

If you're into deep-water fishing, it's hard to beat the Great Lakes. Here you'll find salmon, perch, walleye, whitefish, herring, pike, and more. Contact **E.U.P. Fishing Charters** (724 Cheeseman Rd., 877/475-3474, catchfish@lighthouse.net) or **Dream Seaker Charters & Tours** (888/634-3419, www.dreamseaker.com) for information on charters into the Straits.

Inland fishing is abundant in the area. Inland lakes, rivers, and streams provide famously good fishing from April right up to December's freeze. You'll need a Michigan Department of Natural Resources fishing license. Visitors from outside Michigan will need a temporary nonresident license. Both are available online at www.mdnr-elicense.com and at most fishing charter services.

Other Water Sports

Like the rest of the U.P., St. Ignace can be a summertime paradise. In particular, visitors have come to love the sandy **beaches** and the relatively warm waters, which offer plenty of relaxing recreation. You'll find suitable

swimming spots at **Straits State Park** (720 Church St., 906/643-8620, www.michigan. gov/dnr) or any number of smaller beaches along the Lake Huron and Lake Michigan shores.

If you thought the Straits were beautiful at eye level, imagine seeing them from a harness attached to a parachute and a 600-foot cable. Parasailing excursions are available from **Mackinaw Parasailing** (866/436-7144, www. mackinawparasailing.com, $60 or $70 single, $100 or $130 tandem), which docks at the Star Line Railroad Dock in St. Ignace. For years, Mackinaw Parasailing has been giving tourists a new perspective from a custom boat that allows for easy flight deck takeoffs and landings. You can also catch a ride from Mackinac Island and Mackinaw City. Parasailing is an exhilarating activity, but clearly not for the faint of heart!

Golf

For some stunning scenery, the **St. Ignace Golf and Country Club** (223 U.S. 2, 906/643-8071, www.stignacegolf.com, $14 for 9 holes, $23 for 18) offers a beautifully tended course with stunning views of the Mackinac Bridge, Lake Huron, and the Straits of Mackinac. Rental clubs and power carts are available. The golf course is located off of U.S. 2, a short distance west of I-75, next to the Big Boy restaurant.

WINTER SPORTS AND RECREATION
Ski and Snowshoe Trails

The miles of hiking trails in St. Ignace don't go away in the winter, they just get covered with snow, perfect for **cross-country skiing** and **snowshoeing.** The North Country National Scenic Trail's 35 St. Ignace miles are popular with skiers. There's a warming cabin at the trailhead to Sand Dunes Ski Trail, which has seven groomed trails suitable for every ski level. Trails range between 1.5 and 7.6 miles. While on Loop A, look for claw marks left by black bears climbing the trees in the fall (remember, bears hibernate in the winter). For more information, contact Hiawatha National Forest's

St. Ignace Ranger District office (1900 W. U.S. 2, 906/643-7900, 8 A.M.–4:30 P.M. Mon.–Fri.).

Downhill Skiing

Believe it or not, you can actually find downhill skiing west of town, at **Silver Mountain Ski Area/Tubing Hill** (Cheeseman Rd. and U.S. 2 West, 906/643-6083). While skiing is included—there are a few runs for beginning and intermediate skiers and snowboarders— Silver Mountain is very much an "all around," family-oriented winter resort, also offering snow tubing with rope tow, paddle towing, and groomed runs. Serious skiers will want to head west to the Iron Mountain area for some of the U.P.'s best downhill skiing, but Silver Mountain is an entertaining diversion.

Snowmobiling

There are about 3,000 miles of snowmobile trails that spread across Michigan's Upper Peninsula, and a few of the trailheads are right here in St. Ignace. Bundle up and hit the trails to pristine winter wilderness or popular destinations like Tahquamenon Falls. The local snowmobile club maintains many of the trails, and snowmobiles can be rented from the **Quality Inn** (561 Boulevard Dr., 800/906-4656). If you're bringing your own, be aware that snowmobile crossings are not allowed on the Mackinac Bridge; transportation is provided by the **Mackinac Bridge Authority** (906/643-7600) for $10 per sled.

As a fairly important side note, remember that snowmobiling in the Upper Peninsula can be remarkably dangerous, especially for newcomers. Every year there are snowmobile-related deaths as reckless enthusiasts drive after a few drinks or plunge through the ice—stay on marked trails and stay *off* rivers and lakes. One particularly popular trail is the ice bridge to Mackinac Island, marked by a line of discarded Christmas trees stretching across Lake Huron. If you'd like to make the trip, talk to locals who know what's going on, check trail conditions with the **Straits Area Snowmobile Club** (www.straitsareasnowmobileclub.com),

and consider the risks carefully. And please remember, drinking before operating a snowmobile can be extremely dangerous.

ACCOMMODATIONS

St. Ignace is jam-packed with lodging, which draws tourists who want to visit Mackinac Island without paying the high island prices. Unfortunately, many of St. Ignace's accommodations are run-of-the-mill and utilitarian. Don't expect to find the glitz of high-end lodging or expensive resorts like the island's Grand Hotel—you are in Michigan's Upper Peninsula, after all—but that doesn't mean you have to settle for a chintzy room, either.

Hotels and Motels

Billed as St. Ignace's oldest lodging establishment, the **Boardwalk Inn** (316 N. State St., 800/254 5408, www.boardwalkinn.com, $89–150) was built in 1928, and the lobby has 1929 desk registers to prove it. Located across the street from the Huron Boardwalk, the classic boutique hotel is right in the middle of downtown St. Ignace. From here, it's an easy walk to most any attraction, including ferries to Mackinac Island. The hotel fills up quickly, especially during the Labor Day Bridge Walk and St. Ignace's annual car show, so book your rooms well in advance. The Boardwalk serves a deluxe continental breakfast for guests each morning.

Considering the smashing views of Lake Huron and waterfront access to a private beach and boardwalk, the **Bay View Motel** (1133 N. State St., 906/643-9444, $42–65 mid-May–Oct.) is surprisingly cheap. Don't expect much from the Spartan rooms, of course, but what this motel lacks in decor it makes up for in its thrifty appeal and scenic location. Expect rates to jump during holidays and festivals.

Bed-and-Breakfasts

Although it has seven adjoining motel rooms, the █ **Colonial House Inn** (90 N. State St., 906/643-6900, www.colonial-house-inn.com, $65–185) is first and foremost a bed-and-breakfast, and St. Ignace's only one at that. The

Victorian-style home overlooks the Straits of Mackinac and features a wraparound veranda and second-floor balcony. Each of the B&B's seven rooms is distinctively and individually decorated, and has a double or queen-sized bed and a private bath. Occupancy is limited to two people per room, so families will have to stay in the adjacent motel or find rooms elsewhere. Pets are not allowed.

Camping

Of St. Ignace's many campgrounds, the most popular is **Straits State Park** (720 Church St., 906/643-8620, $16–28). With 275 campsites, many with electrical service and all with access to modern restrooms, the park's popularity is driven by a number of can't-say-no perks, including Lake Huron waterfront access, stunning views of the bridge, and the Father Marquette memorial and interpretive trail, which are located here. Close to town, the campground is right in the thick of it, and with easy access to Mackinac Island ferries and other attractions, it's almost worth putting up with the summertime crowds. Of the four modern campgrounds, aim for East Loop or West Loop, which have nicely wooded sites right on the Straits.

Smaller crowds can be found at **Brevort Lake Campground** ($18 single, $26 double) in the Hiawatha National Forest some 20 miles west of St. Ignace. The 4,233-acre lake has about 70 large, forested campsites with tables and fire rings. Campers have access to the lake for boating, fishing, and swimming, and three hiking trails explore the surrounding forest. You'll find boat and canoe rentals, as well as groceries and other necessities, at a small store adjacent to the campground. You might also want to try one of the 54 sites at **Foley Creek Campground** ($16). Although still in Hiawatha National Forest, Foley Creek is only six miles outside town. Smaller and more secluded than Straits State Park, this campground is close enough to the St. Ignace tourist scene to use as a home base. Private campsites are set among large shade trees; Lake Huron beach access is a one-mile hike up Horseshoe Bay Trail. Contact

Hiawatha National Forest's St. Ignace Ranger District office (1900 W. U.S. 2, 906/643-7900, 8 A.M.–4:30 P.M. Mon.–Fri.) for additional information about both campgrounds.

Other Lodging

The cabins at **Balsams Resort** (1464 West U.S. 2, 906/643-9121 June–Labor Day, 313/791-8026 rest of the year, www.balsamsresort.com, $110 daily, $655 weekly) are cozy, fully furnished homes away from home. Balsams Resort can put you up in a one- or two-bedroom log cabin, where you can prepare your own meals in the kitchen, relax in front of the fireplace, or wander over the streams and through the 40-acre woods. You won't be able to see Lake Michigan from all of its nine cabins, but the motel,($45) which isn't quite as quaint, affords a decent view and guests have access to a private beach.

Several area cabins and cottages are available for rent on a nightly or weekly basis, which is an attractive option for families or vacationers looking for an extended, comfortable stay. With a wide range of rooms, locations, and availability, prices can be as low as $100 a night and can easily surpass $1,000 for weeklong rentals. Pets are welcome, but with significant restrictions. Full details are on their website. For information and availability, contact the **St. Ignace Visitors Bureau** (6 Spring St., Ste. 100, 800/338-6660, www.stignace.com).

FOOD

It's not impossible to visit the U.P. without sinking your teeth into the crust of at least one pasty (pronounced PASS-tee), but it's pretty near sacrilegious if you don't at least try one. Stop by **Bessie's Original Homemade Pasties** (1106 N. State St., 906/643-8487) for the traditional Yooper nosh, a potpie creation of beef (or chicken), potatoes, onions, rutabagas, and other vegetables. Bessie's also serves deli subs, old-fashioned ice cream, and smoked fish. **Suzy's Pasties** (1020 W. U.S. 2, 906/643-7007) also serves a great version of this delicacy.

Clyde's Drive-In No. 3 (U.S. 2, just west of

the bridge, 906/643-8303) is another perennial St. Ignace favorite. Known throughout the U.P. as home of the best burgers you'll find on either side of the bridge, Clyde's Drive-In is not only an authentic curbside restaurant, but it's also the best place for a low-priced meal. You can choose to eat in if you prefer, but it gets pretty cramped. Clyde's menu includes fried shrimp, chicken, and perch, light breakfasts, old-fashioned malts and shakes, and the famous three-quarter-pound C Burger. Oh, in case you were wondering, Nos. 1 and 2 are in Sault Ste. Marie and Manistique, respectively.

You'll find more old-fashioned dining at **Bentley's B-n-L Cafe** (62 N. State St., 906/643-7910), a fourth-generation diner that has a vintage soda-fountain look.

Some of the town's best pizza, as well as steak, seafood, and sandwiches, can be found at **Driftwood Restaurant & Sports Bar** (590 N. State St., 906/643-9133, 8 A.M.–12:30 A.M., bar until 2 A.M.), a family restaurant and sports bar. If you miss breakfast, the restaurant also offers a great lunch special for less than five dollars. Dinner entrées can climb as high as $27, a little steep for family dining, but more moderately priced plates can be had for around $10.

For the best of St. Ignace's fine-dining scene—which manages to stay stubbornly unpretentious—grab a table the **Mackinac Grille Restaurant & Waterfront Patio Bar** (251 S. State St., 906/643-7482, www.mackinacgrille.com, $5–8 lunch, $10–18 dinner) specializes in locally caught whitefish. The restaurant is located on the marina and has views of the Straits, Mackinac Island, and the Star Line ferry dock. Mackinac Grille is open 11 A.M.–midnight Monday–Saturday and 9 A.M.–midnight Sunday during the summer tourist season. Off-season hours are 11 A.M.–9 P.M. Monday–Saturday and 9 A.M.–2 P.M. Sunday.

INFORMATION

For traveling assistance and information, contact the **St. Ignace Visitors Bureau** (6 Spring St., Ste. 100, 800/338-6660) or the **St. Ignace Chamber of Commerce** (560 N. State St., 800/970-8717). Both can be found online at

www.stignace.com. More particulars on the trails, camping, and recreation available in Hiawatha National Forest are available from the **St. Ignace Ranger District** office (1900 W. U.S. 2, 906/643-7900, 8 A.M.–4:30 P.M.).

GETTING THERE AND AROUND
Car

Traveling from the south, follow I-75 north across the bridge to St. Ignace. From the north, I-75 drops into St. Ignace from Sault Ste. Marie, while travelers coming east from Wisconsin can take U.S. 2 into the city. If you're crossing the bridge from Mackinaw City, the 2012 passenger vehicle toll is $4, with an additional $2 for each axle if you're pulling a trailer. Tolls will increase every few years until they reach $4.50 in 2014; additional axles will bump up to $2.50. Motor homes will be on an incremental toll schedule, too: the $3.50/axle toll will jump up every few years until it reaches $6/axle in 2014.

Air

The two closest airports with regularly scheduled service are **Pellston Regional Airport (PLN),** south of Mackinaw City in the Lower Peninsula, and **Chippewa County International Airport (CIU)** in Sault Ste. Marie. For information on shuttles and car rentals, see *Mackinaw City* or *Sault Ste. Marie.*

If you'd rather fly into St. Ignace's Mackinac County Airport directly, you can charter a flight through **Great Lakes Air** (906/643-7165, www.greatlakesair.net) from a number of nearby locations, including Detroit and Chicago Midway or O'Hare, but it can be very costly.

Boat

Boaters can make reservations at one of the 120 slips at **St. Ignace Marina** (906/643-8131, www.michigan.gov/dnr). The harbormaster is on duty from mid-May through late September; you can reach the marina on radio channel 9. The location is 45° 51.58 N, 84° 43.06 W.

Public Transportation

Greyhound (800/231-2222, www.greyhound.com) has a bus terminal just across from the ferry docks, providing service to St. Ignace from all points across the country. **Amtrak** (800/872-7245, www.amtrak.com) has partnered with Greyhound to provide transportation to St. Ignace from several major cities in southwest Michigan. **Indian Trails** (800/292-3831, www.indiantrails.com) offers motor coach service to St. Ignace from Chicago and a number of Michigan cities.

Getting Around

Since you're in St. Ignace, odds are you'll want to head across to Mackinac Island before too long. You can catch a ride on a ferry at Arnold Transit Company (906/847-3351, www.arnoldline.com), Shepler's Mackinac Island Ferry (231/436-5023, www.sheplersferry.com), or the Star Line (800/638-9892, www.mackinawferry.com).

Mackinaw City

Mackinaw City, located at the very tip of the Lower Peninsula, serves mostly as a launching pad for tourists bound for Mackinac Island. A community of strip malls and souvenir shops, the downtown also offers some "serious" merchants, including bookstores, antique shops, and clothing stores that don't specialize in T-shirts. The area also boasts Michigan's excellent historic parks—and, of course, the always-beautiful Great Lakes view. You can find some good food and lodging here as well.

SIGHTS
Mackinac Historic State Parks

With a history as long and rich as Mackinac's, it isn't surprising to find a collection of historic sites that, together with Mackinac Island's Fort Mackinac and historic downtown, explore nearly 300 years of Michigan history. If you'd like to explore the park's lighthouse, sawmill, blacksmith shop, churches, homes, and two

forts (and you really should), it's best to purchase a combination ticket, which gives you seven-day admission to three of the four parks (Fort Mackinac, Colonial Michilimackinac, Old Mackinac Point Lighthouse, and Historic Mill Creek) for $23 adults, $14 children 5–17. Families might want to take advantage of the Mackinac Family Heritage Membership for season-long unlimited entry to all of the sites for up to two adults and all dependent children or grandchildren 17 or younger. The $65 membership includes 15 percent off museum store purchases.

Historic Mill Creek Discovery Park (9001 S. U.S. 23, 231/436-4100, www.mackinacparks.com, $8 adults, $4.75 children 5–17) is located in an exceptionally pretty glen with a rushing stream; this pleasant oasis for visitors was once an innovative industrial site. When the British made plans to move from Fort Michilimackinac to Mackinac Island,

the Mackinac Bridge, as seen from Mackinaw City

© PAUL VACHON

PONTIAC'S REBELLION

At the end of the French and Indian War, the Treaty of Paris gave the Great Lakes region to the British, who had a very different way of dealing with Native Americans. While the French had, for the most part, cultivated alliances with the tribes, giving them gifts and engaging in trade, the British were openly hostile – they saw Native Americans as a conquered people instead of as allies.

Native American resentment increased and came to a head in Detroit and throughout the Great Lakes area in 1763. An uprising was planned. The tribes passed messages in war belts made of wampum, encouraging the Native Americans to band together and push the British out of the region. Pontiac, the Ottawa chief who eventually gave the war its name, laid siege to Fort Detroit in May 1763, effectively beginning the war. The conflict quickly spread to other British forts in the region, including Fort Michilimackinac, one of the eight forts successfully taken.

On June 2, 1763, local Chippewa played a match of baggatiway, an early form of lacrosse, against visiting Sac just outside the fort. Soldiers watched the entertainment, unaware that the Chippewa had a violent surprise planned. One of the men threw an errant ball into the fort; when the players chased after it, they grabbed hidden weapons that had been smuggled in by Native American women and turned on the unsuspecting British, killing 16 soldiers within minutes. Five others were tortured to death after the fighting had subsided.

The Native American victory was short-lived. Just over a year later, the British returned to Fort Michilimackinac. Pontiac's siege of Fort Detroit, which ended in October 1763, ended even sooner. Today, Pontiac's Rebellion is considered a draw of sorts: the Native Americans failed to push the British out, but neither could the British conquer them. And, insofar as it forced the British to change their policies toward Native Americans, it was at least a partial success.

Scotsman Robert Campbell recognized the obvious need for lumber. He purchased 640 acres of land surrounding the only waterway in the area with enough flow to power a sawmill. He built the mill in 1790 and later added a blacksmith shop and gristmill.

When the fort ceased operation, the site was no longer profitable, and was abandoned in the mid-1800s. Archaeologists and historians have worked together since the 1970s to re-create the water-powered sawmill on its original site. Today, visitors can see the splashing waterwheel in action and visit the Orientation Center, which has an audiovisual presentation and displays on other artifacts uncovered during the dig. Make sure to walk the park's 3.5 miles of trails, which wind through three kinds of forest or along the creek and mill pond, rising up to scenic overlooks with views of the Straits and Mackinac Island.

An extra $7 will gain you access to the park's new Treetop Discovery Tour, where you can stroll through the treetops on a canopy bridge, fly over a pond on a 350-foot zip line, or scale a climbing wall. Children have access to the Water Power Station and the Forest Friends Children's Play Area. Mill Creek is located just southeast of Mackinaw City, and is open from early May through mid-October 9 A.M.–4 P.M., until 5 P.M. early June to late August.

Old Mackinac Point Lighthouse (550 N. Huron Ave., 231/436-4100, www.mackinacparks.com, $6 adults, $4 children 5–17) is Mackinaw City's third historic state park. Located on a point just east of the Mackinac Bridge, this 1892 light guided ships through the busy Straits of Mackinac for nearly 70 years. When the Mackinac Bridge was completed in 1957, it became obsolete, since vessels could navigate using the bridge's high lights instead of this diminutive 50-foot tower. Today this charming lighthouse, topped with

a cherry-red roof, houses a maritime museum, complete with hands-on exhibits, a tour to the top of the tower led by a costumed interpreter, and historic images. The lighthouse grounds serve as their own delightful little park, with impressive views of the Mackinac Bridge, and a beach, as well as picnic tables scattered across the tidy lawn.

C Colonial Michilimackinac State Park

Believed to be the nation's longest-running archaeological dig, the site of Colonial Michilimackinac State Park (102 Straits Ave., 231/436-4100, www.mackinacparks.com, $10 adults, $6.50 children 5–17) has provided archaeologists with treasures since 1959. The 18th-century military outpost and fur-trading village is the finest of the Mackinac Historic State Parks. The site was long a well-traveled Native American hunting and trading ground; the French built a post here in 1715. The French exploited the Native Americans, bribing them with gifts and alcohol as an incentive to assist them in the fur trade. Though this unfortunate relationship led many Native Americans to abandon their traditional ways of life, the two groups rarely fought. Instead, the French feuded with the British, who sought to expand their landholding in the region. For the next 65 years, the fort along the Straits alternately fell under French and British control.

The fort's most violent episode occurred while it was under British rule. In 1763, Pontiac, the Ottawa war chief, ordered an attack on British posts all over Michigan, an attempt to drive the growing British population out of Ottawa native land. While Pontiac laid siege to Detroit, local Ojibwa stormed the fort, killing all but 13 soldiers. In the end, though, it was the feisty French colonists who sent the British fleeing from Fort Michilimackinac. They dismantled what they could and burned the rest to the ground in 1780, opting for a new, more defensible post on nearby Mackinac Island. In fact, much of the masonry from the original fort was used to build its counterpart in the island.

Today, Colonial Michilimackinac State Park portrays the lives of both the Native Americans and the European settlers, with costumed interpreters reenacting daily life at a Native American encampment and a stockade fort, a modern duplicate of the original. Displays include many of the artifacts excavated by archaeologists. Interpreters demonstrate various crafts and skills, from cooking and weaving to cleaning weapons. They're quite knowledgeable and able to answer most visitors' questions. Don't miss the underground archaeological tunnel exhibit, "Treasures from the Sand." Colonial Michilimackinac is open from early May through mid-October 9 A.M.–4 P.M., until 7 P.M. early June to late August.

Mackinac Bridgemen Museum

It's not slick or fancy, but this small museum is loaded with tidbits and artifacts on the construction of the $100-million Mackinac Bridge. An informative video documents the bridge's design and construction. The original museum (231/436-5937, www.mackinacbridemuseum. com, May 1–Oct. 30 8 A.M.–midnight, free) was destroyed by a fire in 2005—it's since been rebuilt a mile south of Mackinaw City at 13922 Old U.S. 31.

Icebreaker Mackinaw Maritime Museum

When the United States Coast Guard Cutter *Mackinaw* was retired in 2006, ending 62 winters of clearing shipping lanes through the Great Lakes shipping channel, it was transferred to the Mackinaw Maritime Museum and docked in Mackinaw City. Built to help boost wartime production in the early 1940s, the ship was the most cutting-edge icebreaker in the world. Located at the old railroad dock (131 South Huron Ave., 231/436-9825, www. themackinaw.org, $11 adults, $6 children over 5), it's now open for tours from the end of May through August 9 A.M.–7 P.M. and September 9 A.M.–5 P.M.

Downtown

Mackinaw City's downtown is largely what

people refer to as a "tourist trap." Despite the genuine destinations offered elsewhere in the city, downtown seems overrun by a particularly touristy atmosphere and tacky shops, but there are moments when it can seem quaint. You will, of course, want to find one or two of the city's innumerable **fudge shops,** and **Mackinaw Crossings** (248 S. Huron Ave., 231/436-5030, www.mackinawcrossings.com) is an outdoor mall with some good stores and restaurants. One especially noteworthy store is **Enchanted Knights** (231/436-4059, www. shop.enchantedknights.com). This imaginative shop is the perfect place for the serious enthusiast to get outfitted for a Renaissance fair, but also appeals to more modern souls. Here you'll find clothing, gifts, jewelry, and yes, swords—real ones; all of which make you feel like you've just been deputized by the Sheriff of Nottingham.

The **Mackinaw Trolley Company** (231/436-7812) offers tours of Mackinaw City as well as a historical tour that crosses the bridge into St. Ignace. Tours are offered from early May through mid-October and cost around $20 for adults, depending on the tour (prices range $7–15 for children 5–12).

Lighthouses

Mackinaw City is a place where lighthouse lovers will feel at home. The **Old Mackinac Point Lighthouse** stands guard in the shadow of the Mackinac Bridge. The city's second lighthouse, **McGulpin's Point Lighthouse,** a few miles west, recently transitioned from life as a private home. If this weren't enough, there are plenty of historic light stations nearby—enough to make the fascinating **lighthouse cruises** offered by Shepler's Ferry one of the city's more popular attractions.

◀ MCGULPIN'S POINT LIGHTHOUSE

In 2009 Emmett County purchased McGulpin's Point Lighthouse and is gradually restoring it to its early-20th-century appearance (it was decommissioned in 1906) while the residence portion has been reborn as a museum, displaying household items common during the late nineteenth

Historic McGuplin Lighthouse was a private residence until recently.

century. This is one of the oldest lighthouses in the area, built in 1868 and is well preserved today due at least in part to its all-brick construction. The structure is nestled in a heavily wooded area, which belies the fact that it's just outside Mackinaw City. Bringing the structure back to life is expected to be a long-term endeavor. In 2009 the lantern room and light at the top of the tower were replaced. Visitors today can ascend the stairs to get a panoramic view of the Straits. During the summer months, the lighthouse is open 10 A.M.–5 P.M. Saturdays and 11 A.M.–4 P.M. Sundays. Admission is free, but donations for the ongoing restoration of this gem are deeply appreciated.

LIGHTHOUSE CRUISES

The lighthouse cruises offered by Shepler's Ferry (556 E. Central Ave., 231/436-5023, www.sheplersferry.com, $52.50 adults, $27.50 children 5–12) are very popular, and for good reason. Choose between cruising east into Lake Huron or west into Lake Michigan; either way, you'll pass below the Mackinac Bridge for a rare

MACKINAC OR MACKINAW?

First-time visitors to the Straits will often notice the variant spelling of its name and become curious as to the reason. Simply put, the inconsistency can be traced to the area's multi-layered history.

The original name given to the area by the Native Americans was Michilimackinac. Although scholarly opinion is divided, consensus states the term meant "Great Turtle," the giver of life, since the shape of Mackinac Island in fact resembles a turtle. When the French constructed Fort Michilimackinac in 1715, they took the name and attempted to spell it in their language (a process known as transliteration), and ended the word (which is universally pronounced "awe") in "-ac," in keeping with typical French spelling for this particular sound. Shortly thereafter, the name was shorted to Mackinac and the fort was moved to Mackinac Island for strategic reasons. Eventually the new name became associated with the Straits themselves, which probably explains why the French spelling was chosen for the bridge.

When the British established the city on the tip of the Lower Peninsula in 1857, they took the name and spelled it keeping with standard English pronunciation, "aw" for "awe." So while the city's name is distinguished by its spelling, the pronunciation is the same.

Today, the different ways of spelling the name of this beautiful place is a small vestige of Michigan history.

glimpse of its underside and get close enough to at least four historic lights to snap some photos. The trips last about three hours and are narrated by members of the Great Lakes Lighthouse Keepers Association. Historic lights include Mackinac Island's Round Island Light Station and Round Island Passage Light; St. Helena Island Light west of St. Ignace; and the White Shoal and Waugoshance lighthouses. Cruises are offered between June 9 and September 17, though not every day (inclement weather can often force a cancellation), so be sure to call ahead.

FESTIVALS AND EVENTS

Hundreds of actors participate in Memorial Day weekend's **Colonial Michilimackinac Pageant,** which re-creates historical events from the 1700s, including the famous 1763 attack. Perhaps taking a cue from St. Ignace's auto shows, Corvette enthusiasts gather at the **Corvette Crossroads Auto Show** in late August.

Mackinaw City's biggest event is Labor Day's **Annual Mackinac Bridge Walk,** which begins in St. Ignace and ends here. A few days later, in early September, thousands of people turn out for **Hopps of Fun,** the city's annual beer and wine festival, featuring more than 50 microbrews and 60 Michigan wines.

Winter events include an annual **Winterfest** in early January. Information on all these events can be found at www.mackinawcity.com/specialevents. The **Mackinaw Mush Sled Dog Race,** a longtime favorite winter event, usually takes place in early February.

SUMMER SPORTS AND RECREATION
On the Water

One of the more popular **fishing** spots is the Mackinaw City Fishing Pier, built specifically for angling, and where you may have some luck with perch, bass, salmon, or trout. **Cheboygan State Park** (4490 Beach Rd., 231/627-2811, www.michigan.gov/dnr), some 20 miles east of the city, is a favorite among anglers.

St. Ignace's **E.U.P. Fishing Charters** (724 Cheeseman Rd., 877/475-3474, catchfish@lighthouse.net) docks in Mackinaw City for offshore fishing trips with views of Mackinac Island and the bridge. For **parasailing** excursions into the Straits, contact Mackinaw Parasailing (866/436-7144, $55 or $65 single, $100 or $120 tandem).

Beaches

There are miles of shoreline in and around the city, much of it with beaches. About four miles

west of Mackinaw City on Wilderness Park Road, Lake Michigan curves into Cecil Bay, with sandy shores and shallow water. Public restrooms are available.

Golf

South of the city, the **Mackinaw Club** (11891 N. Mackinaw Hwy., Carp Lake, 231/537-4955, http://mackinawclub.com, May 10–October 31, $15–25 9 holes, $35–40 18 holes) was built on the site of an emergency World War II landing strip for B-25 bombers. Today, its 18 holes and driving range are open to the public.

Skydiving

Despite its name, **Mackinaw City Skydiving** (1040 Arbor St., Harbor Springs, 231/242-8822, www.skydiveharborsprings.com, spring–fall, $249 for ages 18 and older, discount for groups of two or more) is actually in nearby Harbor Springs (it's a short drive west of the bridge, and is operated by Skydive Harbor Springs). Still, it has the best view of the bridge. Whether you jump on your own or in a tandem flight, you'll be able to see both peninsulas during one of the most exhilarating experiences in the region.

ACCOMMODATIONS

With the Straits as a major tourism draw, Mackinaw City alone has more than 3,000 rooms. There's nothing quite as extravagant as the island's Grand Hotel or Mission Point Resort, but the city has plenty of lodging at affordable rates.

Hotels and Motels

Families will probably find the prospect of staying at the **Fairview Beachfront Inn and Waterpark** (907 S. Huron Ave., 231/436-8831, http://www.mackinaw-city.com/hotels/aquagrand/) irresistible. The 5,000-square-foot water park, built in 2004, has plenty of room for the kiddies to splash and play with water cannons, waterfalls, and buckets that will douse them with more than 1,700 gallons of continuously recirculating water each minute. There's also plenty of private Lake

Huron beach. The four floors of guest rooms and two- or three-bedroom suites can accommodate families of any size. That said, if you don't have any little ones, you'll definitely want to find rooms somewhere else. Guest rooms begin at $54 and can climb as high as $259 for in-season suites.

Parkside Inn Bridgeview (771 N. Huron Ave., 800/827-8301, www.parksideinn.com) is a very nice hotel located just shy of the bridge, which means that you should be able to get what everyone wants when they stay here—a room with a view—but you'll pay for it, too. Double-occupancy rooms begin at $109 for midsummer weeknights and jump up from there. If you're lucky, you can snag a discount rate and squeeze in for less than $100.

If you're not too picky, there are plenty of no-frills motels offering basic rooms that won't exactly strain your budget. Try **Sunrise Beach** (11416 W. U.S. 23, 231/436-5461), **Bell's Melody Motel** (11460 W. U.S. 23, 231/436-5463, www.bellsmelodymotel.com),

© PAUL VACHON

Accommodations in Mackinaw City include both chains and independents.

or **Northwinds Motel** (11472 W. U.S. 23, 231/436-7434, www.mackinawcitymotels. com). Like a lot of Mackinaw City lodging, you won't be too impressed, but they're about as cheap as they come—you can pay as little as $50, but expect prices for some rooms to go as high as $125 during the busy summer months.

Bed-and-Breakfasts

Located in one of Mackinaw City's oldest homes, the **Deer Head Inn** (109 Henry St., 231/436-3337, www.deerhead.com, $80–225) was built in 1913. The five rooms each try to capture the rustic Northern Michigan spirit, with names like "Hemingway," "Wilderness," and "Hiawatha," and decorations that include bear skins, caribou and fox pelts, and Mission-style furniture. Don't worry—the B&B doesn't compromise elegance to achieve its woodsy charm. Deer Head Inn is open year-round, and room rates rise and fall seasonally.

The **(Brigadoon Bed & Breakfast** (207 Langlade St., 231/436-8882, www.mackinaw-brigadoon.com, May–early Nov., $175–255) is located across the street from Huron Avenue, the Lake Huron shore, and the ferry docks. Its eight rooms mix modern appointments with a taste of the Old World. If you book a stay in the elegant butter-yellow building you'll enjoy king or queen poster beds, heated marble floors in the private baths, and signature breakfasts on the veranda.

Camping

Mackinaw Mill Creek Camping (9730 U.S. 23, 231/436-5584, www.campmackinaw.com, May–Oct.) has more than 600 sites, including full hookups for RVs, tenting sites, cabins, and a mile of shoreline. The amenity-rich campground (free Wi-Fi!) is great for families. Sites range from $19 to $46, depending on the level of amenities desired, while cabin rates swing wildly according to seasonal and holiday demand.

The nearest state campground is 12 miles west at wonderful **Wilderness State Park** (898 Wilderness Park Dr., 231/436-5381, www.

michigan.gov/dnr, Apr.–Dec.), located at the end of a point. It offers 250 modern campsites, rustic cabins, and bunkhouses. The park has two campgrounds, one on the lakeshore and another tucked away in a grove of mature pines.

Twenty miles east of Mackinaw City, **Cheboygan State Park** (4490 Beach Rd., 231/627-2811, www.michigan.gov/dnr) has modern sites near Lake Huron's Duncan Bay. (None are directly on the water.)

Other Lodging

Private, individual cottages are the draw at **The Beach House** (11490 W. U.S. 23, 231/436-5353, www.mackinawcitybeachhouse.com, mid-May–mid-Oct.). While rooms are clean and well kept, they're nothing to write home about—you'll want to stay here for the 250 feet of beach, the view of the bridge (only a mile away), and the cottage-like feel, not so much for the decor. The rooms sleep between one and five people, with kitchenettes available.

FOOD

The **Historic Depot Restaurant** (248 S. Huron Ave., 231/436-7060, www.mackinaw-crossings.com) in Mackinaw Crossings is a casual dining restaurant with nightly entertainment, a full bar, and usually a pretty long wait time for a table. As its name implies, the restaurant channels the bygone days of train travel.

The two-story **(Dixie Saloon** (401 E. Central Ave., 231/436-5449, www.dixiesaloon.com) was a Mackinaw City mainstay in the 1890s. The renovated cedar building is wide open on the inside and features good all-American steak, ribs, and burgers. Stop by the Dixie Saloon on weekends for year-round live entertainment; the restaurant also features a full bar and weekly karaoke. Attached to the Dixie is **O'Reilly's Irish Pub** (www.oreillys-mackinawpub.com), a casual yet elegant bar and grill. Despite the Irish decor, however, the menu is pretty much standard American bar fare.   An excellent choice for quality family dining is **Darrow's Family Restaurant** (Louvigney & Jamet Sts., 231/436-5514, www.darrowsrestaurant.com). A family-run

establishment for over fifty years, Darrow's has evolved from a simple 1950s hot dog stand to a drive-in to today's incarnation as a sit-down restaurant. The eclectic menu includes soups, salads, sandwiches, and entrées such as Mackinaw-style smothered chicken breast, Southern-style chopped steak, and plenty of fish offerings from the Great Lakes.

Fudge

If you put on a blindfold and walk into a random building in Mackinaw City, odds are it'll be a fudge shop. They're all over the place here. The first Murdick's Fudge Store was opened on Mackinac Island in 1887, and **Fran Murdick's Fudge** (222 Central Ave., 888/436-5415, www.franmurdicksfudge.com) is continuing the tradition more than 130 years later. Other fudge shops include **Joann's Fudge** (2 Main St., 303 East Central Ave., 231/436-5611, www.joannsfudge.com), **Marshall's Fudge Shop** (308 E. Central Ave., 231/436-5082, www.marshallsfudge.com), and two **Kilwin's** locations (226 East Central Ave., 231/436-5939, and 176 South Huron Ave., 231/436-7200, www.kilwins.com).

INFORMATION

The **Mackinaw Area Visitors Bureau** (10800 West U.S. 23, 231/436-5664, www.mackinawcity.com) can be reached for helpful information, adventure guides, or brochures. Another option is the **Mackinaw City Chamber of Commerce** (216 E. Central Ave., 231/436-5574, www.mackinawchamber.com), which offers plenty of visitor information, a comprehensive calendar of events, and additional community information.

GETTING THERE AND AROUND
Car

Mackinaw City is accessed by I-75, north from Lansing or south from Sault Ste. Marie. If you're driving east from Wisconsin, take U.S. 2 to St. Ignace and join I-75 south across the bridge. The 2012 passenger vehicle toll is $4, with an additional $2 for each axle if you're pulling a trailer. Tolls will increase every few years until they reach $4.50 in 2014; additional axles will bump up to $2.50. Motor homes will be on an incremental toll schedule, too: the $3.50 per axle toll will jump up every few years until it reaches $6 per axle in 2014.

Air

Delta Airlines currently schedules several flights daily to Pellston Regional Airport (PLN), about 15 miles south of Mackinaw City. Shuttle transportation is available from **Wolverine Stages** (800/825-1450, www.wolverinestages.com, reservations preferred) and **Mackinaw Shuttle** (231/539-7005, www.mackinawshuttle.com). Make sure you call ahead for reservations and current rates. **Top of the Hill Taxi** (800/825-1450) provides taxi service, or you can rent a car through **Avis** (231/539-8302, www.avis.com) or **Hertz** (231/539-8404, www.hertz.com).

Boat

The **Mackinaw City Municipal Marina** (231/436-5269, www.michigan.gov/dnr) has a total of 104 slips and can be reached on radio channels 9 and 16. The harbormaster is on duty from May 1–October 10, from 7 A.M.–9 P.M. The marina is located at 45° 46.55 N, 84° 43.12 W.

Public Transportation

Although **Greyhound** (800/231-2222, www.greyhound.com) offers limited service stops to Mackinaw City, there is no public transportation and no rental services in the city itself, so having your own vehicle at the ready is a must. **Amtrak** (800/872-7245, www.amtrak.com) has partnered with Greyhound to provide service from some cities in southeast Michigan.

Getting Around

To book a spot on one of the three **ferries** with service from Mackinaw City to Mackinac Island, contact **Arnold Transit Company** (906/847-3351, www.arnoldline.com), **Shepler's Mackinac Island Ferry** (231/436-5023, www.sheplersferry.com), or the **Star Line** (800/638-9892, www.mackinawferry.com).

ESCANABA AND THE LAKE MICHIGAN SHORE

U.S. 2, the main road that heads west from St. Ignace and hugs the Lake Michigan shoreline, has plenty of places to pull over for an admiring gaze of the lake. The beaches here are sandier than Lake Superior's, and the water is warm enough in late summer for a swim (though it might be a bit chilly) if the spirit moves you. Visitors taking a small detour to the north will find that the Seney National Wildlife Refuge is an ideal place for hunting, fishing, and berry picking in the summer and, in the winter, Nordic skiing and snowshoeing.

Like most U.P. towns, Manistique isn't quite the booming city it used to be. Since its heyday as a lumber port in the early 1900s, Manistique has shrunk to a town of just over 3,000 people. It's a quaint little place—the Manistique River flows through the center of town and into Lake Michigan, and the scenic boardwalk is worth strolling when the weather is behaving. Just past Manistique, the Garden Peninsula drops south into Lake Michigan, framing the northern reaches of Green Bay.

Garden, the largest city in the Garden Peninsula, is really only worth driving through on your way to Fayette, the Upper Peninsula's most famous ghost town, yet also a fascinating remnant of the area's industrial past. If you're curious you'll want to spend a morning or afternoon exploring the once-bustling production town where pig iron was smelted during the Civil War.

The Green Bay shoreline, west of the Garden Peninsula, is known for its moderate climate and relatively mild (by Upper Peninsula standards) winters, which average just over four feet of snowfall each year. That's little more than a dusting to

© PAUL VACHON

HIGHLIGHTS

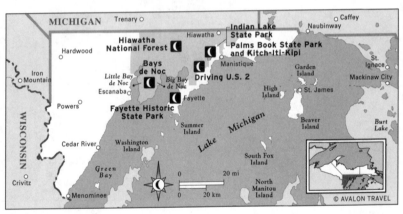

◖ Driving U.S. 2: The few small towns, scenic pull-offs, and other diversions found along U.S. 2 are nothing compared to the drive along the lake (page 63).

◖ Palms Book State Park and Kitch-Iti-Kipi: Looking down to the bottom of this crystal-clear lake, you'll be able to see volcanoes of sand as fresh ground water emerges from the earth (page 65).

◖ Indian Lake State Park: One of the U.P.'s largest lakes is also one of its most popular recreation destinations – stop here for boating, fishing, hunting, skiing, swimming, and hiking (page 66).

◖ Fayette Historic State Park: This historic townsite is one of the U.P.'s most famous ghost towns and a convenient metaphor for the regional rise and fall of big industry. Incidentally, it's a great park, too (page 71).

◖ Bays de Noc: With more than 200 miles of shoreline and 120,000 acres of water (or thereabouts), these bays have irresistible walleye fishing (page 73).

◖ Hiawatha National Forest: The eastern part of the national forest spreads north from U.S. 2 all the way to Lake Superior. If you're looking for wilderness, you'll find it here (page 79).

THE LAKE MICHIGAN SHORE

LOOK FOR ◖ TO FIND RECOMMENDED SIGHTS, ACTIVITIES, DINING, AND LODGING.

Yoopers. The temperate weather year-round makes the last bit of Lake Michigan shoreline a favorite destination for outdoor enthusiasts. Escanaba and Menominee (the U.P.'s third and fourth largest cities, respectively) make this region better than most for dining and lodging choices.

PLANNING YOUR TIME

There's plenty of scenic driving along the lakeshore and a few worthwhile stops along the way. You'll find more activity in Escanaba, Menominee, and Manistique than in the peninsula's smaller towns, but the biggest summertime draw is the fishing. Winter visitors will find miles of snowmobile trails packed into this small region. But unless you're spending a week at one of the forest campgrounds, a day or two to visit the cities or head north to inland recreation will be plenty of time for most tourists.

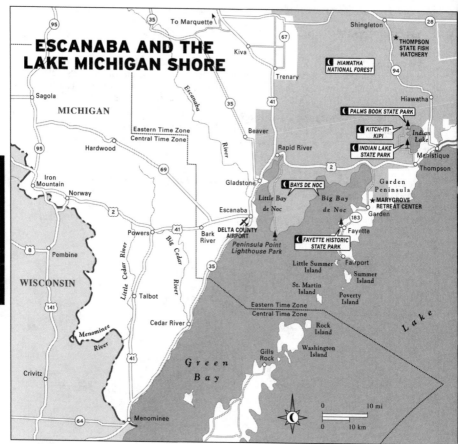

HISTORY

The cities along the Lake Michigan shore have shared the fate of many Upper Peninsula towns: Native American communities gave way to the mining and logging industries, which in turn collapsed as the natural resources became depleted and demand began to wane. Manistique was a thriving port city central to the timber industry, while Escanaba flourished as a conduit for iron ore shipping. Historic Fayette Townsite is a testimony to what could have happened to these once-bustling communities—it's been relegated to a ghost town. But Escanaba, Manistique, and Menominee are still vibrant communities, with economies that are supported mostly by the U.P.'s enduring appeal as a tourism destination.

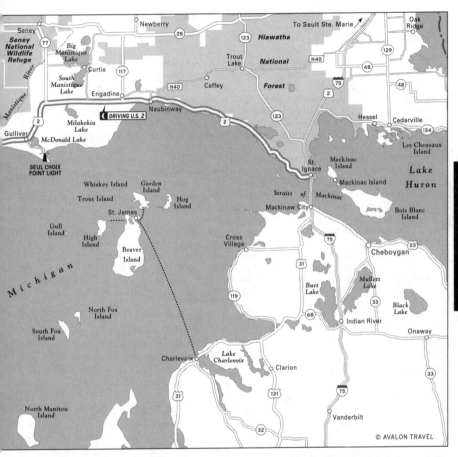

St. Ignace to Manistique

SIGHTS
(Driving U.S. 2

U.S. 2 is one of the main east–west thoroughfares in the Upper Peninsula. There's not much entertainment or lodging along the shore, but the road to Manistique is lined with scenic pull-offs, beaches, and other detours. You'll definitely want to hit one or two of the scenic pull-offs for a stunning view of Lake Michigan.

Heading west along U.S. 2, you'll breeze through Brevort, Epoufette, and Naubinway. You won't have to look far to find a short hiking trail or two, a sandy beach, or a decent restaurant for a touch of local color and off-the-beaten-path dining. A trip north on Highway 33 will bring you to the town of Curtis, nestled between **Big Manistique Lake** and **South Manistique Lake** and home to plenty of outdoor activities. Take a small southern detour

LAKE MICHIGAN

By any standard, the Great Lakes are enormously impressive. Carved away by receding glaciers several thousand years ago, the five lakes are more than beautiful, useful, or recreational – they're massive. According to the Great Lakes Information Network, these lakes (Michigan, Superior, Huron, Erie, and Ontario) cover more than 94,000 square miles and hold an estimated 6 *quadrillion* gallons of water. This equals some six thousand million million gallons (6,000,000,000,000,000), which represents one fifth of the Earth's fresh water, and is enough to cover the 48 contiguous states to a depth of nearly 10 feet.

Compared to those numbers, Lake Michigan itself may seem small. But the second-largest of the Great Lakes (Lake Superior being the largest) and the only one residing entirely within the United States is significant in its own right. Lake Michigan is 307 miles long and 118 miles wide and holds just shy of 1,180 cubic *miles* of water. With an average depth of 279 feet, Lake Michigan is some 925 feet deep at its deepest point. Its surface area is 22,300 square miles, and it has more than 1,600 miles of shoreline.

Scientists who specialize in water studies explain that Lake Michigan and Lake Huron are "hydrologically inseparable," which means they have the same surface elevation and are not separated by a river. The Straits of Mackinac connect the two lakes that are, for all purposes except the most technical, two separate bodies of water.

The southern end of the lake is the warmest and most swimmable, but there are numerous sandy beaches in the U.P. as well. So around all the shores of Lake Michigan, you'll find plenty of good sailing and boating, world-renowned fishing, and sunsets to leave you spellbound.

---

along County Road 432 for a glimpse of Seul Choix Point Light, a spot that offers a better view than the typical lighthouse. On a clear day you can catch a glimpse of Beaver, Garden, and High Islands, not to mention a few passing freighters. The road reconnects to U.S. 2 after passing between **McDonald Lake** and **Gulliver Lake,** two good-sized inland lakes.

Siphon Bridge and Water Tower

Although it isn't nearly as big as Mighty Mac (and not half as impressive, either), Manistique's siphon bridge, which crosses the Manistique River, may very well be the Upper Peninsula's second most interesting bridge. An innovative engineering feat, the 1919 bridge is partially supported by the water underneath it; the roadway is actually sited four feet below water level. Its construction was prompted by a paper mill upstream, which needed to dam the river for its water needs, thus raising the river.

You'll want to stop at the historic water tower for a taste of regional history, too. The 200-foot brick tower is located on the site of the Schoolcraft County Historical Park, which also includes a small historical museum.

Thompson State Fish Hatchery

In Thompson, just a few miles west of Manistique, you'll find a working fish hatchery, which produces a number of different fish for the Great Lakes and inland lakes. It isn't the prettiest stop on a tour of the U.P., but a relatively new interpretive center provides plenty of information about the importance of hatcheries and fisheries, small tributaries to the Great Lakes, and how watersheds work. The Thompson State Fish Hatchery (944 S. State M-149, 906/341-5587, 7:30 A.M.–3:30 P.M. daily, free) offers self-guided tours; you'll be able to read informative signs that help explain what you'll see, and you can watch staff working with the fish in the ponds. Please note that the indoor portion of the hatchery is closed to the public.

◖ Palms Book State Park and Kitch-Iti-Kipi

Located on Indian Lake's western shore, north and west of town, Palms Book State Park (State Highway M-149, 906/341-2355) guards one of the U.P.'s most remarkable natural attractions. Kitch-Iti-Kipi, or "Big Spring," looks like a deep, dark pool tucked away in a grove of cedars—until you get up close. Then you discover it's an enormous spring, where gin-clear water bubbles out of the earth at a staggering 10,000–16,000 gallons per minute.

The park maintains a convenient raft, which allows you to propel yourself across the 200-foot-long spring with the help of a hand-powered cable. It's an amazing view. Take your time to peer 45 feet down (it doesn't appear that deep) into the clear, slightly emerald waters and erupting sand bottom. You'll see lunker brown trout glide among the skeletons of downed trees. The spring is a popular attraction, so come during the early morning or evening, when the surrounding trees cast their reflections on the sill water. You'll have to hike 100 yards or so up the park's gated entrance road, but Kitch-Iti-Kipi is such a magical place that you won't mind. Winter is a particularly special time to visit. Unlike most area lakes, Kitch-Iti-Kipi does not freeze over, while the bubbling water appears even more unique surrounded by snow and leafless trees.

Lighthouses

Ten miles south of Blaney Park at Gulliver, 14 miles east of Manistique, a road leads you down a point to the 1895 **Seul Choix Point Light** (672 NW Gulliver Lake Rd., 906/283-3183, www.exploringthenorth.com/seulchoix/seul.html, 10 A.M.–6 P.M. daily Memorial Day through mid-Oct.; adults $4, children $2, families $10), a worthwhile detour. Pronounced "sul-SHWA"—French for "Only Choice"—it sits at the end of a finger of land that offers boaters the only choice for hiding from storms along this stretch of Lake Michigan shoreline. The township of Gulliver has done a splendid job of restoring the light and creating a maritime museum in the fog signal building.

© PAUL VACHON

Kitch-Iti-Kipi is a natural wonder that will fascinate anyone.

(It includes an admirable scale model of the lighthouse, made by hand with thousands of miniature bricks.) Climb the tower for great views of much of northern Lake Michigan. You'll have a good chance of seeing ship traffic, since Port Inland, just to the east, is an important commercial port. From U.S. 2 at Gulliver, go southeast on County Road 431 (a gravel road) and travel another four miles to the light.

The **Manistique East Breakwater Lighthouse** is located on the east side of Manistique, at the end of the east breakwater arm. The concrete breakwaters were built in the early 1900s as a means of creating safe harbor for large ships. You'll be able to see the red lighthouse, which dates from 1916, from throughout Lakeview Park; access to the pier and lighthouse can be had on the west side of the park. You won't be able to go inside, but you can get close enough for a good view.

ENTERTAINMENT
Kewadin Manistique Casino
Here at Kewadin Manistique (East U.S. 2, Manistique, 800/539-2346, www.kewadinmanistique.com), one of Kewadin's five Upper Peninsula casinos, gamers can try Lady Luck at the slots or hit the tables for blackjack, Let it Ride stud poker and three-card poker. The **Team Spirits Bar** hosts karaoke night on Fridays, and live local entertainment on the last Saturday of each month—during the rest of the week, catch the game on the bar's big screens. If the bar menu isn't enough, visit Mariner's Cove, Kewadin Manistique's 60-seat restaurant, for breakfast, lunch, or dinner at surprisingly good prices.

The casino is located on the north side of U.S. 2 in Manistique—simply take U.S. 2 into town; you can't miss it.

Mackinaw Trail Winery
The small, simply decorated Mackinaw Trail Winery (103 W. Lakeshore Dr., 906/341-2303, www.mackinawtrailwinery.com, 10 A.M.–10 P.M. Mon.–Sat. and noon–5 P.M. Sun. May 1–Oct. 31) tasting room is a testimony to Michigan's growing wine industry. With more than 14,000 acres of vineyards, Michigan is one of the most prolific grape-growing states, producing more than 375,000 cases of different wines (red, white, and fruit) each year. Mackinaw Trail Winery uses grapes harvested from across the state to make their award-winning wines.

SUMMER SPORTS AND RECREATION
Seney National Wildlife Refuge
Several miles north of U.S. 2 (M-77 will take you there), the Seney National Wildlife Refuge (1674 Refuge Entrance Rd., Seney, 906/586-9851, www.fws.gov) has more than 95,000 acres in the area known as the Great Manistique Swamp. Established for resident wildlife, the area provides protection for endangered and threatened species and a habitat for migratory birds. The refuge is one of the U.P.'s most pristine wildlife-viewing areas. Come here to enjoy hiking, biking, paddling, and fishing in the summer and cross-country skiing and snowshoeing in the winter. Stop at the visitors center for an orientation slide show and information about the self-guided audio tour. Seasonal nature programs and special events are offered year-round, provided that sufficient staff is available.

◀ Indian Lake State Park
The Upper Peninsula's fourth-largest lake, Indian Lake is well known among anglers and RV campers. (Be warned that Jet Skiers have discovered it, too.) The anglers come for the perch, walleye, and muskie that thrive in the lake's warm and quite shallow waters. The RV campers come for the convenient location—just north of U.S. 2 and the Garden Peninsula, which includes plenty of campsites and sandy beaches.

The best-known campsites are found at Indian Lake State Park (8970 W. County Road 442, 906/341-2355) with two units, one on the south shore and a second one three miles away on the west shore. Each offers a modern campground and a boat launch. (The

THE CCC CAMP

The Civilian Conservation Corps (CCC) program was begun in 1933 after President Franklin Roosevelt proposed to Congress a program to provide meaningful work to unemployed young men whose families were drawing relief as a result of the Depression.

Participants were initially required to be between the ages of 17 and 25 and were required to be unmarried. They were put to work in a vast network of rural camps performing tasks such as planting trees, building roads, parks, and other recreation facilities, fighting fires, and related duties. Participants were initially paid $30 per week, of which $25 was sent to their parents.

At its peak in 1935 the program enrolled over half a million participants in some 2,900 camps. During the life of the program (1933-1942), a total of 2.5 million men participated, including over 100,000 in Michigan. The sheer volume of work performed by the CCC is amazing. Over nine years the corps planted approximately 3 billion trees and built over 800 parks nationwide. Many of the building projects undertaken by the CCC are still in use today.

The program was so successful that in recent decades the concept has been replicated by many states as an answer to chronically high unemployment.

Noteworthy enrollees in the CCC included actors Walter Matthau, Robert Mitchum, and Raymond Burr, in addition to Admiral Hyman Rickover and test pilot Chuck Yeager.

Several states have museums dedicated to the legacy of the Civilian Conservation Corps. The Michigan facility is located in the Lower Peninsula at 11747 N. Higgins Lake Road, Roscommon, MI 48653. Additional information can be found at www.michigan.gov/dnr.

THE LAKE MICHIGAN SHORE

lake is the focus here, so hiking is limited.) The western unit sites, while not on the water, tend to be less busy. If you're looking for a waterfront site in the southern unit, plan to arrive midweek or during off season, and keep your fingers crossed. This state park offers it all, hunting and fishing, boating, beaches, and picnics, so it's a high demand spot. To reach Indian Lake State Park, take U.S. 2 to Thompson, then go north on M-149 and east on County Road 442. To reach the west unit, stay on M-149.

Hiking and Biking

A lovely trail hugs the Lake Michigan shoreline several miles directly south of U.S. 2. Take Gould City Road south from Gould City until you hit **Gould City Township Park,** which will drop you off in the middle of the pathway. Head east along a moderately difficult off trail route that extends about 3.5 miles before doubling back to your car; you can keep going west for another 2.5 miles or so. The trail here is a little difficult to find, and the footing can be difficult at times, but the solitude and the views of the lake make it worthwhile.

With only two miles of hiking trails, Indian Lake State Park itself probably won't top your list of hiking destinations. However, the **Indian Lake Pathway** has 8.5 miles of trails that are perfect for hikers and bikers. The three loops provide flat-to-rolling terrain and lengths that vary from 1 to 4.5 miles. Don't confuse Indian Lake Pathway with the state park, though, or you're bound to get disappointed. The pathway is located west of the park; the easiest way to reach the trailhead is to take M-149 about 12 miles north of Thompson.

There's a much easier three-mile trail at **Camp Seven Lake Recreation Area,** some 24 miles north of Manistique in the Hiawatha National Forest, which take about two hours to complete. While here, take some time to enjoy the picnic grounds and swimming area. The **Rainey Wildlife Area,** on the north side of Indian Lake, has a hiking trail and boardwalks that lead to a wildlife observation platform, where you've got a decent chance of seeing bald

eagles in spring and early summer. Head north from Manistique on M-94 for about 5 miles, then take a left on Dawson Road. After 1.5 miles, take an access road north to the parking lot. It's definitely worth the detour.

Canoeing and Kayaking

You'll find some of the area's best canoeing in and around Curtis. You can paddle Big Manistique Lake, South Manistique Lake, and the smaller North Manistique Lake, but one of the area's most popular trips will take you down the **Manistique River,** which begins at the west end of Big Manistique Lake and empties into Lake Michigan some 70 miles downstream. There are a few access points just west of Big Manistique Lake and then a long stretch of 27 miles between easy take-outs located at Mead Creek and Merwin Creek campgrounds. Coming from the other direction, put in to the **Indian River** a good distance north, near Steuben, or farther west, where the river passes beneath County Road H-13. From here, take the river about 30 miles west and south to Indian Lake.

Fishing

The abundance of rivers, streams, and large lakes in the area gives this stretch of the Upper Peninsula a bevy of fishing options. Camping or building fires is prohibited in the **Seney National Wildlife Refuge** (1674 Refuge Entrance Rd., Seney, 906/586-9851, www.fws.gov), but you can cast a line at Walsh Creek and the Ditch, Creighton, Driggs, and Manistique Rivers, as well as a number of fishing pools. The water (more than 20,000 acres of it!) of the **Manistique Lakes** is generally less than 30 feet deep. Fishing here includes muskie, northern pike, walleye, bass (large and smallmouth), perch, bluegill, and more. Be warned, though—these waters are accessible to Jet Skis and water skiers. Try **Camp Seven Lake** (906/341-5666) in Hiawatha National Forest for smaller waters. For more information on popular fishing spots, contact the **Manistique Tourism Council** (800/342-4282, www.visitmanistique.com), the **U.S. Forest Service**

(2727 N. Lincoln Rd., Escanaba, 906/786-4062, www.fs.fed.us), or the **Michigan DNR** (906/452-6227, www.michigan.gov/dnr).

Open-water fishing trips can be chartered through **Delta Dawn Charters** (906/428-9093, www.dawndeltachartersup.com), which docks at Manistique for salmon fishing. Morning, afternoon, and evening charters are available. Half-day charters are $325 for up to four people, $50 each for additional persons, up to six total. Full-day charters cost $425 for up to four people, $50 each for additional persons, up to six total.

Golf

If you've come to the U.P. to golf, you can find 18 holes at **Indian Lake Golf and Country Club** (1305 N. Birch St., Manistique, 906/341-5600, www.indianlakegolfclub.com), on the northeast shore of Indian Lake. The course has a pro shop, cart and club rentals, a full bar and restaurant, and all bent grass greens and fairways. There were only nine holes here for more than seventy years, but the club added an additional nine in 2000; 9 holes will cost you $19 (with golf cart, $26), and 18 holes, $37 (with golf cart, $49). Travel north on M-94 from downtown Manistique for 2.5 miles, turn left at the school, and travel a mile to the golf course.

Stony Point Golf Course (8102 W. U.S. 2, Manistique, 906/341-3419, www.michigan.org, $20–28, mid-Apr.–mid-Nov.) is a nine-hole course located just two miles west of Manistique. The par-35 family-owned course has bent grass greens and fairways and is nestled among the Upper Peninsula's renowned scenery.

Off-Road Vehicles

Unlike Michigan's Lower Peninsula, the Upper allows off-road vehicles to operate on any state forest road, so long as it isn't specifically posted as off-limits. Although much of the U.P. is accessible via these roads, a designated trail system has been set aside specifically for ORV use. Plenty of multi-use trails thread through the U.P. along and north of U.S. 2. Try the 36-mile **Sandtown Trail** just east of

the Manistique Lakes. Take M-117 north to Sandtown Road and turn right on Hayes Road to the parking area. The **Brevort/Trout Lake Trail** starts north of Brevort Lake, a short way out from St. Ignace; from there, connect to the Newberry–Rexton Trail and a system of trails that makes its way west. Additionally, all Schoolcraft County roads are open to ORVs, provided you keep to the shoulder at a speed below 25 mph. Detailed off-road vehicle maps are available from Michigan DNR Service Centers (the closest ones are in Newberry and Marquette), or you can contact the **Manistique Area Tourism Council** (800/342-4282, www.visitmanistique.com).

WINTER SPORTS AND RECREATION
Ski and Snowshoe Trails

The **Indian Lake Pathway** provides some of the area's finest groomed ski trails, with 8.5 miles of flat-to-rolling terrain. There are more than nine miles of trails at the **Seney National Wildlife Refuge,** where skiers are likely to see some winter wildlife. Failing that, the wooded surroundings and views of the frozen Manistique River make the trek worthwhile.

Snowmobiling

The area near U.S. 2 and north of Lake Michigan can be traversed by snowmobile on Trail 2, which starts in St. Ignace and makes its way west to Escanaba and beyond. A number of smaller trails (too many to list here) branch off and provide access to much of the U.P., including state and national forests and the Manistique Lakes. Nearing Manistique, Trail 2 skirts the Seney National Wildlife Refuge before dropping south into town. Take Trail 41 or Trail 7 northwest into Hiawatha National Forest.

Ice Fishing

Some people enjoy fishing in sub-zero temperatures on a frozen lake; these people will like the Manistique Lakes near Curtis. The ice tends to form in early December, giving ice-fishers plenty of time for some of the U.P.'s best seasonal fishing for northern pike, walleye, and perch.

ACCOMMODATIONS

Several nice mom-and-pop motels are managing to hang on along U.S. 2, though they're getting more and more competition from chains. Let's hope places like **Star Motel** (1142 E. Lakeshore Dr., 906/341-5363, www.exploringthenorth.com/star/motel.html, $35–65) continue to fend off the big boys. Located a mile or two east of Manistique on U.S. 2, this tidy, vintage 1950s motel has large rooms, rates in the $50 range, meticulous owners, and a nice setting on the lake. It allows well-behaved dogs, too. What more could you ask? Another good non-chain option is the **Beachcomber Motel** (751 E. Lake Shore Dr., Manistique, 906/341-2567, $35–80, open year-round), across from the lake, one mile east of Manistique on U.S. 2.

◖ **Elk Street Lodge** (906 W. Elk St., 906/341-1122) is another excellent option for a comfortable room in a historic building. Visitors get breakfast and a bedtime snack, and you'll find access to the U.P.'s snowmobile trails in wintertime. If you want to do a little gaming while in Manistique, Elk Street Lodge has shuttle service to and from the Kewadin Casino. Lots of **chain motels** are represented along U.S. 2, especially near Manistique.

For Indian Lake lodging, try **Mountain Ash Resort** (3 N. County Road 441, Manistique, 906/341-5658, $45–105 daily during off season, $300–700 weekly July and Aug.). Proprietors Rick and Becky Bayer have 12 log cabins and a three-bedroom lodge (you'll pay considerably more for the lodge) that are open year-round and easily accessible to all sorts of recreation—fishing and hiking in the summertime, snowmobiling and cross-country skiing in the winter. The cabins are stocked with dishes, cooking utensils, appliances, and bed linens. Just bring your own towels and some food, and you'll be good to go. Pets are allowed with a deposit. Take County Road 149 north of U.S. 2 at Thompson, turn right on County Road 442 and left on County Road 441; the lodge is located on the east side of Indian Lake.

Camping

The **Log Cabin Resort and Campground** (W18042 County Road H-42, Curtis, 888/879-6448 or 906/586-9732, www.up-logcabin.com, $22–35 campsites, $45–109 cabins) has some 600 feet of Big Manistique Lake frontage on more than 23 acres of property. Here you'll find boat slips, a game room, a sandy beach, and 50 campsites, 34 of which are full-service RV sites.

Some 20 miles north of Manistique, just off M-94, the **Indian River Campground** (Hiawatha National Forest, 906/341-5666) sits on a bluff overlooking the Indian River. The five private, wooded sites provide plenty of seclusion and the feeling of solitude despite the camp's close proximity to the highway. This is an excellent stop for paddlers making their way down the Indian River Canoe Trail, offering clean drinking water, picnic tables, and grills. **Camp Seven Lake Campground** (906/341-5666) in the Hiawatha National Forest has considerably more campsites—41 of them, each with a table and a fire ring. Camp Seven Lake is perfect for boating, fishing, swimming, and hiking along a three-mile hiking trail. Take County Road 442 eight miles east of Forest Highway 13, 24 miles northwest of Manistique.

FOOD

It seems everyone who drives along U.S. 2 stops for a bite at the **Sunny Shores Restaurant** (906/341-5582, open Apr.–Nov., 7 A.M.–9 P.M. Mon.–Sat., 10 A.M.–6 P.M. Sun.) on U.S. 2 in Manistique. It's known for breakfast, which is available all day long, but also features a number of lunch and dinner options. Also in Manistique, the **Harbor Inn** (238 Cedar St., 906/341-8393) has good whitefish dinners, a bountiful salad bar, and a neat old tavern perfect for a beer after a day of mountain biking or beach-combing. Both restaurants are moderately priced.

If you didn't stop at Clyde's Drive-In No. 3 outside St. Ignace, make a point of going to **Clyde's Drive-In No. 2** (201 Chippewa Ave., 906/341-6021, 9 A.M.–10 P.M. Mon.–Sat.,

11 A.M.–9 P.M. Sun., $10) in Manistique. You'll find the same old-school service, malts, and Big C burgers as at Clyde's other well-known U.P. drive-ins.

Teddy's Pub (100 S. Second St., 906/341-8212, 11:30 A.M.–2 P.M. and 4:30–10 P.M. daily Memorial Day–Labor Day, $8–16 dinner) is well known for its pizza, but you can get a steak or large pan-fried walleye if you're looking for something a little less casual. The prices are modest, the Victorian atmosphere is family-friendly, and the wine list isn't half bad. **Elkhorn Station Restaurant and Sports Bar** (6055 W. U.S. 2, 906/341-2244) is located a mile from Kewadin Casino. It's among Manistique's finer dining spots, with hand-cut steaks and freshwater fish, but the casual atmosphere, full bar, and summer patio dining will tempt you to kick back in your chair and relax. You can get burgers, salads, and sandwiches here, too, all at respectable rates.

INFORMATION AND SERVICES

The **Manistique Area Tourist Council** (800/342-4282, www.visitmanistique.com) is your source for visitor information in Manistique. You can also contact the **Schoolcraft County Chamber of Commerce** (1000 W. Lake Shore Dr., Manistique, 888/819-7420 or 906/341-5010, www.schoolcraftcountychamber.com) and the **Michigan DNR** (906/228-6561, www.michigan.gov/dnr).

Manistique's hospital is the **Schoolcraft Memorial Hospital** (500 Main St., Manistique, 906/341-3200, www.scmh.org), 0.25 miles east of M-94. For banking and an ATM, stop at **Wells Fargo** (226 S. Cedar St., 906/341-1900, www.wellsfargo.com) or one of Manistique's many other banks.

GETTING THERE AND AROUND
Car

U.S. 2 unwinds from St. Ignace, just north of the Bridge, for about 90 miles before it runs into Manistique. It keeps going, of course, into Escanaba and on toward Wisconsin, but

the long, easy stretch between St. Ignace and Manistique parallels the lakeshore for much of the drive. You'll want to detour on highways north and south of U.S. 2 along the way. Coming from Wisconsin, take U.S. 41 north from Green Bay, cross into Michigan at the twin cities of Marinette (WI) and Menominee (MI), then take M-35 north to U.S. 2 and Manistique. From Munising on the Lake Superior shore, simply drive south on M-94.

Boat
There's a small marina in Manistique, where the river flows into Lake Michigan, that offers a small selection of seasonal and transient slips. The **Manistique Marina** (906/341-6841, www.michigan.gov/dnr) has a harbormaster on duty from mid-June through September 1, and can be reached on channel 9 or 68. Marina coordinates are 45° 57.08 N, 86° 14.08 W.

Public Transportation
Regular bus service is provided to Manistique (as well as several small towns along U.S. 2) from St. Ignace and Escanaba, which can be reached from a network of cities throughout Michigan, as well as Green Bay and Milwaukee. Contact **Indian Trails** (800/292-3831, www.indiantrails.com) for current schedules and rates.

Garden Peninsula

The Garden Peninsula is a quiet, peaceful point of land, filled with seldom-used asphalt roads perfect for cycling and a handful of sleepy farms and orchards. Garden, the largest city in the Garden Peninsula, is really just a stop on the way to Fayette, the Upper Peninsula's most famous ghost town. A bit of history, a moderate climate, and scenic beauty make the peninsula one of the U.P.'s more tranquil destinations.

SIGHTS
If you're curious about the town of Garden and its history, stop at the **Garden Peninsula Historical Museum** (State St., 906/644-2398, June–Labor Day). There isn't much here aside from genealogy and community history (logging, fishing, and the like), but the quaint museum, located in a one-room schoolhouse, will likely appeal to local history buffs. If you're looking for an "express" tour of the Garden Peninsula, keep going to Fayette State Park.

◖ Fayette Historic State Park
By far the Garden Peninsula's most notable attraction—and rightly so—is Fayette Historic State Park (13700 13.25 Lane, 906/644-2603, www.michigan.gov/dnr). If you make time for just one stop in this part of the U.P., make it

this outstanding state park. Once the site of a large smelting operation, Fayette's limestone furnaces converted raw iron ore from U.P. mines into pig iron that was loaded onto barges

the dramatic limestone cliffs at Fayette

© DON SIMONELLI, TRAVEL MICHIGAN

THE FURNACES OF FAYETTE

Fayette is now one of the nation's most celebrated ghost towns which typifies the "boom and bust" pattern often associated with towns that sprang up from the California gold rush. In 1867 the Jackson Iron Company established Fayette to serve a very specific purpose: extraction of pure iron (known as "pig iron") from the iron ore being mined nearby, particularly in Negaunee. The site offered the essential combination of limestone (to construct the smelting furnaces), a deep-water harbor, and a large hardwood forest to manufacture charcoal, a necessary ingredient for the smelting process. The 19th-century enterprise made the town hum. In the 1880s, stinky and industrial Fayette boasted a population of 500, and its loud, hot-blast furnaces cranked away seven days a week. By 1891, nearby forests that fueled the furnace were all but depleted, and more efficient steelmaking methods came into vogue. The furnace shut down, and the town died with it.

In modern times, the town was rescued from its demise as a restored historic village, with some 20 historic buildings and scenic overlooks, a visitors center, a dock, and the old furnace complex. Visitors can contemplate this vestige of Michigan's industrial past and try to picture a distant era of thumping industry.

dozen limestone buildings tucked alongside the sheer white bluffs and deep clear waters of Snail Shell Harbor. Start at the visitors center, which gives a good historical overview and features a helpful scale model of the village. You can wander in and out of the hotel, opera house, homes, and other buildings, some intact, some more decayed. Horse-drawn carriage rides around the grounds and boat tours are available from Memorial Day to Labor Day. You're welcome to explore the grounds any time. In fact, a very early morning or off-season visit can add to the ghostly appeal of the place, a big plus when one considers the irony of a crowded ghost town.

With the historic town site acting like a magnet for visitors, the rest of the 750-acre park is often overlooked. It includes a semi modern campground (electricity but no modern restrooms or showers) and several miles of hiking trails, including one that swings north along the bluffs above Snail Shell Harbor.

Marygrove Retreat Center

Although it's clearly a Catholic retreat center (as indicated by the statuary and other decor), Marygrove (6411 State St., 906/644-2771, www.marygrove.org, retreat rates vary) welcomes people of any faith for retreats that provide tranquility, renewal, and rest. It's taken a lot of continuing work to keep the 1920s building—originally a cancer hospital—in top shape, but it's paying off. The 36 guest rooms are clean, well kept, and inviting. Located on Garden Bay, the center has 40 acres of wooded property, gardens, a library, a conference center, and an intriguing labyrinth patterned out of stone. Specialized retreats are offered to guests with specific interests or needs. Take M-139 south of U.S. 2 for nine miles.

Fairport

If commercial fishing interests you, continue down County Road 513 to Fairport, near the tip of the peninsula, where a commercial fleet still operates. There's little else in this simple town, but it's fun to watch the comings and goings of the fishing boats, especially in

bound for Escanaba. In the 1880s, industrial and gritty Fayette claimed a population of 500, and its loud, hot blast furnaces cranked away seven days a week. By 1891, the nearby forests that provided the furnaces with fuel were all but depleted, and more efficient steelmaking methods came into use. The furnaces shut down, and the town died with them.

Nearly a century later, Fayette was reborn as a wonderfully restored historic site and state park. Today, Fayette is surely one of the nation's most scenic ghost towns, its

mid-afternoon, when they usually return with the day's catch.

Fayette Heritage Days

For more than 20 years, Fayette Historic Town site has come to life during the annual Fayette Heritage Days festival, celebrating the town's history. The second Saturday in August brings visitors to the state park for period music, food, and displays that channel the ghost town's once-busy iron-smelting days.

SUMMER SPORTS AND RECREATION
◖ Bays de Noc

With the exception, perhaps, of Green Bay, Lake Michigan's best-known inlets are the Bays de Noc. The Big and Little Bays are positioned at the northwest end of the lake and are known primarily for their world-class walleye fishing. Equally popular, though, are the vast acres of water themselves—more than 120,000 acres between the two bays make them one of the U.P.'s top summer destinations for water lovers. This is a superb destination to fish, boat, paddle, or swim.

Hiking and Biking

There's more to **Fayette State Park** than the historic town site. A five-mile footpath affords views of the ghost town from the area's limestone bluffs, and some 17 miles of trails wind their way through the forests surrounding the town. **Portage Bay State Forest Campground** (906/452-6227, www.michigan. gov/dnr) has just over two miles of nice trails on the Ninga Aki Pathway. Take County Road 483 10 miles south of Garden.

Kayaking

If you're into kayaking—and sea kayaking in particular—you won't want to miss the opportunity to put in to Lake Michigan at **Fayette State Park.** From here, head north to Snake Island and Garden Bay or south to Sac Bay. The waters close to shore are suitable for all but the least experienced kayakers, offering views of towering limestone cliffs and sandy

beaches. Experienced kayakers can head south from the southern point to nose around the offshore islands, but there's plenty of open water involved—caution is advised. No rentals are available, but you're welcome to launch your own.

Fishing

Although you'll be able to find some fishing at **Fayette State Park** and **Portage Bay State Forest** campground (906/452-6227, www.michigan.gov/dnr), you might want a more adventurous option. With **Bay de Noc Charters** (7989 U.S. 2, 906/474-6918, www. baydenoccharters.com) you can set out on a fishing trip in legendary walleye waters. Bay de Noc Charters is located in Rapid River, on the extreme north end of Little Bay de Noc, but fishing excursions are available in Big Bay, too. Visit www.sallmarresort.net/FishingCharters. html for pricing and tour information. Charter tours can run from $300 for five hours, all the way up to $2,250 for a weeklong trip featuring six eight-hour fishing trips.

Boating

There are somewhere around 90,000 acres of water in **Big Bay de Noc.** The larger of Delta County's two bays fills the gap between the Garden Peninsula and Stonington Peninsula to the west, and its open waters provide some of the area's best boating. There are boat landings at the Fayette Historic Townsite and Garden Bay, as well as at Little Fishdam River to the north and Nahma, a few miles south of U.S. 2 on County Road 497. The Fayette Historic Townsite's Snail Shell Harbor has 300 feet of dock available for overnight or day use, and the waters here are deep enough for larger crafts. Boaters in search of larger marinas will have to dock at Gladstone or Escanaba on Little Bay de Noc or Manistique to the east, on the opposite side of the Garden Peninsula. Rates start at $16 for each of these marinas.

Beaches

Located on Lake Michigan's Big Bay de Noc, **Sac Bay Park** (906/786-4902 or

906/786-1020, www.deltacountymi.org) is a 65-acre county park and beach five miles south of Fayette. This is a very basic type of beach, but you will find the sandy lakeshore, a small play area, and some picnic tables—it's basically a rest stop for travelers making their way through the Garden Peninsula. **Fayette State Park** also has a small swimming beach just south of the town.

Golf

There is one adequate but basic golf courses in or near the Garden Peninsula. More serious golfers may wish to head west for the Bays de Noc golf trail near Escanaba. If you want to stay in the Garden Peninsula (you really can't beat the scenery), you can find some good greens at the **Nahma Golf Course** (8588 LL Rd., 906/644-2648, $12). You'll find nine holes on a pretty flat public course. Take County Road 494 south of U.S. 2.

WINTER SPORTS AND RECREATION
Ski and Snowshoe Trails

The same Garden Peninsula trails that make for popular summertime hiking become pathways through the Upper Peninsula's winter wonderland. The five miles of trail that overlook the **Fayette Historic Town site** (13700 13.25 Lane, 906/644-2603, www.michigan.gov/dnr) are regularly groomed for skiing each winter. Although the path is suitable for beginners, more advanced skiers will enjoy the views of Big Bay de Noc and the town, even if they do miss the challenge of a more difficult trail. Strap on some snowshoes for a trek through the town site itself—although it can be brutally cold, you'll bypass the summer tourist crowds.

Snowmobiling

Connect to the U.P. snowmobile trail system via Trail 415 (the only designated snowmobile trail in the Garden Peninsula), which starts in the city of Garden and makes its way north to Trail 2. From there, the U.P. is yours.

ACCOMMODATIONS

On the north end of Big Bay de Noc and the Garden Peninsula, where U.S. 2 and M-183 meet, **Tylene's Motel** (16086 U.S. 2, Cooks, 906/644-7163, open Apr.–Dec., $46) has 12 modestly priced rooms (one with a kitchenette), plus a three-bedroom apartment. The motel offers lake access, beach views, and—best of all—a diner-style restaurant next door. No pets allowed.

Camping

Camping is readily available at dozens of rustic campgrounds within Hiawatha National Forest, and a particularly nice one is the very secluded—and difficult to reach—**Portage Bay State Forest Campground** on the Garden Peninsula's eastern shore. It's southeast of Garden, at the end of Portage Bay Road. For modern campsites, your best bets are often state parks like **Indian Lake** or **Fayette.** For camping reservations at any Michigan state park, call 800/447-2757 or visit www.michigan.gov/dnr.

FOOD

Rosie's at Tylene's (U.S. 2, Garden Corners, 906/644-7155, open daily 7 A.M.–9 P.M. Memorial Day–Labor Day, 8 A.M.–9 P.M. off season) is a must for guests of Tylene's Motel, if only because it's right next door. The unassuming restaurant is a worthwhile stop for everyone else, too, with its good food and convenient location, just west of the intersection of U.S. 2 and M-183. In Garden, you'll want to visit the **Garden House Bar and Grill** (M-183, downtown Garden, 906/644-2844, 11 A.M.–10 P.M.). Dinners are a little on the pricey side for the U.P.—entrees can run upwards of $20—but the fresh fish (locally caught, of course) and prime rib are worth the stop. As its name implies, **Sherry's Port Bar** (4424 M-123, 906/644-2545), south of Garden, is primarily a drinking establishment, but it's managed to become a catch-all family restaurant with cheap food and a good breakfast. Its proximity to Fayette State Park makes it a popular stop.

INFORMATION

For visitor information and assistance for the Garden Peninsula, contact the **Bays de Noc Convention & Visitors Bureau** (230 Ludington St., 906/789-7862 or 800/533-4386, www.travelbaysdenoc.com) and the **Delta County Chamber of Commerce** (230 Ludington St., 888/335-8264 or 906/786-8830, www.deltami.org).

Bank choices are limited in Garden, but you can do some banking at **First Bank Upper Peninsula** (6322 State St., Garden, 906/644-3535, 8:30 A.M.–4 P.M., www.first-bank.com), but note that there is NOT an ATM on site.

Your best bets for medical attention will be to head to Manistique for the **Schoolcraft Memorial Hospital** (500 Main St., Manistique, 906/341-3200, www.scmh.org). Take East U.S. 2, turn left on M-94 north, then turn right on Main Street—the hospital is 0.25 mile up the road.

GETTING THERE AND AROUND
Car

This is really your only viable option for getting to (and around) the Garden Peninsula. There isn't any sort of regular public transportation that makes its way south of U.S. 2, there certainly aren't any airports, and although there are boat landings and docks at Fayette State Park, Garden Bay, and Portage Bay, there are no big marinas like you'll find in Escanaba, St. Ignace, or even Manistique. Besides, even if you managed to get here by some other means, there's nowhere to rent a car—you'll have to drive your own in or rent a vehicle in one of the U.P.'s bigger cities.

Escanaba and Vicinity

A metropolis for these parts, Escanaba and neighboring Gladstone (just a few miles north) are home to some 20,000 people, serving as the industrial and commercial center for the south-central Upper Peninsula. The natural deepwater port gave Escanaba its start back in the Civil War days, when a hastily built rail line linked the iron mines in Negaunee with the port, bringing raw materials to support the Union war effort. Today iron ore is still being shipped out of Escanaba's modern port facilities in the form of iron/clay taconite pellets, bound for steelmakers in Indiana and Ohio.

Unlike M-35 north of Gladstone, the stretch of highway between Gladstone and Menominee runs close to the coast, and it has been designated the **U.P. Hidden Coast Recreation Heritage Route.** Follow it south from Gladstone into Escanaba.

SIGHTS
Downtown

Downtown Escanaba focuses on Ludington Street, an east–west route that runs from M-35 to the waterfront. Here's where you'll find most of the town's restaurants and shops and a growing local arts presence. The town's landmark is the **House of Ludington** (223 Ludington St., 906/786-6300, www.houseofludington.com), a grand old Queen Anne resort hotel built in 1865. After enjoying a second heyday in the 1940s and '50s, the old hotel has stuttered and stumbled with some shoddy interior remodeling and mismanagement. The most recent owners have reopened the hotel's restaurant with an upscale menu (one of the best in the U.P.), and the building's imposing facade continues to anchor the downtown.

At the foot of Ludington Street, lovely **Ludington Park** offers paved pathways along the water and to a small island (in-line skates permitted), interpretive signs explaining local history, a band shell that hosts concerts on Wednesday and Sunday evenings in summer, a playground, a beach, tennis courts, and a boat launch.

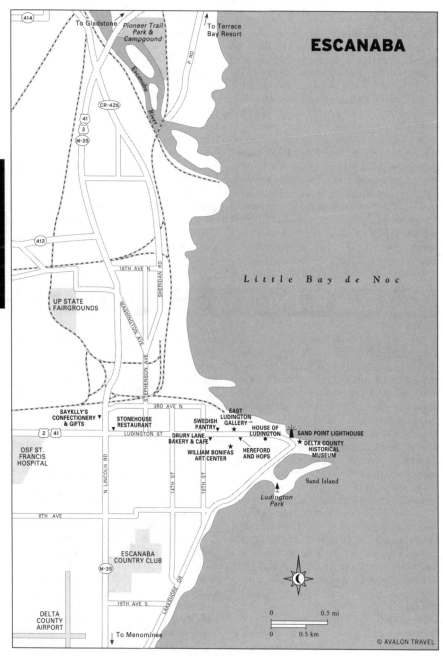

ESCANABA IN DA MOONLIGHT

Travelers who haven't been to the Upper Peninsula and don't quite know what to expect could certainly do worse than to track down a copy of *Escanaba in da Moonlight*, an off-color love song to the beautiful, quirky, often misunderstood Yooper culture.

The movie (starring, written, directed, and produced by Michigan native Jeff Daniels) tells the story of the "buckless Yooper," Reuben Soady, a 42-year-old Escanaba man in the humiliating position of never having shot a buck, considered an essential rite of passage in Soady's Escanaba. Most of the film takes place at the Soady deer camp, and at the core of it, it's about hunting and family and expectations and the spirit of the Upper Peninsula itself. It's really quite good.

That said, the play is rather odd as well. Things get a bit off (even more so in the movie) when talk turns to UFOs, but the rest of the film is, at least to an outsider's eyes, an accurate depiction of area culture: the local vernacular ("Yoobetcha!"), the conviction that euchre is the only card game worth playing, the flannel shirts, the hunting camp. This is the Upper Peninsula seen from a somewhat stereotypical perspective, told by someone who understands and appreciates the land and its people.

Clearly, the movie is not for everyone (the film's website attributes the PG-13 to "uncultured humor") and has not been well received by critics, but may still be worth a place in your rental queue.

THE LAKE MICHIGAN SHORE

Escanaba's art scene can perhaps be best witnessed during a visit to the **William Bonifas Art Center** (700 1st Ave. S., 906/786-3833, www.bonifasarts.org, 10 A.M.–5:30 P.M. Tues.–Fri., 10 A.M.–3 P.M. Sat.), a community art facility housed in a 1938 building that originally served as a gymnasium and auditorium. Today, the center is open for visitors to tour the changing free gallery exhibits, watch theatrical productions, and attend classes. The **East Ludington Gallery** (619 Ludington St., 906/786-0300, www.eastludingtongallery.com) displays and sells works by more than 35 regional artists.

Delta County Historical Society

Just to the south, the **Delta County Historical Museum** (16 Water Plant Rd., Escanaba, 906/786-3428, www.deltahistorical.org, Memorial Day–Labor Day, $3 adults, $1 children) has interesting and informative displays on local logging, native cultures, military history, and maritime history. The four-room museum has been collecting historical artifacts for more than 50 years, and the result is an important documentation of regional heritage.

Waterfalls

They're pleasant enough, and certainly pretty, but with a drop of about five feet spread out over a number of tiers, the **Rapid River Falls** aren't as powerful or impressive as some of the U.P.'s other waterfalls. Still, they're peaceful, relaxing, and visually interesting. A park on the river has picnic tables and grills, as well as a playground. Take U.S. 41 seven miles north of Rapid River and follow the signs to the left.

Lighthouses

One of Ludington Park's most popular attractions is the **Sand Point Lighthouse** (16 Water Plant Rd., Escanaba 906/786-3763), an 1868 brick light that was restored and reopened in 1990 by the Delta County Historical Society. It was a big job: In the 1940s, the Coast Guard remodeled the obsolete light for staff housing, removing the lantern room and the top ten feet of the tower. For a few dollars, you can climb the tower and take a look at the restored keeper's house. The light's first custodian, by the way, was Mary Terry, one of the nation's earliest female light keepers. The Delta County Historical Museum is located nearby.

At the tip of the Stonington Peninsula, across

© HENRYK SADURA/123RF.COM

Sand Point Lighthouse has been lovingly restored by local volunteers.

Little Bay de Noc from Escanaba, **Peninsula Point Lighthouse Park** is the perfect place to sprawl out on a sunny day: an open meadow, a grassy picnic area, a great shoreline for beachcombing, and—the main attraction—an 1865 lighthouse. Climb the spiral stairway for one of the most expansive views around: a 270-degree survey of Green Bay, and even Wisconsin's Door County in clear weather. The lighthouse was abandoned in the 1930s, replaced by a more effective shoal light several miles offshore. Local volunteers restored and reopened the old light, prior to it being ravaged by fire in 1959. While the keeper's home was destroyed, the tower survived the blaze.

ENTERTAINMENT
Island Resort and Casino
Harris, a small town some 13 miles west of Escanaba, has one of the U.P.'s finest gaming resorts. Island Resort and Casino (W399 U.S. 2/U.S. 41, 906/466-2941 or 800/682-6040, www.chipincasino.com) is a 24/7 casino with more than 1,400 slot machines and plenty of table games—craps, blackjack, roulette, poker, Texas Hold 'Em, and more. When you get hungry, stop at the Firekeeper's Restaurant for cheap breakfast and lunch or daily all-you-can-eat dinner specials. Additional on-site dining can be found at the Beachcomber Restaurant and Bar, Coral Reef Grille, and Bingo Snack Bar. The Island Showroom seats more than 1,300 for headliner shows; for lesser-known acts, visit Club Four One for weekly live bands and comedy nights every Sunday. A golf course, a 113-room hotel with indoor pool, a salon, and an RV park round out the experience and cement Island Resort's reputation as one of the Midwest's premier resort destinations. This is an Upper Peninsula casino experience unlike any other.

FESTIVALS AND EVENTS
Upper Peninsula State Fair
On M-35, between Escanaba and Gladstone, you'll pass the U.P. State Fair Grounds. For decades Michigan had the rare distinction of hosting two state fairs, the event in Detroit

as well as its Upper Peninsula counterpart. However, the tumultuous economy of the last several years caused the State of Michigan to end many traditions, and the fairs were unfortunately among them. Since 2010 the U.P. edition has been operated by the Upper Peninsula State Fair Authority, a quasi public body governed by a board consisting of representatives from all fifteen Upper Peninsula counties. Regrettably, Detroit has not managed to continue its fair. The fair continues to be held during the third week of August. For additional information, contact the **Delta County Chamber of Commerce** (230 Ludington St., 906/786-2192 or 888/335-8264, www.deltami.org).

Balloons on the Bay and Pioneer Days

The combination is interesting, to say the least—hot air balloons and pioneer heritage. Every year in late June, the U.P. State Fair Grounds become the staging ground for hot air balloons that fill the sky above Lake Michigan. Jump in the basket for a tethered balloon ride or experience a bit of the old days while watching lumberjack exhibitions, old-fashioned craft demonstrations, and a barbecue cook-off. Again, for more information, get a hold of the **Delta County Chamber of Commerce** (230 Ludington St., 906/786-2192 or 888/335-8264, www.deltami.org).

Monarch Migration

There really isn't anything official about the annual monarch butterfly migration, aside from volunteers, organized by the U.S. Forest Service, who count the populations and help tag the insects for tracking. But when it comes to monarch viewing, you can join the throng of enthusiasts who make the trek to the Stonington Peninsula every August. The peninsula, which extends south into Lake Michigan between the Bays de Noc, is an annual gathering point in the butterflies' great migration south to Mexico—they stop in and around Peninsula Point Lighthouse Park before the long flight across Green Bay

and the open waters of the lake. The brilliant orange and black monarchs are best seen in August, although the migration continues into September, often overlapping with the autumn colors Michigan is known for, and combining to form a spectacular display of color.

SUMMER SPORTS AND RECREATION
◖ Hiawatha National Forest

The 860,000-acre Hiawatha National Forest spans much of the central U.P., with its western unit stretching all the way from the Lake Michigan shoreline of the Stonington Peninsula to the Lake Superior shore near Munising. For information on hiking trails, campgrounds, canoe routes, and other attractions, stop at the **Hiawatha National Forest Visitor Information Station** (906/474-6442) just east of Rapid River on U.S. 2. You can talk with rangers and pick up a wide selection of maps and handouts. The station also includes interpretive displays and a small bookshop.

Hiking and Biking

Hiawatha National Forest's 40-mile **Bay de Noc/Grand Island Trail** follows an old Ojibwa portage route, used to carry canoes and supplies between Lakes Michigan and Superior. Today it ends just short of both lakes, beginning just northeast of Rapid River and ending 10 miles shy of Lake Superior at Ackerman Lake. The trail parallels the Whitefish River, about half a mile to two miles away, tracing its eastern bluff and offering high, sweeping views of the forested river valley. It hopscotches over several streams and passes several lakes. Due to the high density of hardwoods, the route is particularly beautiful in the fall color season.

Horses and mountain bikes are allowed on the Bay de Noc/Grand Island Trail, but not motorized vehicles. Primitive camping is permitted throughout the national forest (no permit required). To find the trailhead, follow East U.S. 2 from Rapid River two miles, then turn left on County Road 509 and drive another 1.5 miles. You'll see a parking area on the west side of the road.

A few miles east of the Hiawatha National Forest Visitor Information Station, turn north off U.S. 2 onto County Road H-13 to reach the great hiking and mountain biking trails of **Pine Marten Run.** The trail network lies between the Indian River to the north, County Road 440 to the south, Forest Road 2258 to the west, and County Road 437 to the east. This newly signed area includes 26 miles of rolling single-track and overgrown double-track. Various loops wind through groves of huge hemlocks and white pines, a dozen lakes, and the beautiful Indian River. From County Road H-13, turn right on County Road 440, and watch for the Forest Service sign directing you to Iron Jaw Lake. Alternatively, head north from County Road 440 on Forest Road 2258, where you'll find another trailhead just before the road crosses the Indian River. Maps and more information are available from the Hiawatha National Forest Visitor Information Station.

Just three miles north of Gladstone, the Escanaba River State Forest maintains the **Days River Pathway,** a fine nine-mile hiking trail that loops through forest and along the scenic Days River, which cuts a deep gorge near the trailhead. This is a good stream for brook trout, so bring a fly rod. Don't forget your binoculars or camera, too, since the area features warblers and other songbirds. To reach the trailhead, follow U.S. 2 east of Gladstone three miles, then turn left onto Days River Road. For more information, contact the **Escanaba Forest Area Office** (906/293-3293, www.michigan.gov/dnr).

On the opposite side of Little Bay de Noc, the Stonington Peninsula is largely bypassed by tourists, as it lacks accessible sandy beaches or significant commercial attractions. It is a soft and peaceful place, with smooth slabs of bedrock shoreline and sunny meadows that have reclaimed abandoned farmland. The Hiawatha National Forest manages a nice stretch of shoreline along the peninsula's west side, including a few campgrounds and hiking trails. Look for the Forest Service signs south of Garth Point. The peninsula preserves several stands of old-

growth hemlocks, hardwoods, and pines. One of the most notable examples is now protected as the **Squaw Creek Old Growth Area,** part of the Hiawatha National Forest. Though these woods are not virgin timber, 19th-century loggers practiced selective cutting (quite unusual in those days) and left behind several large trees, which are now huge. Trails are few—just a couple of abandoned logging roads open only to foot traffic. Walking is easy, however, since the high shade canopy created by the trees crowds out the underbrush usually found in the woods. Be sure to take a compass.

The southern part of the 65-acre tract is particularly scenic, with the clear, tea-colored waters of Squaw Creek slaloming between the fat trunks. You'll find the largest hemlocks south of the creek and huge hardwoods just to the north. Squaw Creek is not marked by a sign and shows up on few maps. To find it, drive south nine miles on County Road 513; just before and after the road crosses the creek, you'll see pull-offs on the east side of the road and old roads leading inland.

Canoeing and Kayaking

Just north of Pine Marten Run and the Indian River, the **Big Island Lake Canoeing Area** offers paddlers a quiet chain of nine lakes. Since there are few launches for powerboats, the lakes usually remain peaceful and pristine even in the height of summer. Again, be sure to obtain information and maps from the Visitor Information Station. It will be a great asset during your adventure.

You'll find good paddling on the **Escanaba River,** too. Put in northwest of Gladstone and take the river all the way to Green Bay. There are more than 40 miles of good paddling between Gwinn and Gladstone, with periodic access points; most of the river is suitable for intermediate paddlers, though some sections are more difficult. You can paddle a few miles along the **Ford River,** southwest of Gladstone. Beginners can take the river between County Road 414 and U.S. 2, but there's some whitewater as you get closer to Green Bay (there's an access point at U.S. 2 if you're nervous

about continuing on). Of course, experienced open-water kayakers can paddle Little Bay de Noc and Green Bay. Rent a canoe or kayak (or a number of other boats) from **Splash Rentals** (2311 9th Ave. N., 906/789-1009) in Escanaba.

Fishing

Although it's the smaller of the two bays, **Little Bay de Noc**'s 30,000 acres of water are nothing to sneeze at. The bay is known for its fishing, particularly for its walleye during the fall. Captain Dick Stafford of **Take Five Charter Fishing** (7262 U.S. 2, 906/789-0110) in Gladstone pilots half- and full-day fishing charters in Little Bay de Noc and Green Bay. Rapid River's **Bay de Noc Charters** (7989 U.S. 2, 906/474-6918, www.baydenoccharters.com), on the northern tip of the bay, can take you on a fishing trip in Little Bay de Noc, and charters into Big Bay de Noc are available as well. Gladstone is home to a bevy of fishing charters—contact the **Bays de Noc Convention & Visitors Bureau** (230 Ludington St., Escanaba, 906/789-7862 or 800/533-4386, www.travelbaysdenoc.com).

If you'd rather set off on your own, get a hold of **U.P. Michigan Boat Rentals** (434 E. Prospect St., Marquette, 877/228-5447, www.upmichiganboatrentals.com). Marquette is some 60 miles north of Gladstone, but U.P. Michigan Boat Rentals can deliver fishing or pontoon boats to Little Bay de Noc (plan on spending at least $1/mile for delivery and pickup). Local tackle shops and outfitters include **Bayview Bait and Tackle Shop** (7110 U.S. 2, 906/786-1488), between Gladstone and Escanaba, and **Walleye's Choice** (10132 M-35, 906/428-1488, www.walleyeschoice.com). Walleye's Choice also offers fishing charters. Cast a line into the **Whitefish River,** which flows into Little Bay de Noc at Rapid River, for trout and smallmouth bass.

Beaches

In Gladstone, visit **Van Cleve Park** (906/428-2916) on Lake Shore Drive. There's a sandy beach for swimming in the waters of Little Bay de Noc, and a number of other facilities make this one of the area's best beaches for family fun—a fitness course, sand volleyball courts, horseshoes, basketball courts, a softball diamond, a gazebo, playground, and more. The Gladstone Harbor is here, too.

Golf

Golfing in the Upper Peninsula is like most U.P. activities—casual and unpretentious, without the pomp and circumstance found at more expensive destinations. One of the U.P.'s finest golf trails, right in Delta County, consists of four top-notch courses, each within 20 minutes of the others. You'll spend somewhere around $25 for 18 holes at each of them. The **Escanaba Country Club** (1800 11th Ave. South, 906/786-1701, www.escanabacc.com) is the oldest country club in Delta County, founded in 1915. The par 71, 18-hole course has a PGA professional on staff and one of the most difficult finishing holes around. Nearby **Gladstone Golf Club** (6514 Days River Rd., 906/428-9646, www.gladstonegolf.com) is surrounded by of thousands of acres of forests. The Days River runs through 5 of the 18 holes. Take U.S. 2 about three miles north of Gladstone and turn left on County Road 446 for two miles. Rated one of the best courses in the area, the 18-hole **Terrace Bluff Golf Club** (7146 P Rd., Gladstone, 906/428-2343, www.terracebay.com) features views of the bay and is suitable for golfers of every skill level. The amenities of Terrace Bay Resort and Convention Center are close at hand. Finally, seven miles west of Escanaba on U.S. 2, the **Highland Golf Club** (906/466-7457, www.highlandgolfclub.net) was Delta County's first 18-hole course.

Off-Road Vehicles

The **Forest Islands Trail** begins about 10 miles south of Escanaba, west of M-35 (take 4.25 Road to H Road and turn right, then turn left on F Road to parking). The 33-mile trail ends in Cedar River, and is broken into the Limpert Road Loop, the Seven Mile Marsh Loop, and the Westman Road Loop near Cedar River at the south end of the trail.

THE LAKE MICHIGAN SHORE

WINTER SPORTS AND RECREATION
Downhill Skiing

The Escanaba area is only a short distance east of Iron Mountain and the Upper Peninsula's best-known skiing runs, but beginning and intermediate skiers can try **Gladstone Sports Park** (900 North Bluff Dr., 906/428-9130, $10/day ski, $8/day tube), just east of the city. It's a relatively low-key resort but its combination of easy hills and tubing runs makes it ideal for families who want to avoid the crowds and prices of the bigger resorts to the west. There are a few rope tows and a T-bar, three tube runs (with the only return lifts in the U.P.), and a snowboard terrain park that includes a half-pipe for riders. Concessions are sold in the Ski Chalet.

Ski and Snowshoe Trails

The nine miles of **Days Rivers Pathway** (906/293-3293, www.michigan.gov/dnr), three miles south of Rapid River, are among the most popular groomed ski trails in the area. Choose from loops of between one and eight miles, suitable for beginners as well as experts. Six miles north of Rapid River, the **Rapid River Ski Trails** (906/786-4062, www.fs.fed.us) provide an especially beautiful excursion through varied terrain. Pay attention to the signs, and stay off the 10-mile loop unless you're an expert skier—the other loops are suitable for less-experienced cross-country enthusiasts. Snowshoers can make tracks alongside both trails. Both trails have donation boxes to help support trail maintenance and upkeep, so if you have a few spare dollars, it wouldn't hurt to help out. The surprisingly secluded **Escanaba Cross Country Pathway** is located inside the Escanaba city limits, but it's so quiet you wouldn't know it.

Dog Sledding

In the winter, the Bay de Noc and Grand Island Trail area serves as the stomping grounds for the sled dogs of **Triple Creek Sled Dog Kennels** (906/439-5242 or 877/275-7533). Owner Bob Johnson, one of the U.P.'s most experienced mushers, offers a variety of two-hour to five-day dogsled trips in the region. Package tours include a stay at **Johnson's Buck Sporting Lodge,** his solar-powered wilderness lodge north of Rapid River.

Snowmobiling

Gain access to the Michigan's seemingly endless 6,100 miles of interconnected snowmobile trails via the **Nahma Grade Snowmobile Trail**; the trailhead is a couple miles east of Rapid River. After following a natural gas pipeline for 11 miles, the trail heads north. From Escanaba, Trail 2 takes you west toward Iron Mountain.

ACCOMMODATIONS

The typical sprawl of chain motels runs along M-35 between Escanaba and Gladstone, but some nice family-owned operations are still holding their own along the waterfront, with rates in the $50–100 range. The ◖ **Terrace Bay Resort** (7146 P Rd., 906/786-7554, www.terracebay.com, $72–92), on Little Bay de Noc between Escanaba and Gladstone, has nice, clean motel rooms with great bay views. The 200-acre golf resort complex includes an 18-hole golf course, indoor and outdoor pools, tennis courts, a game room, and more. To find Terrace Bay, watch for signs on U.S. 41 south of Gladstone. About six miles south of Escanaba on M-35, **Fishery Pointe Beach Cottages** (E5043 M-35, 616/361-1386, www.fisherypointe.com, Memorial Day–Labor Day, $570–700 per week) and **Sandy Shores Resort** (4717 M-35, 906/786-3625, $65, $575–725 per week for cabins, May–Nov. 1) offer housekeeping cottages (simple accommodations with no cleaning service provided) on a nice stretch of sandy beach.

Downtown Escanaba's ◖ **House of Ludington** (223 Ludington St., 906/786-6300, www.houseofludington.com, $55–85) hasn't exactly been restored to its former glory, but the current owners, Ed and Suzell Eisenberger, have certainly made a good faith effort. The hotel's 17 guest rooms are decorated with different themes, each with an eye to highlighting the hotel's storied past. The

© PAUL VACHON

THE LAKE MICHIGAN SHORE

The historic House of Ludington is a local legend in dining and lodging.

House of Ludington was conceived in 1865, renamed in 1871, and torn down and rebuilt in 1883. It's passed through numerous hands in the decades since. It was closed for a few years during the 1990s. A new bar occupies the spot that was once a courtyard, and the building also includes two dining rooms and modern amenities in each guest room.

A few miles south of Escanaba, travelers can find some of the remote peace and tranquility the U.P. is known by visiting **St. Michael's in Cedar Dells** (2726 M-35, Bark River, 906/786-4541, www.escanabacottages.com, $55–150). St. Michael's is a resort tucked away in a cedar grove overlooking Lake Michigan. The rustic but clean one- to three-bedroom cottages are perfect for families. Pets are welcome, too.

Camping

Haymeadow Creek Campground (Rapid River Ranger District, 499 East Lake Shore Dr., Manistique, 906/474-6442, www.fs.fed. us) is about 10 miles north of U.S. 2 on County Road 509 in Hiawatha National Forest. Each

of the 15 campsites has a fire ring and a picnic table, and drinking water is available on site. You'll be able to connect to the Bay de Noc–Grand Island Trail from here, too.

Closer to town, you'll find both tent and RV camping at the **Pioneer Trail Park and Campground** (906/786-4902, www.delta-countymi.org, $15–17 tents, $23–26 RVs), a county park a few miles north of Escanaba. Of the 75 sites, only 17 are for tenting, but these include fire pits and picnic tables. The rest of the campsites have electric hookups for RVs, and most of them have water. Pioneer Trail is ideal for families: Amenities include a playground and a playing field, a picnic area, showers, and optional cable TV. The campground is on U.S. 2/M-35 between Gladstone and Manistique. There are 25 additional campsites at the **O. B. Fuller Park and Campground** (906/786-4902, www.deltacountymi.org, $24–26), another county park on Lake Michigan, 15 miles south of Escanaba. The campground features more than 80 wooded acres, Lake Michigan shoreline, fishing on the

Bark River, and electricity and water at each campsite. Follow M-35 south from Escanaba to the Bark River crossing.

FOOD

You'll find your best dining options in downtown Escanaba. The hottest spot in town is **Hereford and Hops** (614 Ludington St., 906/786-1945, www.herefordandhops.com, 11 A.M.–10 P.M. Mon.–Sat. and 4 P.M.–9 P.M Sun.), a cook-your-own-steak place and microbrewery in the 1914 Delta Hotel. You'll find excellent seafood choices, too, such as grilled salmon and tilapia bruschetta. Entrée prices range $20–24. For homemade soups, sandwiches, and wonderful Finnish baked goods, don't miss the **Drury Lane Bakery and Cafe** (906 Ludington St., 906/786-0808). You can get traditional American meals at the **Swedish Pantry** (819 Ludington St., 906/786-9606, www.swedishpantry.com), but you'll also find that—true to its name—the cute little restaurant serves up traditional Swedish food that's tough to resist. No one will stop you from ordering the meatloaf or roast beef, but you really should try the Swedish meatballs, potato sausage, and rutabaga. The Swedish Pantry is open for breakfast, lunch, and dinner. Grab a massive fresh-baked cookie from the bakery, and browse the traditional Scandinavian merchandise at the gift shop.

The **Stonehouse Restaurant** (2223 Ludington St., 906/786-5003, www.stonehouseescanaba.com, 11 A.M.–2 P.M. and 5–9:30 P.M. Mon.–Thurs. and 5–10 P.M. Fri. and Sat.) doesn't look like much on the outside, but it's got some fine food and a casual atmosphere. Lunch runs around $10 for sandwiches, salads, and entrées (look for the daily plate special), but plan on spending $18–28 for a dinner entrée—steak, lobster, scallops, duck, and more. The Carport Lounge serves mixed drinks and a passable list of wines by the glass.

Of course, you can always make reservations at an Escanaba landmark. The historic **House of Ludington** (223 Ludington St., 906/786-6300, www.houseofludington.com,

11:00 A.M.–2 P.M. lunch Tues.–Thurs., 5–8 P.M. dinner Mon.–Thurs., and 5–9 P.M. dinner Fri. and Sat.) has two dining rooms: the King George Dining Room is an elegant choice (you'll dine with antique silver here), while the Emerald Dining Room is slightly more casual. The restored hotel serves gourmet meals for both lunch and dinner. The varied menu offers something for everyone, including a roast chicken breast in pesto sauce and portabella mushroom pie. Special mention, however, must be given to the outstanding cashew strawberry salad. Dinner prices are in the range of $12–24.

Sayklly's Confectionary & Gifts (1304 Ludington St.) is one of those unexpected, special places you find that make a vacation more memorable. A community institution since 1906, Sayklly's has been producing and selling delicious treats including assorted chocolates, peanut brittle, and salt-water taffy to generations of tourists and locals alike. They even ship anywhere in the world! Its local notoriety earned them national attention when the company was featured on the Food Network's show "Unwrapped" in 2011. The store also features unique gift items from manufacturers such as Lladro, Waterford, Swarovski, and Dept. 56.

INFORMATION AND SERVICES

Visitor information for Escanaba and the surrounding area can be obtained from the **Bays de Noc Convention & Visitors Bureau** (230 Ludington St., 906/789-7862 or 800/533-4386, www.travelbaysdenoc.com) and the **Delta County Chamber of Commerce** (230 Ludington St., 906/786-8830 or 888/335-8264, www.deltami.org). For recreation information, contact the **Michigan DNR** (6833 U.S. 2, Gladstone, 906/786-2351, www.michigan.gov/dnr) or the **U.S. Forest Service/Hiawatha National Forest** (2727 North Lincoln Rd., Escanaba, 906/786-4062, www.fs.fed.us).

Dial 911 for emergencies, and seek medical attention at **OSF St. Francis Hospital** (3401 Ludington St., Escanaba, 906/786-5707,

© PAUL VACHON

Sayklly's Confectionary ships their delicious treats worldwide.

www.osfstfrancis.org). There are plenty of banks and ATMs in downtown Escanaba and in Gladstone, including **Wells Fargo** (1205 Ludington St., 906/789-5236, www.wellsfargo.com) and a number of smaller local and regional banks.

GETTING THERE AND AROUND
Car

If you're coming from the Mackinac Bridge or south on I-75 from Sault Ste. Marie and Ontario, you really couldn't have an easier time of driving to Escanaba—you simply take East U.S. 2 from St. Ignace until you hit the city. Since Escanaba is far closer to Wisconsin than it is to the Lower Peninsula, many drivers will want to drive along Green Bay (the bay) from Green Bay (the city) on U.S. 41 to M-35 and take it into Escanaba from the south.

Boat

There are two quality marinas in the vicinity of Escanaba, one in Escanaba itself and the other in Gladstone, a few miles north. The **Escanaba Municipal Marina** (906/786-9614, www. michigan.gov/dnr) has 37 transient and 128 seasonal slips. The marina is open seasonally from May 9 to October 7, and the harbormaster can be reached on channel 9, 7 A.M.–4 P.M. The marina offers showers, gas and diesel fuel, day-use dockage, pump out, launch, bicycle rentals, a dog run, and snacks, plus cable TV hookup and free Internet access. Its location is 45° 44.34 N, 87° 02.05 W. The **Gladstone Marina** (906/428-2916, www.michigan.gov/ dnr) is located at 45° 50.15 N, 87° 01.00 W, and the harbormaster is on duty from May 15 to September 1. Gladstone Marina monitors radio channels 9 and 68.

Air

Delta Airlines services **Delta County Airport** (ESC, 3300 Airport Rd., 906/786-4902, www. deltacountymi.org), a small, two-runway airport located just southwest of Escanaba. Service is offered to and from Detroit, Minneapolis–St. Paul, and Iron Mountain. You can rent a car

from **Alamo Car Rental** (3300 Airport Rd., 906/786-0603, www.alamo.com) that'll take you where you want to go (and you really will need a car while you're here). Though not as close to the airport, rentals are also available at **Delta Economy Car Rental** (2920 Ludington St., 906/786-1947).

Public Transportation

Regular bus service to Escanaba is provided from Green Bay, Ironwood, Marquette, and St. Ignace by **Indian Trails** (800/292-3831, www.indiantrails.com). You can reach Escanaba from Chicago and Detroit, too, on a combination of Indian Trails and Greyhound buses.

Menominee and Vicinity

Spiking like a canine tooth between Wisconsin and the waters of Green Bay, the triangle of land comprising Menominee County and southern Delta County has been dubbed the peninsula's "banana belt." It's a fitting name, as it does have the U.P.'s most temperate climate, thanks to the relatively warm waters of protected Green Bay, and the lightest snowfall in the Upper Peninsula—just 50 inches a year on average, a quarter of what typically falls on the rest of the U.P.

Locals take advantage of this quirk of nature not for growing bananas, but for raising dairy cattle and crops like corn and soybeans. Farms dot the countryside here, many on land long ago clear-cut by loggers. The longtime logging industry still echoes through the region, however, in the historic waterfront district of Menominee and the mammoth Mead Paper plant near Escanaba—a key factor in the area's stable economy. Many visitors, though, have a tough time getting past the big lake always looming on the eastern horizon. The lapping waters of Green Bay are infinitely enticing and easily accessible here.

Don't forget that Menominee is located in the Central Time Zone, an hour behind Escanaba and the majority of the Upper Peninsula.

SIGHTS

The Menominee River spills into Green Bay between the twin cities of Marinette, Wisconsin, and Menominee, Michigan, once the region's richest lumber port. Menominee's bustling business district is centered on 1st Street, along the waterfront. Fortunately, most of the 19th-century brick and sandstone buildings have survived intact, and their restoration is an ongoing task. You can explore the **historic district** guided by a walking tour brochure available at **Spies Public Library** (940 1st St.). Its 1905 Beaux Arts facade happens to be one of the tour's most handsome buildings. A growing number of shops and restaurants along 1st Street are adding new life to this pleasant area.

The Menominee County Historical Society maintains the **Menominee County Heritage Museum** (904 11th Ave., 906/863-9000, www.menomineehistoricalsociety.org, 10 A.M.–4 P.M. Mon.–Sat. Memorial Day–Labor Day) in an old Catholic church. Like many of the Upper Peninsula's regional history museums, the very local focus may be of limited interest to outsiders, but it does outline the county's history since its beginnings, and has displays about logging, Native American artifacts, and other aspects of Menominee's heritage, making it worth the stop for those who appreciate local history.

Just north of Menominee you'll find the **De Young Family Zoo** (N5406 County Road 577, Wallace, 906/788-4093, www.deyoungfamilyzoo.com, 10 A.M.–5 P.M. daily during the summer months, 10 A.M.–4 P.M. Mon.–Sun. the rest of the year, $12 adults, $8 children 5–15, children 4 and under free), a pleasant diversion at the end of a long day's drive. Here you'll find some of the animals you'd expect in big city zoos, including big cats, bears, primates, and canines (wolves, foxes, etc.). They also offer special

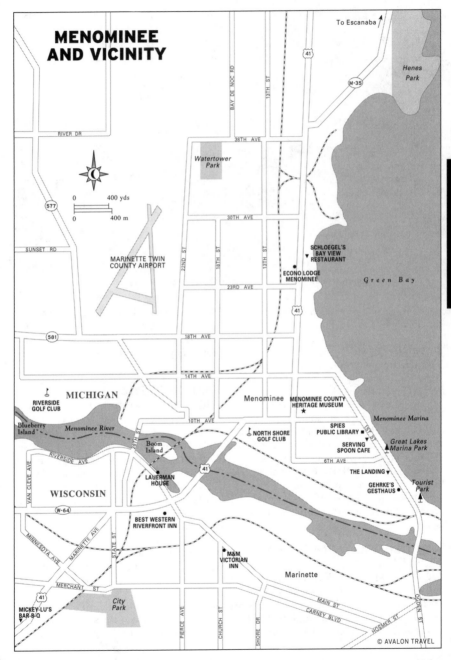

THE LAKE MICHIGAN SHORE

THE LAKE MICHIGAN SHORE

The drive to Menominee along M-35 offers plenty of scenic lookouts.

© PAUL VACHON

programs including animal shows and feeding demonstrations.

Bayside Parks

The waterfront district is also home to bayside parks, easily accessible on foot. **Great Lakes Marina Park** stretches along the water between 6th and 10th Avenues, flanked by a new marina and a band shell that hosts summer concerts on Tuesday and Thursday evenings. For a longer walk or bike ride, head south along the water to the **Tourist Park** swimming beach. Continue farther south to the **North Pier Light,** which marks the entrance to Menominee Harbor with a beacon at the end of a rocky breakwater. Although the light is attractive, it isn't open to the public.

MENOMINEE WATERFRONT FESTIVAL

Pay a visit to Menominee's Historic Waterfront district for the **Waterfront Festival,** a popular four-day celebration that offers plenty of traditional activities and events, including live music at the band shell, parades, boat races,

and food vendors. Be sure not to miss the amateur lumberjack competition or the stunning fireworks display. The Waterfront Festival is held every year in early August.

SUMMER SPORTS AND RECREATION
Hiking and Biking

Menominee's most popular park is a bit farther afield. Located at the north end of town off M-35, **Henes Park** (906/863-2656) occupies a 50-acre point that juts out into Green Bay. Designed by noted landscape architect Ossian Simonds, this unusual park combines tracts of virgin hemlock and pine with traditional park amenities like walking trails, swimming beaches, and playgrounds.

At the Cedar River, the **Escanaba River State Forest** (906/786-2351) offers a network of hiking and mountain biking trails, with four loops (ranging from two to seven miles) that travel over hilly terrain sculpted by Ice Age glaciers. The Cedar River Trail and Timber Trail in **J. W. Wells State Park** (906/863-9747) both follow the Green Bay shoreline.

MINING AND THE CIVIL WAR

Much of Michigan's contribution to the war effort came from the Upper Peninsula in two forms: the men who fought as part of the Iron Brigade, famous for suffering the highest casualty rate during the war, and from those who labored tirelessly in the iron mines.

There are three iron ranges in the Upper Peninsula, and during the years of mining's heyday (which overlapped with the Civil War), they yielded several million tons of product needed for munitions, armaments, and other hardware. In fact, the North's overall industrial capacity is frequently cited by historians as a decisive factor in its victory over the South. This wartime demand for high-quality iron was met by the mines of the Menominee, Marquette, and Gogebic ranges. As a result, the Upper Peninsula experienced considerable prosperity; railroad lines were built and shipping ports thrived, providing a high standard of living to area residents.

But like other industries built on finite resources such as the fur and lumber trades, mining's profitability could not be sustained. When supplies began to run thin and demand decreased, the industry collapsed, taking with it towns like Fayette, which was famously left behind as an empty shell of the community it once was.

Canoeing and Kayaking

The 100-mile stretch of the Menominee River from above Iron Mountain all the way through Menominee separates the Upper Peninsula from Wisconsin—and gives paddlers an intense, high-current ride. You'll have to portage around several dams and reservoirs, but the wildlife viewing and rugged scenery make the effort worthwhile. The upper reaches of the river shouldn't be tried by amateurs, though. The Class IV and V white water is some of the U.P.'s fastest. If you're an inexperienced or timid paddler, put in at an access point closer to Menominee, where the flow is gentler and the rapids (much slower here) are more easily navigated.

Beaches

In the 55 miles between Menominee and Escanaba, several parks and beaches lure you off the highway. About 13 miles north of Menominee, **Bailey Park** is a favorite swimming beach of the locals, with fine sand and low dunes on a point that stretches away from the highway. Just to the north, **Kleinke Park** is more exposed to M-35, but offers campsites overlooking the bay, as well as a sandy beach. There are small swimming beaches at **Tourist Park,** near the Menominee Harbor and the North Pier Light, and at **Henes Park,** on M-35 just north of town.

Fishing

There's some fishing available at Cedar River, north of Menominee, as well as at the Menominee River and several smaller, local lakes and rivers—try Hayward Lake or Walton River. In town, anglers can cast a line off the Menominee Municipal Pier (the same pier that leads to the North Pier Light), but some of the best fishing is in Green Bay and Lake Michigan. Contact **Fish Tales Guide Service** (W4565 9.5 Rd., 906/863-2267, http://user.cybrzn.com/fishtales) for open-water charters lasting five to eight hours. Some packages even include lodging and a continental breakfast. Inland and river fishing is also available.

Boating

Green Bay, Little and Big Bays de Noc, and northern Lake Michigan are among the Midwest's most beautiful, temperate, and sailable waters. Along with sites in Escanaba and Gladstone to the north, boaters can put in at the **Menominee Marina** (906/863-8498, www.michigan.gov/dnr). Although primarily a fishing charter service, **Fish Tales Guide Service**

THE LAKE MICHIGAN SHORE

(W4565 9.5 Rd., 906/863-2267, http://user. cybrzn.com/fishtales) also offers scenic and lighthouse tours.

Golf

In Stephenson, several miles north of Menominee on U.S. 41, golfers can enjoy a relaxing game at the rural **Indian Hills Golf Course** (N8881 Walnut Rd., 906/753-4781, http://nuttall.net/ihills/index.htm, $12–18). Perhaps due to its remote location, surrounded by fields of grain and corn, this nine-hole course holds a certain quaint attraction. Closer to Menominee, golfers can visit the **North Shore Golf Club** (2315 M-35, 906/863-3026, www. northshoregolf.net, $30 greens fees, including cart) a few miles north of town on M-35. The club's 18 holes are well maintained, and (one of the most compelling reasons to swing a club here) a few holes provide views of Green Bay. You'll find many of the amenities you'd expect at a higher-level course: a PGA professional, a restaurant, a banquet hall, a pro shop, a driving range, and more.

WINTER SPORTS AND RECREATION
Ski and Snowshoe Trails

One of the best places for non-groomed ski trails is **J. W. Wells State Park** (906/863-9747), on M-35 some 25 miles north of Menominee. The park, open year-round, has almost 700 acres of land available for public use, crossed by eight miles of ski and snowshoe trails, some of which usher skiers along the Green Bay shoreline. You'll find the groomed trails of **Cedar River Pathway** (906/786-2354, www.michigan.gov/dnr) several miles north of J. W. Wells State Park, where M-35 and County Road 551 meet. The pathway has several loops (ranging from two to nine miles) that are perfect for beginning skiers.

Snowmobiling

The expansive Michigan DNR trail system doesn't extend south into Menominee County—your best bet for snowmobiling is to head north on U.S. 41 to Powers, where the trailhead for Trail 331 connects to Trail 2 a few miles north. Take 2 west toward Iron Mountain or east to Escanaba.

Many of Menominee County's unpaved roads and the shoulders of paved roads are accessible by snowmobile; double-check local ordinances for exceptions. Always use extreme caution when riding on public roads. More information about state-wide snowmobile regulations is available from the **Michigan DNR** website (www.michigan.gov/dnr). Remember, safety first.

ACCOMMODATIONS

Lodging choices are pretty much limited to a few franchise motels in both Menominee and neighboring Marinette, Wisconsin. Two of the best values are **Econo Lodge** (2516 10th St., Menominee, 906/863-4431, rates start at $59), which has rooms overlooking the bay, and, in Wisconsin, **Best Western Riverfront Inn** (1821 Riverside Ave., Marinette, 715/732-1000, rates start at $84), just west of U.S. 41 at the river.

Cross the river into Wisconsin for comfortable lodging at one of the area's nicest historic inns, the 🄲 **M&M Victorian Inn** (1393 Main St., Marinette, 715/732-9531, www.lauermanhouse.com, $90–150). Named after the twin cities of Menominee and Marinette (not the candy) the M&M is a stunning, restored 1893 Queen Anne–style home with elegant, original woodwork, stained glass, and five rooms. Travelers can also stay at Marinette's **Lauerman House Inn** (1975 Riverside Ave., 715/732-7800, www.lauermanhouse.com, $90–170).

Camping

J. W. Wells State Park (906/863-9747 or 800/447-2757, www.michigan.gov/dnr), about 25 miles north of Menominee on M-35, is the most extensive park along the highway. Flanking both sides of M-35, the 800-acre park is known for its three-mile stretch of rocky beach and large modern campground. The campground doesn't offer much privacy, but all 178 sites are near the beach and 30

back up right to the water. All sites often fill on summer weekends. If you've planned well ahead, you might be able to claim one of the park's five rustic cabins ($50), stone and log buildings built as a Civilian Conservation Corps (CCC) project in the 1930s and tucked in secluded woods near the water. They sleep 8–16 and feature barrel stoves for both warmth and cooking.

The **Cedar River North State Forest Campground** (906/786-2354, $15, no reservations) in Escanaba River State Forest is a quiet, rustic campground right on the banks of the river, just a few miles upstream from the mouth. The 18 sites are for tent and small trailer use, and 4 of them are walk-in tent-only sites. You'll find vault water and potable water from a rustic hand pump. From M-35 at the village of Cedar River, follow County Road 551 west for eight miles.

Fox Park (906/753-4582), seven miles north of Cedar River, has a 25-site primitive campground that rarely fills and a nice sandy beach. The more popular **Fuller Park** (906/786-1020), nine miles north, has 25 modern sites, a sandy beach, a bathhouse, a boat launch, and access to the Bark River.

The biggest problem with **River Park Campground** (502 5th Ave., 906/863-5101, www.cityofmenominee.org) is that it's located behind a Kmart. Otherwise, the modern campground's 58 sites are clean, with paved parking pads and a playground. If you expect convenience, you'll be within walking distance of a coin laundry. But this is the exception more than the norm. In Michigan's Upper Peninsula, most people come to find a campsite within walking distance of absolutely nothing at all.

FOOD

Dining in Menominee features mostly classic American fare, with an emphasis on fish from the local waters. **Berg's Landing** (450 1st St., 906/863-8034, 5–9 P.M. Mon.–Thurs., 5–10 P.M. Fri.–Sat., 5–8 P.M. Sun., $12–22) offers terrific views of Green Bay and good, reliable steaks, seafood, chicken

and vegetarian dishes. Locals will likely point you to **Schloegel's Bayview Restaurant** (2720 10th St., 906/863-7888, http://tastefullydifferent.com, 6 A.M.–8 P.M. Mon.–Sat., 7:30 A.M.–8 P.M. Sun., $15–23), right on U.S. 41, for pies (baked daily), generously built sandwiches, and ethnic items like Swedish pancakes and Cornish pasties. There's a good view of Green Bay, too.

In addition to the traditional café offerings—coffee, espresso, soups—the **Serving Spoon Cafe** (821 First St., 906/863-7770, 7 A.M.–3 P.M. Mon., 7 A.M.–8 P.M. Tues.–Fri., 8 A.M.–8 P.M. Sat., and 8 A.M.–3 P.M. Sun., $10) has earned a reputation for its Mediterranean style foods; pitas, light salads, and vegetarian sandwiches. Across the river on the Wisconsin side, **Mickey-Lu's Bar-B-Q** (1710 Marinette Ave., 715/735-7721) looks like a hole in the wall, but it's the place to go for cheap food—authentic, old-fashioned butter burgers, malts, and ice cream sundaes. Menu items top out at only $10.

INFORMATION AND SERVICES

Perhaps the most important piece of information (or at least the one plenty of tourists forget) is that Menominee County is in the Central Time Zone with Wisconsin. Most of the Upper Peninsula, like the entire Lower Peninsula, is set firmly in the Eastern Time Zone, but the counties that share a border with Wisconsin share a common time, too. When traveling between Menominee and Escanaba, set your clock forward an hour when heading north to Escanaba and back an hour when driving south.

For visitor information, contact the **Marinette/Menominee Area Chamber of Commerce** (601 Marinette Ave., Marinette, WI, 906/863-2679, www.marinettechamber. com).

Menominee banks include two **Wells Fargo** locations (M&M Plaza, 906/863-5523, and 962 1st St., 906/863-5515, www.wellsfargo. com) with ATMs, **Stephenson National Bank and Trust** (1111 10th St., 906/863-2526,

www.snbt.com), and **First National Bank and Trust** (3805 10th St., 906/863-7861, www.fn-bimk.com).

In case of emergency, call 911. The closest hospital is Marinette's **Bay Area Medical Center** (3100 Shore Dr., 715/735-4200 or 888/788-2070, www.bayareamedical.com) in Wisconsin. Take U.S. 41 south to Main Street and turn left, then go right on Shore Drive for a mile and a half.

GETTING THERE AND AROUND
Car
Menominee is located on the border of Michigan and Wisconsin, across the river from Marinette. You'll get to town by taking U.S. 41 from the north or south, or driving along the Green Bay coast south from Escanaba on M-35.

Boat
The **Menominee Marina** (906/863-8498, www.michigan.gov/dnr) has 20 transient slips and a whopping 243 seasonal slips. Open from mid-May through mid-October, the marina has restrooms and showers, gasoline, laundry, and a picnic area with tables and grills. Contact the harbormaster on channel 22 or 16. Menominee Marina is located at 45° 06.21 N, 87° 35.58 W.

Air
The airport most accessible to Menominee is the Delta County Airport in Escanaba, north of Menominee on M-35. You can rent a car in Escanaba.

Public Transportation
Regrettably, there is currently no public transportation serving the greater Menominee area.

THE SUPERIOR UPLAND

The western Upper Peninsula is defined by its land, which is both austere and beautiful. Known as the Superior Upland, this portion of the peninsula is filled with rocky crags, rugged landscape, and old growth forest. In short, it's the wildest region of an already remote destination. Here the eastern U.P.'s flat and tame landscape gives way to the Porcupine Mountains, roaring streams, and unbridled forests.

Gogebic County and the region surrounding Ironwood are known as the Big Snow Country and are the U.P.'s top destinations for downhill skiing. Though Michigan's "mountains" don't reach 2,000 feet, the resorts at Bessemer and Wakefield make for some of the best skiing in the Midwest. Summertime visitors can enjoy the region's numerous waterfalls and hiking trails.

The Porcupine Mountains, or the Porkies, as they're affectionately known, are among the oldest highland ranges in the United States. Bring your hiking boots. Much of the Porkies—particularly the 85 miles of trails in Porcupine Mountains Wilderness State Park—are only accessible by foot. If you're looking for old-growth hemlock, rustic cabins, remote backpacking—plus fishing, canoeing, or camping—this is the place for you.

PLANNING YOUR TIME

The western U.P. is made for rugged isolation during the summers. In winter, it's where you'll find the best of Michigan's downhill skiing. Plan on two or three days to explore—and longer for ski trips or backcountry hiking. No matter why you came to the Upper

HIGHLIGHTS

◖ **Piers Gorge:** Just what you'd expect the ultimate wilderness stream to be: rugged, tranquil and picturesque, with rolling rapids to boot (page 99).

◖ **Iron County Heritage Trail:** A complex of attractions, with the Iron County Historical Museum as its centerpiece, this is a great destination for history buffs. Learn about the area's iron mining past while having a great deal of fun at the same time (page 105).

◖ **Sylvania Wilderness and Recreation Area:** Between the wilderness and recreation areas, Sylvania's more than 20,000 acres are among the U.P's finest spots for outdoor enjoyment (page 106).

◖ **Bond Falls:** With a reputation as one of the Upper Peninsula's most beautiful water-

falls, this one should near the top of visitor's list – second only to Tahquamenon Falls, of course (page 111).

◖ **Little Girl's Point:** A dramatic spot high on a bluff over Lake Superior, you'll find superb recreational facilities and a spectacular view of both the lake and the mountains (page 114).

◖ **Copper Peak:** No longer a ski resort, this spot boasts a spellbinding view (page 114).

◖ **Downhill Skiing:** The Superior Upland offers truly world-class skiing despite being located east of the Rockies (page 116).

◖ **Porcupine Mountains Wilderness State Park:** Virgin Forest, Lake Superior shoreline, and miles of trails make the Porkies a rugged, secluded paradise that's perfect for getting away from the crowd (page 120).

LOOK FOR ◖ TO FIND RECOMMENDED SIGHTS, ACTIVITIES, DINING, AND LODGING.

Peninsula—or in what season, you'll want to set some time aside for the Porkies. Speaking of time, don't forget the time change in the counties bordering Wisconsin. Set your clocks back one hour.

HISTORY

This corner of the Upper Peninsula traces its heritage to iron. You can see it reflected in the town names: Iron Mountain, Iron River, Ironwood, National Mine, Mineral Hills. You see it on the faces of the residents, descendents of immigrant mine workers from Scandinavia, Italy, and Cornwall, England.

Federal surveyors first discovered iron ore in 1844 near present-day Iron River. As workers systematically surveyed this unfamiliar land recently acquired by the state Michigan, their compasses swung wildly near Negaunee, where iron ore was so plentiful that it was visible on the surface, intertwined in the roots of a fallen

tree. The tree is the official symbol of the city of Negaunee. The symbol became both literal and metaphorical, as the fortunes of the community became intertwined with the rise and fall of the iron industry.

Apart from a handful of small mining operations, the potential wealth of the Upper Peninsula's iron deposits remained largely untapped for decades until the nation's ever-expanding web of railroad lines reached the area. In the 1870s, the arrival of the railroad prompted the development of the first major mines. World War II and its insatiable demand for iron drove area mines to peak production, driving some of them to depletion. By the 1960s and 1970s, the western U.P. iron ranges had grown quiet, after producing nearly two billion tons of ore. All underground iron mines in the U.P. were closed by 1978, casualties of foreign steelmakers and newer manufacturing methods that relied more on plastics.

Iron Mountain and Vicinity

Iron Mountain lacks the glamour of a typical tourist destination. You have to look a little harder here. The surrounding forest is beautiful, and the area's long heritage of logging and mining yields a trove of compelling historical sites.

Iron Mountain was first settled in about 1880 when vast deposits of iron were discovered underfoot. The Chapin Mine, located near present-day U.S. 2 and Kent Avenue on the north end of downtown, boosted the town's population to almost 8,000 by 1890. Italians were among the numerous groups of European immigrants working at the Chapin Mine. Italian neighborhoods still thrive today around the mine on Iron Mountain's north side, evidenced by the number of Italian restaurants and corner markets.

The city's long-abandoned mines still serve an important role—as a magnet for brown bats. An estimated two million bats winter in the Millie Mine shaft, protected from predators

yet still able to enter and exit freely. This is due to the bat-friendly grates installed at the mine entrance. As the weather turns cool in the fall, the bats congregate all around Iron Mountain, creating an amazing sight, before returning to the mine.

While iron mining formed the backbone of the local economy, Henry Ford added some measure of diversification in the 1920s, when he bought up huge tracts of nearby forest and built his first company sawmill on land southwest of town, which he dubbed Kingsford, in honor of Iron Mountain's Ford dealer, Edward Kingsford. Soon Ford's Kingsford empire included the main plant for making floorboards for the Model T, residences for workers, a refinery, and even a chemical plant to make newfangled charcoal briquettes. All of it was eventually closed or was sold, including the briquette plant, which relocated to Oakland, California, and has since been acquired by the Clorox Company, but still

manufactures the ever-popular Kingsford charcoal briquettes.

During World War II the facilities were devoted to production of military hardware. The sawmill began building Waco CG-4A gliders for the Army Air Force, an indispensible element during the Allied invasion of France.

Henry Ford's handprints can also be found in some surprising places. The local airport and main city park bear his name, and the nickname of the athletic teams at Kingsford High School is the "Flivvers," an early nickname for the Ford Model T. But perhaps the most telling example is a name Kingsford shares with Detroit. Both cities' main streets are named Woodward.

SIGHTS
Iron Mountain Iron Mine

If you're going to spend any amount of time in Iron Mountain and the rest of the Superior Uplands, it's helpful to get a firsthand look at the mining industry that made the area what it is today. You can't miss the Iron Mountain Iron Mine (906/563-8077, www.ironmountainiron-mine.com, June 1–Oct. 15) in Vulcan, nine miles east of Iron Mountain. Big John, a towering two-dimensional miner with a pickax in his hands, welcomes westbound motorists on U.S. 2. The mine tour takes visitors 400 feet below the surface on a half-mile journey. Equipped with rain slickers and hard hats, tourists board an underground train to learn about the history and process of mining, including equipment demonstrations. You'll get outfitted for the tour in the gift shop, where you can also browse rock and mineral samples.

IXL Museum

A lot of museums bill themselves as a "step back in time," but you truly feel it at the IXL Museum (906/498-2498, www.hermansville.com/IXLMuseum, 12:30–4 P.M. Memorial Day–Labor Day) in downtown Hermansville, 28 miles east of Iron Mountain. For more than a century, this wood-frame building served as the northern office of the Wisconsin Land & Lumber Company, which in the 1860s began

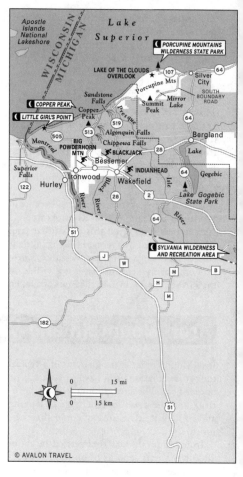

© AVALON TRAVEL

building doors and window sashes in central Wisconsin. After the Great Chicago Fire of 1871, founder C. J. L. Meyer moved north to tap into the vast pine reserves of the Upper Peninsula. He built the Hermansville office and adjacent sawmill in 1881. "IXL" stands for "I excel," and was used as a logo on all the company's products.

Today, the preserved IXL building exists in a time warp and is one of the most fascinating museums in the Upper Peninsula; the Dictaphones, mimeograph machine, and payroll records...are all still here, in place, as if

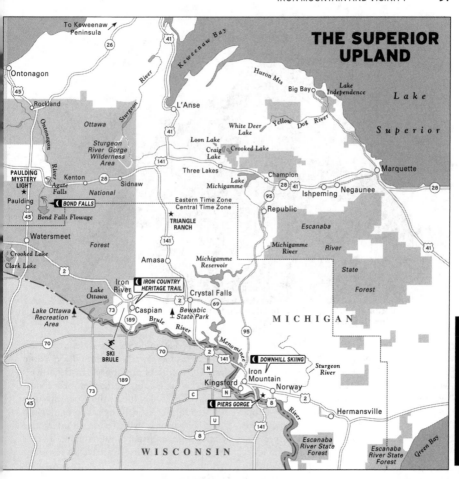

THE SUPERIOR UPLAND

THE SUPERIOR UPLAND

you stepped into the office on a weekend when everyone was off duty. The second floor, which was originally apartments for Meyer and his family, now, displays a variety of machinery from the logging days. When Meyer expanded the business into Michigan, he came up with a clever little innovation: tongue-and-groove flooring, precision-milled in one operation. The Hermansville operation quickly became the largest flooring plant in the country, crafting the floors for the Mormon temple in Salt Lake City and Yellowstone National Park's main lodge, in addition to other notable clients.

At its peak, it held 30 million board-feet of lumber in its yards and operated three railroads to handle ever-increasing shipments.

Cornish Pump and Mining Museum

Iron Mountain's Chapin Mine once led Menominee Range mining production, but it was also one of the wettest mines ever worked. In 1893, an immense steam-operated pump, a 54-foot-high, 725-ton behemoth—the largest in the world at the time—was put into service. Though electric pumps replaced

© JOSH BISHOP

The Iron Mountain Iron Mine, in Vulcan, offers underground mine tours as a means of experiencing the Upper Peninsula's past.

it just 20 years later, the pump is on display today at the Menominee Range Historical Foundation's Cornish Pump and Mining Museum (906/774-1086, www.menomineemuseum.com, 9 A.M.–5 P.M. Mon.–Sat. and noon–4 P.M. Sun. Memorial Day–Labor Day), one block east of U.S. 2 in downtown Iron Mountain. Along with the impressive pump, this comprehensive museum includes a good-sized collection of mining equipment, photos, and period clothing, as well as a small theater. Recently opened was the adjacent World War II Glider and Military Museum, which tells the compelling story of the Waco World War II glider and also contains some small military planes, displays of uniforms, equipment, etc.

Menominee Range Historical Museum

The Menominee Range Historical Foundation's other museum, the Menominee Range Historical Museum (300 E. Ludington St., 906/774-4276, www.menomineemuseum.com, mid-May–mid-Oct.), provides a overview of the area's history from the 1800s on. More than 100 exhibits are housed in the town's former Carnegie Library, most of them focusing on the everyday life of those who lived in the Menominee Iron Range. You can visit a Victorian parlor, a livery stable, an interactive general store, and much, much more. There's also a historical archive available for research.

Badwater Ski-ters Water Ski Show

Sure, this one is in Wisconsin, but it's worth a trip into America's Dairyland to catch the Badwater Ski-ters Water Ski Show (skiters@charter.net, www.exploringthenorth.com/ski/ski.html) at Vagabond Park on the Menominee River, just five miles west of Iron Mountain. The world-class, nationally renowned water-ski team performs jumps, trick and barefoot skiing, and the pyramid. Best of all, the shows are free. Catch the Ski-ters every Wednesday and Sunday throughout the summer, from early June through mid-August. Take U.S.

MINING

Mining in the Upper Peninsula falls into two categories: copper mining in the Keweenaw Peninsula and iron mining in the Superior Upland. The U.P.'s iron industry stretched from the peninsula's western border east some 150 miles, to the Lake Superior port of Marquette and the Lake Michigan port of Escanaba. It comprised three major ranges: the Gogebic Range, with operations centered near Ironwood; the Menominee Range, based largely around the Iron River and Iron Mountain areas; and the Marquette Range, located near Marquette and the Ishpeming/Negaunee area.

Iron mining was somewhat limited during its early years. From its initial discovery in the 1840s until the arrival of the railway some 30 years later, yields were minimal due to the limitations of equipment, transportation, etc. The Menominee Range saw the first major mines, followed by the Gogebic Range. Many of the early mines were open pit affairs, but soon the need for iron ore drove miners deeper and deeper underground. Today communities like Ishpeming sit atop patches of earth riddled with mine shafts and adits. Occasionally, sections of land will sink, leaving behind tilted and abandoned homes. Near Iron Mountain, the entire town of Norway was moved twice due to street cave-ins.

Depleted supplies, combined with a drop-off in demand, caused most of the mines to close by the late 1970s. A few open-pit mines remain in operation; you can see one in Republic, where a small viewing platform (free) overlooks a gargantuan crater in the earth. Republic is located just off M-95, about six miles south of U.S. 41 in Marquette County.

2/141 west from Iron Mountain and look for the signs.

Millie Mine Bat Cave

Sure, bats can be a little creepy, but there's something impressive about the million or so bats that spend winters in the abandoned mine shaft. Bats have free access into the mine through a grate, which was constructed to prevent people from falling several hundred feet to the floor of the mine shaft—a good idea all around. The mine's constant 40°F temperature makes it ideal for the bats, which can be viewed entering or leaving the mine each spring (late April to early May) and autumn (August and September). The best viewing time is at dusk. Take Park Street north from U.S. 2 East until you get to the marked viewing area.

Pine Mountain Music Festival

The annual Pine Mountain Music Festival (906/482-1542, www.pmmf.org), now in its 22nd year, has a lineup of musical performances that take place all across the region, from Marquette and Houghton to Munising and Iron Mountain. The annual festival features opera, symphonies, and chamber music. During the 2011 season, the opera *Rockland* made its debut. The show tells the story of a 1906 incident in the nearby town of Rockland when a small group of striking Finnish copper miners were confronted by sheriff's deputies. The incident escalated until shots were fired and two of the miners were killed. *Rockland* is slated to be performed over the next several seasons.

◖ Piers Gorge

Where the U.P. isn't bordered by lakes, it's bordered by rivers: The grand Menominee rambles from near Iron Mountain all the way to Lake Michigan's Green Bay, forming nearly half the boundary between Wisconsin and the Upper Peninsula.

Just south of Norway, it narrows through Piers Gorge, a pretty run of frothing white water and waterfalls. In the mid-1800s, loggers relied on the Menominee to float logs to the river's mouth; they cursed this stretch of river for the logjams it caused, and they built

a series of wooden piers here in an attempt to slow the current and channel the flow—hence the name. To view the gorge, follow U.S. 8 south from Norway and turn right on Piers Gorge Road just before you cross the river into Wisconsin. Follow the road about half a mile until it ends at a trail. Along the mile-long trail, you'll be treated to several views of the gorge, which become progressively more dramatic, some as high as 70 feet. These, however, can only be accessed via several side trails, of varying degrees of safety. Some of the trails wind down to the river itself. This is not a good choice for those with small children, since there are several steep dropoffs.

SUMMER SPORTS AND RECREATION
Hiking and Biking
The trails that encircle the large lake of **Fumee Lake Natural Area** give hikers the chance to see plenty of natural beauty, still untouched by motorized vehicles and development. There are five miles of shoreline and more than 500 acres of water in Fumee Lake and Little Fumee Lake. Choose between loops of one, two, or seven miles. Each offers different views of the lakes and wildlife. Bring your camera, or at least a pair of binoculars. Fumee Lake Natural Area is located east of Iron Mountain, near Norway. Take Upper Pine Creek Road north of U.S. 2.

Canoeing and Kayaking
Only experienced white-water kayakers who can handle Class III and IV rapids should consider running the **Menominee River.** The narrow canyon walls of Piers Gorge produce some of the Midwest's most thrilling (and difficult) white water. For an easy paddle on the nearby Brule or Pine Rivers, though, contact **Northwoods Wilderness Outfitters** (N4088 Pine Mountain Rd., 906/774-9009, www.northwoodsoutfitters.com) in Iron Mountain. This excellent shop will set you up for an afternoon or an extended trip, with canoe and kayak rentals as well as drop-off/pickup service, a real plus.

Fishing
Even though Lakes Michigan and Superior don't border the Iron Mountain region, there's still plenty of great fishing here. Try **Bass Lake** near the Wisconsin border, north of Iron Mountain and two miles west of U.S. 2, or larger **Lake Antoine**, four miles north of Iron Mountain (take U.S. 2 to Lake Antoine Rd.). **Carney Lake** is a little farther away, 16 miles northeast of Iron Mountain on M-95 and Merriman Truck Trail, but this one is over 100 acres and includes a boat launch and rustic campgrounds to make it worth the drive. For more sites and advice on fishing the area's rivers, contact the **Dickinson Area Partnership** (800/236-2447, www.ironmountain.org).

Off-Road Vehicles
When the mining and logging industries waned, they left behind a vast network of unpaved roads, making the backcountry around Iron Mountain perfect for off-road vehicle riders. There are also nearly 30 miles of ORV routes on the **Norway Trail.** Take County Road 573 east of Norway to Norway Truck Trail, then go north to parking, or take Foster City Road several miles north of U.S. 2 in Waucedah.

Golf
The **Pine Grove Country Club** (1520 W. Hughitt St., Iron Mountain, 906/774-3493, http://pinegrovecc.org, rates vary widely, check website for details) has been around for more than 100 years, but the semi-private course's elegant new club house is less than a decade old. Since the club is semi-private, there is limited open play time for nonmembers: Monday, Thursday, and Friday before noon, and Saturday and Sunday after 1:00 P.M. You'll have a better choice of tee times at **Oak Crest Golf Course** (N1475 U.S. 8, 906/563-5891,www.oakcrestgolf.com, $17–22 for 9 holes, $28–38 for 18 holes) in Norway. The 18-hole course is edged by oak trees, which gives the course

both a naturally stately feel as well as its name. You can also play at **TimberStone Golf Club** (N3332 Pine Mountain Rd., 906/776-0111, www.pinemountainresort.com, $50–60 for 9 holes, $89–100 for 18 holes), part of Pine Mountain Resort. The course's 18 holes are set on 240 wooded acres. TimberStone has been certified a five-star course by *Golf Digest* magazine, an honor granted to only 24 courses nationally from a pool of some 6,000. Look for package deals on lodging and golf.

Waterfalls

You'll find a couple of waterfalls in the area, although they aren't the Upper Peninsula's most dramatic. The pretty but small **Fumee Falls** has a minimal water flow but is very easy to get to. A trail and viewing platform just off U.S. 2 allow you to see the more than the 20-foot drop without fairly easily. The **Sturgeon Falls Dam** (not to be confused with Sturgeon Falls) isn't quite as accessible, but is worth your while. The falls are 3.5 miles south of Loretto on the Menominee River.

WINTER SPORTS AND RECREATION
Ski and Snowshoe Trails

Perhaps the most appealing feature about **Fumee Lake Natural Area** is its year-round accessibility. The summer hiking trails transition nicely into cross-country ski and snowshoe pathways during the long and intense Upper Peninsula winters. There are loops of varying distance and difficulty, all wonderfully isolated from the nearby towns. An excellent example is the **Upper Pine Creek Road** north of U.S. 2, a few miles west of Norway and east of Iron Mountain. Also, the **Merriman East Pathway,** some 13 miles northeast of Iron Mountain on M-95 and Merriman Road, has nearly 10 miles of trails that make for pleasant Nordic skiing.

Downhill Skiing

Although Michigan's biggest and best ski resorts are farther west in the Ironwood area, the Iron Mountain region holds its own with two downhill ski resorts—plus a little something

© PINE MOUNTAIN RESORT

THE SUPERIOR UPLAND

Pine Mountain Resort offers some of the best skiing in the western U.P.

extra. **Norway Mountain** (N2090 Briar Mountain Rd., 906/563-9700 or 800/272-5445, www.norwaymountain.com, $36–39 adults, $30–33 ages 10–18, children free) has three lifts and runs from beginner slopes to black diamond terrain. There are two terrain parks open to both skiers and boarders, too, with a quarter-pipe, large jumps, and plenty of rails and boxes—as well as a less-intense area for beginners. Norway also hosts a good number of special events throughout the ski season. Details are available on the website. Not to be outdone, **Pine Mountain Resort** (N3332 Pine Mountain Rd., 906/774-2747, www.pinemountainresort.com, $30–39 adults $25–36 ages 13–17, $10–15 children), in Iron Mountain, has multilevel skiing and lighted nighttime runs, two terrain parks, and a half-pipe. But that pales in comparison to the **Pine Mountain Ski Jump** (N3330 Pine Mountain Rd., 800/236-2447, www.kiwanisskiclub.com), a towering scaffold that tops out at more than 175 feet tall, with a run of 380 feet. There's an international competition here that draws some 20,000 people each year to what is the world's largest artificial ski jumps; the current Pine Mountain record is a 468-foot jump by Austria's Stefan Kaiser.

Snowmobiling

More than 120 miles of snowmobile trails cross Dickinson County, connecting to trails throughout the rest of the U.P. and northern Wisconsin. Iron Mountain and Norway are connected by a trail that skirts Fumee Lake (you can take it east to Escanaba), while Trail 5 will take you north toward Marquette and Lake Superior.

ACCOMMODATIONS

The [**Pine Mountain Resort** (N3332 Pine Mountain Rd., 877/553-7463, www.pinemountainresort.com, $50–100 rooms, $50–100 condos) anchors a full-service ski and golf resort on the northwest side of town, complete with dining room, indoor pool, outdoor pool, sauna, tennis courts, hiking and mountain biking trails, and more. Choose from standard lodge rooms or condominiums. Just off U.S. 2, the [**Edgewater Resort** (4128 N. U.S. 2, 800/236-6244, www.edgewaterresort.com, $430–680 per week) makes the most of its fine setting overlooking the Menominee River, with 10 log cabins scattered across its grounds, along with a picnic area, a playground, a volleyball court, canoes and fishing boats available for rent, and more. Single-bed, two-bedroom, and three-bedroom cabins with kitchens rent by the week, but can also be rented by the day subject to availability. Pets are permitted. Two miles north of Iron River, the mom-and-pop **Woodlands Motel** (N3957 U.S. 2, 906/774-6106, $50–75) offers standard motel rooms with small kitchenettes. Look for standard chain motels in downtown Iron Mountain.

The **Edgewater Log Cabin Resort** (W8176 S. U.S. 2, Iron Mountain, 800/883-5335, www.edgewaterresortmi.com, $445–745, weekly—call for daily rates) is a cozy cluster of cabins located on the Menominee River, each equipped with a kitchen, king or queen beds, and cable TV with a DVD player. The resort also offers wireless Internet, laundry facilities, a playground for children, and a boat for fishing. Either a Michigan or Wisconsin license is valid for fishing on the Menominee.

The **Mountain Host Motor Inn** (1451 S. Stephenson Ave., Iron Mountain, 888/776-0701 or 906/776-0700, www.mountainhostmotorinn.com, $50–70) is a very reasonably priced motor lodge in the Iron Mountain area which offers some unusual amenities. Each room is equipped with a fax modem in addition to wireless Internet plus hair dryers and in-room cable with movies. The motel offers an exercise room with a sauna and tanning bed, a copy service for the business traveler, and a daily continental breakfast.

The **Woodlands Motel** (N3957 U.S. 2, Iron Mountain, near the junction with M-25 906/774-6106 or 800/394-5505, reservations only, www.exploringthenorth.com/wlandsim/wood.html, $50–80) is a classic mom-and-

pop operation. Each of the 19 clean and comfortable rooms has a kitchenette, queen-sized beds, and wireless Internet access. There's a playground for kids and as an extra bonus for winter vacationers, it's close to the area's snowmobile trails.

In Norway, you'll love the comfort and serenity of the **ⓒ AmericInn** (W6002 U.S. 2, Norway, 906/563-7500 or 800/634-3444, www.americinnofnorway.com, $80–120) at the end of a long day's drive. The rustic feel of the lobby and the soothing water of the hot tub will ease your tension and recharge your batteries for the next day. Offers a complementary continental breakfast, a cocktail lounge and a pool with a dry sauna. All rooms are nonsmoking.

Camping

At **Carney Lake State Forest Campground** (906/875-6622, www.michigan.gov/dnr, $15), campers will find 16 rustic sites suitable for tents and trailers. You won't find showers or laundry here, but there are vaulted toilets and clean water from the campground's hand pump. You'll have the best luck during the off season, since there are no reservations and the first-come, first-served sites can be claimed rather quickly. The fishing is worth it, however. Take M-95 north of Iron Mountain and head east on Merriman Truck Trail. **Summer Breeze Campground** (W8576 Twin Falls Rd., 906/774-7701, www.summerbreezecampground.com, May 1–Oct. 15, $18 tent, $24–28 hookup; weekly and seasonal rates also available) is pretty much the opposite—amenity rich, busy, and plenty of room for even the largest RVs. Amenities go beyond heated showers and a camp store (they do have those, of course) to a heated swimming pool, DVD rentals, wireless Internet, and a book exchange. There are fire rings and tables at every site. Speaking of sites, the 70 campsites here are grassy and shaded, 28 with full hookups and 42 with water and electricity. Take M-95 North to Twin Falls Road and then turn left. You can find campsites at **Lake Antoine Park** (N3393 Lake Antoine, 906/774-2573) and **Rivers Bend Campground** (N3905 Pine Mountain Rd., 906/779-1171) as well.

FOOD

Italian is the way to go if you're eating out in Iron Mountain. Homemade ravioli, slow-roasted pork, Italian sausage, Roma red sauce… you'll find it all in Iron Mountain's unassuming Italian eateries. **Bimbo's Wine Press** (314 E. Main St., 906/774-8420) dishes out mouthwatering Italian sandwiches like porketta and Italian hot beef for incredibly reasonable prices ($5 on average). More upscale is **ⓒ Fontana's Supper Club** (115 S. Stephenson Ave./U.S. 2, 906/774-0044, $15) for steaks and, yes, Italian specialties. Save room for cheesecake. The food at **Romagnoli's Restaurant** (N. Stephenson Ave./U.S. 2, 906/774-7300, closed Sun.) is made from original family recipes. Known for their ribs as much as for their gnocchi, Romagnoli's also serves steaks, fish, and, perhaps as a nod to Midwest America, fries on the side. With the exception of the thin-crust pizzas, **Famers** (N3332 Pine Mountain Rd., 906/774-2747, www.pinemountainresort.com) is the place to go when you're looking for something a bit less Italian. The restaurant, which is part of Pine Mountain Resort, is a sports bar, complete with good appetizers, five televisions, cocktails, and big steaks. It's the perfect place to catch the big game.

In Norway, you'll want to stop at the appropriately named **Norway Deli** (1028 Main St., 906/563-8180, 11 A.M.–7 P.M. Mon.–Fri., 8 A.M.–2 P.M. Sat.), a casual breakfast, lunch, and dinner restaurant. Stop in on Friday for the fish fry if you like, but don't miss the Saturday breakfast, which is both good and inexpensive. For slightly heartier fare (try the half-pound burger), head to the **ⓒ Thirsty Whale Bar and Grill** (825 Murray Rd./U.S. 2, Norway, 906/563-5466, open daily for lunch and dinner) west of town. A good choice for families is the **Maple Creek Restaurant** (1052 Stephenson, Iron Mountain 906/774-1777,

THE SUPERIOR UPLAND

www.maplecreekim.com), where you'll find satisfying family-style fare at very attractive prices.

INFORMATION AND SERVICES

For information on Iron Mountain and the surrounding area, contact the **Tourism Association of the Dickinson County Area** (600 S. Stephenson Ave., 800/236-2447, www. ironmountain.org). Also remember that Iron Mountain is on Central Time, an hour behind most of the Upper Peninsula.

If medical attention is necessary, the **Dickinson County Hospital** (1721 S. Stephenson Ave., Iron Mountain, 906/774-1313, www.dchs.org) is located on U.S. 2/141 heading southeast out of town. In addition to a few local banks, **Wells Fargo** (www.wellsfargo. com) has locations both in Iron Mountain (1805 S. Stephenson Ave., 906/774-0930) and north in Crystal Falls (1352 U.S. 2, 906/875-6651).

GETTING THERE AND AROUND
Car

Iron Mountain is located on Michigan's border with Wisconsin, at the intersection of two major highways. Driving into town from the east, take U.S. 2 (which is U.S. 2/141 when you come from the west). North from Wisconsin or south from other parts of the U.P., U.S. 141 will take you right into town. Take U.S. 2/141 north to Crystal Falls, U.S. 2 east to Norway, and U.S. 2 west to Iron River.

Air

There are a few nearby options for people flying into Iron Mountain. **Ford Airport** (IMT, 906/774-4870, www.fordairport.org) in Kingsford offers service on Delta Airlines to Detroit, Chicago, Minneapolis–St. Paul and other Midwestern cities. **Delta County Airport** (ESC, 3300 Airport Rd., 906/786-4902, www. deltacountymi.org), a small airport just southwest of Escanaba, provides service to Detroit and other regional airports through Delta. You can rent a car from **Alamo Car Rental** (3300 Airport Rd., 906/786-0603, www.alamo.com) that'll take you where you want to go (and you really will need a car while you're here). You can fly into **Sawyer International Airport** (MQT, 125 G Ave., Gwinn, 906/346-3308, www.saw-yerairport.com), too. American Eagle offers daily scheduled flights to and from Chicago. Mesaba Airlines (in conjunction with Delta) offers daily service to Detroit. You'll find a good number of car rental agencies, too: **Avis** (906/346-6398), Budget (906/372-9240), **Alamo/National** (906/346-6378), **Dollar** (906/346-4355), and **Thrifty** (906/346-4355). Sawyer is just south of Marquette and a good distance from Iron Mountain (the drive is about two hours, maybe less), but its regular service makes it one of the most attractive options.

Public Transportation

Currently, there is no regularly scheduled bus service to the Iron Mountain area. For taxi service, call **Tri-City Cab** (906/774-7878).

THE SUPERIOR UPLAND

Iron River and Ottawa National Forest

Iron County's population centers around Iron River, an iron mining center, and Crystal Falls, the picturesque county seat 15 miles to the east. Both retain their small-town charm. Like Iron Mountain, Iron River is just a simple town to pass through while on your way to some great skiing or backwoods campsites. Still, it makes for a quaint visit and a convenient stop.

The real draw to the region is the Ottawa National Forest. Sprawling across nearly 100,000 acres, the Ottawa National Forest blankets much of the western peninsula from the Wisconsin border to U.S. 141, which runs north from Iron River. Unlike a national park with contiguous boundaries, the Ottawa National Forest is a patchwork of protected lands, pieced together around towns, private property, and various state parks and forests.

Named for the Ottawa Indians who lived and traded in this region (though they actually populated the eastern half of the U.P. in greater numbers), the Ottawa National Forest encompasses more than 400 lakes, seven major river systems, some of the U.P.'s most outstanding waterfalls, 27 campgrounds, and three wilderness areas: Sylvania, the Sturgeon River Gorge, and the McCormick Tract.

SIGHTS
◀ Iron County Heritage Trail
There are 12 total stops along the Iron County Heritage Trail, a path of historic places scattered throughout the county. You won't find a lot of dramatic lighting and fancy display cases at the **Iron County Historical Museum** (906/265-2617, www.ironcountyhistoricalmuseum.com, daily mid-May–Oct., adults $8, children 5–18, $3), two miles south of U.S. 2 off M-189 in Caspian. What you will find is an interesting, appealing, and eclectic blend of local history and culture at this rambling, funky, and homegrown museum. Located on the site of the once productive Caspian iron mine—the mine's rusting headframe still looms over the complex—it runs largely on

donated money and volunteer labor. In the main museum building, displays cover everything from Native American history to logging, mining, and sporting equipment and kitchenware from the early 1900s. The perennial favorite display is the mechanized iron mine and railroad model: for five cents, a miniature ore skip hauls rocks to the surface and loads them on the railroad.

Other displays not to miss: the Mining Memorial, with a database of area mines and miners along with a video of life in the mines; a 3-D acrylic mine diagram which will enable to appreciate the depths of the mine, precisely where the ore has been extracted—and where it remains. You'll also see a 50-foot-long diorama of a logging camp, complete with hundreds of folk-art figures by local artist William Monogal; newspaper clippings on Iron River's 1920 "rum rebellion," when federal agents from Chicago stormed the home of the priest and discovered eight barrels of rum, only to be defied by the county prosecutor. Topping it off is an exhibit depicting the history of the local labor movement, which helped boost miners' earnings from $365 per year in 1931 to $1,886 per year a decade later.

Outside, several relocated buildings occupy the grounds, including a streetcar barn, as well as the streetcar that once traveled between the mines in Caspian and Iron River.

Head to Crystal Falls for a look at the small-town life of miners at the turn of the century. Tour the **Harbor House Museum** (906/875-4341, www.ironheritage.org, 11 A.M.–4 P.M. Tues.–Sat. June 1–Sept. 1), a restored Queen Anne Colonial Revival home that houses a two-story museum, complete with authentic furnishings and decorations and several exhibits displaying regional artifacts. Pay a visit to **Mile Post Zero and Treaty Tree,** too. As you might expect, this spot is simply a mile post and a treaty tree, but its historical significance is certainly noteworthy: The site marks the precise location of the survey point that set the

boundary between Michigan and Wisconsin in 1840.

Other sites on the trail include the **Amasa Museum,** the **Iron County Courthouse,** and **Mansfield Location and Pioneer Church.** Contact **Friends of the Heritage Trail** (906/875-6642, www.wuppdr.org/iron_heritage) for maps and additional information.

Triangle Ranch

Much of the U.P. is dotted with ghost towns, but Triangle Ranch may be its only ghost farm. In the 1920s, one developer had grand plans for some of Iron County's clear cut logging land. He purchased nearly 10,000 acres, building pens, corrals, barns, and a rancher's home, with the intention of raising beef cattle. The idea went bust after just one year—it proved too costly to care for the animals over the long U.P. winter. Most of the land was sold back to a pulp/paper company (and has since been reforested), but the skeletons of the operation remain. Triangle Ranch remains on the Michigan state map; from Crystal Falls, take U.S. 141 north about 15 miles to the marked Triangle Ranch Road (a few miles north of Amasa). Follow the road east about a mile to the remains of the ranch.

Paulding Mystery Light

If inexplicable, supernatural happenings fascinate you (or if you don't believe in them and would like a little convincing), a fun evening pastime is visiting the Paulding Mystery Light in Watersmeet. Believe it or not, the mysterious light reportedly appears in the distance almost every night. According to the sign at the site, "Legend explains its presence as a railroad brakeman's ghost, destined to remain forever at the sight [*sic*] of his untimely death. He continually waves his signal lantern as a warning to all who come to visit." To get here, take U.S. 2 east of Iron River, then follow U.S. 45 about five miles north of Watersmeet to Robbins Pond Road—brown signs will help you find the way from there. Several attempts have been made over the years to explain this bizarre phenomenon, though none have proved conclusive.

🄲 Sylvania Wilderness and Recreation Area

Sylvania protects its assets well—36 crystalline glacial lakes hidden among thick stands of massive, old-growth trees. For anglers who dream of landing (and then releasing) that once-in-a-lifetime smallmouth bass; for paddlers who yearn to glide across deep, quiet waters and along untrammeled shoreline; for hikers who wish to travel under a towering canopy of trees and hear nothing more than the haunting whistle of a loon, Sylvania can be a truly magical place.

One of three wilderness areas within Ottawa National Forest, Sylvania stretches across 18,000 acres near Watersmeet, an area roughly bordered by U.S. 2 to the north, U.S. 45 to the east, and the Wisconsin border to the south. The adjacent Sylvania Recreation Area acts as a buffer, extending by an additional 3,000 acres this area of lakes and woodlands. There are a few developed services, including a drive-in campground, a nice beach, flush toilets, and running water.

Ottawa National Forest occupies much of the Superior Upland.

Once viewed as just another tract of good timber, Sylvania's fate turned in the late 1890s, when a lumberman who purchased 80 acres near the south end of Clark Lake decided it was too lovely to cut, and instead kept it as his personal fishing retreat. He invited his wealthy friends—some of them executives at U.S. Steel who were also captivated by the land. Together, they purchased several thousand additional acres and formed the private Sylvania Club.

Like other upscale U.P. "great camps," the Sylvania Club soon had grand log lodges along its shores, guards to keep trespassing anglers away from its bountiful lakes, and caretakers to squelch forest fires as they cropped up. Ownership changed a few times over the decades, eventually ending up in the hands of Lawrence Fisher, one of the seven brothers of the famous Fisher Body Works, which eventually became part of General Motors. When he died, his heirs sold the property to the federal government for $5.7 million. It was operated as a recreation area from the late 1960s until 1987, when the bulk of it was converted to wilderness status.

We can partly thank Old Money for the condition of the land today. With the public previously barred from fishing here, Sylvania's lakes are now a paradise for anglers, especially those looking for smallmouth bass. Its waters remain pristine, due to the lack of development and powerboat access, as well as the area's topography. Sylvania lies on the divide between Lake Superior and the Mississippi, so it doesn't suffer from runoff of nearby lands. And whatever your thoughts on fire management, Sylvania's decades of fire protection mean that visitors today can marvel at a virgin forest of white pine and hardwoods—hemlocks, maples, and basswood trees more than 200 years old.

Begin a trip to Sylvania with a call or visit to the **Watersmeet Visitors Center** (906/358-4724) at the intersection of U.S. 2 and U.S. 45. The staff can help you with maps, regulations, campsite reservations, and other information. Sylvania's rules can be quite unique, especially the fishing regulations. Take time to ask questions and read through the materials rangers provide. To reach Sylvania itself, follow U.S. 2 west about four miles from the visitors center and turn south on Thousand Island Lake Road. Travel about four miles, and follow the signs to reach the entrance building. All visitors are required to register upon arrival.

The entrance sits in the recreation area, near the drive-in campground on Clark Lake. If you intend to travel into the wilderness area, plan on treating your own water; you'll find water pumps only in the recreation area. Cookstoves are highly encouraged, too, to lessen the number of feet tramping through the forest in search of dead wood. During summer months, make sure you also have ample insect repellent or, better yet, a head net to combat mosquitoes and black flies.

ENTERTAINMENT

If you're looking for local U.P. gaming, you can find it at **Lac Vieux Desert Resort Casino** (N5384 U.S. 45, Watersmeet, 906/358-4226 or 800/583-3599, www.lvdcasino.com) in Watersmeet. It's a bit of a drive west on U.S. 2 and then north on U.S. 45, but it's worth the trip from Iron River. The 24/7 gaming room has more than 700 video and reel slots, roulette, blackjack, craps, bingo, a poker room, and plenty more gaming fun. Stop by the Thunderbird Sports Lounge for food, drinks, and free live entertainment every Friday and Saturday night until 1 A.M. There's a snack bar for light fare and a restaurant with several buffets in addition to a full menu.

RODEO

One of the biggest events to hit Iron County is the annual **U.P. Championship Rodeo** (Iron County Chamber of Commerce, 888/879-4766, www.upprorodeo.com), which has been hosting professional rodeo events since 1968. The event is usually held during the third weekend of July. Popular events like steer wrestling, bull riding, and bareback riding, among others, continue to draw crowds each year for a good serving of Western-style fun.

SUMMER SPORTS AND RECREATION
Biking and Hiking

In the far south of the Ottawa National Forest, a few miles south of Iron River, the **Lake Ottawa Recreation Area** (Lake Ottawa Rd., 906/265-9259, www.fs.fed.us) has about nine miles of trails. One of the more popular is the primitive but nice Ge-Che Trail, which follows a 2.5-mile loop from the boat landing area. Try the two-mile Brennan Lake Loop, too. The Lake Ottawa Recreation Area is listed as part of the Iron County Heritage Route. Hikers in search of a short, easy trail will find it at **Bewabic State Park** (1933 U.S. 2 West, Crystal Falls, 906/875-3324, www.michigan. gov/dnr), located just off U.S. 2 between Iron River and Crystal Mountain, closer to the Crystal Mountain side. The two-mile nature trail ushers visitors from the campground to the day-use area and back—expect to spend about an hour on the trail.

Sylvania Wilderness Area and Recreation Area maintains 15 miles of trails, including a seven-mile trail (marked with blue blazes) around Clark Lake. It provides access to campsites and trails to other lakes. Most of Sylvania's trails are old roads left over from its fishing-camp days. While not always well marked, the trails are quite easy to follow. These same roads become a great **cross-country ski** network in winter months. National Forest staff grooms 15 miles of trails within Sylvania.

The marked and mapped **Pines and Mines** trail system gives a glimpse of the enticing opportunities for mountain biking in the western Upper Peninsula. A joint effort of local tourism and economic development groups, the Ottawa National Forest, and TRALE-UP (a local trail-access organization), Pines and Mines comprises some 200 miles of trails in three networks. Routes range from tame gravel roads to single-track trails deep in the woods. As a bonus, many showcase waterfalls, remote lakes, and historical landmarks.

Near Marenisco in Gogebic County, the **Pomeroy–Henry Lake network** offers 100 miles of gentle biking on wide gravel roads around a national forest area peppered with small lakes. It's a good choice for families. The **Ehlco network,** just south of the Porcupine Mountains Wilderness State Park, includes more single-track deep in the forest, on grass or dirt paths. This area can be wet, thanks to some lowlands and the work of local beavers, so avoid it after a rain. Arguably the best of the three networks is the one located outside the national forest: the Iron County (Wisconsin) system. Trails radiating out of Hurley, Wisconsin, lead you past waterfalls, large flowages, and old mining relics like the Plummer headframe near Pence, Wisconsin. Good interpretive signs help make sense of historic sites. Routes in this system range from gravel to single-track roads, though the map makes it difficult to distinguish between them. Single-track trails 6 and 13 are recommended.

While the Pines and Mines trails are great, the provided map is mediocre. It's best to bring your own topographical map, and before you set out get a little local advice from national forest rangers, local bike shops (**Trek and Trail** in Ironwood, 906/932-5858), or the Pines and Mines organizers. Pick up a map at the Wisconsin or Michigan state information centers. Both are on U.S. 2 near the border. You can also find them at local bike shops or the Ottawa National Forest office in Ironwood.

Canoeing and Kayaking

Seven major river systems flow within the Ottawa National Forest; a staggering total of 1,000 miles of navigable waters. Congress has designated more than 300 of those miles as "wild and scenic" or "recreational" rivers, keeping them largely in a pristine state. In general, rivers like the Ontonagon and Presque Isle offer quiet water in their southern reaches, winding through relatively flat woodlands. North of M-28, they begin a more rugged descent through hills and bluffs, requiring more advanced skills and boats appropriate for white water. For strong paddlers with good white water skills, these rivers offer some of the finest paddling in the Midwest.

Of course, all of this can change depending

upon rainfall and the time of year. Rivers that normally flow gently can become torrents in the spring. Always check with Forest Service officials before setting out. Also, the Forest Service distributes an extensive *River Digest*, a free publication that outlines navigable rivers, launch areas, and liveries, in addition to high and low flow times. Pick one up at a district ranger's office.

The three branches of the mighty Ontonagon spread across the western U.P. like a spider web. At times it seems every road you travel crosses one branch or another. While many parts of the river system are worth exploring, one spot gets particular attention: the upper reaches of the middle branch of the Ontonagon, where **Bond Falls** cascades down a series of black boulders.

Paddling is the best way to explore the Sylvania Wilderness. Most of the lakes are linked by water or by relatively easy portages, though there are a couple "grunt portages" of two miles or more. Many campsites are accessible only by water. Motors and other "mechanized equipment" are forbidden, including even sailboats. The one exception is Crooked Lake, which allows electric motors of 4 horsepower or less.

From the entrance road you can park your vehicle and put in at Clark Lake or Crooked Lake. According to a ranger, Clark (the largest), Crooked, and Loon Lakes are the three busiest lakes. Some of the smaller lakes; Mountain and High Lakes, which are both accessible from Crooked Lake, see less traffic and are just a short portage away. One ranger recommends bringing snorkel gear. The crystal-clear waters provide great visibility for viewing special species of large fish. Canoes and kayaks can be rented from **Sylvania Outfitters** (23423 U.S. 2, 906/358-4766, www.sylvaniaoutfitters.com) in Watersmeet. You can outfit your entire trip here: boat, food, fishing gear, and maps. You and even arrange to have your equipment delivered to and picked up from the water's edge.

A small but pleasant chain of lakes is the highlight of **Bewabic State Park** (1933 U.S. 2, 906/875-3324, www.michigan.gov/dnr),

located five miles west of Crystal Falls. Boaters can put in at the first of the Fortune Lakes and make their way to Fourth Lake, an easy day's paddling adventure. Though First Lake can be somewhat frenetic on summer weekends, the waters get quieter and downright pristine as you proceed down the chain. Paddlers can escape fishing boats by darting under the low U.S. 2 bridge to Mud Lake. The park itself has a modern 144-site campground with good privacy, a small stretch of sandy beach, tennis courts, and other amenities. Camping reservations are generally not necessary, but can be made via the state park reservation system (800/447-2757, www.michigan.gov/dnr).

Fishing

Bewabic State Park (1933 U.S. 2, 906/875-3324, www.michigan.gov/dnr) has some fine fishing, too. Fishing for perch and bass is best on First Lake, the park's largest (192 acres) and deepest (72 feet). There are more than 300 lakes here, and miles of rivers and streams for fishing. Iron County is home to five of the Upper Peninsula's 13 blue-ribbon trout streams, the highest certification the state DNR confers. Try the 12-mile stretch of **Iron River** extending upstream from the city, wade into **Brule River** between M-73 and M-189 south of town, or head to **Cooks Run**, south of U.S. 2. For more information on fishing in Iron County, contact the Chamber of Commerce (50 E. Genesee St., 906/265-3822 or 800/879-4766, www.iron.org/chamber).

Golf

Iron County is also home to some of the most interesting golfing in the entire U.P. You won't want to miss the 18 holes at the **George Young Recreational Complex** (159 Young's Lane, 906/265-3401, www.georgeyoung.com, $46/day). Not only is it the area's only 18-hole venue, but as a professional course measuring 7,030 yards, it's also the U.P.'s longest. You can play the standard course at just shy of 5,400 yards if you prefer. The elegant complex is run by a nonprofit corporation dedicated to recreation and preservation. Its lands include miles

of trails for biking, hiking and Nordic skiing. The **Crystal View Golf Course** (602 Wagner St., 906/875-3029, www.crystalfalls.org, $10) in Crystal Falls is a nine-hole course owned by the city, located on the banks of Paint River. Another nine-hole course, **Iron River Country Club** (110 Hiawatha Rd., 906/265-3161, $13) is located nearby in Iron River.

Off-Road Vehicles

Off-road enthusiasts can find a designated ORV route stretching some 67 miles from Iron River northwest to Marenisco. There are miles of additional trails that network throughout Ottawa National Forest, some of which used to be the roadbeds of railroad tracks. Be careful to stay on designated, marked roads and trails. Contact the **U.S. Forest Service** (E6248 U.S. 2, Ironwood, 906/932-1330, www.fs.fed.us) for maps and more information.

Waterfalls

Just off the Black River Road National Scenic Byway, the Black River rolls and tumbles over seven magnificent waterfalls north of Bessemer before rushing into Lake Superior. The site is believed to be the largest concentration of waterfalls in the state. The first two, **Chippewa Falls** and **Algonquin Falls**, 9.5 and 9 miles north of Bessemer, are a little tough to find without a topographical map, since they don't lie near well-marked trails. The next five are a different story. The national forest has marked and mapped a good trail network, beginning from a parking lot off M-513, about 13 miles north of Bessemer. From this lot you can hike, from south to north, to **Great Conglomerate, Potawatomi, Gorge, Sandstone,** and **Rainbow Falls.** Only strong hikers and serious waterfall enthusiasts should try to cover them all in one 10-mile outing—there are many steps and several waterfalls.

Like babies and sunsets, each waterfall is beautiful in a different way, and it's impossible to name the "best." Potawatomi is the closest, just a few minutes' walk from the lot, and accessible by wheelchair. And it is lovely, a delicate fretwork of foam cascading over

Bond Falls is a breathtaking sight in winter as well as in summer.

remnants of an ancient lava flow. The last falls, Rainbow, is the largest of the group, cascading 40 feet. The resulting spray sometimes creates a rainbow effect, hence the name. The best view of Rainbow Falls is from the east side of the river, which you can access from a suspended foot bridge near the river's mouth at **Black River Harbor.**

C BOND FALLS

Some consider Bond Falls one of the most spectacular falls in the Upper Peninsula, a mighty big claim—while others feel the setting is far too developed with walkways and viewing platforms, distorting its natural beauty. Decide for yourself, and head for Paulding on U.S. 45 in Ontonagon County. Bond Falls is three miles east on Bond Falls Road and is well marked by signs. Though virtually surrounded by national forest land, the falls themselves sit on power company property, just below a dam that forms the adjacent **Bond Falls Flowage,** a popular area for fishing, swimming, and camping. To view the falls, follow the trail down the west side of the river. Ignore the spillway, cement retaining wall, and other power company additions. Once you begin descending the stairs the falls come into your view to the right, close enough to touch. Continue down the path to a footbridge that spans the base of the falls for an up close and personal view. Water gushes down a 50-foot face of chiseled rocks, so dramatic it almost looks like a Disney creation. A few miles north of Bond Falls **Agate Falls** is another striking waterfall, this one offering a bridge for easy viewing. Take U.S. 45 north from Watersmeet, then M-28 east from Bruce Crossing.

WINTER SPORTS AND RECREATION
Downhill Skiing

Without the benefit of the "Big Snow Country" marketing muscle that serves the ski resorts of Gogebic County, **Ski Brule** (397 Brule Mountain Rd., 906/265-4957 or 800/362-7853, www.skibrule.com) is left to its own devices to sell this appealing ski area six miles

south of Iron River. Its gimmick is that it's "first to open, last to close," which translates to about six months of skiing. Brule is reliably open for downhill skiing by mid-November and continues through April. The terrain is nice, too, with 500 feet of vertical, eight chairs and T-bars, and a decent half-pipe for snowboarders. Contact Ski Brule for information on lift rates, rentals, and resort lodging.

Ski and Snowshoe Trails

Ski Brule (397 Brule Mountain Rd., 906/265-4957 or 800/362-7853, www.skibrule.com) is also an ideal place for cross-country skiing. Nordic skiers can check out 14.2 miles of groomed and tracked trails, some of which wind along the Brule River. Because they aren't covered by the resort's snowmaking, the Nordic trails don't always open as soon as the downhill area. There are some 8.5 miles of groomed trails at **The Listening Inn** (339 Clark Rd., Crystal Falls, 906/822-7738, www.thelisteninginn.com, trail use $6/day), a splendid log lodge and B&B located nine miles north of Crystal Falls. Two beginner loops, separate snowshoe trails, and ski rentals make the inn an ideal ski destination. As with hiking, one of the finest trails for Nordic skiing in the **Lake Ottawa Recreation Area** (Lake Ottawa Rd., 906/265-9259, www.fs.fed.us) is the groomed and marked Ge-Che Trail.

Also, the national forest grooms 15 miles of trails within the Sylvania Wilderness Area and Recreation Area which provide a great cross-country ski network in winter months.

Snowmobiling

As with ORV trails, a network of snowmobile trails leaves Iron River and scatters through Ottawa National Forest. Snowmobile Trail 2 heads west into the forest, eventually reaching Ironwood, while plenty of routes branch off to the north and south into Wisconsin. Trails 2 and 16 head east for Escanaba.

ACCOMMODATIONS

The **Lakeshore Motel** (1257 Lalley Rd., 906/265-3611, www.lakeshoremotelicelake.com,

THE SUPERIOR UPLAND

$51–96) sits on the edge of spring-fed Ice Lake in Iron River (just east of downtown on U.S. 2), with tidy motel rooms, some with kitchenette units, and cabins from $60 a night. It's a great find, complete with a sandy beach and a boat launch. Iron River also has an ◖ **AmericInn** (40 East Adams St., Iron River, 906/265-9100, www.americinn.com, $104–150) on U.S. 2 just east of downtown, with a nice indoor pool, whirlpool, and sauna. Suites are available. You'll find great lodging at ◖ **Chicaugon Lake Inn** (1700 County Road 424, 906/265-9244, chicaugonlakeinn.com, $50–99), predictably located near Chicaugon Lake in Iron River. The year-round hotel has sparsely decorated but well-kept rooms, whirlpool suites, and free wireless Internet. Check out their special rates for the fall color season. **Lac O' Seasons Resort** (176 Stanley Lake Dr., 906/265-4881 or 800/797-5226, www.lacoseasons.com, $125–308) rents 14 cabins and cottages on the shores of Stanley Lake; in Crystal Falls, **Michi-Aho Resort** (2181 M-69, 906/875-3514 or 800/875-0904, www.michiahoresort.com, $59–70) has rooms and cottages on the banks of the Michigamme River.

Camping

The ◖ **Ottawa National Forest** maintains 27 auto-accessible campgrounds, all with tent pads, fire grates, and some sort of toilet facilities. Many are located along rivers and lakes. Most tend to be quite rustic and secluded, with the exception of Black River Harbor, Sylvania, and Bobcat Lake. A few, like Black River Harbor, require a fee and allow reservations through a central reservation system, 800/283-2267 or 800/280-2267. For more information on a specific campground, contact a district ranger station or the **Ottawa National Forest Headquarters** (2100 E. Cloverland Dr., 906/932-1330 or 800/562-1201) in Ironwood.

FOOD

The namesake of ◖ **Alice's** (402 W. Adams St., 906/265-4764) produces Italian specialties just as her immigrant mother did in Iron River before her, with homemade ravioli and other pasta dishes, gnocchi (Italian dumplings), and soups. Entrées run about $14. For picnics, pick up supplies at **Angeli's Foods,** in Riverside Plaza on U.S. 2 East (906/265-5107, http://angelifoods.com). An ordinary-looking modern supermarket from the outside, inside it surprises with a superb bakery, produce department, and deli. The family-run operation also has stores in Menominee and Marinette. For something a little out of the ordinary, try eating in a train car at ◖ **The Depot Restaurant & Bakery** (50 4th Ave., 906/265-6341), which serves more than 50 types of sandwiches at the site of the St. Paul Railroad Depot. Although it's a casual atmosphere (since you are dining in a train car), fine dining selections include steak and seafood.

INFORMATION AND SERVICES

For more information on the Iron River area and Iron County, contact the **Iron County Chamber of Commerce** (50 E. Genesee St., 906/265-3822, www.iron.org) in Iron River. All of Iron County is in the Central Time Zone.

Iron County Community Hospital (1400 W. Ice Lake Rd., Iron River, 906/265-6121, www.icch.org) can see to your medical needs (dial 911 for emergencies). For financial needs, including ATMs and branch locations, try **Wells Fargo** (234 W. Genesee St., 906/265-5144, www.wellsfargo.com) or **Miners State Bank** (312 W. Genesee St., 906/265-5131, www.msbir.com).

To make sense of what the Ottawa National Forest has to offer, start with a map. You can pick up a small brochure (free) or large topographical map ($4) at the **National Forest Headquarters** in Ironwood (2100 E. Cloverland Dr., 906/932-1330) or at the **Watersmeet Ranger District** office at the intersection of U.S. 2 and U.S. 45 in Watersmeet (906/358-4551). Other district offices, in Bessemer, Bergland, and Ontonagon, should have maps and brochures, although budget cuts have forced them to curtail other visitor services.

GETTING THERE AND AROUND
Car

Like many of the larger cities in the U.P.'s western reaches, Iron River is located where Michigan and Wisconsin meet. If you're coming up from Wisconsin, take Wisconsin Highway 139 (WIS 139) across the border. U.S. 2 arrives in town from Ironwood to the west and Iron Mountain to the east. If you're coming in from (or going to) the Keweenaw Peninsula, U.S. 141 is the way to go.

Air

Generally, the farther west you go in the Upper Peninsula, the farther you get from convenient airports. One of the downsides to all this rugged isolation is that no matter where you fly, you'll have a good amount of driving to do.

Thankfully, both **Delta County Airport** (ESC, 3300 Airport Rd., 906/786-4902, www.deltacountymi.org) near Escanaba and **Sawyer International Airport** (MQT, 125 G Ave., Gwinn, 906/346-3308, www.sawyerairport.com) near Marquette have plenty of options for car rentals. Wisconsin's **Rhinelander-Oneida County Airport** (RHI, 3375 Airport Rd., 715/365-3416, www.fly-rhi.org) is a bit closer, and has daily service to and from Milwaukee via Frontier Airlines and vehicle rentals through Avis and National/Alamo.

Public Transportation

Getting to Iron River can be done easily enough on **Indian Trails motor coaches** (800/292-3831, www.indiantrails.com), which run regular trips from Escanaba to Ironwood. Call for schedules and rates.

Ironwood

With mammoth Lake Superior providing the requisite moisture, the northwestern corner of the U.P. isn't exaggerating when it markets itself as "Big Snow Country." Cool air moving across the warmer waters of Lake Superior creates lake-effect snow when it hits land, generating an astounding average of 200 inches per season. This combines nicely with the area's rugged hills, home to many of the Midwest's largest downhill ski resorts. As a result, the western U.P., especially around Ironwood, is one of the Upper Peninsula's more heavily marketed tourism areas, luring sizable crowds of skiers up I-39/U.S. 51 every weekend from Wisconsin and the Chicago area.

Ironwood hugs the border and merges with its sister city of Hurley, Wisconsin, once the center of civilization for the iron miners of the Gogebic Range. Ironwood had the stores and services; Hurley provided the bars and brothels. During the heyday of iron mining—from the early 1900s to about 1930—the population topped 15,000. But as the mining industry

grew less profitable, the fortunes made from iron left the region, without leaving behind opulent mansions or other monuments of wealth, as was the case in copper country.

Consequently, Ironwood today is a hardscrabble town that barely hints at its prosperous past. Still, locals are friendly, and they would probably agree that Ironwood isn't the tourist attraction—the natural beauty of the surrounding land is.

SIGHTS
Downtown Ironwood

There are a few interesting diversions in Ironwood's downtown, one of which is the **Ironwood Memorial Building,** a beautiful building that serves as a memorial for area residents killed in combat. World War I scenes are portrayed in stained glass, a statue of a soldier stands guard in the lobby, and displays outline the history of the region. Stop by the **Old Depot Park Museum,** once the train station and now an interesting museum devoted to the area's history. You can also visit the **Historic**

Ironwood Theater to learn more about the town's heritage.

Hiawatha

After encountering Big John, the absurdly tall miner at Iron Mountain Iron Mine, you'd be correct for thinking the Upper Peninsula has a thing for oversize historical figures. Case in point: Hiawatha, the 50-foot fiberglass Native American that serves as a very touristy roadside attraction.

◖ Little Girl's Point

Just minutes from the strip-mall world of U.S. 2, a real U.P. experience awaits. Follow M-505 north from Ironwood to reach Little Girl's Point, an area favorite. Perched high on a bluff over Lake Superior, this county park features a sandy beach, a boat launch, picnic tables, grills, and fantastic views. Take time to absorb the stunning sights of the Porcupine Mountains to the east and the Apostle Islands to the west.

Black River Road National Scenic Byway

Gogebic County tourism folks heavily promote this 15-mile stretch of County Road 513 from Bessemer north to Lake Superior, and for good reason. The two-lane road itself is pleasant enough, a wooded drive that twists in tandem with the Black River, hidden away in the forest just off the road's eastern shoulder. But even better, it links together several noteworthy attractions.

The end of County Road 513, Black River Harbor, is a popular national forest campground on Lake Superior, with a large dayuse area, sand beach, and boat launch. You can also pick up the North Country Scenic Trail here. For campground reservations, call the national forest central reservation system, 800/280-2267 or 800/283-2267.

◖ Copper Peak

You'll see the peak long before you reach it. About nine miles north of Bessemer, the rocky outcrop of Copper Peak rises 364 feet above the surrounding countryside, crowned by the 421-foot **Copper Peak Ski Flying Hill** (906/932-3500, www.copperpeak.org). Ski flying is similar to ski jumping but uses different equipment to achieve even *longer* distances. The current record is 512 feet. Copper Peak, built in 1970, is the only ski flying hill in the Western Hemisphere and the highest artificial jump in the world.

From Memorial Day to Labor Day, and weekends through mid-October, a chairlift, elevator, and steps will bring you to the top for a heart-thumping skier's eye view of the chute. This is not a trip for the faint of heart. But if you can get over a little knee-knocking, you'll be wowed by the panorama of the surrounding countryside, with views stretching across the undulating green of the national forest, the serpentine Black River, and the aqua blue horizon of Lake Superior. The Copper Peak complex also offers 12 miles of mountain biking trails.

SUMMER SPORTS AND RECREATION
Hiking and Biking

The lengthy **North Country National Scenic Trail** has been mentioned before, but the footpath really is the area's best hiking. When it's completed, the North Country Trail's 4,600 miles will make it the longest off-road hiking trail in the United States, longer even than the renowned Appalachian Trail. The section that passes through Ontonagon and Gogebic Counties cuts through Ottawa National Forest and Porcupine Mountains Wilderness State Park before bowing out of Michigan and into Wisconsin near Ironwood. Although it's one of the nation's longest trails it's also one of the least traveled, providing plenty of solitude for long stretches along the path.

In a land filled with stunning views, you'll find one of the best on the **Gogebic Ridge Hiking Trail,** a spur from the North Country Trail, about 40 miles northeast of Ironwood. The trail is eight miles long, and reaches its pinnacle at an overlook on one of the longest, tallest cliff faces in the state, complete with views of Lake Gogebic and the forested countryside. The south end of the trail skirts Weary

Lake. Contact the Forest Service (906/884-2411) for additional information about both the North Country and Gogebic Ridge trails.

When the snow isn't on the ground, the extreme western U.P. is prime **mountain biking** territory. More than 100 miles of the **Pines and Mines Mountain Bike Trail** cut through Gogebic County alone, while nine miles of trails comprise the **Wolverine Mountain Bike Trail.** One of the fat-tire highlights is **Copper Peak,** where bikers can enjoy a ride up the hill that would be a ski lift in the wintertime, then tear through the woods on the way back down.

Canoeing and Kayaking

Some of the best paddling the U.P. can offer is in Ottawa National Forest's 1,000 or so miles of streams and rivers. Paddlers in the Ironwood region will likely want to make the short trip east to the forest.

Fishing

Two companies in Ironwood charter fishing trips in Lake Superior, the largest, deepest, and coldest of the Great Lakes. Try **Bud's Charter Service** (128 E. Larch St., 906/932-5652, www.budscharters.com, full day $470, half day $360) or **Nomad Lake Superior Fishing Charters** (211 W. Lime St., 906/932-1576, www.nomadcharters.com, full day $550, half day $400). Your best bet for stream, river, and inland lake fishing will be to head east to Ottawa National Forest's almost 2,000 miles of waterways and some 500 lakes.

Golf

One of the western U.P.'s finest golf courses can be found in Ironwood itself. The **Gogebic Country Club** (200 Country Club Rd., 906/932-2515, $23 for 18 holes, $9 for holes) has been a favorite Michigan golf spot since the early 1920s, when the attractive stone clubhouse was constructed. Its 18 holes measure around 6,000 yards. Take U.S. 2 a few miles west of Ironwood and turn south on Country Club Road. For a shorter nine-hole course, check out **Indianhead Mountain Resort** (500

Indianhead Rd., Wakefield, 906/229-5181 or 800/346-3426, www.indianheadmtn.com) or **Boulder Creek Golf Course** (N11868 Heron Lane, Bessemer, 906/932-9066, www.bouldercreekgolfmi.com).

Contact each golf course for current hours and greens fees, which fluctuate seasonally.

Off-Road Vehicles

The closest major off-road vehicle trail in Ottawa National Forest is the 67-mile route that runs from Marenisco, 25 miles east of Ironwood on U.S. 2, to Iron River. There are, of course, smaller trails closer to Ironwood, but remember that ORVs are prohibited in the national forest except on designated, marked trails. Maps are available from the **U.S. Forest Service** (E6248 U.S. 2, Ironwood, 906/932-1330, www.fs.fed. us), or you can contact the Department of Natural Resources (906/353-6651).

Waterfalls

From Little Girl's Point, continue west on M-505 to reach **Superior Falls.** The rushing Montreal River puts on its final spectacular show here, plummeting more than 40 feet, then squeezing through a narrow gorge before spilling into Lake Superior a short distance away. You can also reach the falls by taking U.S. 2 about 11 miles west from Ironwood and turning north on Wisconsin Highway 122 (WIS 122), traveling through Wisconsin and back into Michigan in the process. In about 4.8 miles, watch for a small brown sign that directs you west into a small parking area near a Northern States Power substation. From there, it's a short walk to the falls. You also can continue down the path past the falls to Lake Superior, an excellent place to watch the sunset.

As you can no doubt guess from its name, **Interstate Falls** is located on the border of—and shared by—Michigan's Upper Peninsula and Wisconsin. Like Superior Falls, Interstate Falls is part of the Montreal River, but this waterfall is less towering (though still more than 20 feet) and wider, with a fairly impressive flow when the water level is high. You'll

want to cross into Wisconsin to see it. Take U.S. 2 west across state lines to an unpaved road about 0.25 miles past the border and follow the signs for **Peterson Falls,** which is a short walk upstream.

Heading north from Bessemer on the Black River Road National Scenic Byway will take you to a beautiful and popular lineup of five waterfalls on the Black River, which runs roughly parallel to the byway. Within the last few miles before reaching Lake Superior, you'll be able to see the **Great Conglomerate, Potawatomi, Gorge, Sandstone,** and **Rainbow Falls.**

WINTER SPORTS AND RECREATION
◖ Downhill Skiing

With the exception of the ski area in the Porcupine Mountains Wilderness State Park, the area's downhill ski resorts line up conveniently along a short stretch of U.S. 2 just east of Ironwood. Each one welcomes both downhill skiers and snowboarders. Ticket prices vary with age and season. Package rates that include lodging usually offer the best deals. For those who want to explore all the area's terrain, ask about the interchangeable lift ticket, which is available at each participating resort. It's good on weekdays only at the area's four major resorts: Powderhorn, Blackjack, Indianhead, and Whitecap Mountain (located just over the border in Wisconsin).

Heading east from Ironwood, the first resort you'll reach is **Big Powderhorn Mountain** (N11375 Powderhorn Rd., 906/932-4838, www.bigpowderhorn.net) in Bessemer. Powderhorn radiates an early 1970s feel, and the giant fiberglass skier at its entrance—complete with red and blue vintage '70s skiwear—says it all. The resort's 25 downhill runs wrap across two faces, with 700 feet of vertical drop and nine double chairlifts. Perhaps more than the others, Big Powderhorn Mountain caters to families, with affordable lift tickets, mostly tame runs, and plenty of ski-in/ski-out lodging bordering its slopes. In the main lodge at the base you'll find a cafeteria, ski rental and repair,

ski school, a bar, and other services. The resort is open daily.

Also in Bessemer, the smaller, family-run **Blackjack Ski Resort** (888/906-9835, www.skiblackjack.com) carves out a niche in the market by making the most of its terrain. Cameron Run and Spillway often are left ungroomed and offer up good bump skiing, and Blackjack is arguably the best resort for snowboarders, with the area's best half-pipe (served by its own rope tow) and a great terrain park on Broad Ax. Look to Blackjack for a variety of snowboard events, including camps and competitions. It's also a good place to avoid the weekend crowds that can plague Powderhorn and Indianhead. Blackjack offers 16 runs, four double chairlifts, and 465 feet of vertical. A day lodge at the base offers food service along with ski rental and repair. A limited number of condo accommodations line the slopes. The Loggers Lounge upstairs hosts the area's liveliest after-ski scene. Blackjack generally is open daily only during high season, and is can be closed on Tuesday and Wednesday other times. Call or check the website for a current schedule.

A few more miles down the road brings you to Wakefield and **Indianhead Mountain Resort** (500 Indianhead Rd., 800/346-3426, www.indianheadmtn.com), the area's largest resort, with 638 feet of vertical, five chairlifts, two T-bars, and 22 runs. Indianhead offers some of the region's most challenging (although overly groomed) skiing and pleasant runs that wind for more than a mile through the woods. Indianhead's lodging and skier services (sales, rentals, and repairs) are located at the top of the resort and offer more choices than area competitors. The day lodge even offers great views of Ottawa National Forest spilling out across the valley and far beyond the slopes. Indianhead is open daily.

Ski and Snowshoe Trails
Active Backwoods Retreats (E5299 W. Pioneer Rd., Ironwood, 906/932-3502, www.michiweb.com/abrski/), or ABR for short, grooms 25 miles of trails for skiing and striding on hundreds of acres of private

SKI THE U.P.!

When thinking of downhill skiing, places such as the Rocky Mountains or the Alps are usually the first to come to mind – certainly before the Great Lakes region. And while it may be misleading to say that Ironwood has the same caliber of skiing as the western U.S., it is fair to say that the abundance of ski runs and resorts, combined with the impressive snowfalls of the western Upper Peninsula, make it one of the finest destinations for Alpine skiers between the Rockies and the Appalachians.

There are numerous ski resorts within a short drive of Ironwood: **Big Powderhorn Mountain, Blackjack Ski Resort, Indianhead Mountain Resort, Whitecap Mountain, Porcupine Mountains, Ski Brule,** and a few other, smaller hills. Whether you like carving a halfpipe or leaving the first tracks on a backcountry slope, you'll find enough variety and deep snow to keep you satisfied, often for a fraction of what you'd pay at one of the large Colorado resorts.

As an added draw, the U.P. is home to some of the United States' largest ski jumping and ski flying hills: the **Pine Mountain Ski Jump** and the **Copper Peak Ski Flying Hill.**

© PAUL VACHON

Big Powderhorn Mountain beckons tourists year-round with a classic billboard.

land three miles south of Ironwood. Daily fees range from $9 to $12. The trails are open daily, as well as some nights for lighted skiing or moonlight skiing. A warming hut, lessons, and rentals are available.

South of Wakefield, **Miljevich Cross Country Ski Trail** (906/229-5267) has 6.8 miles of groomed trails winding through the woods, along with a warming hut, rentals, and more. This is an easygoing kind of place; trails open when Rollie Miljevich can get the parking lot plowed open. There's no fee, but donations are appreciated. To find Miljevich's, turn south off U.S. 2 at Sunday Lake Street (the stoplight) and drive about 2.5 miles.

Between Ironwood and Bessemer, take

Section 12 Road north from U.S. 2 to reach **Wolverine Nordic Trails,** (www.wolverinenor-deic.com). Situated on private land and maintained by volunteers, the 9.3 miles of groomed trails wind through the hilly country south of the Big Powderhorn ski area. In fact, you can ride one of Powderhorn's chairlifts ($3 per ride) to access the network. Otherwise, begin at the lot with the warming hut on Sunset Road off Section 12 Road. A donation is requested.

If solitude is more important to you than track set trails, don't overlook the vast terrain available in the 982,895-acre Ottawa National Forest. The **U.S. Forest Service** office (2100 E. Cloverland Dr., Ironwood, 906/932-1330) has national forest maps and can suggest trails to try.

Snowmobiling

Of the western U.P.'s snowmobile trails (hundreds of miles of them), plenty are accessible from Ironwood. Trail 2 leaves the city, heading east before fanning out to cross the rest of the U.P. Take Trail 11 north to Porcupine Mountains State Park and Lake Superior. Heading the opposite direction, Trail 11 runs northwest to find Lake Superior where Michigan and Wisconsin meet. Plenty of these trails drop south into the neighboring state and connect with Wisconsin's network of snowmobile trails.

ACCOMMODATIONS

You'll find a large selection of mom-and-pop motels along U.S. 2, many of which offer great deals and clean, comfortable, if simple, rooms. A couple of good choices are the **Classic Motor Inn** (1200 Cloverland Dr., 906/932-2000) and the **Crestview Motel** (906/932-4845) at the west end of U.S. 2. Both run $36–58, although rates may be higher during peak ski season.

The larger area ski resorts have slopeside (or near slopeside) accommodations that range from dormitories to simple motel rooms to deluxe condominiums. Prices range widely enough to fit almost every budget, and they can be a good value outside of ski season. Try

Indianhead reservations (800/346-3426) or **Big Powderhorn Mountain and Lodging** (800/222-3131) for plenty of choices. Ask about package deals with lift tickets if you're traveling in winter. The handy Big Snow Country **lodging referral service** (906/932-4850) can fill you in on even more lodging options throughout the region—not just those near downhill ski resorts—from the Wisconsin border to just east of the Porcupine Mountains.

For something a little more intimate, you can't beat the **Bear Track Inn** (N15325 Black River Rd., Ironwood, 906/932-2144). National forest land practically surrounds the inn's three log cabins, which have a great location one mile from Lake Superior's Black River Harbor and near scores of hiking/biking/ski trails. Each cabin has a full kitchen and use of the Finnish sauna. From the outside, the **Regal Country Inn** (1602 E. U.S. 2, Wakefield, 906/229-5122, www.westernup.com/regalinn) looks nothing like an old Victorian home, but you're in one of its historic or Victorian rooms you'll swear you've booked a B&B. Antique beds and decorations, pictures of local historic figures, quilted bedspreads, and a gourmet breakfast (for an additional charge; continental breakfast is included) all add to this inn's charm. Free wireless Internet is an added plus.

Finally, chain motels cluster near the U.S. 2/U.S. 51 interchange, including the **Days Inn** (715/561-3500, $50–100) in Hurley, Wisconsin, with an indoor pool. Some rooms include microwaves and refrigerators.

Camping

True to Michigan state park form, **Lake Gogebic State Park** (800/447-2757, www.michigan.gov/dnr) offers a fine modern campground, with large (but rather open) sites on the western shore of Lake Gogebic. A boat launch, small sandy beach, and nice picnic area are nearby. Lake Gogebic is known for great walleye and perch fishing, so pack a rod even if you don't come with a boat. Though reservations are rarely needed, you can obtain one through the state park central reservation system.

FOOD

It looks like a classic corner tavern, but **Don & GG's** (906/932-2312) on U.S. 2 in Ironwood might surprise you with its vegetarian dishes and smoked trout salad. Don't worry—you can still get burgers and chicken dinners, too. The **Hoop 'N' Holler Tavern** (115 Hoop 'N' Holler Rd., Merriweather, 906/575-5555) is a tavern in the classic mold, complete with plenty of good cheer and some very good tavern food, including burgers, sandwiches, and pizza. Located on Lake Gogebic's northwest side, Hoop 'N' Holler has a beach available in the summertime. Unlike Ironwood, the tavern is located in the Eastern Time Zone: add one hour.

The **C Kimball Inn** (715/561-4095) is actually in Wisconsin, but it's worth the extra four-mile drive west on U.S. 2 from the Michigan–Wisconsin border to sample its smoked barbecue, charbroiled steaks, grinders, and more. It's closed on Mondays. Also in Wisconsin, **Petrusha's Supper Club** (715/561-9888) in downtown Hurley serves up good Italian and classic American fare, from prime rib to seafood. There are some interesting Austrian dishes, too, like the filet with chicken livers and cognac sauce. Back in Ironwood, the **Royal Bakery** (906/932-1931) at the corner of Cloverland Drive (U.S. 2) and Douglas Boulevard is a good bet for fresh homemade pasties, as well as basic doughnuts and pastries.

INFORMATION AND SERVICES

For tourism information, assistance, and planning, get ahold of the **Ironwood Area Chamber of Commerce** (150 N. Lowell St., 906/932-1122, www.ironwoodmi.org) or the **Western Upper Peninsula Convention and Visitor Bureau** (906/932-4850 or 800/522-5657, www.westernup.info).

Ironwood's hospital is the **Grand View Hospital** (10561 N. Grand View Lane,

906/932-2525, www.gvhs.org), just north of U.S. 2 between Bessemer and Ironwood. There's no shortage of banks in Ironwood and Bessemer. You'll find both local and regional banks, or you can go to one of Wells Fargo's two locations.

GETTING THERE AND AROUND
Car

Ironwood is tucked about as far into the U.P.'s western corner as you can get. Take U.S. 2 in from the east or west. From the south, drive up Wisconsin Highway 77 or U.S. 51. M-28 serves as the connection from the north and east in the Upper Peninsula.

Air

In addition to the distant **Sawyer International Airport** (MQT, 125 G Ave., Gwinn, 906/346-3308, www.sawyerairport.com) near Marquette, you can find a closer facility in Houghton County, in the Keweenaw Peninsula. **Houghton County Memorial Airport** (CMX, 23810 Airpark Blvd., Calumet, 906/482-3970, www.houghtoncounty.org) has regularly scheduled flights to and from Chicago, as well as vehicle rentals through National/Alamo. In Wisconsin, the **Rhinelander-Oneida County Airport** (RHI, 3375 Airport Rd., 715/365-3416, www.fly-rhi.org) has daily service to and from Milwaukee and vehicle rentals through Avis, Budget, and National/Alamo.

Public Transportation

Getting to Ironwood via bus is actually pretty easy, even if you're coming from Chicago, Detroit, or other far-off locations. A combination of **Greyhound** and **Indian Trails** (800/292-3831, www.indiantrails.com) routes can get you there without too much trouble. Call Indian Trails for current rates and schedules for its St. Ignace–Escanaba–Ironwood line.

THE SUPERIOR UPLAND

Porcupine Mountains and Ontonagon

SIGHTS
◖ Porcupine Mountains Wilderness State Park

Anchored along the Lake Superior shore in the northwest corner of the U.P., Porcupine Mountains Wilderness State Park covers 60,000 acres, making it the largest member of Michigan's excellent state park system. The Porcupine Mountains were considered as a national park site in the 1940s, but came under state authority in 1945 when loggers threatened the virgin timber resources before the federal government took action.

Someone once decided that this rumpled landscape of low mountains and tall pines looked like the silhouette of a porcupine. The name stuck, along with an endearing nickname: "the Porkies." The area is a focal point for casual hikers and hardcore backpackers alike, home to 90-plus miles of well-marked and well-maintained trails—more than you'll find in many national parks, and certainly more than you'll find in most of the Great Lakes region.

And in this case, bigger means better. The park preserves vast stands of virgin hemlock, pine, and hardwoods, the largest tract of virgin hardwoods between the Rockies and the Adirondacks. There are also secluded lakes, wild rivers, and some of the Midwest's highest peaks. Summit Peak tops out at 1,958 feet. Unlike most state parks, Porcupine Mountains is large enough to provide a sense of wilderness and serenity, a treasured escape from the civilized world.

Ontonagon County Historical Museum

The Ontonagon Boulder was pried from its namesake riverbank a few miles upstream from the Lake Superior shoreline community of Ontonagon. Today the two-ton mass

The majestic Porcupine Mountains provide Michigan's most stunning scenery.

© PAUL VACHON

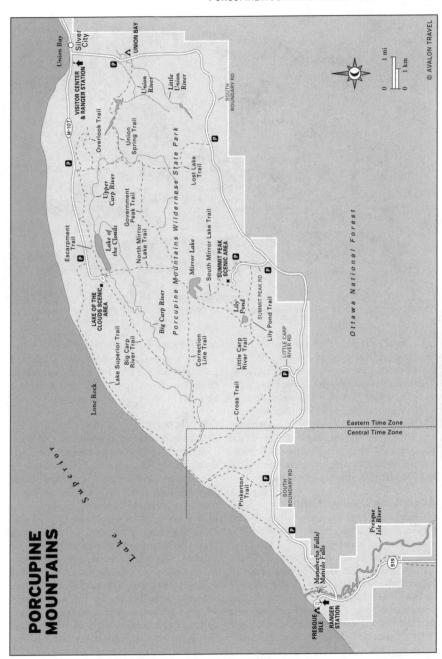

PORCUPINE MOUNTAINS

THE SUPERIOR UPLAND

© AVALON TRAVEL

THE SUPERIOR UPLAND

An array of old Michigan plates is displayed in the Ontonagon County Historical Museum.

© PAUL VACHON

of native copper resides at the Smithsonian Institute, and Ontonagon's mining heritage thrives only in museums, especially since the mine and smelter in nearby White Pine closed in 1995. White Pine now is little more than a creepy ghost town of 1950s tract housing. Check out Ontonagon's happier heyday at the very worthwhile Ontonagon County Historical Museum (422 River St., 906/884-6165, www.ontonagonmuseum.org), a lavender building on U.S. 41/M-38, downtown's main street.

Adventure Copper Mine

In Greenland, 12 miles southeast of Ontonagon, the Adventure Copper Mine (906/883-3371, www.adventureminetours.com, 9 A.M.–6 P.M. Mon.–Sat. and 11 A.M.–6 P.M. Sun. late May–mid-Oct., tours $12.50–$55) operated for 70 years without turning a profit. Today, it's more successful as a tourism destination, offering a number of surface and underground tours that last from 45 minutes to 3 hours. One of the tours re-creates the experience of old-time miners by having visitors rappel down a mine-shaft in total darkness, explore small areas, and get a little dirty. There are some tamer underground tours, too. To get there, take Adventure Road off of M-38 in Greenland.

Old Victoria

Originally established by copper miners in the 1840s, the tiny town of **Rockland** was nearly destroyed by fire in 1890. It was rebuilt in the popular Victorian style of the day. Several Victorian facades still decorate this small community in the Ontonagon River valley, which is 14 miles south of Ontonagon on U.S. 45. From downtown Rockland, follow Victoria Dam Road southwest two miles to Old Victoria (906/886-2617, www.oldvictoria.net), a cluster of miners' log homes huddled around a once-lucrative copper mine shaft. Locals have worked strenuously to save this historic site, which is still a work in progress. Its new designation as a Keweenaw National Historic Park cooperating site may attract new attention and

needed funds. The homes are open on most summer afternoons when guides are available. Donations are both needed and much appreciated. Visitors are welcome to wander the grounds at any time. Continue past Old Victoria to the **Victoria Dam,** a hydroelectric facility and yet a surprisingly pretty spot popular with local anglers.

Ontonagon Lighthouse

The Ontonagon County Historical Society's current project is the restoration of the 1866 Ontonagon Lighthouse, which replaced the original built in 1853. Contact the **Ontonagon County Historical Society** (906/884-6165) to learn more about public tours and the restoration effort.

SUMMER SPORTS AND RECREATION
Hiking and Biking Trails

Many visitors to the Porkies head immediately toward the justly famous **Lake of the Clouds Overlook.** From the parking lot at the end of M-107, it's just a few steps to the overlook, where the placid lake slices a long sliver of blue through a thick blanket of jade forest hundreds of feet below. The exquisite view is arguably the most dramatic in Michigan and is truly the stuff postcards are made of.

The overlook also serves as the trailhead for some the park's most rugged and scenic routes. To fully appreciate the Lake of the Clouds view, hike the aptly named **Escarpment Trail,** which winds east and skims over Cloud Peak and Cuyahoga Peak. Bordered by a sheer cliff, the four-mile trail is considered by many to be the most beautiful in the park. Allow ample time to stop and enjoy the shimmering lake and valley floor spreading out around you.

At its eastern trailhead, the Escarpment Trail links up with the 7.5-mile **Government Peak Trail.** This secluded route drops south over the Upper Carp River and past Trap Falls, then swings west and scales Government Peak. As quickly as it rises, the trail drops down to quiet

Mirror Lake, a perfect spot to soak weary feet after a full day of hiking.

From Mirror Lake, the dull and heavily wooded **Correction Line Trail** heads west, where it meets the **Big Carp River Trail,** another good choice. Running nine miles from Lake Superior to the Lake of the Clouds Overlook, this fine route leads hikers along a shaded river valley of hemlocks and ferns, past the park's highest waterfall (25-foot Shining Cloud Falls), and along a dry ridgetop with more dramatic peeks at the unspoiled Lake of the Clouds.

Several miles south, visitors get another soaring view from the **Summit Peak observation tower.** At 1,958 feet, Summit Peak grows even taller with a 40-foot observation tower at its crest. It's an inspiring panorama, a vast landscape unscarred by humans. In fact, the only sign of civilization is a spindly ski jump 18 miles away, rising above the tree line like a circus clown on stilts. On a clear day, you can scour the horizon for a glimpse of Lake Superior's Apostle Islands, nearly 40 miles to the west.

One of the park's most spectacular trails is probably its most accessible: the **East and West River Trail** parallels the wild and turbulent Presque Isle River. From the Presque Isle Campground at the park's west end, you can follow the river one mile upstream and down the opposite bank as it roils and boils through narrow rock walls and tumbles into Lake Superior. Keep a tight hold on children and pets along this trail, and don't think about wading—the current is swift and dangerous. To dangle your toes or let your dog take a swim, there's a wonderfully deep, clear, and placid backwater pool just east of the main channel right near Lake Superior.

Long before the Porcupine Mountains were preserved for their virgin timber and natural beauty, miners harvested the rich minerals buried in their bedrock. At the east end of the park, the **Union Mine Trail** provides a glimpse into life in the 1840s, when the Porkies pulsed with the excitement of the area's copper rush.

Marked with white mine shovels to indicate points of interest, this self-guided interpretive trail forms a mile loop along the spring-fed Union River and the site of an old copper mine, now largely reclaimed by nature. In the shadow of lofty hemlocks, you'll see how miners tunneled shafts into the riverbank and learn about their lives in the wilderness—a wilderness still untamed today.

Fishing

Fishing is one of the many recreational benefits in this vast expanse of wilderness. The park's most striking location, Lake of the Clouds, is accessible to anglers along with a number of other lakes and streams. Try Mirror Lake and any number of rivers—the Carp River, Presque Isle River, and Union River. Contact the DNR park headquarters (906/885-5275) for regulations and information.

Beaches

Porcupine Mountain State Park is known, in part, for its beaches and more than 50 miles of Lake Superior shoreline. The most popular is **Union Bay,** in part because of its pleasant but chilly swimming and because it's easily accessible by car.

Golf

Golfers will have to turn to the nine holes at **Ontonagon Golf Course** (19906 Firesteel Rd., Ontonagon, 906/884-4130, $17 for 9 holes, $27 all day), which isn't a bad thing at all. The clubhouse is fairly spartan, but the par-35 course makes for a nice round, and the pro shop can provide you with everything you need for an afternoon on the links.

Off-Road Vehicles

The old Copper Range Railroad grade bisects Ontonagon County and the southern Keweenaw from Mass City north to Houghton, a distance of more than 41 miles. Throughout the state, the DNR has purchased many of these old grades and removed the rails, maintaining them as multi-use trails. In the U.P., that usually means snowmobiles and ATVs. Near the

The Lake of the Clouds is an excellent choice for fishing.

© PAUL VACHON

PORCUPINE MOUNTAINS CONSERVATION

Long before Europeans arrived and began harvesting the area's abundant resources, the Ojibwa people had already (inexplicably) named the peaks and crags along the Lake Superior shore the Porcupine Mountains. In the 1700s the area was a principle trapping area of the fur trade. In the mid-1800s copper was first discovered. During the last half of the 19th century and into the early 20th, there were 45 copper mines operating inside what is now Porcupine Mountains Wilderness State Park. Loggers soon discovered the area as well, and began to pursue their trade.

Due to absence of modern conservation methods, logging has had a drastic, often damaging impact on the landscape, and the threat to the Porcupine Mountains became real. As tree cutting began to encroach on the virgin forests in the early 1920s, the issue of preservation came up in discussion. The dream became a reality some 20 years later, when the Michigan state legislature established the park and the Porcupine Mountains (nicknamed the "Porkies") were saved. Despite some minor conflicts with copper mining companies, the park is now in nearly untouched condition.

Today, the Porkies are home to one of the Great Lakes region's largest remaining old-growth forests, hardwoods, and eastern hemlock trees. It's a remarkably beautiful park, offering almost boundless recreational opportunities.

intersection of M-26 and M-38 at Lake Mine, the trail spans the Firesteel River on three bridges which range from 65 to 85 feet high. Stop at the DNR office in Baraga for a map of the rail trail that shows access points. Where the trail crosses roads, look for a yellow-and-black snowmobile crossing sign on the highway or a DNR ATV wooden trail sign on the trail.

Waterfalls

The Porcupine Mountains' more than 60 waterfalls can seem a bit overwhelming, but despite the overwhelming choices, some falls stand out above the others. Make the brief trek to **Presque Isle Falls** in the western portion of the park. Take South Boundary Road southwest from the visitors center to a boardwalk that follows the river to a number of falls, including **Manabezho Falls** and the smaller, less impressive **Manido Falls.**

WINTER SPORTS AND RECREATION
Downhill Skiing

Downhill skiers are often surprised to find a state-run downhill ski area within the park, and even more astonished to find it offers 42 runs, including a 787-foot vertical. The runs vary in difficulty from bunny to advanced and span a north-facing flank served by two chairlifts, one T-bar, and a rope tow. The ski area recently added more than 100 acres of backcountry terrain when it opened Everest, a half-mile wide section of virgin forest with more than 17 runs and snowcat service. A day lodge at the base offers food service, rentals, and a small ski shop. The lifts may be old and a bit creaky, but the terrain is wonderful, the snow is reliable (the annual average tops 175 inches), and the views of Lake Superior from the top are phenomenal. But for all its charms, this is not a good choice on a day when a strong north wind is blowing—you'll feel the wind chill all the way from Canada.

Located just west of the park headquarters on M-107, the ski area is open 9:30 A.M.–5:30 P.M. weekdays, 10 A.M.–5 P.M. weekends. Call the **park headquarters** (906/885-5275) for information on ticket prices and snow conditions.

Ski and Snowshoe Trails

The same chalet and base area serves cross-country skiers, who can access a terrific network of trails. The park service grooms and tracks 14.2 miles of the park's hiking trails, which wind through the eastern end of the

park. Some skirt the Lake Superior shoreline, where snow and ice sculptures form. Others scale the hilly terrain in the interior of the park and can be reached via one of the downhill ski area lifts. Skiing is free, but there is a charge for lift service and park admission. Call the park headquarters for more information.

Snowmobiling
In addition to the marked trails in Ottawa National Forest, you can take unplowed M-107 to Lake of the Clouds for a great, groomed snowmobile trail in the Porkies that ends at a spectacularly beautiful location.

ACCOMMODATIONS
You'll find a string of motels along M-64 between Silver City (two miles east of park headquarters) and Ontonagon. Many are plain, somewhat spartan mom and pop–type establishments, but they'll work just fine after a long day outdoors. **Mountain View Lodges** (906/885-5256, $225–275) feature two-bedroom cottages on Lake Superior with amenities like fireplaces and fully equipped kitchens including dishwashers. The **Americinn Porcupine Mountain Lodge** in Silver City (906/885-5311, $100–150) offers the full array of motel services, including an indoor pool, a sauna, meeting rooms, and a dining room. For other options, contact the Ontonagon Chamber of Commerce (906/884-4735).

Camping
Campers have their choice of two modern campgrounds, both with a number of sites overlooking Lake Superior: **Union Bay** (full hookups) at the east end of the park or **Presque Isle** (no hookups) near the mouth of the Presque Isle River on the park's western edge. Both offer flush toilets and showers. In addition, three rustic campgrounds (called "outposts") with 3 to 11 sites each are located off the South Boundary Road, accessible by car, but with no facilities. They tend to offer more privacy than the modern campgrounds. Reservations

for all campsites are recommended in summer (800/447-2757, www.michigan.gov/dnr).

As another option, the park offers 16 hike-in **rustic cabins.** These are great retreats after a day on the trail. They come with two to eight bunks, mattresses, a woodstove, basic utensils, and protection from the elements, but no electricity or running water. Bring your own stove for cooking. Cabins situated on inland lakes even come with a rowboat, so you can finish the day with a lazy drift across the water. Reserve a cabin as much as a year in advance by calling 906/885-5275.

Two more options for backpackers: there are three hike-in **Adirondack shelters** with sleeping platforms, available only on a first-come, first-served basis, and backcountry camping. Trailside camping is permitted throughout the backcountry, as long as you stay a quarter mile or more from cabins, shelters, scenic areas, and roads. All backpackers must register at the visitors center before setting out.

FOOD
Paul's Restaurant (906/885-5311), in Silver City's Porcupine Mountain Lodge, gets high marks for fish and other supper-club fare. In Ontonagon, **Syl's** (713 River St., 906/884-2522) is a classic small town café, with some of the best pasties around. Fifteen minutes south of Ontonagon on U.S. 45, **◖ Henry's Never Inn** (906/886-9910) in Rockland draws crowds in from far and wide for its enormous buffets with various fish dishes on Friday night and Italian delicacies on Saturday. Soups and sandwiches are great, too, but it's really the spirited locals who add flavor to this old mining haunt. Henry's has a very colorful history, having served as a "blind pig" during Prohibition.

If you're camping in the Porkies, your closest full-service grocery is in Ontonagon, 17 miles east of the park. For last-minute supplies, try the **Silver City General Store** (906/885-5885) on M-107. It has basic camping and fishing supplies, and picnic staples like cheese and bread.

INFORMATION AND SERVICES

Tourism information can be had from the **Porcupine Mountains Convention and Visitor Bureau** (906/884-2047, www.porcupinemountains.com) or the **Western Upper Peninsula Convention and Visitor Bureau** (906/932-4850 or 800/522-5657, www.westernup.info) in Ironwood. For maps and information about Porcupine Mountains Wilderness State Park, visit the **park headquarters** (412 S. Boundary Rd., Ontonagon, 906/885-5275, www.michigan.gov/dnr).

If you need a hospital, you'll find one in Ontonagon. To get to the **Aspirus Ontonagon Hospital** (601 South 7th St., 906/884-4134, www.aspirus-ontonagon.org), take Greenland Road (M-38) to 7th Street and turn north. Banking can be done at **Citizens State Bank of Ontonagon** (501 River St., 906/884-4165, www.csbont.com).

GETTING THERE AND AROUND
Car

M-38, M-64, and U.S. 45 all converge on Ontonagon, which is located on the shores of Lake Superior. From Ironwood, take U.S. 2 to M-28/64 before branching north on M-64. From Ontonagon, take M-64 to M-107 to get to Porcupine Mountains Wilderness State Park—the headquarters are on South Boundary Road, just south of M-107.

Boat

Ontonagon has a small marina that has 29 seasonal slips and 7 transient slips. The **Ontonagon Village Marina** (906/884-4225, www.michigan.gov/dnr) operates from May 1 to October 5 and can be reached on radio channels 16 and 68. Coordinates are 46° 52.57 N, 89° 19.58 W.

Air

Ontonagon's county airport doesn't offer commercial flights, but you'll be able to catch a plane into **Houghton County Memorial Airport** (CMX, 23810 Airpark Blvd., Calumet, 906/482-3970, www.houghton-county.org), which has regularly scheduled flights from and to Chicago via United Airlines. National offers vehicle rentals, and taxi and limo service are available. Marquette's **Sawyer International Airport** (MQT, 125 G Ave., Gwinn, 906/346-3308, www.sawyerairport.com) is a more distant option.

KEWEENAW PENINSULA AND ISLE ROYALE

If Lake Superior resembles the head of a wolf, then the Keweenaw Peninsula (KEE-wuh-naw) is seized firmly in its jaw. Parts of the land look like they've been gnawed on, too; remnants of long, hard decades of mining during the 19th-century copper boom. This narrow strip has justly earned the name "Copper Country."

Today, the Keweenaw's wealth is measured not in copper but in its boundless natural beauty. The peninsula is a mother lode of wild rivers, hidden waterfalls, and lonely Lake Superior beaches. There's civilization here too, but the Keweenaw is pretty thinly populated even by Upper Peninsula standards. Houghton is the largest city, with Hancock, just across the river, a close second. Together they have a combined population of around 11,000. The cities are separated by Portage Lake, part of the Keweenaw Waterway that splits the peninsula nicely in half. Some locals refer to the upper portion, the part containing Hancock and Copper Harbor, as "Copper Island."

Copper Harbor, on the shores of Lake Superior at Michigan's extreme north, is literally the end of the road. Specifically, it's the end of U.S. 41, a long, black, asphalt ribbon that originates in Miami, Florida. Copper Harbor enjoys a well-burnished reputation as an outdoor destination, even in the outdoorsy U.P. It's a destination for scores of kayakers, bikers, and snowmobilers. Rugged pleasure-seekers on the way to Isle Royale National Park can catch a ferry here.

Some 48 miles north, and also part of Michigan, Isle Royale National Park lies in

© PAUL VACHON

HIGHLIGHTS

《 Quincy Mine: North of Hancock, this historic mine tops the list of stops among the Keweenaw Historic Sites. The full two-hour tour takes you deep into the mine (page 134).

《 Downtown Calumet: A true diamond in the rough, Downtown Calumet provides a three-dimensional reminder of the once prosperous copper industry. Friendly townspeople make it all the more enjoyable (page 137).

《 Fort Wilkins Historic State Park: Another of many U.P. historic forts, this one is also well worth your time. Don't miss the costumed interpreters (page 149).

《 Brockway Mountain Drive: Only slightly out of the way, you won't want to miss this scenic lookout on the way to Copper Harbor, or the view of the city on the way back down (page 150).

《 Lighthouses: Sand Hills. Eagle Harbor. Copper Harbor. Some of the U.P.'s finest historic lighthouses are here in the Keweenaw. A few of them double as bed and breakfasts (page 150)!

《 Hiking Isle Royale: It takes some work to get here, but once you do, you'll have around 165 miles of trails beneath your feet – and some of America's last true wilderness at your fingertips (page 167).

LOOK FOR **《** TO FIND RECOMMENDED SIGHTS, ACTIVITIES, DINING, AND LODGING.

Lake Superior, a wild, craggy, roadless archipelago of lakes and forests, of moose and hiking trails. This wonderfully remote location makes possible the park's status as the least-visited property in the National Park Service system.

The remote Keweenaw has never had the tourist appeal—and subsequent amenities of a larger community like Marquette. But tourists are beginning to find out. With the national park as a draw, more museums and other attractions are opening, and more people every year are discovering the Keweenaw's unspoiled beauty. Some locals may be uneasy about the growing tourism interest. The backcountry is filled with amazing hiking and mountain biking trails, which lead to waterfalls and other

gems, but you'll find little guidance in where to go or how to get there.

Yet for those who crave adventure and solitude, the Keweenaw Peninsula and Isle Royale offer it up generously. As it was for those early copper miners, the Keweenaw remains a remarkable land of discovery.

PLANNING YOUR TIME

It's only about a two-hour drive from the base of the Keweenaw to Copper Harbor, but with scenery this stunning and outdoor activities this isolated, you're going to want to plan on spending considerably more time here. Houghton and Hancock make a great home base for outdoor excursions—you can

KEWEENAW PENINSULA

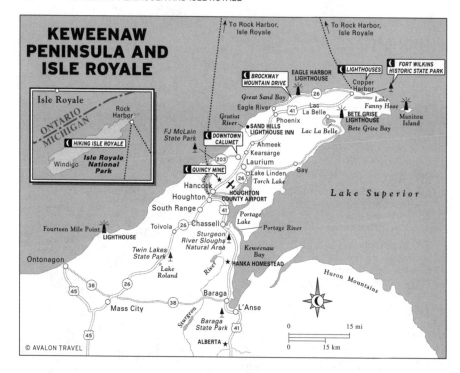

get pretty much anywhere in the peninsula in a little more than an hour at most. Depending on how many hours you're looking to spend on the trail or in that kayak, visitors often find that a weekend is plenty of time for a good recreation and sightseeing vacation. If you're planning on a visit to Isle Royale, you'll want to add several days. The island wilderness is vast, with over 165 miles of trails, several inland lakes, and other natural curiosities.

HISTORY

Raking off the back of the Upper Peninsula like a ragged dorsal fin, the Keweenaw Peninsula was quickly shunned by early European immigrants hopelessly remote and rugged. Nearly surrounded by Lake Superior. Smothered in snow half the year. Blanketed by impenetrable forests, which grew out of untillable rock and infertile sand. They dismissed it as nothing more than a wasteland, even more so than the rest of the Upper Peninsula.

But then in 1840, state geologist Douglass Houghton confirmed the presence of copper. Vast deposits of pure, native copper, much of it right below the surface, at the time unclaimed. The young United States had an insatiable appetite for the metal, first for new industrial machinery and later for Civil War hardware, electrical wiring, and other innovations. The value of Houghton's discovery seemed virtually incalculable.

The Copper Rush began almost overnight, beginning with prospectors followed by large mining enterprises flocking to the "wasteland" of the Keweenaw. It was the nation's first mineral rush. Copper employed thousands of immigrant laborers, built cities, made millionaires, and financed extravagant luxuries like opera houses and "copper baron" mansions. Before it was over, King Copper generated more than

$9.6 billion in wealth, exceeding the value of the California Gold Rush by more than tenfold.

Today, the aftermath of the copper boom looms large, evidenced by abandoned mines, ghost towns buried in the forest, and the odd juxtaposition of lavish buildings in almost-forgotten towns. Neglected for most of the 20th century, the efforts of historic preservationists began in the 1970s. The result is the Keweenaw National Historic Park, which was established in 1992 and is still very much a work in progress. Unfortunately, a great deal of this rich history has been demolished, thrown away, or crushed under the weight of winter snows. But an astounding amount remains. While chain restaurants across the United States line their walls with fake tools and other "junque," here you'll find the real thing: scores of mining artifacts decorating restaurants, front porches, and other public venues.

Houghton, Hancock, and Vicinity

When the hip outdoor sporting magazine *Outside* listed Houghton (HOE-ton) among America's "next wave of dream towns," it became obvious that change had arrived. *Outside* may indeed have something here. Houghton and the adjacent city of Hancock offer great sporting diversions, and boast an ethnic flair. Streets lined with beautifully preserved early 1900s buildings and a university add an atmosphere of culture and liveliness.

While the cities provide a refreshing dose of civilization, there are plenty of outlying towns and destinations that are also worth your time. This makes Houghton and Hancock a great place for hub-and-spoke traveling—find your lodging, spend the evenings in the city, and make your way out on engaging day trips.

SOUTH OF HOUGHTON AND HANCOCK

The Keweenaw Peninsula begins at Ontonagon on its western shore and at L'Anse on the east; an imaginary line traced roughly by M-38. Between this highway and the Portage Waterway, the southern Keweenaw is quiet and sparsely populated. It's quite a change from the turn of the century, when the Copper Range Company operated successful mines across this whaleback of a peninsula. Like elsewhere in the Keweenaw, the tall skeletons of mining shaft houses occasionally lurch skyward out of the pines, dying relics of the Copper Rush.

Logging subsequently came to fill the void.

Today, a sawmill operated by Mead Paper in South Range (south of Houghton on M-26) ranks as one of the area's largest employers. The facility mills the rare and prized bird's-eye maple that grows just to the north. Today the economy struggles, and locals have made insufficient efforts to capitalize on the tourism trade.

At the foot of Keweenaw Bay, between Baraga (BARE-a-ga) and L'Anse (LAHNTS), the enormous wooden statue *Shrine of the Snowshoe Priest* looms 35 feet above Red Rock Bluff. It commemorates the life of Bishop Frederic Baraga, a Catholic missionary from Slovenia who gained recognition for his work with local Ojibwa in the mid-1800s, traveling by snowshoe to reach distant communities. Unlike most missionaries in his day, Baraga is believed to have worked in support of the Ojibwa's rights by helping them gain title to their land, a stance unpopular with the local European fur traders and government Indian agents. Baraga spoke the native language fluently, and his guidebook of Ojibwa vocabulary and grammar is still consulted today.

A few miles south of L'Anse, on U.S. 41, a white clapboard lumber mill marks your arrival in **Alberta.** In 1935, Henry Ford built the mill, dammed nearby Plumbago Creek for the mill's water supply, and constructed housing for the mill's workers. It's a classic example of a "company town," one that has changed little since operations shut down in

the early 1950s. Today the facility is operated by Michigan Technological University as a forestry research center. The grounds, including a small museum, are open to the public.

Hanka Homestead

The Hanka family from Finland established this farmstead in 1896, hidden away in the creases of the landscape above Keweenaw Bay between Baraga and Houghton. The buildings include a log house, a barn, a milk house over a spring for natural refrigeration, and a sauna, in keeping with Finnish tradition. The self-sufficient Hankas raised dairy cows and chickens, grew vegetables and grains, and tanned hides to eke out a living and get through the harsh winters. What they didn't do much was modernize. Even though Jalmar Hanka, the last surviving family member, lived here until the mid-1960s, the Hanka Homestead (906/353-7116, noon–4 P.M. Tues., Thurs., and Sat.–Sun. Memorial Day–Labor Day, $3 adults, $1.50 children) remains suspended in time at about 1920, complete with the Hankas's belongings filling the home and its nine outbuildings. Guides offer comprehensive tours, and the homestead is a cooperating site of the Keweenaw National Historic Park. It's best to call ahead before you make the drive. To find the homestead, head north about 10 miles on U.S. 41 from Baraga, turn west on Arnheim Road, and follow the small wooden signs, which may refer to it as the "Finnish Homestead Museum."

HOUGHTON AND HANCOCK

Houghton (population 7,000) and Hancock (population 4,000) face each other across the Portage Waterway, with homes and churches tumbling down steep 500-foot bluffs reminiscent of San Francisco, especially on the Hancock side. The Portage Waterway effectively slices the Keweenaw in two, a 21-mile passage that saves boaters the 100-mile-trip around the peninsula.

Native Americans had used the route for centuries to cross the peninsula, traveling from

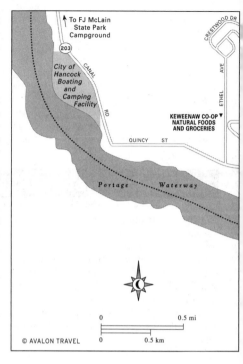

Keweenaw Bay across Portage Lake and along the ancient Portage River, then crossing over land the rest of the way to the shores of Lake Superior. In the late 1800s, a dredged canal eliminated the need for the west-end portage. Commercial traffic plied the waterway, largely to serve the smelters, stamping plants, and vibrant cities of the burgeoning copper trade.

A unique lift bridge spans the waterway to link Houghton and Hancock. Functioning in a way similar to a drawbridge, its huge center section rises like an elevator to let water traffic pass. Today the Portage Waterway largely serves pleasure boaters and the 125-foot *Ranger III,* a ferry that transports hikers to Isle Royale National Park. Houghton and Hancock are considered the gateways to the Keweenaw and to Isle Royale, but visitors just whizzing through will miss an appealing slice of the region.

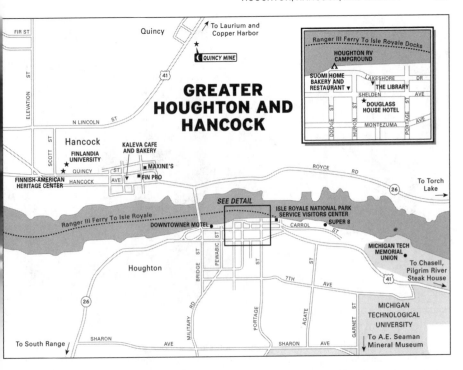

Downtown Houghton and Hancock

You can conduct your own historic walking tour of Houghton by strolling down Shelden Avenue, the city's main street. Tall facades of red brick and red sandstone line the street, including the **Douglass House Hotel** (517 Shelden Ave.), built in 1860 as a luxury hotel and dining establishment for travelers through the Portage Waterway. An addition in 1899 made it the lavish building you see today. Inside, the Victorian interior of the **Douglass House Saloon** (906/482-2003) still reflects those genteel days, with original Tiffany chandeliers, leaded glass windows, and frilly curtains.

On the east end of town, the campus of **Michigan Technological University** stretches out along the Portage Waterway. Nearly 6,300 students attend Michigan Tech, almost three-quarters of them in some type of engineering program. Not surprisingly, geology, mining, and industrial archaeology are some of the school's most notable fields of study. Students interested in mining management get real-life experience here, actually learning hands-on mining practices deep inside the nearby Quincy Mine.

Michigan Tech is home to the highly regarded **A. E. Seaman Mineral Museum** (1400 Townsend Dr., 906/487-2572, 9 A.M.–4:30 P.M. Mon.–Fri. yearly, noon–4 P.M. Sat.–Sun. July–Sept., closed Sat.–Sun. Oct.–June, donations welcome, children 12 and under free), the official mineralogical museum of the state of Michigan. The Keweenaw is considered one of the most geologically rich and fascinating regions in the world, and the Seaman Museum holds the premier collection of area minerals and gemstones, including

© PAUL VACHON

Houghton offers a downtown that's both historic and cool.

crystallized copper, silver, datolites, greenstones, and agates. Don't miss the informative exhibit of an iron mine and glowing fluorescent minerals. The museum also houses an impressive collection of minerals from around the world. All in all, its collection numbers more than 30,000 specimens. The museum is on the fifth floor of the Electric Energy Resource Center (EERC) Building, behind the J. R. Van Pelt Library. Obtain a parking pass at the Hamar House, a few buildings to the east of the library.

Michigan Tech isn't the only local university. Across the waterway sits **Finlandia University,** which began in 1896 as a Finnish academy to serve the area's ever-growing number of immigrant miners' families. Today, enrollment is approximately 550. The institution's **Finnish-American Heritage Center** (601 Quincy St., 906/487-7367, 8 A.M.–4:30 P.M. Mon.–Fri.) maintains a gallery open to the public that highlights Finnish artists and the archives of the area's Finnish settlement.

Even nonshoppers might be drawn into some of Hancock's stores, with their emphasis on unusual Finnish products. Where else do you shop for sauna supplies but **Fin Pro** (208 Quincy St., 906/482-9202)? The shop owners, who retired here from Helsinki, also carry an excellent selection of Finnish textiles, glassware, books, and music. You'll also find a good array of Finnish glassware and gifts at **Maxine's** (119 Quincy St., 906/482-5101).

Quincy Mine

Just north of Hancock, the mammoth shaft house of the Quincy Mine (906/482-3101, www.quincymine.com, 9:30 A.M.–5 P.M. daily early June–mid-Oct., 9:30 A.M.–5 P.M. Fri.–Sun. mid-Oct.–early June, hoist and mine tour $18 adults, $8 children 6–12, under six free; surface tour and tram ride $12.50 adults, $5 children) dominates the skyline. The Quincy ranked as one of the world's richest copper mines in the late 1800s, producing over a billion pounds of copper. Today, a few of its buildings still stand, and the land beneath it remains stitched with the shafts (vertical tunnels)

MICHIGAN TECHNOLOGICAL UNIVERSITY

The copper industry in the Keweenaw had become both productive and highly profitable by 1885. Despite this success, state mining authorities saw the need to improve both efficiency and safety in the mines. In 1885 the state established the Michigan Mining School in Houghton with just a handful of students. The new school's mission was to train engineers and managers to improve mine operations.

Over the next several decades the school (which soon changed its name to the Michigan College of Mines) steadily grew in enrollment and influence, developing new programs to serve the evolving industry. By World War I, the college's resources were put at the disposal of the military, and several graduates served in the Army Corps of Engineers.

As the twentieth century progressed, the college (then known as the Michigan College of Mining and Technology) added new programs in forest management and assembly line production. These were followed by the addition of graduate programs in chemical, electrical, and civil engineering.

By the 1960s the campus had evolved to a large complex of buildings on the east end of Houghton. The now-diverse school had outgrown its original focus on mining and was therefore renamed Michigan Technological University. MTU today is a first-rate educational institution with over 6,500 students and more than 400 faculty members.

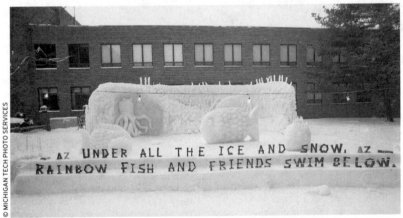

© MICHIGAN TECH PHOTO SERVICES

a snow sculpture produced by MTU students during the Winter Carnival

and adits (horizontal tunnels) of the mammoth mine, which stretch more than a mile and a half deep—92 levels—and two miles wide.

The Quincy Mine is a key site in the Keweenaw National Historic Park, and it offers a fascinating tour that takes you through the historic buildings and deep into the mine itself. Many of the tour guides are mining students at nearby Michigan Tech, so they can

handle just about any mining or engineering question. The tour begins with a look at the gargantuan steam hoist, the world's largest. A giant spool of sorts, it powered the steel pulleys that hauled the miners and mine cars loaded with copper in and out of the mine. The machine's mammoth size (more than double the size of the average hoist) was necessitated by the extreme depth of the mine.

U.S. 41 begins its gradual uphill climb at Hancock.

As interesting as the hoist is the building itself. In an era when miners made $1 a day (a good wage for the time), the Quincy Mining Company built its hoist house of poured concrete, then decorated it with lovely arched windows, lined the walls with Italian tile, and topped it off with green tiles imported from Spain. Thanks to all that concrete, the immense room today remains in excellent shape. It also houses plenty of artifacts and photos, including bilingual safety instructions posted next to the machinery, an indication of the predominance of immigrant Finnish miners.

From the hoist house, the tour continues with a rather dramatic ride in a glass-enclosed tram down the side of a steep hill. Views of Houghton and Hancock are terrific as the tram descends to an entrance to the mine, an adit at Level 7. A tractor carries you about 2,000 feet into the mine, where guides demonstrate mining techniques and give you a feel for what it was like to work deep inside the earth; a drippy, damp environment with only hand tools and candles. Contact the **Quincy Mine**

Hoist Association (49750 U.S. 41, 906/482-3101, www.quincymine.com) for tour times and other information.

Lighthouses

Two of the lighthouses in the Houghton and Hancock area are the **Portage Lake Upper and Lower Entry Lights,** the Upper located at the end of the breakwater at McLain State Park. Built in 1950, the steel tower is one of the Keweenaw's newest lights, which takes away nothing from its beauty. Take M-203 about 10 miles north of Hancock to F. J. McLain State Park and the light. The Portage Lake Lower Entry Light is on the east side of the Keweenaw Peninsula at the Portage River in the town of Lake Linden. This light was built some 30 years earlier than its companion on the other side of the river. A long walk along the breakwater pier will allow you to get close.

Near the Lower Entry Light, the **Portage River Light** (also called the Jacobsville Light) has been converted into a pleasant, unique bed-and-breakfast in Lake Linden. The **Jacobsville**

Lighthouse Inn (38741 Jacobs St., 906/523-4137, www.jacobsvillelighthouse.com) offers regular tours of the lighthouse and grounds. Call ahead for an appointment, or just stop by to check availability.

NORTH OF HOUGHTON AND HANCOCK

At the height of the Keweenaw's copper mining glory, the Calumet and Hecla Consolidated Copper Company, which operated largely in Calumet, proved the grandest operation of all. At the turn of the 20th century, C&H employed some 11,000 workers who extracted more than 1.5 billion tons of copper from a web of mines that tunneled under Calumet and adjacent Laurium. A surface plant in town, considered the most efficient in the nation, roared and whistled with the sound of 50 steam engines at work.

C&H ultimately generated more than $72 million in revenues. It built low-cost housing for its miners, consisting of some 1,000

© PAUL VACHON

This thermometer records the area's annual snowfall.

dwellings lined up like chess pieces. Groups of homes formed towns and were given colorful names like Swedetown and Limerick, which duplicated cites in their homelands. Most significantly, C&H spawned the city of Calumet, known then as "Red Jacket," a booming community of more than 60,000 residents. Striking red sandstone buildings with false fronts and cornices lined the 12-square-block business district. Downtown Calumet was filled with elegant shops, soaring churches, some 70 saloons, and even a lavish theater that attracted the nation's leading vaudeville stars. The city buzzed day and night, both above and below ground.

After the mining industry declined, Calumet's economy became stagnant and the city remained largely frozen in time. However, downtown's sturdy sandstone buildings have survived years of harsh winters and neglect beautifully. As a result, Calumet is a trove of early 1900s architecture, and was a deciding factor in the area achieving national park status. "We are fortunate that this area has been little disturbed since those glory days," said a park supporter. "Few modern intrusions have marred the area's scale and the feeling of its mining heritage." Today, Calumet (pop. 800) anchors the new Keweenaw National Historic Park, one of the park's two key units and a designated historic district.

◆ Downtown Calumet

Thanks to the new national park and renewed civic pride, downtown Calumet looks more like a movie set every day. Ugly 1960s facades are coming down off the elegant sandstone and brick buildings, and new money is coming in to further restore and preserve them. To appreciate this architectural legacy, stop by the **Keweenaw Convention and Visitors Bureau** (56638 Calumet Ave., 906/337-4579 or 800/338-7982, www.keweenaw.info) and pick up a walking tour guide. A few stops of particular note: The **Union Building** at 5th Street and Red Jacket Road was home of one of the area's first banks in 1888 and remains in excellent shape, with a decorative metal

cornice. **Shute's Bar** (322 6th St.) doesn't look that special on the outside, but inside you can see the preserved ornate plaster ceilings and the magnificent back bar with a stained-glass canopy. Across the street, the **Red Jacket Fire Station** typifies the Romanesque style favored for public buildings and churches at the time. At 340 6th Street, examine the detail on the **Red Jacket Town Hall and Opera House,** now called the **Historic Calumet Theatre** (340 6th St., 906/337-2610, www. calumettheatre.com, tours 11 A.M.–2 P.M. Mon.–Fri.). Perhaps more than any other, this building was truly the pride of the community. The theater portion, added in 1898 and the first municipally owned theater in the country, was a showy extravagance of plaster Rococo in cream, crimson, green, and gilt. It even had electric lights, a rarity at the time. Referred to as "the greatest social event ever known in copperdom's [*sic*] metropolis" when it opened in 1900, the theater attracted A-list celebrities including John Philip Sousa, Harry Houdini, Douglas Fairbanks, Jr., and Sarah Bernhardt.

Keweenaw National Historic Park

The Keweenaw National Historic Park (200 5th St., 906/337-3168, www.nps.gov/kewe) is not so much a place on a map but a place in time. One of the nation's newest national parks, it was established in 1992 "to commemorate the heritage of copper mining on the Keweenaw Peninsula; its mines, its machinery, and its people."

Rather than a park with simply defined boundaries, the Keweenaw National Historic Park consists of historic attractions throughout the peninsula. Two units anchor the park, the Quincy Unit at the Quincy Mine in Hancock and the Calumet Unit in historic downtown Calumet, although some of this land remains privately owned. The National Park Service owns just a limited amount of land outright to preserve key sites and conduct interpretive activities. In addition, the park has designated "cooperating sites" throughout the peninsula, including mine tours and museums which

remain in private ownership but will benefit from increased visibility and federal funding.

The park will continue to be under development for several years, while continuing to restore buildings, create interpretive displays, and develop educational programs. While the overall project is still a work in progress, the park headquarters in Calumet now consists of a full administrative staff administrative staff. For visitor information, contact the offices located at 25970 Red Jacket Road in Calumet (located in the historic former offices of the Calumet & Heda Company). The park superintendent can be reached at 906/483-3020.

C&H Industrial Core

One of Calumet and Hecla's mines was located right in town, in an area bisected by Red Jacket Road, just west of U.S. 41. Beginning at the Coppertown USA museum, a self-guided "industrial core" walking tour takes you past a drill shop, a powder house, a machine shop, and several other mining buildings in various states of restoration. The park service is adding interpretive signs to guide you along and share mining information, but you'll also want an information sheet that maps the route, available from the Keweenaw Tourism Council, the park headquarters, or the Coppertown USA museum.

Coppertown USA

The mine's pattern shop, where wooden patterns were made as molds for machine parts, now serves as the home of Coppertown USA (25815 Red Jacket Rd., 906/337-4354, http:// uppermichigan.com/coppertown/main.html, 10 A.M.–5 P.M. Mon.–Sat. and 12:30 P.M.– 4 P.M. Sun. June 1–Sept. 1, $3 adults, $2 with National Park Pass, $1 teens 12–18, free under 12), a privately run museum and national park cooperating site that traces the region's copper industry. It includes numerous artifacts, a display of area minerals, a replica of a mining captain's office, a diorama of Native American mining and more, with all the exhibits close enough to really examine. Don't miss the pattern shop area, which

COPPER MINING IN COPPER COUNTRY

The Keweenaw Peninsula nickname as "Copper Country" is well earned. After the discovery of Upper Peninsula copper in the mid-1800s, copper mines in the tip of the Keweenaw Peninsula were among the first to open. The copper business limped along for several years until just before the Civil War. By 1860, Copper Country was producing about 12 million pounds of the metal per year. By 1890 the region was sending about 100 million pounds of copper annually by ships that traveled through the Great Lakes or by trains headed to Chicago and the rest of the nation. For some 40 years, Michigan produced more copper than any other state, occasionally accounting for as much as 90 percent of the nation's copper output.

As the boom began to flourish, the Upper Peninsula soon saw an influx of workers from elsewhere in North America, followed by immigrants from Cornwall, England. Cornish miners were later joined by large numbers of Norwegians, Finns, Danes, and Swedes, who came to the Upper Peninsula to work tirelessly in the copper and iron mines and make an honest living. These newcomers brought with them their culture, foods, languages, and customs. Many of the old mining communities in Keweenaw and other areas of the U.P. are still influenced by their heritage. Even today, Finns are among the most prominent ethnic groups in Michigan's Upper Peninsula.

Copper Country mining camps and small towns grew seemingly overnight to become large cities and industrial centers. In Hancock, the region's mining and immigrant heritage survives, exemplified by the Quincy Mine, a national historic site, and Finlandia University, founded in 1896. Other towns born of the copper boom include Calumet, Laurium, and Lake Linden.

As the area's copper deposits became exhausted; the industry began to decline, which culminated with the last mines closing by the 1970s.

The economic impact on the area was severe, and long lasting. In most U.P. communities, the hole left by demise of mining has yet to be filled with another industry. Today, logging (conducted in a responsible and sustainable manner) and tourism hold the best hope for the area's economic future. These industries permit utilization – but not exploitation – of the Upper Peninsula's prized natural resources.

still houses thousands of patterns, lined up on shelves as if they haven't been touched for 50 years (some have been relocated to the Smithsonian Institute). Another interesting exhibit is a 1976 scale model that shows elaborate plans for Calumet, including a cultural center, a festival plaza, and a products exhibit center. The museum is located near the intersection of U.S. 41 and Red Jacket Road.

Downtown Laurium

Just across U.S. 41 from Calumet, Laurium was largely a residential district for the area mines. The west end of town (closest to Calumet) has a few streets of plain company homes remaining, looking rough and dilapidated—like much of Laurium. But a few blocks farther east, around Pewabic Street and 3rd Street, mining management officials built their homes, and today the area is a quiet and stately neighborhood well worth visiting. Pick up a *Laurium Walking Tour* guide from the Keweenaw Convention and Visitors Bureau (56638 Calumet Ave., 906/337-4579 or 800/338-7982, www.keweenaw.info) in Calumet. It will direct you to impressive homes like the one at 305 Tamarack Street, where a wise mining investor created this grand home with seven fireplaces, a third-floor ballroom, and a carriage house.

The finest home of all belonged to Captain Thomas Hoatson, founder of the Calumet and Arizona Mining Company, who built his dream mansion at 320 Tamarack Street. Today it operates as the **Laurium Manor Inn** (906/337-2549, www.laurium.info, tours 11 A.M.–5 P.M.

daily, $6 adults, $3 children), which means the public can enjoy a glimpse of this remarkable place. Sprawling across 13,000 square feet, the 45-room mansion includes ceilings covered in silver leaf, elephant-hide wall coverings, a triple staircase of hand-carved oak, and a turntable in the carriage house so that carriages could be rotated to face forward. The inn is open year-round, with most guest room rates ranging $90–175.

Football or cinema fans may want to view the decidedly less dramatic home at 432 Hecla Street. Laurium's most famous citizen was born here—**George Gipp,** the Notre Dame football star. "The Gipper" was undoubtedly Ronald Reagan's most famous role, that is, until he became president. A George Gipp Memorial decorates the corner of Tamarack Street and M-26.

Ghost Towns

Ghost towns litter the Keweenaw, faded testaments to the boom-and-bust days of copper. The ruins of old mines and stamping plants (facilities that separated copper from rock) line M-26 between Hancock and Calumet. The gray piles of residue are mine tailings or stamping plant leftovers called "stamp sand." Several bona fide ghost towns hide in the woods, too, especially between Calumet and Copper Harbor. At **Central** (watch for the small brown sign on U.S. 41, about 11 miles north of Mohawk), an exceptionally rich mine produced nearly $10 million worth of copper by 1898 while the surrounding town grew to 1,200. Today, nature has all but reclaimed Central, with just a few clapboard houses creaking in the breeze. Turn right near the top of the hill for a look at the mine ruins and rows of house foundations. Be sure to watch your step while walking.

Just south of Copper Harbor on U.S. 41, another sign announces your arrival in **Mandan,** directing you down a dirt road disappearing into birches. Follow it south for about 50 yards and a tidy row of homes suddenly erupts out of the woods. Welcome to Mandan, the last stop on a trolley line from Hancock.

ENTERTAINMENT
Ojibwa Casino

The Ojibwa Casino (16449 Michigan Ave., 906/353-6333 or 800/323-8045, www.ojibwacasino.com) in Baraga is tucked away in the southeast corner of the Keweenaw Peninsula, where the long land formation meets the rest of the U.P. There's enough gaming here to satisfy all but the choosiest players, with more than 300 slot and video poker machines that take denominations as low as a penny and up to five dollars. If you prefer table games, the casino offers craps, roulette, blackjack, poker (including 3-5-7 and Texas Hold 'Em), and more. Get something to eat at the Pressbox Sports Bar, which serves up exactly the type of food you'd expect at a sports bar. You'll find other sports bar trappings here, too, like happy hour specials and big-screen televisions. You'll also see a few things you might not expect, such as an eight-lane bowling alley and a dance floor. The Pressbox hosts DJs or live bands on weekends. The lodging here is good, too. The Ojibwa Casino hotel has gone through a series of renovations to their 40 guest rooms, which include double rooms and whirlpool suites at remarkably modest rates ($69 d, $85 suite with hot tub). To get there from Houghton and Hancock, take U.S. 41 south to M-38, turn right, and go a little more than a mile. From Ontonagon, take M-38 east.

Calumet Theatre

Built more than a century ago, the Calumet Theatre (340 6th St., Calumet, 906/337-2610, www.calumettheatre.com) was Keweenaw's destination for live opera. The theatre enjoyed a good run, hosting greats such as John Philip Sousa among others. But its fortunes faded as the era of live theater began to decline. After about 30 years, as copper mining started to wane and motion pictures grew in popularity, the Calumet was converted into a cinema. Summer stock took hold a few times in the '50s and in the '70s, but didn't enjoy a permanent resurgence until the Calumet

© BILL FINK

The interior of the Calumet Theatre recalls the Gilded Age.

Theatre Company was incorporated in 1983 and brought year-round entertainment back to this glamorous hall. And it *is* glamorous. The auditorium, with its bowl-shaped proscenium, stunning paintings, and elegant woodwork, was restored in the 1970s with the exterior following suit in the late '80s. Today, it's a National Historic Landmark that regularly hosts theater and opera performances as well as symphony concerts and dance shows. Some 30,000 people come through the doors each year. You can take a guided tour of the historic theater from Monday through Friday during the summer season, while self-guided tours are available year-round at limited times. Take U.S. 41 into town and turn north on 6th Street to get to the theater.

FESTIVALS AND EVENTS

Leave it to those engineering students at Michigan Tech to design and build elaborate snow sculptures at the university's **Winter Carnival** in January. Houghton also hosts the **Bridgefest and Seafood Fest** in June, with food and music on a parking deck overlooking the Portage Lift Bridge. Chassell's **Strawberry Fest** is held the second week in July, just in time for the sweet and juicy harvest.

SUMMER SPORTS AND RECREATION
Hiking and Biking

Mountain bikers new to the area can hardly believe the wealth of terrific trails in the Keweenaw, literally hundreds of miles of old mining and logging roads, overgrown double track routes, and technical single track. They loop through towering pines to backwoods waterfalls, to otherwise inaccessible Lake Superior shorelines and even past ghost towns now buried deep in the woods. But please note that many trails may turn into dead ends suddenly.

Vast tracts of land in the Keweenaw are privately owned by large corporations; either mining firms or paper companies. In exchange

KEWEENAW PENINSULA

for a break in state taxes the companies allow public use of the land for recreation, including hiking, fishing, and mountain biking. Still, for liability reasons some outfitters and bike shops are hesitant to hand out maps or endorse these lands for riding. If you ask though, most bike shops tend to be quite helpful about suggesting trails, especially the **Keweenaw Adventure Company** (145 Gratiot St., 906/289-4303, www.keweenawadventure.com) in Copper Harbor. If you're going on your own, snowmobile maps make decent trail guides. Cross reference them with a topographical map. Snowmobile trails often cross frozen lowlands that are impassable during summer months.

Always remember to use common sense. Don't venture out without a map and compass and the skill to use them. Stay away from active logging areas, which are usually marked by signs, and the audible presence of buzzing logging equipment. If you hear a logging truck coming, don't just move to the side, get completely off the trail. Logging trucks are wide and heavy, and they can blaze down roads at surprising speeds. They aren't expecting to see you and probably wouldn't be able to stop in time if they did.

Old railroad grades threading across the northern Keweenaw have been converted to public multiuse trails, intended for snowmobiles, ATVs, and perhaps to a lesser extent, mountain bikes. For cyclists not comfortable venturing deep into the woods, they're a nice way to get off the road. The **Jack Stevens-Rail Trail** runs 14 miles from Hancock north to Calumet on the former Soo Line grade. Somewhat less appealing, because it parallels M-26 for a lengthy stretch, is the **Keweenaw Rail-Trail,** an 18-mile route from Hancock along Torch Lake, also ending in Calumet. Trail surfaces can be a rough collection of rock, gravel, wood, and sand or whatever happened to be there when they removed the rails, so they're not appropriate for narrow-tire bikes. For more information and a map listing access points, contact the Keweenaw Tourism Council at 800/338-7982.

If you're handy with a map and compass,

some fine single track winds down along the **Gratiot River** about five miles north of Calumet. As a bonus, you can check out the seldom-visited Upper and Lower Gratiot Falls as the river rolls and tumbles its way to Lake Superior. For other ideas, check in at **Cross Country Sports** (506 Oak St., Calumet, 906/337-4520). Most of the staff is willing to divulge at least a couple of favorite trails.

For something a little less adventurous, pedal the **Swedetown Trails,** a cross-country trail network on the southwest edge of Calumet. From 6th Street near St. Ann's Church, pick up Oceola Road and follow it south. The trail network has about 25 kilometers of trails over rolling hills and through woods and all are great for biking except the northernmost loop (the Red Trail), which is usually too wet. From this small network, you can veer off onto what seems like an endless network of side trails. In winter, these trails offer great Nordic skiing, along with a warming chalet (open noon–5 p.m.). For information, contact the Keweenaw Convention and Visitors Bureau (906/337-4579 or 800/338-7982).

Canoeing and Kayaking

Rivers in the Keweenaw tend to be somewhat rocky, so white-water kayaking is limited, although this varies with each year's level of precipitation. Sea kayaking, on the other hand, is outstanding. It's the perfect way to access bluffs, caves, sea stacks, and rocky islands all along the Lake Superior shoreline. The Keweenaw Water Trail, still under development, guides small craft around the peninsula and through the Portage Waterway. Canoeing is popular on inland lakes, but open boats are not recommended on Lake Superior.

The **Keweenaw Water Trail** provides a mapped passageway of more than 100 miles through the Portage Waterway and along the Lake Superior shore, indicating accommodations, campgrounds, launches, and more. For more information and to purchase a water trail map, contact the Keweenaw Convention and Visitors Bureau (906/337-4579 or 800/338-7982). For white water boaters, **Down Wind**

Sports (308 Shelden Ave., Houghton, 906/482-2500, www.downwindsports.com) is your best source for local information on river conditions.

Fishing

One of the finest fishing rivers in the Houghton and Hancock area is the Salmon Trout River. Flowing for about 12 miles from tiny Perrault to Lake Superior, the river is an excellent spot to cast for steelhead and brook trout. Take M-26 a few miles south of Houghton to Old M-26/Erickson Drive in the village of Atlantic Mine. Turn right, then right again on County Highway A-65, which continues as Obenhoff Road to an access point a couple of miles west.

Another popular site for fishing is **McLain State Park** (906/482-0278, 18350 Highway M-203, www.michigan.gov/dnr) seven miles north of Hancock on M-203. You can also try both Portage Lake and Torch Lake for walleye, bass, and northern pike.

Golf

The only choice for 18 holes in the Keweenaw Peninsula is **Portage Lake Golf Course** (46789 U.S. 41, Houghton, 906/487-2641, www.portagelakegolfcourse.com, 8 A.M.– 7:30 P.M. daily May–mid-Oct., 18 holes $37, 9 holes $22), a fine course belonging to Michigan Technological University. Although it's located off the main drag as you enter town, the well-kept greens are peaceful and the holes have the tree-lined horizons you'd expect from a U.P. golf course. The clubhouse has a pro shop and a bar and grill, which is cleverly named the Par and Grill. The bar is actually a newer addition, since the P&G only received its liquor license in 2008. Players can get a beer at the grill or from one of the beverage carts. There's also a putting green and a driving range that closes at dusk.

About 15 miles south of Houghton, in Toivola, the **Wyandotte Hills Golf Club and Resort** (5821 East Poyhonen Rd., 906/288-3720, www.wyandottehills.com, May–Oct., 18 holes $23, 9 holes $18) is a nine-hole

course that does double duty as an overnight getaway, with four cabins that can be rented year-round. The wooded and watered course makes for good golfing, while the clubhouse serves an excellent lunch and dinner Monday through Friday and lunch only on Saturday. In Calumet, you'll find the **Calumet Golf Club** (1501 Golf Course Rd., 906/337-3911, http:// calumetgolfclub.com/, 18 holes $25, 9 holes $15), which features club rentals, a restaurant, and more.

Bird-Watching

Birders find good habitat and a variety of northern species, including red- and white-winged crossbills, Canada geese, hawks, peregrine falcons, and bald eagles. An estimated 20 species of warblers are frequently spotted in the Keweenaw.

Just north of the Hanka Homestead, the Sturgeon River bleeds across the lowlands before emptying into Portage Lake, forming sloughs that attract migrating waterfowl. For the best access, stop at the **Sturgeon River Sloughs Natural Area,** marked by an observation tower along U.S. 41 near Chassell. The 1.5-mile De Vriendt Nature Trail follows a series of dikes and boardwalks back into the slough, with interpretive signs describing herons, osprey, eagles, kestrels, ducks, and dozens of other species that frequent the area.

Off-Road Vehicles

The Michigan DNR's ATV route, Hancock–Calumet Trail, stretches all the way between Hancock and Calumet. Like all other DNR trails, this one is kept lightly groomed. Also remember that all state forest roads are open to ORV use, unless specifically marked otherwise. The rail trails and other old railroad grades that can cause headaches for mountain bikers are more suitable for ORV riders. Bear in mind that you'll likely be sharing the pathway with nonmotorized travelers.

Waterfalls

Far south of Houghton and just north of the imaginary line that forms the base of the

Keeweenaw Peninsula, the **Wyandotte Falls** drop some 20 feet down multiple steps in a beautiful display. Take Wyandotte Hills Golf Course Road less than a mile west of M-26 to the parking area, then follow the trail to the falls. The **Hungarian Falls,** north of Hancock, are better still. Take M-26 north to Hubbell, then turn left on 6th Street. Take the left fork two blocks up, and turn left on the second trail road. Both forks lead to the falls. The right fork leads to the Upper Falls while the left heads to the Lower. At some 25 feet, the Upper Falls drop farther, but the Lower Falls are more beautiful, at a still impressive 15 feet.

WINTER SPORTS AND RECREATION
Downhill Skiing

If you're into serious skiing, head north to Mt. Bohemia near Copper Harbor, but for novices or skiers who appreciate tamer terrain, **Mont Ripley** (906/487-2340, www.aux. mtu.edu/ski, $38 full day, $30 half day) near Houghton and Hancock (owned and operated by Michigan Technological University) also offers some good downhill runs and is lit for night skiing.

Ski and Snowshoe Trails

A giant snow gauge on U.S. 41 south of Phoenix proudly marks the Keweenaw's record snowfall, a staggering 390.4 inches in the winter of 1977–1978. It wasn't an aberration; the surrounding waters of Lake Superior routinely generate colossal lake effect snows, often averaging over 300 inches per year. That reliable level of snow, combined with the remarkable local terrain, makes the Keweenaw a haven for snowmobilers.

Thankfully, skiers and snowshoers will find there's enough wilderness to go around. Many towns have developed Nordic ski trail systems. For backcountry skiing and snowshoeing, pick up a snowmobile map and avoid the marked trails. Also note that some accommodations located on signed and groomed trails cater to snowmobilers, and the roar can get pretty deafening. Don't be afraid to ask about the presence of "sleds," as they're sometimes referred to, before booking lodging in winter months.

Snowshoers should stay off groomed ski trails, but Michigan Tech in Houghton has a series of marked snowshoeing trails. In Calumet, try the marked Swedetown trails.

Snowmobiling

There are more than 2,000 miles of snowmobile trails in the U.P., and at last count, the Keweenaw had more than 200 of them. They stretch from south of Houghton all the way into the tip. Most are clearly identified, well groomed, and between 10 and 16 feet wide. And they do connect to the other 1,800-plus miles above the bridge. The Keweenaw Trail (Trail 3) is the main route into and out of Houghton and Hancock, and connects to numerous other branches: The North and South Freda trails lead towards Lake Superior, while Stevens Trail connects to Calumet.

Keweenaw Trail joins the 55-mile Bill Nichols Trail, which ends farther south in Mass City, near Ontonagon. A popular multiuse trail during warmer weather, this converted rail line is one of the most popular scenic snowmobile routes in the Keweenaw. For a detailed map, including the locations of gas stations, contact the Keweenaw Convention and Visitors Bureau (56638 Calumet Ave., Calumet, 906/337-4579 or 800/338-7982, www.keweenaw.info).

ACCOMMODATIONS

There are a few good options south of Houghton. **Carla's Lake Shore Motel** (906/353-6256,www.carlasinn.com, starting at $52), on U.S. 41 north of Baraga, has both clean, inexpensive motel rooms and a few cabins, all with a stunning view of Keweenaw Bay. Pets are welcome in the motel. Baraga also has a few chain motels, including **Super 8** (790 Michigan Ave., 906/353-6680, www.super8baraga.com) and **Best Western Baraga Lakeside Inn** (900 S. U.S. 41, 906/353-7123, www.bestwestern.com). Rates for both run $75–125. After a visit to Hanka Homestead, you can step back in time and sample a stay at a Finnish farm at

❰ Palosaari's Rolling Acres B & B (906/523-4947, $55). A tidy dairy farm near Chassell, it offers three simple rooms, a shared bath, a sauna, a nearby swimming beach, and a big country breakfast. Four miles south of Chassell, take North Entry Road east 1.3 miles.

For such a small metropolitan area, Houghton accommodations can run a bit on the pricey side, perhaps due to the presence of the university. But bargains are available. Tucked below downtown Houghton along the Portage Waterway, **Super 8** (1200 E. Lakeshore Dr., 906/482-2240, www.super8. com, $50–100) offers one of the best locations in town, right on the water and the bike path. It also offers an indoor pool and free continental breakfast. A good mom-and-pop operation is the **❰ Downtowner Motel** (110 Shelden Ave., 906/482-4421 or 800/430-0083, reasonable rates).

East of town, on the Lake Superior shore in the town of Lake Linden, the comparatively expensive but charming **Jacobsville Lighthouse Inn** (38741 Jacobs St., 906/523-4137, www. jacobsvillelighthouse.com, $180–300) offers five guest rooms in a well-maintained keeper's home with attached lighthouse tower. The 50-foot tower offers stunning panoramic views of Lake Superior and the surrounding land, plus more than 350 feet of lakeshore.

The **❰ AmericInn Motel and Suites** (5101 6th St., 906/337-6463, www.americinn.com, $90–130) in Calumet, north of Hancock, is the area's only full-service motel with an indoor pool and other amenities. The **Wonderland Motel and Cabins** (787 Lake Linden Ave., 906/337-4511), in Laurium, offers good budget accommodations with kitchens in the cabins. At the other end of the spectrum, you have the option of the opulent copper baron mansion at the **❰ Laurium Manor Inn** (320 Tamarack St., 906/337-2549, www.lauriummanorinn.com, $90–140) in Laurium. Across the street, the owners have also restored the 1906 opulent and historic **Victorian Hall** (906/337-2549, www. laurium.info) into an upscale B & B. Room #1, the Laurium Suite, is purported to have hosted Teddy Roosevelt during his presidential campaign of 1912. Rates vary widely depending on the season, specific room requested, and the particular week. Check the website for particulars. All rooms have private baths.

Camping

At Toivola, head 6.2 miles west on Misery Bay Road, then north and west on Agate Beach Road for 4 miles to **Agate Beach Park** (906/288-3644), a rather unknown little spot on Lake Superior. There's no modern plumbing, but the idyllic and quiet sandy beach, Lake Superior sunsets, and a mere $7 tent fee ($9 for sites with electricity) make up for it. **Baraga State Park** (1300 U.S. 41 S., 906/353-6558, www.michigan.gov/ dnr, $16–18) is almost entirely campground. Most come for its modern sites (more than 100, with electricity and showers) with a convenient location: just off U.S. 41, a mile south of the town of Baraga. Reservations are usually not necessary. Across the highway, a day-use area offers a sand beach and a bathhouse. The Bill Nichols Rail–Trail passes through **Twin Lakes State Park** (6204 E. Poyhonen Rd., 906/288-3321, www.michigan.gov/dnr, $20–22) in the southern Keweenaw. Though situated along the highway, many of its modern sites sit on the shores of Lake Roland, which was once determined was the warmest lake in the Upper Peninsula. For campsite reservations at any Michigan state park, call 800/447-2757 or visit www.midnrreservations.com. To rent rustic cabins or walled tents, contact the parks directly.

Sunsets get top billing at **McLain State Park** (18350 M-203, 906/482-0278, www.michigan. gov/dnr, $16–26 campsites, $60 cabins), where the sky often glows in peach and pink hues before the sun melts into Lake Superior. Like most Michigan state parks, the 98 campsites are fine, too, and many come with those waterfront views. Continuing up M-203 seven miles north of Hancock, the **City of Houghton** maintains an RV-only campground (1100 W. Lakeshore Dr., 906/482-8745). Each site is located near the water. No pets allowed. Tent campers will be more attracted to the **Hancock Recreation**

Area (2000 Jasberg St./M-203, 906/482-7413, www.cityofhancock.com, May 15–Oct. 15) which sits on the Portage Waterway. Following M-203 a mile from downtown, the primitive sites are situated in a quieter area apart from the 50 RV sites that are so modern they even include cable TV. Showers and laundry are on the premises.

FOOD

Combine a college town with a large ethnic population, and you come up with a good range of eating options in the Houghton and Hancock area. Houghton offers a number of fine places to eat. **The Library** (62 N. Isle Royale St., 906/487-5882, 11 A.M.–10 P.M. daily) ranks as the most popular place in town, offering home-brewed beers, plus salads, pizza, pastas, and a bevy of sandwich choices. The **Pilgrim River Steak House** (47409 U.S. 41, 906/482-8595,www.pilgrimriver.com, 11 A.M.–10 P.M. Mon.–Sat., noon–9 P.M. Sun.) on U.S. 41 on the southeast end of Houghton, is *the* place to go for beef of all sorts, especially prime rib. Along with your basic eggs-and-hash-browns fare, **Suomi Home Bakery and Restaurant** (54 N. Huron St., 906/482-3220) includes a few Finnish specialties on the menu. Try the *pannukakku,* billed as a "Finnish pancake" (but more like deep-dish custard pie), topped with raspberry sauce. Most breakfasts come with *nisu,* a Finnish yeast bread spiced with carda-mom. The restaurant can be a bit hard to find. It's tucked under Houghton's covered walkway, a block down the hill from Shelden.

On Hancock's main street, the **Kaleva Cafe and Bakery** (234 Quincy St., 906/482-1230) draws the locals for its baked goods, including its self-proclaimed "famous" whipped-cream cakes. Kaleva makes a good pasty, a potpie creation of beef, potatoes, onions, and ruta-bagas—just the kind of hearty, self contained meal miners could take with them deep under-ground. You'll also find pasties at coffee shops and grocery store deli counters throughout the Upper Peninsula.

Though you'll find plenty of traditional grocery stores along M-26 south of town and U.S. 41 North, a better choice just might be the **Keweenaw Co-op Natural Foods and Groceries** (1035 Ethel Ave., 906/482-2030, www.keweenaw.coop/, 10 A.M.–8 P.M. Mon.–Sat., 10 A.M.–5 P.M. Sun.) in Hancock. A friendly staff, excellent organic produce, and plenty of reasonably priced staples make this a great option for picnic supplies. As you head up the hill on U.S. 41, veer left onto Ethel when the highway swings hard right. Watch for the colorful wooden sign. The co-op is a couple blocks ahead on your right.

Heading north towards downtown Calumet, you'll want to visit **Thurner Bakery** (315 5th St., 906/337-3711), which churns out hearty pasties, soups, and baked goods.

You can also find similar homemade coffee shop fare and Finnish bakery items like saffron bread at **Toni's Country Kitchen** (79 3rd St., 906/337-0611, Laurium). At the **Lindell Chocolate Shoppe** (300 Calumet St., Lake Linden, 906/296-0793, www.lindellchoco-lateshoppe.net), visitors come to marvel at the beauty of this untouched 1920s shop, gleam-ing with golden oak, stained glass, and marble. Locals, though, come for the food, especially its very extensive breakfast offerings and its Friday night fish fry.

INFORMATION AND SERVICES

The twin towns of Houghton and Hancock represent the area's largest population cen-ter, where you'll find the lion's share of area services, including tourism information and medical care. The area also serves as the un-official gateway to the upper Keweenaw. With an office in Calumet, the **Keweenaw Convention and Visitors Bureau** (56638 Calumet Ave., 906/337-4579 or 800/338-7982, www.keweenaw.info) serves as an ex-cellent one-stop source for attractions and lodging information. If you're interested in Copper Country's history, you won't want to miss the fascinating **Keweenaw National Historic Park** (200 5th St., 906/337-3168, www.nps.gov/kewe, 9 A.M.–5 P.M. Mon.–Fri.) in Calumet.

If you need medical attention while in Houghton and Hancock, **Portage Health** (500 Campus Dr., 906/483-1000 or 800/573-5001, www.portagehealth.org) in Hancock is the place to go. The hospital is located just west of U.S. 41. Take U.S. 41 north or south to Campus Drive, turn west, and follow for 0.5 miles until you reach the Portage Health sign. Farther north, just outside Calumet in Laurium, go to **Keweenaw Memorial Medical Center** (205 Osceola St., 906/337-6500, www.kmmc.org). Take U.S. 41 into town to M-26/School Street and go east to 2nd Street. Turn right on 2nd, and then left on Osceola to arrive at the hospital.

There are several **banks** on either side of the river. You can find national banks (Wells Fargo, 600 Sheldon Ave., Houghton, 906/482-5500, www.wellsfargo.com), Midwest banks (Citizens Bank, 400 Quincy St., Hancock, 906/482-6002, www.citizensbanking.com), and local banks (Superior National Bank and Trust, 235 Quincy St., 906/482-0404, www.snb-t.com). There's another branch of Superior National Bank in Calumet (56788 Mine Street Station, 906/337-5983, www.snb-t.com) and in Lake Linden (53115 M-26, 906/296-6611, www.snb-t.com).

GETTING THERE AND AROUND
Car

For those traveling by car, U.S. 41 and M-26 are the main routes to the peninsula (U.S. 41 west from Marquette and M-26 north from Mass City), meeting and crossing in Houghton and Hancock and then merging again at Calumet. Many of the secondary roads in the Keweenaw are dirt or gravel. For old logging roads and other questionable routes, a four-wheel drive vehicle is highly recommended.

Air

Houghton County Memorial Airport (CMX, 23810 Airpark Blvd., Calumet, 906/482-3970, www.houghtoncounty.org) is located a short ways northwest of Hancock. Skywest Airline, which runs regional flights as an airlink for United Airlines (800/864-8339), offers the only commercial airline service, with two daily departures to and arrivals from Chicago. If you're coming from elsewhere, you'll have a layover in the Windy City.

Ground transportation is available for both local and long distance trips. Contact **Neil's Taxi** (906/482-5515) or **Copper Country Limo** (906/370-4761). Houghton County Memorial Airport also offers car rentals through **National Car Rental** (906/482-6655).

It's not entirely accurate to say that the only air service to and from Houghton is offered by **Northwest-Royale Air Service** (218/721-0405 or 877/359-4753) offers daily one-way ($185) or round-trip ($269) seaplane flights to Isle Royale National Park.

Boat

You have multiple options for boating into Houghton and Hancock, since there's a marina in each city. Despite its name, **The Houghton County Marina** (906/482-6010, www.michigan.gov/dnr) is actually located in Hancock. It provides 44 seasonal 10 transient slips. The marina is amenity rich and offers close up views of the lift bridge. It's open seasonally from May 1 through October 1, and you can contact of the harbormaster on channels 16 and 68. Entry into the Portage Waterway is at 47° 14.08 N, 88° 34.19 W (coming in from the east) or at 46° 57.40 N, 88° 26.00 W (from the west), with the marina itself located at 47° 07.30 N, 88° 34.19 W. Your other option (albeit a limited one) is to put in at Houghton City Marina, which is located just across the Portage Waterway and has 300 feet of broadside dockage but no overnight use. Channel entrances are the same; the dock is located at 47° 07.21 N, 88° 34.20 W.

Public Transportation

Bus service tends to be spotty in the U.P., especially in the Keweenaw. The city's **Houghton Motor Transit Line** (906/482-6092, www.cityofhoughton.com, $2 adults) runs a regularly scheduled Downtowner Route loops around from the Michigan Tech

campus and ends at the Copper Country Mall. It's convenient, but doesn't go much farther than you could get walking or on bike. It does offer on demand service for locations inside ($5) and outside ($6) city limits, but its scope is limited to the immediate area. Likewise, **Hancock Public Transportation** (906/482-3450, www.cityofhancock.com, $4 adults) runs a door-to-door, on-demand service within a limited area.

Copper Harbor and Vicinity

Wedged between Lake Superior to the north and long and lovely Lake Fanny Hooe to the south, Copper Harbor has always been an outpost in the wilderness—for the copper prospectors who came in the mid-1880s, for the military who built a fort to keep the miners and the Native Americans at peace, and today for those who come for its water and woods.

Copper Harbor marks the end of the road in the Keweenaw Peninsula. Literally. Even U.S. 41 peters out here, ending in a small, unceremonious loop some 1,990 miles from its other terminus in Miami. The tip of the peninsula probably draws people precisely because it is the end of the road. And when they get here, they discover one of the Upper Peninsula's most scenic natural areas and one of its most appealing little towns.

The city is a favorite vacation spot for kayakers, canoers, and boaters. With its location in the far north of the U.P. and surrounded on three sides by Lake Superior, Copper Harbor feels like the ends of the earth, or, at the very least, the end of Michigan.

SIGHTS
Downtown Copper Harbor

Tiny Copper Harbor, population 75, offers much more than you might expect from its size. If you enjoy shopping, check out the Finnish pottery at **Sataman Ruukku** (906/289-4636), a shedlike storefront on U.S. 41, and the artwork and gifts at the **Laughing Loon** (906/289-4813). In a town just a few blocks long, street addresses are only used by the postal service. Rock hounds will like the **Keweenaw Agate Shop** (906/353-7285) and **Swede's Gift Shop** (906/289-4596), both with a good selection

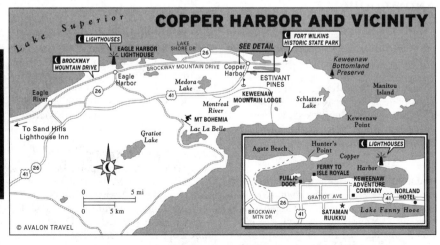

COPPER HARBOR AND VICINITY

© AVALON TRAVEL

© PAUL VACHON

Serving a very small community, this one-room school house still operates.

of local minerals and, as the Keweenaw Agate Shop advertises, "advice and stories."

The **Thunderbird Shop** at the **Minnetonka Resort** (562 Gratiot St., 906/289-4449, www. minnetonkaresort.com) is a terrific source for books on mining, shipwrecks, and other historical subjects. The shop also has a lot of interesting artifacts for sale, such as lanterns and clay pipes discarded long ago by miners. The motel's adjacent **Astor House Antique Doll and Indian Artifact Museum** is well worth a visit, too.

You won't find a full-service grocery store in Copper Harbor, so load up in Houghton or Calumet if you're planning a campout or cabin stay. However, the exceptionally friendly **Gas Lite General Store** (906/289-4652) has all the basics, and also happens to be the spot to catch up on local news. What you don't learn there, you'll hear about at the Pines across the street. For fresh or smoked fish, head to the ferry dock and **Jamsen's Fish Market** (906/289-4285), run by the last commercial fishing family still working the local waters.

Around Town

You can enjoy a couple of nice walks just a few blocks from downtown. From the parking lot of the municipal marina west than the ferry dock, a 3.2-mile round-trip trail winds through the woods and over twisted roots to Hunter's Point. This small appendage of land forms the west end of the harbor. On the open Lake Superior side, Agate Beach is a good spot to look for the namesake banded rocks. Downtown, a sign will point you south toward **Estivant Pines,** a 377-acre sanctuary of virgin white pines just a few miles south of town. As recently as the 1970s, local conservationists like the late Jim Rooks saved the magnificent trees from loggers. Some tower nearly 10 stories high and date back nearly 1,000 years. At first the pines will seem hidden by the maturing oaks and maples. But just look up, up, and up.

◖ Fort Wilkins Historic State Park

The history of Fort Wilkins (15223 U.S. 41, 906/289-4215, www.michigan.gov/dnr) reads like one of those overblown military spending stories of the 20th century. With miners pouring north during the Copper Rush, the federal government feared fighting would surely erupt between the newcomers and the local Native

KEWEENAW PENINSULA

American tribes, so it ordered the construction of a garrisoned fort. In 1844, the government sent around 100 men, who built barracks, a mess hall, a hospital, and other buildings behind a tall stockade fence; then hunkered down to fend off the fighting. Only no fighting ever erupted, and the winters proved long, cold, and desolate. By the following year, half the troops were sent south, where the country faced the threat of war with Mexico. By 1846 the rest were gone.

Today, Fort Wilkins stands as one of the only remaining wooden forts east of the Mississippi, with 16 whitewashed buildings wonderfully restored and filled with exhibits of life on the northern frontier. From mid-June to late August, costumed "inhabitants" even re-create military life. Along with the fort, the state park includes rocky and scenic Lake Superior frontage, a few short hiking trails, and the 1866 **Copper Harbor Lighthouse** (accessible only by boat), plus an excellent campground on Lake Fanny Hooe. For campsite reservations, call 800/447-2757 or visit www.midnrreservations.com.

◖ Brockway Mountain Drive

Dubbed "the most beautiful road in Michigan," this 10-mile route traces the spine of a high ridge between Copper Harbor and Eagle Harbor. Rising 735 feet above Lake Superior, it is the highest paved road between the Rockies and the Allegheny Mountains. A parking area midway allows you to stop and soak in the panorama of Lake Superior and the rolling forests of the Keweenaw, an incredible vista no matter how many times you've seen it. Watch for ravens, bald eagles, and peregrine falcons, which sometimes soar below you. Traveling west to east, the end of the drive is marked by a postcard quality shot of Copper Harbor, tucked between Lake Superior and Lake Fanny Hooe.

Scenic Lakeshore Drive

This stretch of M-26 between Copper Harbor and Eagle River lives up to its name: Lake Superior looms just alongside the road, studded with rocky islands and swelling dunes.

Unfortunately, you miss about 10 miles of the route if you take Brockway Mountain Drive. Plan to do both on your trip to Copper Harbor—Brockway is better headed east, while this drive is better headed west.

About five miles south of Copper Harbor, **Hebard Park** is a good picnic, sunset, or agate hunting spot. Where M-26 and Brockway Mountain Drive meet, watch for the small sign marking **Silver Falls**. It's a short downhill walk to this pretty little waterfall, splashing and pooling in the forest.

West of Eagle Harbor, the road climbs above **Great Sand Bay** toward Eagle River. From this high vantage point, you can sometimes see huge 1,000-foot lake carriers out in the shipping lanes, which squeeze close to shore to round Keweenaw Point. Inland, beach peas, sand cherries, and wild roses cling to windswept, volatile mounds of sand. Like beach grasses, the plants' spreading root systems help trap the sand, stabilizing and building dunes.

The Keweenaw's tilted fault line is particularly pronounced in this part of the peninsula. To the south rises the exposed basalt face of the Cliff Range, while to the north, the fault line drops away so quickly that Great Sand Bay plummets to depths of more than 1,000 feet. In between, deep ridges allow microclimates to thrive. Along the south side of the road, watch for faintly marked **Michigan Nature Association trails** that dip into dark, deep forests, where lichen drapes from the pines and deep cushions of moss cover the rocky path.

◖ Lighthouses

You can't reach the **Copper Harbor Lighthouse** by land because adjacent property owners refuse to grant a right of way, so the Park Service has arranged for boat tours of the light and keeper's house, which contains a worthwhile small museum. Originally built in 1849, the stone lighthouse is the oldest operating light on Lake Superior. An adjacent tall steel tower now does duty, however. Just wandering around the lovely rocky point is worth the trip. It was on this point, by the way,

where Douglass Houghton first spotted a thick green stripe in the rock indicating the presence of copper, a discovery that unleashed the Keweenaw's copper boom. The 90-minute tour leaves from the municipal marina several times daily from Memorial Day to early September. Call 906/289-4966 for specific times and reservations (adults $15, children 12 and under $10). Also ask about sunset cruises. There are a few other lighthouses around Copper Harbor: Gull Rock Lighthouse and Manitou Island Lighthouse, the oldest light on the Great Lakes. Like the Copper Harbor light, they're only accessible by boat.

One of the Keweenaw's most charming little towns, Eagle Harbor has a sleepy, comfortable feel to it, with a wonderfully protected natural harbor, a perfect crescent of beach, and even a historic lighthouse with an observation deck out on the rocky point. In short, it's a classic summer getaway. "Everybody in Copper Harbor is trying to make money…everybody in Eagle Harbor has already made it," noted one local. The red-brick **Eagle Harbor**

Lighthouse (906/289-4990, mid-June–mid-Sept., $4), built in 1861, is one of the area's prettiest. Its outbuildings contain a small museum filled with information on shipwrecks, mining, and commercial fishing. The one-room schoolhouse in Eagle Harbor (two blocks west of the harbor on Center Street) was the birthplace of the **Knights of Pythias,** a secret fraternal society known for its elaborate rituals and fanciful costumes.

A few miles west of Eagle Harbor, the **Eagle River Lighthouse** is worth a brief look and makes for a nice picture, even if it is closed to the public. The light went out of service in the early 1900s; today it's a private residence. On the other side of the peninsula, in Bete Grise, historic lighthouse aficionados will want to track down **Mendota Lighthouse** for a picture, but should bear in mind that it's a private residence. The owner does, however, maintain an excellent website (www.mendotalighthouse. com) which offers an abundance of information on the history, evolution, and ongoing restoration of this historical gem. If you're

Isolated Copper Harbor Lighthouse can only be reached by boat.

© PAUL VACHON

KEWEENAW PENINSULA

A DYNASTY OF PINE

In the mid-1800s, a young and growing United States suddenly had an insatiable appetite for timber. Virtually all structures at the time were constructed of wood, creating an enormous demand on this one material. Settlers were moving west, into the treeless plains, and in need of lumber to build their new towns. Burgeoning cities needed lumber to build homes and businesses. Railroads needed lumber as they laid mile after mile of track to connect it all.

Michigan's natural resources proved the perfect mix to fuel a hungry nation. Immense white pines and other conifers grew thick and tall throughout the Upper Peninsula and across more than half of the Lower Peninsula. Rivers honeycombed these vast forests, providing a route to the Great Lakes, which in turn connected the northern wilderness to Chicago, Detroit, and other railroad centers in the south. Nature had created the perfect delivery system for the logging industry.

Around 1850, logging camps began appearing deep in the woods, from the western U.P. to the shores of Lake Huron. Young men streamed north, some of them farm laborers looking for winter wages, others newly arrived immigrants looking to gain a foothold in their new homeland. It was difficult and dirty work. The lumberjacks worked by hand, with ax and saw, tree after tree, acre after acre. With a shout of "timber!" the old pines came down with an earth-shaking thud, some of them as much as 20 feet in circumference and 100 feet tall.

The logging camps operated primarily during the winter months, to allow for easy transport of the huge logs. With horses and sleighs, workers hauled the logs from the woods to the river's edge, branded the ends with the lumber company's mark, and stacked them there until spring, when they were floated downriver to waiting sawmills on the Great Lakes.

In the spring the colorful and chaotic log drives began. Thousands of logs were placed into the north woods rivers, guided downstream by fearless workers known as "river pigs," who danced across the dangerous mass of moving wood, using hooks, poles, and sometimes dynamite to dislodge log jams. It was the most dangerous job in the trade: With one misstep, a river pigs could end up crushed between tons of logs or trapped underwater.

Once at the mills, the jumble of logs was sorted according to the mill owner's mark and floated into mill storage ponds. From there, buzzing sawmills sliced the logs into lumber and loaded it onto lumber schooners (barges and steamers in later years) which headed primarily to Chicago, the nation's largest lumber market and railroad hub.

In its heyday, the logging industry gener-

---

looking to get inside a lighthouse, and especially if you'd like to stay the night, try the **Sand Hills Lighthouse Inn** (906/337-1744, www.sandhillslighthouseinn.com) in Ahmeek. The 1917 lighthouse, made for three keepers and their families, underwent a three-year restoration in the early 1990s. Amazingly, it's just as stunning inside as out.

FESTIVALS AND EVENTS

Copper Harbor hosts the peninsula's best **Fourth of July** fireworks show, and Sam Raymond, owner of Copper Harbor's Keweenaw Adventure Company, puts on a growing **Fat Tire Festival** the day before Labor Day. For more information on all area festivals and celebrations, contact the Keweenaw Convention and Visitors Bureau (56638 Calumet Ave., 906/337-4579 or 800/338-7982, www.keweenaw.info).

SUMMER SPORTS AND RECREATION
Hiking and Biking

You'll need a map to reliably navigate the area. A snowmobile trail map (available through local shops and the Keweenaw Convention and Visitors Bureau) is adequate for major

ated billions of board-feet of lumber and billions of dollars, the actual number almost incalculable. Lumber companies were given to making all sorts of grandiose proclamations: Michigan's mills claimed they produced enough lumber to lay an inch-thick plank across the state. Given the immense profitability of the industry, such claims may not have been too far off the mark.

Success stories were everywhere. A sawmill in Hermansville, Michigan, came up with the idea of tongue-and-groove planks and quickly became the largest flooring plant in the country, crafting the floors for the Mormon Temple in Salt Lake City and the main lodge in Yellowstone National Park. Timber baron homes were marvels of hand-carved mahogany, gold leaf inlay, and cut crystal chandeliers.

But the era thought to last forever ended after less than 50 years. By 1900, nearly all the big trees were gone, leaving behind a scorched, denuded landscape of stump prairies. When farmers were able to convert some of the southernmost pineries into useful crop land, ambitious entrepreneurs sought to do the same in the north. A newspaper publisher in Menominee extolled the virtues of Upper Peninsula cutover land for farming or ranching. "No matter where the first Garden of Eden was located," he proclaimed, "the present one is in the Upper Peninsula."

Thousands of hard-working folks were lured north by the promise of cheap land in exchange for the back-breaking labor of removing pine stumps and tilling soil. But by the late 1920s, their work proved futile. Nearly half of the U.P. was tax-delinquent cutover land. Most ranches and farms failed, the stock market crashed, and the nation's economy was soon in the grips of the Great Depression.

Soon the federal government stepped in to repair the damage. In 1911, it established the first national forests in Michigan and Wisconsin, setting aside land and creating tree nurseries as a first step in reestablishing the Midwest's great forests. The Civilian Conservation Corps, established in 1933 in part to combat unemployment, continued the reforestation efforts, planting trees, fighting fires, and slowly nursing the remaining great forests back to health.

Although we can never recreate the magnificent old-growth forests of yesteryear, pines once again stretch skyward across Michigan. Logging continues, too, though with sophisticated forest management and reforestation practices that help ensure the sustained livelihood of the state's lumber and paper industries. And a few stands of virgin old-growth timber remain, giving us an awe-inspiring glimpse of a lost Michigan landscape.

routes, the *DeLorme Atlas and Gazetteer* includes a few more, although a topographical map is best. However, no map yet shows even half the trails in the area. Sam Raymond, owner of the **Keweenaw Adventure Company** (145 Gratiot St., 906/289-4303, www.keweenawadventure.com) in Copper Harbor, has mapped and signed (although the signs keep disappearing) dozens of miles of mountain biking routes. He's also clearing and maintaining the trails with only the help of a few friends. It's a huge undertaking for minimal return, so show Sam your appreciation by giving him your business. Keweenaw Adventure

Company rents and services mountain bikes and sells those ever-helpful maps.

Not surprisingly, Keweenaw Adventure Company is also your best source for trail suggestions in the area. The **Red Trail** is the region's classic route, a single-track trail with plenty of technical twists and turns. It runs roughly from the gravel **Burma Road Trail,** past the south end of the Keweenaw Mountain Lodge golf course and the north shore of Lake Manganese, where you can pick up **Paul's Plunge** back to Lake Fanny Hooe. Another good loop is the two-track **Surprise Valley Trail,** which hooks up with the **Kamikaze**

KEWEENAW PENINSULA

Trail that traces the southern side of Lake Fanny Hooe.

In the same general area, the **Clark Mine Trail** dips south away of Copper Harbor at the south end of Lake Fanny Hooe. Just outside town, brown and white signs will direct you to **Manganese Falls,** a pleasant walk down into a ferny oasis; **Manganese Lake,** a popular fishing and swimming hole; and the **Clark Mine,** where the old brick furnace chimney still stands against a backdrop of mine tailings. Where the Clark Mine Trail swings east, make your way south to meet up with the Montreal River if you're interested in a little trout fishing.

In addition to the trails south of Copper Harbor, here are a few other destinations to consider. From the end of U.S. 41, the road continues east as a wide dirt-and-gravel road. Follow it for about a mile to the first main left branch, which winds north and east to the Lake Superior shore and **Horseshoe Harbor,** a fine place to spend an afternoon scrambling around the rock ledges and beaches. This picturesque sliver of a harbor is owned by the Nature Conservancy, so keep mountain bikes off the property as requested. Backtracking to the main road, continue east about three miles to another left (northeast) turnoff, which skirts **Schlatter Lake** and continues on to **High Rock Bay** at the tip of the peninsula. Don't be surprised to see a camp or two set up here.

Copper Harbor lies at the top of the Keweenaw Peninsula, but it doesn't lie at the end. The tip of the peninsula curves to the east and continues about 10 more miles beyond town, leaving about a 60-square-mile tract to the east and south of Copper Harbor with no pavement, development, or attractions, unless you like to hike, mountain bike, fish, or just get out alone in the woods.

Probably more than 100 miles of trails crisscross the tip of the peninsula; there is no accurate count. They range from deer trails to tight single-track to wide gravel and dirt roads used by logging trucks and snowmobiles. Aside from a few tracts held by the state and the Nature Conservancy, the vast majority of the land is owned by International Paper, which uses it for logging. The paper company has put the land in what is called "Commercial Forest Reserve." CFR lands, common throughout the U.P., provide tax breaks to companies that agree to keep the land open to the public for recreation. That means you are free to hike, bike, and otherwise explore this area. Avoid any active logging areas and follow the same guidelines you would anywhere: Respect all "no trespassing" signs and leave nothing but footprints.

Canoeing and Kayaking

Paddling is at its finest in the Keweenaw, where there are plenty of islands, rock formations, and wilderness coastlines to explore. **Keweenaw Adventure Company** (145 Gratiot St., 906/289-4303, www.keweenawadventure.com) rents kayaks, guides trips, and offers lessons. Beginners should try the 2.5-hour introductory paddle, which includes novice dry-land instruction and a fine little trip around the harbor and along the Lake Superior shoreline. Keweenaw Adventure Company also offers some daylong trips around the peninsula to Horseshoe Harbor, Agate Harbor, and the mouth of the Montreal River as scheduling permits. Check the website or give them a call for specifics.

If you have your own boat, don't overlook the peninsula's inland waters. Fanny Hooe, Medora, and other nearby lakes offer classic north woods peace and scenery, often with the company of bobbing loons or black bears on the shoreline.

Fishing

The Gratiot River, which crosses M-26/U.S. 41 north of Amheek and Mohawk and continues west to Lake Superior, is a good place to cast a line for brook and rainbow trout, as well as the occasional steelhead. There's an access point on M-26/U.S. 41. To find access where the Gratiot River crosses Cliff Drive, take the turnoff in the village of Amheek and follow Cliff Drive to the water. For another fishing spot, follow Five Mile Point Road from Amheek to Farmer's Road and turn left to the river and its Upper Falls.

You can cast a line at Gratiot River Country Park, too. To get there, take U.S. 41 to Allouez and turn at the gas station onto Bumbetown Road and continue onto Gratiot River Road for just over four miles.

Boat Trips and Tours

The Kilpela family, who run the Isle Royale ferry service, also offer sunset cruises on the *Isle Royale Queen IV* every evening from July 4 to Labor Day. From mid-May through the end of September, the *Queen* earns her keep by ferrying passengers from Copper Harbor to Isle Royale National Park, a 4.5 hour trip. Call 906/289-4437 for reservations and to check the schedule, which varies throughout the summer (one-way cost is $65 adults, $31 children 11 and under; canoes and kayaks an additional $25; fuel surcharge may apply).

Diving

The cold, crisp, freshwater of Lake Superior offers outstanding visibility for divers. Though there's little in the way of plant and animal life—the cold waters make for a pretty sterile environment—the waters provide plenty of entertainment in the form of interesting geologic formations and shipwrecks.

Ships have been running aground for well over a hundred years around the Keweenaw Peninsula, a major navigational hazard. Within the 103-square-mile **Keweenaw Underwater Preserve,** divers can explore the *Tioga,* a freighter that ran aground near Eagle River in 1919, and the *City of St. Joseph,* which met its fate north of Eagle Harbor in 1942. Both ships lie in less than 40 feet of water, with large sections of their hulls, deck machinery, and other artifacts clearly visible.

One of the Upper Peninsula's oldest shipwrecks, the *John Jacob Astor,* lies just offshore from Copper Harbor, near the Fort Wilkins State Park Lighthouse Overlook. An Underwater Trail marks the location of the rudder, anchor, and other remnants of the *Astor,* which sank in 1844. Local lore explains that before the Keweenaw Underwater Preserve was established in 1989, townspeople learned

of a small group of salvage divers who were planning on retrieving one of the anchors. Without the legal protection of an underwater preserve, the divers took the matter into their own hands: They hauled up the anchor themselves and hid it in nearby Lake Fanny Hooe, where it remained until a few years ago when it was safely returned to its original wreck site. Today, disturbing or removing any artifact is a felony under Michigan law.

The U.S. Coast Guard has to be more than a little humiliated about the preserve's most popular dive site, the cutter *Mesquite.* In 1989, the 180-foot *Mesquite* ran aground on a reef off Keweenaw Point while tending to a navigational buoy. Efforts to free the ship failed and winter winds battered it so badly that the Coast Guard decided to sink it as a dive site rather than pay the costs of retrieving and repairing the aging vessel. Today the *Mesquite* sits in 110 feet of water in Keystone Bay with virtually all its equipment on deck. Experienced divers can explore the *Mesquite's* interior. For dive services, contact **A Superior Diver's Center** (12811 M-26, 906/289-4259) in Eagle Harbor.

Golf

The nine holes at ◖ **Keweenaw Mountain Lodge** (906/289-4403 or 888/685-6343, www.atthelodge.com, $19 for 9 holes, $26 for 18 holes, cart fees $16 for 9 holes and $25 for 18 holes) have as much of a reputation for their beautiful scenery as they do for a good game of golf. The truth is, even if the scenery wasn't quite as eye catching, this place would be a better than average golfing destination—one of the Keweenaw's best. There's a pro shop for all your golfing needs, and meals can be had at The Lodge. If the weather's nice and the black flies aren't circling, try dining on the porch. After a full day on the links, you'll appreciate the full bar, wine list, and great food. It's a great way to top off the day before tucking in for the night.

Off-Road Vehicles

Since there aren't any DNR-designated trail systems this far north in the Keweenaw

Peninsula, your best bet for off-roading will be the state forest roads in Copper Country State Forest. All state forest roads are open to ORV use unless they're specifically marked otherwise.

Waterfalls

The Montreal River tumbles over some beautiful waterfalls before joining Lake Superior just to the southeast, but they're difficult to reach. The best way is to start at Bete Grise (bay-duh GREE). Just before you reach Bete Grise Bay, you'll see two dirt routes heading east into the woods. One is signed "This is not the road to Smith Fisheries." Take the unsigned road. It will lead you around Bear Bluff to an old commercial fishing enterprise, which is now private property. Continue on the smaller trail behind the fishery, a terrific path that traces the steep bluffs of the bay shore. It's about another 1.5 miles to the mouth of the Montreal and its stellar waterfalls. West of Bete Grise, the pleasant **Haven Falls** are located at a roadside park. Take Lac La Belle Road south for 4.5 miles, then turn right at the fork and take it to the park.

In Copper Harbor, you won't want to miss the **Manganese Falls,** a thin but inspired flow that drops about 45 feet into a narrow gorge just outside of town. To get there, turn south on Manganese Road for less than a mile; the falls are located a short walk from the roadside. Eagle Harbor has a few shorter falls, each about seven feet. There are taller, more impressive falls in the Keweenaw Peninsula, but these are pretty easy to get to. **Silver River Falls** is a short walk from M-26, a little more than four miles east of Eagle Harbor. The falls are wide and reasonably picturesque, with a picnic area and roadside park nearby. **Copper Falls** is located about three miles south of Eagle Harbor, on the cutoff road between U.S. 41 and town. As you pass Owl Creek on your way south, take the second trail road to the left and park the car. The falls are a very short walk straight off the end of the road.

Eagle River's falls are much more impressive than Eagle Harbor's and even more convenient to get to. Both **Eagle River Falls** and **Jacob's Falls** are more or less on the shoulder of M-26. There's a parking area and pedestrian bridge just off the highway as it enters Eagle River, providing great access to the 60-foot falls. You can see the smaller Jacob's Falls as you drive past on M-26, three miles northeast of Eagle River, but you'll want to stop the car and admire the 40-foot drop.

WINTER SPORTS AND RECREATION
Downhill Skiing

Downhill skiers can check out Michigan's most challenging terrain at **Mt. Bohemia** (100 Lac La Belle Rd., 906/360-7240 or 888/937-2411, www.mtbohemia.com, lift tickets $45/day), near Lac La Belle. Mt. Bohemia offers one of the Midwest's highest vertical drops (900 feet), with some steep pitches, rocky outcrops, and gladded terrain that may make you think you're somewhere in the Rockies.

Ski and Snowshoe Trails

A few trails stand out from the northern Keweenaw's many miles of Nordic skiing possibilities. First among these is the **Copper Harbor Pathway.** With a number of regularly groomed loops and trails that range from beginner to expert, the miles in and around Copper Harbor provide pleasant skiing and include marked snowshoe trails. The **Fort Wilkins State Park Loop** travels the region between Copper Harbor and the north shore of Lake Fanny Hooe, while the long Kamikaze Trail (not for beginners) hugs the lake's southern shore for more than two miles. Snowshoers will want to make their way into Estivant Pines Nature Sanctuary, 350 acres of virgin pine and towering hardwoods that are purported to be the oldest living trees in the state. You'll be able to choose from three loops of distances between 1 and 2.5 miles, and the ancient woods are worth going out of your way for. It's going to be quiet, too, since no snowmobiles (or any other motor vehicles) are allowed.

Snowmobiling

The Copper Harbor region is no different that the rest of Keweenaw: There are well-groomed snowmobile trails, and plenty of them. The Keweenaw Trail curves north to east as it ascends from Hancock, eventually connecting with the Lac La Belle Trail (steer clear of the Mt. Bohemia skiers), Eagle's Loop, Mandan Trail, Harlow Trail, and other snowmobile routes with trail numbers in the 130s. Take the Brockway Mountain or Powder House Trails into Copper Harbor, and for an end-of-the-road journey to the point of the Keweenaw, take the High Rock Trail to Lake Superior, east of the city. A good trail map is available from the Keweenaw Convention and Visitors Bureau (56638 Calumet Ave., 906/337-4579 or 800/338-7982, www.keweenaw.info) in Calumet.

ACCOMMODATIONS

Located high on a ridge above Copper Harbor, the log lodge and cabins of the **Keweenaw Mountain Lodge** (906/289-4403 or 888/685-6343, www.atthelodge.com, $95 motel, $129–165 cabin) were built as a public works project in the 1930s. Reservations here can be tough, but shoot for a cabin rather than the uninspired motel rooms (added much later than the other buildings). At the northern boundary of Fort Wilkins State Park and just a short bike ride from town, the **◖ Norland Motel** (15526 U.S. 41, 906/289-4815) is the kind of find you almost hate to share. Mom-and-pop motel rooms are made special with knotty pine paneling, a wonderful setting on Lake Fanny Hooe, extras like canoes and in room refrigerators (great for picnic lunches), and prices that don't get much higher than $50.

Though not as good a deal, the no-frills rooms at the **King Copper Motel** (906/289-4214 or 800/833-2470, www.kingcoppermotel.com, $65–85) come with great views of the harbor and are just a few steps from the ferry dock—perfect for a warm shower and real bed after a week on Isle Royale.

Between Copper Harbor and Eagle Harbor on M-26, **Eagle Lodge** (13051 Lakeshore Dr./M-26, 906/289-4294 or 888/558-4441, www.eaglelodge-lakeside.com, $75–130) offers simple housekeeping cabins perched on Lake Superior's shore. In Eagle River, the **Eagle River Inn** (5033 Front St., 906/337-0666, www.eagleriverinn.com, $85–115) offers motel style accommodations with a similarly outstanding setting, right at the water's edge and flanked by a long sand beach. All rooms come with lake views. In Ahmeek, south of Eagle Harbor, check out the **◖ Sand Hills Lighthouse Inn** (906/337-1744). It may not be cheap—rooms run $135–200—but with a 90-foot tower to climb and rooms with balconies overlooking Lake Superior, you can justify the cost. Owner Bill Frabotta has restored the 1919 lighthouse, filled it with antiques, and decorated it in lavish Victorian style. There's a great breakfast, too. Take M-26 west out of Ahmeek to Five Mile Point Road.

Camping

Fort Wilkins State Park (15223 U.S. 41, 906/289-4215, www.michigan.gov/dnr) has 165 modern sites in two campgrounds, both on Lake Fanny Hooe. Many sites back up to the water and offer decent privacy. To reserve a spot (but not a specific site), call the Michigan state parks central reservation line, 800/447-2757, or visit www.midnrreservations.com. **Lake Fanny Hooe Resort and Campground** (505 2nd St., 906/289-4451 or 800/426-4451, www.fannyhooe.com, $28–38) offers uninteresting sites in an open grassy area, but with a decent location near town and the south shore of Lake Fanny Hooe.

West of Ahmeek on Five Mile Point Road, **Sunset Bay Campground** (2701 Sunset Bay Beach Rd., 906/337-2494, www.sunset-bay.com, late May–mid-Oct.) indeed offers a fine view of the sunset from your tent flap. Several of its 12 primitive sites sit on Lake Superior. There are 18 RV sites available. Many locals simply head out into the woods on weekends and set up camp near a favorite stretch of beach or river. If you choose to do the same, respect "no trespassing" signs and observe all

backcountry camping practices (bury waste, hang packs, stay 50 feet from water, etc.)—you'll be sharing the woods with plenty of black bears.

FOOD

The **Pines** (160 Gratiot St., 906/289-4222, www.pinesresort.net), a small café, is an unbeatably warm, inviting place complete with knotty pine, a stone fireplace, and good basic Yooper fare: burgers, hearty sandwiches, and a delicious turkey dinner offered on Sundays. Get a booth beside a window and take in a true "up north" experience. The adjacent **Zik's Bar** is the hangout for Copper Harbor locals. The **Harbor Haus** (77 Brockway Ave., 906/289-4502, www.harborhaus.com, $19–35 dinner entrées) in Copper Harbor offers top-notch dining overlooking the harbor. When the *Isle Royale Queen IV* passes by, the staff drop what they're doing to rush outside and perform the cancan. Though the ever-changing menu highlights some excellent German specials, you can't do better than the whitefish or lake trout. Another good choice for whitefish is the **Mariner North** (245 Gratiot St., 906/289-4637, until 2 A.M. daily), featuring steaks and seafood. This Copper Harbor institution lost some of its spirit when the original log building burned to the ground several years ago, but it remains a popular gathering place.

In Eagle Harbor, the **Shoreline Restaurant** (906/289-4441) draws a good crowd for homemade pies, but there's enough other homestyle favorites such as soups, sandwiches, and well-prepared fresh lake trout to make it worth the stop.

Inside the Eagle River Inn, **Fitzgerald's Restaurant** (5033 Front St., 906/337-0666, www.eagleriverinn.com, $15–25 dinner entrées) offers upscale dining overlooking Lake Superior. The menu features filet mignon, Memphis-style ribs, fresh fish and seafood, inventive vegetarian dishes, and a comprehensive wine list.

INFORMATION

For Copper Harbor tourism information, contact the **Copper Harbor Improvement Association** (P.O. Box 86, 906/289-4212, www.copperharbor.org) or stop in at the visitors center in the Grant Township building on the corner of U.S. 41 and 2nd Street. The booth is staffed during the summer months, but not to worry—even if you stop by when the booth isn't manned, you can grab brochures from the lobby at any time. The **Keweenaw Convention and Visitors Bureau** (56638 Calumet Ave., 906/337-4579 or 800/338-7982, www.keweenaw.info) in Calumet is a great source for information and maps.

Medical emergencies are going to take you south again, though not all the way to Hancock, unless you really want to skirt past the **Keweenaw Memorial Medical Center** (205 Osceola St., 906/337-6500, www.kmmc.org) in Laurium. Heading into Laurium from Copper Harbor or northern Keweenaw, take U.S. 41 to M-26/School Street and turn left. Take School Street to 2nd Street, turn right on 2nd, then left on Osceola to the hospital.

Just like for the hospitals, you'll have to head south of Copper Harbor to find a bank, but not quite as far this time. Keweenaw's regional bank, **Superior National** (80 Mohawk St., 906/337-6807, www.snb-t.com) has a branch in Mohawk, about six miles north of Calumet on U.S. 41. You can find an ATM at the Gas Lite General Store on the corner of U.S. 41 and 1st Street.

GETTING THERE AND AROUND
Car

The two main roads that lead north and east to Copper Harbor are the same highways from the base of the Keweenaw to Houghton and Hancock. U.S. 41 and M-6 merge into one highway at Calumet and stay that way for several miles until hitting Phoenix, where they split again. U.S. 41 doubles as the Copper Country Trail Scenic Byway (it actually starts back in Hancock), and it really does make for a pleasant drive, striking more or less through the middle of the peninsula. The trail pairs Keweenaw's natural beauty (especially striking during the fall) with a smattering of history;

This sign tells the story of U.S. 41, which runs all the way to Miami, Florida.

old mines, museums, and other heritage sites. While it's certainly very scenic, drivers may want to consider M-26 for the journey between Phoenix and Copper Harbor. Not only does it pass through Eagle Harbor, a pleasant town in its own right, but it also hugs the Lake Superior shore the entire way through. As pleasant as the Copper Country Trail is, you'll get a more scenic drive on the detour north. The best combination would be to take one route into Copper Harbor and the other on the way back.

Air

If you're flying in on your way to Copper Harbor, the closest airport is south in Houghton and Hancock area. The **Houghton County Memorial Airport** (CMX, 23810 Airpark Blvd., Calumet, 906/482-3970, www.houghtoncounty.org) has daily flights to and from Chicago. For car rentals at the airport, contact **National Car Rental** (906/482-6655).

Boat

The northern part of the Keweenaw is small,

but it's got a lot of shoreline and a couple of harbors and marinas to boot. The **Copper Harbor State Dock** (906/289-4966, www.michigan.gov/dnr) is small, with only 10 transient slips available, but there are basic amenities (gas, showers, restrooms, etc.), unlike Eagle Harbor. The harbormaster is on duty from 9 A.M.–5 P.M. and can be reached on radio channel 9. Copper Harbor's dock is located at 47° 28.42 N, 87° 51.50 W.

The **Eagle Harbor State Dock,** about 14 miles west of Copper Harbor, has transient docking, but no other amenities. There's an emergency phone number (906/289-4215) and a harbormaster on duty. You can find the dock at 47° 27.52 N, 88° 09.33 W.

Public Transportation

There is no public transportation in the Copper harbor area, save for limited taxi and shuttle service. Services are located in Houghton and Hancock and at the airport, but realize that this is a very expensive option. There is no bus service to the area.

KEWEENAW PENINSULA

Isle Royale

Stranded in the vast waters of Lake Superior, Isle Royale is perhaps the model of what a national park is supposed to be: wild, rugged, and remote. No roads touch the 45-mile-long island, and its only contact with the outside world remains ship to shore radio. The least visited property in the National Park Service system, Isle Royale attracts just 18,000 visitors a year; fewer visitors than Yosemite receives in a single weekend.

Civilization on Isle Royale (ROY-al, as if there is no "e") is concentrated in two small developments at opposite ends of the island. Windigo, on the southwest end, includes a National Park Service information center, camp store, and marina. Rock Harbor, near the east end, offers the same, plus a no-frills lodge and restaurant across from the ferry dock, and a handful of cabins overlooking Tobin Harbor. The rest of the island is backcountry, 210 pristine square miles of forested foot trails, rocky bluffs, quiet lakes, and wilderness campsites.

Those who make the trek by boat or seaplane to Isle Royale come primarily to hike its 165 miles of trails, fish its 46 inland lakes, and paddle its saw toothed shoreline. Wildlife viewing is popular, too, especially for the moose that swam across from Ontario several decades ago, and the eastern timber wolves that later followed their prey across the rock-solid winter ice. Though the wolves are notoriously elusive, rest assured that your sightings of wildlife will far outnumber your human contacts while on Isle Royale.

THE LAND
Geography
Backpackers will take note of Isle Royale's distinctive topography as they traverse the long, narrow island, which runs southwest to northeast and is less than nine miles across at its widest point. A series of ridges and valleys fall away from the park's high interior backbone, the Greenstone Ridge, creating a washboard of forest and rock. Mt. Desor marks the highest point

on the island, rising from the Greenstone Ridge to 1,394 feet.

The same Precambrian lava flows that formed the Keweenaw Peninsula more than one billion years ago also formed Isle Royale. After each lava flow, wind and rain carried sand and other sediments into the area, producing slabs of softer rock sandwiched between the hard layers of basalt, and creating the island's characteristic ridge and trough pattern. Hikers crossing the width of the island will feel this layout in their quads, as the trail continually rises and falls with each ridge. This feature becomes most apparent on the park's northeastern edge where it meets Lake Superior. The ridges become long rocky fingers, and the valleys become narrow slivers of water wedged between the rocky points.

When the center of the Superior Basin began to subside, it thrust the layers of rock on Isle Royale upward at an angle, giving the island a northeast side of steep ridges and bluffs, and a southwest shore that slopes gradually to the water and includes lowlands and bogs. The northern Keweenaw Peninsula is a near mirror image of Isle Royale, with a gradual northern shore and more steeply angled southern side.

The geography of Isle Royale is inseparable

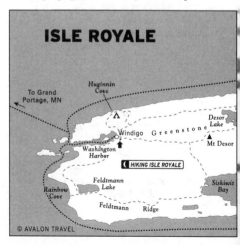

from the water that surrounds it. Along with its namesake island, the largest in Lake Superior, Isle Royale National Park actually consists of an archipelago of some 400 islands, all of them remnants of the same landmass. More than 80 percent of the national park lies underwater, beneath shallow ponds, bogs, inland lakes, and the clear, cold water of Lake Superior. An interesting bit of trivia: Ryan Island, located on Isle Royale's Siskiwit Lake, is the largest island in the largest lake on the largest island in the largest freshwater lake in the world.

Climate

Isle Royale is the perfect escape from a hot, sticky summer. With its water temperature rarely exceeding about 45°F, Lake Superior does a fine job as North America's largest natural air conditioner. It also has a significant moderating effect on the island: summers are generally a little cooler than on the mainland, with daytime temperatures from mid-May to mid-August ranging from about 65–75°F. Nights are north woods cool, often dipping into the 40s and even 30s. Clouds obscure the sun more than half the time in summer. And be aware that fog can strike at anytime. More than one disappointed backpacker has returned from Isle Royale without any memories of the island's lovely vistas.

Lake Superior's moderating effect works in reverse during the cold weather months. Winters on Isle Royale are slightly warmer than on the mainland, though that can be small consolation in this part of the world. Once Lake Superior turns from cobalt to dark gray in late autumn, and its infamous winter storms begin churning, the island becomes shrouded in fog, whipped by wind, and buried under several feet of snow.

Isolation isn't the only reason Isle Royale has low visitor numbers. Come mid-October, it closes down much like a summer resort, and is the only national park to do so. The ferries stop running, the concessionaires in Rock Harbor shut down, and the rangers head for Houghton or take seasonal work in warmer climes. Only the wildlife researchers are in their glory, able to track free-roaming wolves and moose by air.

FLORA AND FAUNA

Isolated from the effects of civilization, Isle Royale acts as a living laboratory, a study of how plants and animals interrelate in the ebb and flow of nature's cycles. Owing to these unique natural qualities, the United Nations declared the park an International Biosphere Reserve in 1980.

Flora

Spruce, firs, and jack pines share the island with beech and maple forests. But numerous

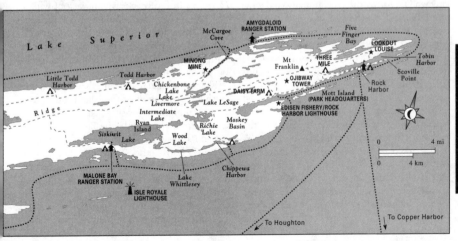

KEWEENAW PENINSULA

varieties of wildflowers take center stage in June and July. Forests can be dotted with yellow lady slipper and American starflower; lowlands are brightened by wild iris, calla lilies, and yellow pond lilies. In July and August different species of berries make their appearance; look for blueberries, thimbleberries, and red raspberries, especially in the sunnier, rockier high areas.

The Island's Most Famous Mammals

The island's **moose** provide the best example. Naturalists believe moose first came to Isle Royale in the early 1900s, several of them swimming the 15 miles from mainland Ontario. With ample vegetation for food and no natural predators, the moose multiplied rapidly, their numbers soaring to somewhere between 1,000 and 3,000 by the late 1920s. Soon after, their numbers outstripped their food sources. Starvation and a succession of harsh winters killed off hundreds of the huge mammals in the 1930s. A fire in 1936 prompted a regrowth of vegetation. With revived food sources, the moose population skyrocketed again, followed by another round of starvation.

The seesaw pattern might have continued for decades, but nature intervened in the form of the eastern **timber wolf** (also known as the gray wolf). During the exceptionally cold winter of 1948–1949, the lake iced over between Ontario and Isle Royale, and a small pack of wolves made its way to the island. The wolves found a bountiful food source in the local moose and multiplied, reaching a peak population of about 50 animals in 1970.

Since then, the wolves and moose, fenced in by the waters of Lake Superior, have provided scientists with a fascinating study of the predator vs. prey relationship. In 2008, the island marked its 50th year of wolf–moose research and study. The study is a joint effort by the National Park Service and Michigan Technological University, and it has become the longest predator–prey study ever undertaken. In a large moose herd, wolves cull the sick, old, and young, preventing overpopulation. In fact,

moose make up around 90 percent of wolves' diet. But a smaller, stronger moose herd means more difficult hunting, which in turn reduces wolf breeding.

Populations of both animals have fluctuated rather dramatically over the decades. Today, the moose population hovers around 557. Hikers have an excellent chance of spotting these 1,000-pound mammals, which often feed in ponds and lowlands or along inland lakeshores. Hidden Lake, across Tobin Harbor south of Lookout Louise, is an exceptionally good spot since moose have a taste for its mineral licks. If you're lucky enough to come upon a moose, give it very, very wide berth. Although they look cartoonish and friendly, moose can be exceptionally dangerous if approached too closely. Cows safeguarding their calves and males behaving aggressively during the fall mating season are capable of inflicting lethal blows with their hooves.

For reasons not clearly understood, Isle Royale's wolf population plummeted in the 1990s. By 1998, just 14 wolves roamed the island in three packs. Biologists feared a lack of genetic diversity might the critical factor that could cause the demise of the island's wolves. In the years since, however, the wolves have rebounded. The winter 2008 count recorded 23 wolves in four packs, the newest of which formed in 2007 (the other three packs have existed since 2000). Whether the wolves will continue to thrive remains one of the most compelling questions this living laboratory has yet to answer.

The wolves tend to hide mostly in the remote southwestern corner of the island, but lately have been migrating east, where moose populations are higher. Only the rare backpacker ever spots one of the shy and stealthy creatures, and "wolf howls" often heard at night are most likely the haunting calls of loons. But the notion that wolves are there, somewhere, and perhaps even watching from deep in the forest, is compelling enough for most, especially those lucky enough to spot a paw print along the trail.

MOOSE AND WOLVES ON ISLE ROYALE

Moose and wolves are the most noteworthy large mammals on Isle Royale. Neither of these species is indigenous to Isle Royale: Moose arrived around 1900, by swimming from the nearby Canadian mainland; wolves made their appearance some fifty years later by walking from Canada – across an ice bridge formed during the severe winter of 1948-1949.The resulting predator-prey relationship has been extensively studied ever since.

The island's isolation, lack of human interaction, and limited, quantifiable populations have created an ideal place for studying the relationship for the last 50 years. The animals don't readily leave the island, nor is it easy for them to get there. So, while the populations are by no means stagnant, the ups and downs can be tracked with relative ease and attributed to natural causes: Illness and hard winters are among them, but the easy majority of the moose deaths are caused by wolves.

The wolf-moose relationship has contributed to an ongoing study that confirms that the two large animals are uniquely interdependent. Wolves are the only natural predator for the moose, and moose make up some 90 percent of the wolves' diets (the rest comes from beaver and snowshoe hare). The fates of the creatures are thus tied together. A spike in one population or a drop in the other provides invaluable information to the researchers from Michigan Technological University, who study the animals' relationship.

In the summertime, researchers and volunteers head into the wild to study elements of the moose population: examine the carcasses, check the impact of moose ticks, observe the moose as they forage, measure the amount of available food, and collect droppings for dietary analysis. The researchers also give attention to the wolves, analyzing their droppings to gather DNA identifications for each of the predators on the island. There's no guarantee that they'll get every wolf, but since they tend to collect a large quantity of droppings, the list is fairly exhaustive.

Much of the work takes place in the winter, while the park is closed to visitors. From mid-January through early March, wolf and moose populations are measured through observation from flyovers. Researchers also estimate kill rates and perform studies on the carcasses.

For the fifth year in a row, 2008 saw the moose afflicted by infestations of ticks (a heavily infected moose can carry tens of thousands of the blood-sucking parasites), and a series of overly hot summers have negatively impacted the moose, which need to maintain a relatively low body temperature.

For their part, the wolves are split into four packs, with a single lone wolf wandering the island.

As the study continues, each year brings with it new, and sometimes surprising information.

Other Animals

Some of the other large mammals common in the northern Great Lakes region are notably absent from the island. Black bears never made it here, and white-tailed deer introduced for hunting vanished early in the century. Likewise, caribou and lynx, present in the 19th century, also disappeared. Instead, hikers may spot red foxes (which love to scavenge around campsites, so hang your pack), beavers, muskrats, hares, red squirrels, otter, and mink.

Birdwatchers will enjoy scouring the water's surface for the common loon, which is indeed common here, along with the Canada goose, bufflehead, black duck, merganser, and mallard. Smaller birds frequenting the island include warblers, chickadees, thrushes, woodpeckers, and kingfishers.

None of Isle Royale's inland lakes can be reached by car or motorized boat, and many of them require serious effort to reach even by foot. This combination makes for great **fishing.** Sport fishing boats ply the Lake Superior waters around Isle Royale for lake trout. But

nearly all of the island's inland waters offer the ultimate fishing experience. Northern pike is considered the prime fish in these parts for its fighting spirit, and can be found in almost any of the local lakes. Hungry hikers will be pleased to know that walleye, perch, and trout abound here, too. Wise backpackers tote along a pack rod to fish with from shore. Many lakes, like Feldtmann, Desor, Siskiwit, Richie, and Chickenbone have foot trails leading directly to them. Other more remote lakes are open to fishing but require good backcountry skills to reach. No license is needed to fish Isle Royale's inland lakes, though Michigan regulations apply. If you plan to drop a line in Lake Superior, you'll need a Michigan license, which are sold at the island's two camp stores.

A discussion of Isle Royale's animal life is not complete with mention of the island's insects. Like much of the Upper Peninsula, and many other wilderness areas, Isle Royale provides a fine home for **mosquitoes** and **black flies,** especially in low lying areas. From mid-June to mid-August or so, keep insect repellent close at hand. In general, insects are less of a problem on higher trails, which often catch a lake breeze.

THE NATIONAL PARK

While many national parks struggle with their fates as islands of wilderness surrounded by a more developed world, Isle Royale represents the opposite scenario. It has the advantage of a much larger buffer zone protecting it from outside encroachment and influence. As a result, it's one of the most closely managed holdings in the national park system. That's good or bad depending on your opinion of the Park Service, but it does present some unique opportunities for conservation. Isle Royale is one of the few parks that regulates the number of visitors who pass through its gates. Though logistics have done a sufficient job of keeping numbers down thus far, the National Park Service need only cut back on ferry service or the number of campsites to further reduce the flow.

Limited access also allows the Park Service to enforce rules more effectively. Dogs, for

© TRAVEL MICHIGAN

Isle Royale's isolation helps perserve its natural beauty.

example, are not allowed on the island for fear they might bring rabies and other diseases to the island's wolf pack. The Park Service also takes great pains to preserve the island's backcountry solitude, with a park brochure reminding hikers to "refrain from loud conversation," "avoid songfests," and "select equipment of subtle natural tones rather than conspicuous colorful gear."

Information

For general information on the park, camping, transportation options, and more, contact **Isle Royale National Park** (906/482-0984,www. nps.gov/isro).

Isle Royale was one of the first national parks to charge a "park user fee." Daily fees are $4 per person per day. If you're traveling to the island by ferry or seaplane, the concessionaire will collect your fee. If you're traveling by private boat, you can pay at the ranger station at Windigo or Rock Harbor, or at the Houghton Visitors Center prior to your departure.

The National Park Service has long

discussed charging admission fees to national parks as a way to compensate for shortfalls in federal funding. In the past, the incentive wasn't there, since all gate fees were fed back into the federal government's general treasury. With the new user fee program, however, 80 percent of the monies gathered is spent at the collecting park. The remaining 20 percent is spent at national parks with priority maintenance projects. In Isle Royale's case, that means hundreds of thousands of dollars that will be spent maintaining trails and repairing or replacing docks.

Getting There

If getting there is half the fun, you'll be very excited by the time you arrive at Isle Royale. Travel to the island is not particularly convenient or cheap, which probably accounts for the average visitor stays—they're considerably longer than most other national park destinations. The average visit to Rocky Mountain National Park is a few hours; to Isle Royale, three days, including day-trippers who flow off the ferry, wander around the harbor for a few hours, and leave that afternoon.

Many, however, come to appreciate even the trip to and from Isle Royale, a mental decompression chamber of sorts that eases the passage between island wilderness and the civilized world.

Your options for travel to Isle Royale are seaplane, ferry, or personal boat. The National Park Service operates the largest ferry, the 165-foot *Ranger III*, which celebrated its 50th birthday in 2008. It departs from Houghton twice a week (Tuesday and Friday) from the beginning of June through mid-September for the six-hour passage to Rock Harbor. The one-way cost is $60 adults, $20 children 6–12; kids under 6 are free. Canoes and kayaks are an additional $20–50 if they're longer than 20 feet or weigh more than 90 pounds. Make reservations through the national park (906/482-0984, www.nps.gov/isro).

If you'd rather see more of the Keweenaw and spend less time on the ferry, drive another hour up the peninsula to Copper Harbor, where you can catch the *Isle Royale Queen IV* for a three-hour trip to Rock Harbor. It operates from mid-May through the end of September, with a varying schedule (adding additional departures as needed in July and August). The one-way cost is $65 adults, $33 children 11 and under. Canoes and kayaks are an additional $25. The *Queen* is notoriously reliable and has happily surprised weary backpackers by showing up to retrieve them on even the stormiest of days. But the ship is most deserving of its nickname "the Queasy." In heavy seas, its hull can rock and roll at a pretty good pitch. To check the schedule and make reservations, contact the **Royale Line** (906/289-4437, www.isleroyale.com).

A third and fourth ferry run from Grand Portage, Minnesota. The 65-foot *Wenonah* makes the three-hour passage to Windigo, on the island's west end, daily from mid-June to mid-September. The round-trip cost is $49 adults, $27 children under 12. Day trips are essentially just a boat ride, since you'll have less than three hours on the island. Reserve a spot through **Grand Portage-Isle Royale Transportation Line** (651/653-5872 or 888/746-2305, Nov.–Apr.; 218/475-0024 or 218/475-0074 May–Oct.; www.isleroyale-boats.com).

A faster but more expensive boat, the 63-foot *Voyageur II,* travels to Windigo from Grand Portage in two hours, then continues on to Rock Harbor. On its way to Rock Harbor, it circumnavigates the island, offering drop-off and pick-up service along the way. This makes for a slow but interesting trip. One way between Grand Portage and Windigo is $64; call for prices to other locations. *Voyageur II* can also carry canoes and kayaks for an additional $56. Again, make arrangements through Grand Portage–Isle Royale Transportation Line.

Seaplane service from Houghton is the most expensive and is usually the quickest way to the island. The 35-minute flight is often delayed by wind and fog. The plane flies on demand (except Sunday) and can carry up to five passengers for $290 round-trip per person ($195 one-way). The plane cannot carry stove

fuel, but you can purchase it on the island at the park store. Contact **Royale Air Service** (877/359-4753 or 218/721-0405, www.royaleairservice.com).

Arriving by private boat is also popular in midsummer; perhaps a bit too popular for many who resent the whine of powerboats jarring the silence. The Rock Harbor and Windigo marinas offer docking and refueling for powerboats and sailboats; boats also are permitted to drop an anchor in a secluded bay overnight and save the marina fee. Protected harbors are plentiful on the east end of the island, although most remain exposed on an east wind, but are nonexistent on the west end. Every boat arriving at the island must first stop at a ranger station in Windigo or Rock Harbor to obtain a permit and pay the park user fee.

Those with boats under 20 feet are strongly urged not to attempt a Lake Superior crossing. Even if you have a larger vessel, consider the passage only if you possess strong navigation skills and a good marine radio. Think ocean, not lake. Remember, these are the waters that were capable of sinking the 729-foot *Edmund Fitzgerald.*

Accommodations and Food

Those just looking for a quiet island stay and some swell day hikes can set up a base in comfort at the **Rock Harbor Lodge** (866/644-2003 or 906/337-4993, www.isleroyaleresort.com). Lodge rooms are pretty much your basic motel-style accommodations, but they sit right at the water's edge with a glorious view of nearby islands and the open waters of Lake Superior. This slice of civilization in the wilderness comes at a high price. Rates for a double average $245–254; the dining room is open daily for breakfast, lunch, and dinner. Dinner offerings often include fresh lake trout from the restored Edisen Fishery. Guests also have use of an adjacent day lodge with a comfortable wood-burning fireplace. Nearby housekeeping cottages include small kitchens, one double bed, and two bunk beds. Rates average $222–246 per night. Reservations are a must.

The Rock Harbor Lodge dining room is open to the public, and its meals taste like a gourmet feast after a week of freeze-dried fare. The Marina Store in Rock Harbor carries a good supply of food, camping supplies, film, fuel…just about anything important you forgot to pack. There's no lodging available at Windigo but you will find an equally well-equipped camp store. Both stores also offer shower and laundry facilities.

If you want to see more of the island, **camping** is the way to do it. Rustic campsites are located throughout the island, with three types of sites available: tent sites for one to three tents, group sites for parties of 7–10 campers, and three-sided shelters that hold up to six people. You must obtain a free camping permit outlining your itinerary from the ranger station (groups of 7–10 pay a $25 processing fee), but reservations are not available. All sites are on a first-come, first-served basis. Should you reach a site at the end of the day and find it full (this can happen, especially in August, and especially at sites a day's hike from Rock Harbor), the unwritten rules ask that you double up. No one expects you to hike off into the dwindling light to the next campsite.

Come prepared. The camp stores, though very well supplied, are not the best places to outfit your trip. Carry a stove and fuel, since many sites do not permit fires, and dead wood is limited anyway. A water filter is another good idea, unless you plan to boil everything. Potable water is only available in Rock Harbor and Windigo, and chemical purifiers like Halizone tablets will not kill the hydatid tapeworm that can be found in Isle Royale waters.

Boat Tours

The Park Service shuttles visitors to various island attractions on its 25-passenger *Sandy.* For information on destinations, schedules, and fares, contact the **Park Service** (906/482-0984, www.nps.gov/isro). Twice a week, the *Sandy* makes the short trip across the mouth of Moskey Basin to the historic fishery of Peter and Laura Edisen, restored to show what life was like at the commercial fisheries that once thrived on the island. From Edisen Fishery,

it's a quarter-mile walk to the stout and simple Rock Harbor Lighthouse, a white edifice built in 1855 to guide ships to Isle Royale's then-busy copper ports.

The *Sandy* also cruises once a week to the Minong Mine. In the 1870s it was the island's largest copper mining operation. The boat excursion alone is worth the trip, rounding Blake Point and cruising past Five Finger Bay and Belle Harbor, one of the park's most scenic areas. Once at the mine, you can examine ancient copper mining pits dug by the island's first inhabitants, which later lead miners to the area's underground wealth. Relics like ore cars and rails remain visible, too. Hikers can view the remnants of another mine on the Island Mine Trail. A wagon road, an old powder house, and mine tailings are all that remains of the island's second largest mining operation. Around all mine areas, watch the ground carefully. Shafts and pits remain, and are often obscured by undergrowth.

◖ HIKING ISLE ROYALE
Day Hikes from Rock Harbor

Several day hikes are doable if you choose to "motel camp" in Rock Harbor. Don't miss **Scoville Point,** a 4.2-mile loop with interpretive signs that traces a rocky finger of land east of Rock Harbor. Another popular short hike (3.8 miles) is the loop to Suzy's Cave, formed by the wave action of a once much-deeper Lake Superior. **Lookout Louise,** north of Tobin Harbor, offers one of the island's most spectacular views, gazing over its ragged northeastern shoreline. If you have a canoe, it's a short paddle and then a two-mile hike. Without a canoe, it's a fine but lengthier hike along lovely Tobin Harbor and the eastern end of the Greenstone Ridge. You'll have to retrace your steps to return to Rock Harbor, making the trek a total of about 20 miles.

For another all day hike, follow the Lake Superior shoreline to the Daisy Farm campground and the Ojibway Trail, which heads north and brings you to the **Ojibway Tower,** an air-monitoring station. The tower marks the highest spot on the eastern end of the island, and you can climb its steps (but not enter the tower room) for an unmatched view of the island's interior lakes and bays on both the north and south sides of the island. Travel back via the Greenstone Ridge and along Tobin Harbor for a varied 18-mile hike that will take you through blueberry patches, wildflower meadows, and serene shorelines. For a similar but shorter hike (about 10 miles) turn north at the Three Mile campground to ascend Mt. Franklin, another high point on the Greenstone Ridge.

Day Hikes from Windigo

If you'd prefer not to haul your possessions on your back, it's possible—but a little more difficult—to do day hikes out of Windigo. Because fewer trails exist here, most hikes will be of the out-and-back variety. The best loop option is to **Huginnin Cove,** a 9.7-mile route that passes through prime moose habitat before emerging onto the Lake Superior shore. There's a campground here if you choose to make it an overnighter. The east side of the trail passes an old mine, which was last active in 1892. Another excellent option is the **Feldtmann Lake Trail,** which winds along Washington Harbor before heading inland to one of the island's least visited lakes. You can hike the 17-mile route out and back in a day, but you'll enjoy your adventure more if you plan it as an overnight. Set up camp here and you'll likely be treated to moose sightings, unmatched fishing, and maybe the howl of a distant wolf. Plus, if you stay overnight, you'll have the time and energy for the short side trip to Lake Superior's pretty Rainbow Cove.

Longer Hikes

With 165 miles of trail, Isle Royale has far more outstanding hiking options that it's possible to outline here. Consider a comprehensive guide like Jim DuFresne's excellent *Isle Royale National Park: Foot Trails and Water Routes,* published by The Mountaineers. If you prefer to avoid the more bottlenecked areas of Windigo and Rock Harbor, consider arranging for the *Voyageur II* ferry (218/475-0024 or

218/475-0074) or the island's water-taxi service (906/337-4993) to drop you off and pick you up at another location.

In general, the **Greenstone Ridge** is the main route to traverse the island, a 42-mile trail of mostly high and dry terrain. It also is the most popular, though "crowds" are relative on Isle Royale.

The park's second-longest trail, the 26-mile **Minong Ridge Trail,** easily ranks as its most challenging. Traversing the north side of the island from near Windigo to McCargoe Cove, the rough and lightly used trail meanders over a rocky ridge and disappears through bogs. If you like surroundings that are primitive and peaceful, and don't get nervous about some poorly marked stretches, this trail is for you. Wildlife sightings, especially moose, are likely here. Though campgrounds are far apart on this trail, they're worth the effort. Little Todd Harbor and Todd Harbor are some of the nicest on the island.

Finally, the **Feldtmann Ridge Trail** loops along the southwestern shore, a well-marked but also lightly used route of 22 miles. The trail offers outstanding variety, from the shoreline of Washington Harbor, through gentle bogs, up the high Feldtmann Ridge, and finally to the open wildflower meadows and waters of Siskiwit Bay.

PADDLING THE ISLAND

For paddlers, Isle Royale is a dream destination, a nook-and-cranny wilderness of rocky islands, secluded coves, and quiet bays interrupted only by the low call of a loon. First-time visitors can't do better than the **Five Fingers,** the collection of fjord-like harbors and rocky promontories on the east end of the island. Not only is it well protected (except from northeasterlies), it offers some of the finest and most characteristic Isle Royale scenery and solitude. Though Isle Royale is generally better suited to kayaks, open canoes can handle these waters in calm weather.

For kayaks, the entire island offers paddling opportunities, though some areas require long stretches of paddling with little shoreline access. Note that open-water passages on Lake Superior should be attempted by experienced paddlers only, and are not at all recommended in an open boat like a canoe. Capsizing in Lake Superior is not an unfortunate experience; it is a life-threatening one. With water temperatures rarely exceeding the 40s, hypothermia can occur in a matter of minutes.

You can avoid open water passages and still explore other areas of the island by making use of the *Voyageur II* ferry or the island's water-taxi service, which will transport you and your boat to various docks on the northeastern half of the island. For more information and rates, call the **Voyageur II** (218/475-0024 or 218/475-0074) or the water taxi (906/337-4993).

Ferries can transport your boat, provided it is less than 20 feet long. You also can rent canoes, 14-foot fishing boats, and outboard motors at Windigo and Rock Harbor. For rental information, call 906/337-4993. For Rock Harbor visitors, a wonderful day can be spent exploring Tobin Harbor, where rental canoes await.

Exploring the inland lakes is a remarkable experience on Isle Royale. Fishing is often superb, and moose often loiter near the shore, unaware of your presence. Plan your routes carefully to avoid grueling portages. Again, your best bet is to arrange for the water taxi or the *Voyageur II* ferry to drop you and your boat at a mid island spot like Malone Bay, Chippewa Harbor, or McCargoe Cove. From there you'll have manageable (and even easy) portages to more than a half dozen lakes, including Siskiwit, Wood, Whittlesey, Intermediate, Richie, LeSage, Livermore, and Chickenbone. There's nothing quite like drifting across a wilderness lake in the middle of a wilderness island.

MARQUETTE AND THE LAKE SUPERIOR SHORE

As home to the Upper Peninsula's largest, most metropolitan city, the Lake Superior shore is deserving of a good portion of your time. Marquette is modern and cosmopolitan, especially for a city located in Michigan's most remote region. It's a college town, which means there's plenty to do whether you're a fan of bars or live performances, college-level sports, or the arts and culture scene. If you're here for the great outdoors, you'll find plenty of it just over Marquette's doorstep: The rugged and undeveloped Huron Mountains lie to the west, while Presque Isle truly is one of the U.P.'s gems.

And while Lake Superior may not have the sandy beaches and swimability of Lakes Michigan and Huron, it's almost impossible to be unmoved by the rough, wild shoreline. The rocks, bluffs, and icy water all make the largest of the Great Lakes in many ways the most awesome.

Both Munising and Grand Island are located on a picturesque bay that would rival any in the world for sheer beauty. Continue east and it only gets better, as the remarkable colors, cliffs, and rock formations of Pictured Rocks National Lakeshore stretch out like an artistic masterpiece being unveiled before you. If you've never kayaked before, this would be a good place to start. The national lakeshore is perfectly bookended on the opposite side by Grand Marais.

Don't forget to take a detour inland, where many of the U.P.'s renowned outdoor recreational activities are at your fingertips. Of particular interest is the Seney National Wildlife

© PAUL VACHON

HIGHLIGHTS

◖ **Downtown Marquette:** Enjoy a respite from nature by taking in the offerings of the Upper Peninsula's most cosmopolitan city (page 173).

◖ **Presque Isle Park:** Just a stone's throw from Northern Michigan University's campus, some of the area's most beautiful scenery is beautifully preserved. Take a car through the park, or better still, bike, hike or ski (page 179).

◖ **Hiawatha Water Trail:** The 120-mile Hiawatha Water Trail isn't for everyone, but the journey from Big Bay to Grand Marias is a beautiful and adventurous one. There are shorter segments for those short on time or stamina (page 182).

◖ **Grand Island:** Take a ferry ten minutes off the shore of Munising and spend a day or

a weekend exploring the island by bike or foot (page 194).

◖ **Hiawatha National Forest:** Several hundred acres of national forest provide seemingly endless recreational opportunities, no matter what the season (page 195).

◖ **Pictured Rocks National Lakeshore:** These unusual scenic rocks with their fascinating colors rank among the very top tier of U.P. attractions. Kayaking is the best way to appreciate their grandeur (page 205).

◖ **Iverson Snowshoe Company:** One of the very few manufacturers of snowshoes and related products that still produce their wares by hand, Iverson's offers fascinating tours of their small factory in Shingleton (page 214).

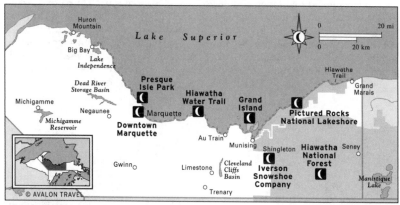

LOOK FOR ◖ TO FIND RECOMMENDED SIGHTS, ACTIVITIES, DINING, AND LODGING.

Refuge, which has 95,000 acres of wetlands, bog, and wilderness. It's home to hundreds of species of birds and other animals, and is an ideal place for hiking or biking.

PLANNING YOUR TIME

You'll probably want to spend at least two or three days in Marquette. There's enough to do that it'll stave off the small-town ennui

that can strike up here. Marquette can also serve as an ideal launching pad for hub and spoke explorations of the surrounding areas. Set aside a day each for Munising, Pictured Rocks, and Grand Marais—longer if you plan to explore the lakeshore by foot. Try to get out onto Lake Superior, whether it's by sea kayak, charter boat, or a tour. Four or five days will do you just fine. Book a nice hotel,

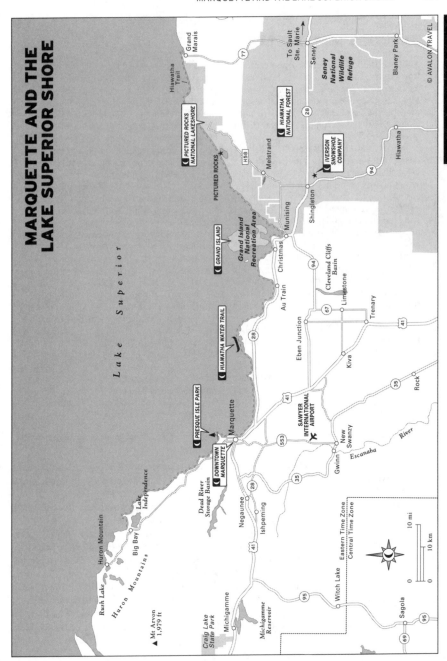

MARQUETTE AND THE LAKE SUPERIOR SHORE

© AVALON TRAVEL

JACQUES MARQUETTE

A Roman Catholic missionary and explorer from France, Jacques Marquette (1637–1675) established a mission among the Ottawa at St. Ignace. He, along with Louis Jolliet, was probably the first European to explore much of the Great Lakes region and the Upper Mississippi.

Born in Laon, France, Marquette joined the Jesuit order in 1654 and spent the next 10 years studying and teaching in France. In 1666, Jesuit priests sent him to New France (present-day Quebec) as a missionary. Like many Jesuits, he lived among the Native Americans and studied their languages. In 1671, he was appointed missionary to the Ottawa tribe, and he established the St. Ignace mission on the north shore of the Straits of Mackinac.

In 1672, French explorer Louis Jolliet arrived at the mission, sent by the governor of New France, Comte de Frontenac, to search for a trade route to the Far East. They had heard from the Native Americans about a great waterway, "MissiSipi" ("Big River"), which they thought might flow to the Pacific Ocean. Marquette, with his knowledge of tribal languages, was to accompany Jolliet.

Marquette, Jolliet, and five other explorers set out in canoes across the northern shore of Lake Michigan in May 1673. They traveled down Green Bay and up the Fox River in present-day Wisconsin, where local Native Americans led them to a portage to the Wisconsin River. The team followed the Wisconsin to its confluence with the Mississippi, which they followed to the Arkansas River. They grew alarmed by both the swiftness of the water and word from the Native Americans about possible Spanish colonists downstream. Fearing an attack by Spaniards and deducing that the river's southerly flow would not lead to the Pacific, the explorers turned back. They paddled the Illinois River to the Chicago River, and then followed the western shore of Lake Michigan to Green Bay – a staggering journey of more than 2,900 miles. Along the way, they peaceably traded with dozens of Native American tribes.

Suffering from a case of dysentery contracted during the Mississippi expedition, an ailing Marquette spent the winter at a mission in Wisconsin, returning to Illinois the following spring to work with the Native Americans he had met along his voyage. In 1675, he died on Lake Michigan, near present day Ludington, Michigan, en route back to Sault Ste. Marie. Marquette and Jolliet's exploration added greatly to the Europeans' knowledge of North American geography. The Native Americans who treated them so well would later suffer when that new knowledge spurred increasing European settlement.

make some dinner reservations, and spend your days exploring.

HISTORY

Marquette and the Lake Superior shore weren't immune to the influence of trade and industry that shaped the rest of the Upper Peninsula. Indeed, its history is remarkably similar, albeit a bit tamer. French missionaries, including the city namesake, Jacques Marquette explored the area in the mid-1600s. Trappers arrived several decades later, and in the mid-1800s the mines opened up. But it took more than mining to put the city on the map. A combination of industries gave Marquette its prosperity. Iron ore mining, shipping, and a stream of wealthy vacationers each capitalized on the area's natural resources to make Marquette prosperous.

Not all of the Lake Superior shore was exploited, however. The Huron Mountains remained largely untouched. The conservation wasn't the result of happy accident, however. Beginning around the 1880s, the Huron Mountains became the wilderness retreat of choice for several millionaire industrialists. Cyrus McCormick, head of the lucrative farm implement company that would become

International Harvester, amassed a huge wilderness estate around White Deer Lake, now part of the Ottawa National Forest's McCormick Tract Wilderness Area. Frederick Miller of Miller Brewing acquired his piece of wilderness at Craig Lake, now a wilderness state park. Dozens of others established "camps" at the Huron Mountain Club, an organization so exclusive that even Henry Ford was turned downed for membership when he first applied. The members easily had enough clout to stop construction of a road that was to link L'Anse with Big Bay. County Road 550 unceremoniously ends just west of Big Bay—terminated by a gate and a security guardhouse.

Today, the 25,000-acre enclave is shared mostly by the descendants of those original members, who quietly protect and preserve this spectacular landholding. Though locals grumble about the lack of access to the property, no one can argue that the Huron Mountain Club has proved to be an exceptional steward of the land. It has kept away loggers, miners, and developers, leaving what some consider the most magnificent wilderness remaining in the state, perhaps in the entire Midwest.

The Pictured Rocks National Lakeshore joined the Huron Mountains as an exceptional specimen of nature in 1966, after areas of the Great Lakes shore were considered for inclusion in the national park system. The 43 miles of scenic shoreline between Munising and Grand Marais became the first national lakeshore in the United States.

Marquette and Vicinity

With just over 20,000 hardy year-round souls, Marquette ranks as the largest city in the Upper Peninsula. Tucked in a well-protected natural harbor almost exactly midway across the U.P.'s northern shore, it grew and continues to thrive due largely to its central location that has made it the U.P.'s center of commerce and government. Marquette also enjoys the status of being a central port for the iron industry.

Don't be deterred by the excess of strip malls along U.S. 41. Head toward downtown where the action is. Here you'll discover the city's rich architectural heritage, a U.S. Olympic Training Center, Northern Michigan University, and a beautiful setting along the high, rocky Lake Superior shoreline. Marquette has never really promoted itself as a tourist destination, but this may actually be to the visitor's benefit. Lodging and good restaurants are plentiful, the downtown and lakefront are ideal for strolling, and the U.P.'s natural attractions: rugged hills, waterfalls, wildlife, and wild rivers all await you just outside the city limits—often with the absence of crowds and typical "tourist trap" blight.

SIGHTS
◖ Downtown Marquette
Third Street, running north–south, and Washington Street, running east–west, represent Marquette's main cross streets, and where they meet is a good area to begin an exploration of the downtown. This puts you in the heart of the shopping and historic district. Buildings like the 1902 **Marquette County Courthouse**, at 3rd and Baraga Avenue, and the 1927 MFC First National Bank, at 101 West Washington Street, showcase the city's affinity for **Beaux Arts architecture.** Step inside the courthouse for a better look, and also to check out a display about Michigan Supreme Court Justice and author John Voelker, better known by his pen name, Robert Traver. Traver, an Ishpeming native, wrote the novel *Anatomy of a Murder,* among other works. Based on a real murder that occurred in nearby Big Bay, the book was made into a movie of the same name in 1959. Scenes from the film, starring Jimmy Stewart and George C. Scott, were filmed in the third-floor courtroom and in Big Bay. The **Marquette County Historical Society** (213

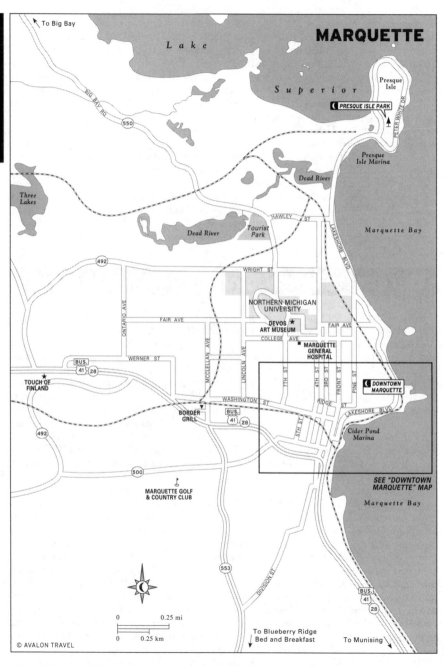

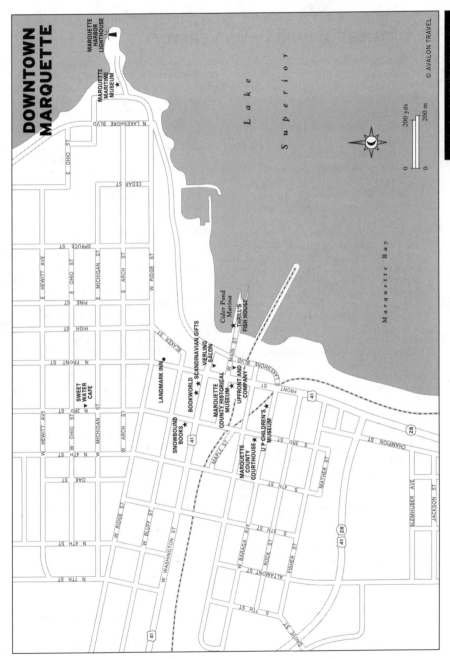

DOWNTOWN MARQUETTE

MARQUETTE HARBOR LIGHTHOUSE

MARQUETTE MARITIME MUSEUM

Lake Superior

© AVALON TRAVEL

0   200 yds
0   200 m

Marquette Bay

N LAKESHORE BLVD

CEDAR ST

SPRUCE ST

E OHIO ST

E HEWITT AVE

E OHIO ST

E MICHIGAN ST

E ARCH ST

W RIDGE ST

PINE ST

HIGH ST

N FRONT ST

BLAKER ST

Cider Pond Marina

THILL'S FISH HOUSE

SCANDINAVIAN GIFTS

VIERLING SALON

W MAIN ST

N LAKESHORE BLVD

SWEET WATER CAFE

LANDMARK INN

BOOKWORLD

MARQUETTE COUNTY HISTORICAL MUSEUM

UPFRONT AND COMPANY

FRONT ST

41

28

N HEWITT AVE

N OHIO ST

N 3RD ST

N MICHIGAN ST

W ARCH ST

SNOWBOUND BOOKS

41

MAPLE ST

U.P. CHILDREN'S MUSEUM

MARQUETTE COUNTY COURTHOUSE

S 3RD ST

MATHER ST

CHAMPION ST

OAK ST

W 4TH ST

W RIDGE ST

W BLUFF ST

W WASHINGTON ST

N 6TH ST

S 4TH ST

S 5TH ST

W BARAGA AVE

ROCK ST

FISHER ST

ALTAMONT ST

41   28

BLEMHUBER AVE

JACKSON ST

N 7TH ST

S 7TH ST

GROVE ST

41

NORTHERN MICHIGAN UNIVERSITY

*Hail Northern, we thy sons
and daughters
Now bring thee tribute long deserved
Thou beacon light – mid nature's
grandeur
Through passing decades well
preserved
Oh, may we labor with untiring zeal
That when these golden days have
flown
We may with honor face the future
And match thy courage with our own.*

Students at Northern Michigan University are a rare and special breed. Not everyone can tolerate spending their winters in Marquette, on the frozen shores of Lake Superior, where the average daytime high temperature drops into the low 20s each January and where, in 1996, the lowest recorded temperature was a shockingly frigid -24°F. It's a place where class is more often cancelled for cold than for snowfall. Michigan has other options for higher education; two Big Ten schools, the University of Michigan and Michigan State University, are located in the warmer climate of the Lower Peninsula. These students are here, for the most part, because they like it here.

Founded in 1899, NMU is the largest university in Michigan's Upper Peninsula. Founded more than 100 years ago with 32 students, the school has grown to an enrollment of slightly more than 9,000 students, still quite small compared to some other schools (U of M has 41,000 students and MSU has 46,000). The school offers a fairly traditional liberal arts education with 180 academic majors and 120 academic minors in such subjects as business, technology, education, and sociology. Northern Michigan takes special pride in its technology programs, founded upon the vision of providing a "learning environment that embraces technology to enhance student access, promote the development of independent learners, and encourage greater student faculty communication and collaboration." It was this vision that led the school to become the first state university in Michigan to become a "laptop campus," providing each of its students with a laptop computer and a standard set of software tools for use during the school year. The university upgrades students' computers every two years.

NMU's campus consists of more than 50 facilities located just off the Lake Superior shoreline. The most interesting of these is undoubtedly the Superior Dome, which has the distinction of being the world's largest wooden dome structure. A fascinating sight, the dome is 14 stories high, has a diameter of 563 feet, and covers more than five acres. It's impressively built from Douglas fir, a natural choice considering its location. Containing 781 beams and more than 100 *miles* of fir decking, the dome can withstand up to 60 pounds of snow per square foot. Inside, removable artificial turf (also the largest of its kind in the world) can host football, soccer, and field hockey. Beneath the turf are three basketball or volleyball courts, two tennis courts, and a 200-meter track.

But the real action takes place at the Berry Events Center. An Olympic-sized ice sheet (200 by 100 feet) hosts ice hockey, the sport of choice here, where the long winters and proximity to Canada make the sport popular. While NMU competes in NCAA Division II for most sports – basketball, football, and the like – hockey is a Division I sport, and catching a game is highly recommended if you're in town.

There are other reasons to visit NMU's campus, too. The school's drama department stages several theatrical productions each year, and the DeVos Art Museum offers scores of intriguing pieces by regional artists.

© PAUL VACHON

the courtroom in the opulent Marquette County Courthouse

N. Front St., 906/226-3571, www.marquette-cohistory.org, 10 A.M.–5 P.M. Mon.–Fri., open until 9 P.M. on the third Thurs. of the month) offers a walking tour brochure.

Downtown Marquette is home to distinctive shops worth a little browsing time. **Bookworld** (136 W. Washington St., 906/228-9490) and **Snowbound Books** (118 N. 3rd, 906/228-4448) offer a good selection of local and regional titles. Follow Main down to the waterfront, where **Thrill's Fish House** (250 E. Main St., 906/226-9851) sells fresh catch and smoked whitefish spread from a little shop at the marina, in the shadow of the old wooden ore dock.

The U.P.'s Scandinavian heritage looms large in Marquette. **Scandinavian Gifts** (1025 N. 3rd St., 906/225-1993) showcases the sleek and simple lines of classic Scandinavian design in its selection of glassware and silver (lots of Norwegian sweaters, too). Back on the highway, **Touch of Finland** (2853 U.S. 41, 906/226-2567, www.touchoffinland.com), on

U.S. 41 across from Kmart, has a bit of almost everything in its 4,000 square feet, including housewares, textiles, and a complete sauna department.

The old red brick waterworks building now houses the **Marquette Maritime Museum** (300 Lakeshore Blvd., 906/226-2006, http://mqtmaritimemuseum.com, 10 A.M.–5 P.M. daily May 25–Oct. 31, $7 adults, $4 children under 13). This worthwhile stop includes exhibits on everything from Native American birch bark canoes to Great Lakes shipwrecks, lighthouses, an interactive display of a freighter's pilot house, and a working submarine periscope. The **Marquette County Historical Museum** (213 Front St., 906/226-3571, www.marquettecohistory.org, Mon.–Fri. year round, $3 adults, $1 children over 12) features excellent Native American exhibits, as well as lots of mining and logging photographs and a large collection of old maps. There's a good bookstore, too. If you've got kids in tow, head for the **U.P. Children's Museum** (123 W. Baraga

Ave., 906/226-3911, www.upcmkids.org, 10 A.M.–6 P.M. Mon.–Wed., 10 A.M.–7:30 P.M. Thurs., 10 A.M.–8 P.M. Fri., 10 A.M.–6 P.M. Sat., noon–5 P.M. Sun., $4 adults, $0.50 children), where they can climb into a tree habitat to learn about its root system, crawl into a replica wasp nest, or explore life in the aquifer under a pond.

The **Marquette Arts and Culture Center** (217 N. Front St., Peter White Public Library's lower level, 906/228-0472 www.mqtcty.org/arts.html, 9 A.M.–9 P.M. Mon.–Thurs., 9 A.M.–6 P.M. Fri.–Sat., 10 A.M.–5 P.M. Sun., free) offers a gallery featuring the work of local artists which changes every month. You'll also find a museum shop offering many of the pieces for sale, as well as occasional informal concerts and plays.

For a unique type of Upper Peninsula experience, stop by Presque Isle Park to watch an ore carrier being loaded at the **Marquette Ore Dock,** located on Lakeshore Boulevard, shortly before the entrance to Presque Isle Park (pronounced *presk ahyl,* which translates from the French as "almost an island" or "peninsula") about four miles northeast of downtown) This behemoth structure, which extends almost a quarter mile out into Lake Superior, is designed to interface with the 600-foot-long ships as they're loaded with taconite pellets deposited by overhead railway cars. It's a noisy spectacle, and a pleasant reminder that a small part of the U.P.'s mining heritage still survives today. Check www.boatnerd.com/passage/marquette.htm for a schedule of vessel passages.

Where would you expect to find the world's largest wooden dome? In the heart of logging country, of course, and along Lake Superior, where hostile weather regularly foils outdoor sporting events. In 1991, Northern Michigan University completed the 8,000-seat **Superior Dome** (1401 Presque Isle Ave., 906/227-2850), affectionately known as the "Yooper Dome." Enclosing some five acres, the dome is fashioned from a framework of 781 huge fir beams, strong enough to withstand substantial amounts of snow. Along with hosting a variety of school sporting events and practices, the

Watching freighters arrive at the dock is a thrill.

dome is open to the public for walking and running on weekday mornings. Call or stop by for specific times.

⟨ Presque Isle Park

A thumb of land thrust out into the big lake, Presque Isle Park, about four miles north of downtown, off Lakeshore Boulevard, is a microcosm of the area's beauty: rocky red bluffs, tall pines, and lovely Lake Superior vistas. You can drive through the 323-acre park, but you'd do better to get out and stroll or ski along its many trails. Watch for albino deer (white-tailed deer lacking pigment), which survive in this protected setting. Near the park's entrance, there's a playground, a picnic area, tennis courts, and a marina. The park is the perfect spot to watch huge 800-foot freighters arrive at the towering **railroad ore dock.** Trains carrying taconite pellets (an iron–clay mixture) from one of the nearby open-pit iron mines chug out onto the 70-foot-high elevated track, where they empty their loads into the hold below. Chutes transfer the taconite into

the bellies of the ore freighters, which transport their cargo to the industrial centers in the southern Great Lakes.

DeVos Art Museum

Although it had its beginnings in the 1975 Lee Hall Gallery, the DeVos Art Museum (1401 Presque Isle Ave., 906/227-2235, http://art.nmu.edu/department/museum, 10 a.m.–5 p.m. Mon.–Wed., 10 a.m.–8 p.m., Thurs., 10 a.m.–5 p.m. Fri., 1–4 p.m. Sat.–Sun., free; donations accepted) part of Northern Michigan University's School of Art and Design, got a facelift with its 2005 reopening, complete with a new larger building, made possible by a grant from the DeVos Foundation of Grand Rapids. The museum's permanent collection (which represents work from numerous well-known artists, including Salvador Dalí) is displayed on a rotating basis, while other areas of the museum host temporary exhibits. You'll also enjoy the sculpture walk, where an inviting pathway snakes through one of the university's wooded areas.

© VITO PALMISANO, TRAVEL MICHIGAN

Presque Isle Park takes on a special charm in winter.

Lighthouses

The **Marquette Harbor Lighthouse** is one of Lake Superior's most attractive lighthouses. The light and some of the land surrounding it was recently acquired by the Marquette Maritime Museum under a lease from the Coast Guard. The lease will expire in 2032, so there's plenty of time to make it to the beautiful red light for a tour. As part of the lease agreement, all tours must be escorted by a member of the museum staff. Built in 1866 and expanded in 1906, the Marquette Harbor Lighthouse serves as an interpretive display and an extension of the museum.

To see another, slightly less scenic lighthouse (one which is still active), head to Presque Isle Park for a look at the **Presque Isle Upper Harbor Lighthouse.** The light is still guiding ships into the railroad ore docks nearby. Stannard Rock Lighthouse is a little harder to get to, since it's located in Lake Superior, about 50 miles from Marquette's shoreline. Ask around for charters to the light. Two operators offering cruise are **Uncle Ducky Charters** (434 E. Prospect St., 877/228-5447, www.uncleducky.com) in Marquette or Shelter Bay Charters (E3394 Old M-28, 906/892-8230, www.shelterbay-charterfishing.com) in Au Train. **Granite Island Lighthouse** is also located offshore, but only by six miles. It's a little more than 10 miles northeast of Marquette.

Ishpeming and Negaunee

In many ways, these twin towns 15 miles west of Marquette represent the heart of the iron range. One of the Upper Peninsula's earliest iron mines, the Jackson Mine, opened here in 1847; the nearby Empire and Tilden Mines mark the end of the era, the last operating iron mines in the range.

Ishpeming and Negaunee pretty much faded right along with the glory days of mining. The economy never quite recovered from the closing of the area mines in the 1960s, and the once-vital downtowns were further displaced by the commercial strips along U.S. 41, which passes just north of Ishpeming. But anyone who enjoys history will find these towns intriguing, with their vintage ornate storefronts, ramshackle antique shops, and fenced off "cave in" areas, where the land has succumbed to decades of tunneling.

One of the finest museums in the Upper Peninsula, the state-run **Iron Industry Museum** (73 Forge Rd., Negaunee, 906/475-7857, www.michigan.gov/dnr, consult website for hours, which vary by season, free.) is well worth the short detour off U.S. 41 to its picturesque location along the Carp River. The spot wasn't chosen for its scenery; it marks the site of one of the area's earliest iron forges, built in 1848. This small facility packs a lot of information and well-produced displays into a single exhibit hall. It tells the story of Michigan's $48 billion iron mining and smelting industry, which dwarfed the California Gold Rush ($955 million), Michigan's lucrative logging industry ($4.4 billion), and even Michigan's venerable copper mining empire ($9.6 billion). You'll learn how iron prompted the development of dozens of port towns and the giant 1,000-foot ore freighters that now ply the Great Lakes. The "Technology Timeline" traces the advancements in exploration, working conditions, and mining methods.

Few people think of Ishpeming as the center of the U.S. ski industry, but many of the large resorts in the Rockies can trace America's interest in the sport to Michigan. In 1887 residents of northern Michigan, many of them Scandinavian immigrants, established the Ishpeming Ski Club, one of the oldest continuously operating clubs in the nation. In 1888 they organized the country's first ski jumping competition. Everett Kircher, visionary founder of Michigan's Boyne Mountain resort, invented the first successful snowmaking machine. As a result Ishpeming was chosen as the site of the **U.S. National Ski Hall of Fame and Ski Museum** (610 Palms Ave., 906/485-6323, www.skihall.com, 10 A.M.–5 P.M. Mon.–Sat. year-round, free), the sport's official hall of fame, just like the Football Hall of Fame in Canton, Ohio, and the Baseball Hall of Fame in Cooperstown, New York.

The museum, on U.S. 41 between 2nd and 3rd Streets, covers the sport from *way* back, beginning with a replica of a 4,000-year-old ski and pole found in Sweden. Most interesting are the displays of early ski equipment (including early poles, which "often doubled as weapons"), an examination of the evolution of chairlifts, and an account of the skiing soldiers of the 10th Mountain Division, who played an important role in the mountains of Italy during World War II. The Hall of Fame plaques offer insightful short biographies of those who shaped the sport, from racers to resort owners.

ENTERTAINMENT

If you're looking for Marquette gaming, look no further than the **Ojibwa Casino** (105 Acre Trail, 888/560-9905 or 906/249-4200, www.ojibwacasino.com) in Marquette. Table games include blackjack, roulette, craps, and poker, while more than 300 reel video and video poker machines play from one cent to $5. There are seven sites available at the Ojibwa Casino RV Park and free shuttle service to and from a number of chain hotels in the area. The snack bar serves up all sorts of food right on the casino floor, from soup, pizza, and burgers to shrimp and fish dinners. Be sure to check with the casino for Snack Bar specials.

FESTIVALS AND EVENTS

The **U.P. 200** (www.up200.org) is a sled dog race held in mid-February that begins and ends in Marquette and loops all the way down to Escanaba on the Lake Michigan shore. An estimated 30,000 people watch the annual race, which has quickly grown into one of the U.P.'s most beloved spectator events. The start and finish are the big draws, but the race has prompted a weeklong calendar of activities, from broomball tournaments (hockey with boots instead of skates, balls instead of pucks, and brooms instead of sticks) to fireworks. Serious mushers will be interested to know that the U.P. 200 is an Iditarod qualifying event. For information and upcoming dates, visit www.up200.org, or contact the Marquette

Country Convention and Visitors Bureau (337 W. Washington St., 906/228-7749 or 800/544-4321, www.marquettecountry.org).

Summertime brings the **Hiawatha Traditional Music Festival** during the second to last full weekend each July. Featuring traditional music such as bluegrass, acoustic blues, folk, old time, and more, the Hiawatha is the only festival of its type and size in the U.P. Contact the **Hiawatha Music Co-op** (906/226-8575, www.hiawathamusic.org) for tickets and more information. June brings music of a different type to the Marquette area as part of the **Pine Mountain Music Festival** (906/482-1542, www.pmmf.org), a celebration of opera, symphony, and chamber music that takes place in locations around the Upper Peninsula and runs from mid-June through mid-July.

Head to Presque Isle Park for the annual **Art on the Rocks** (www.artontherocks.org) festival, featuring a juried exhibition and sales. Check out the **International Food Festival,** too. For information and dates for these and other events, contact the Marquette Country Convention and Visitors Bureau (337 W. Washington St., 906/228-7749 or 800/544-4321, www.marquettecountry.org).

SUMMER SPORTS AND RECREATION
Hiking and Biking

As County Road 550 heads north out of Marquette toward Big Bay, you'll travel just six miles before the sign and parking area before **Sugar Loaf Mountain** lures you to pull over. Heed your instincts; for a relatively easy 15-minute hike. A stairway makes for a gradual ascent up the rock, you'll be rewarded with a sweeping view of Lake Superior to the north, the city of Marquette to the east, and the undulating landscape of the wild Huron Mountains stretching all the way to the western horizon.

There's great hiking and mountain biking in the surrounding terrain, much of it part of the **Little Presque Isle State Forest Recreation Area.** Several miles of trails wind around nearby Harlow Lake, up Hogsback Mountain, and along the Lake Superior shore. Parking is

available in the unmarked lot on the west side of County Road 550. It's near an old gravel pit, about a mile north of the Sugar Loaf Mountain lot. The South Marquette Trails are part of the **Noquemanon Trail Network** (906/228-6182, www.noquetrails.org) and provide for miles of hiking and biking. The Mount Marquette Loop is a five-mile trail, while the Carp River and Pioneer loops run for a combined total of nine miles. The Noquemanon Trail Network was ranked among *Bike* magazine's top 10 trails in 2005.

First, however, pick up the free *Marquette Region Hike and Bike Trail Guide* from the Marquette Country Convention and Visitors Bureau (337 W. Washington St., 906/228-7749 or 800/544-4321, www.marquettecountry.org) or local shops.

The entire Ishpeming–Negaunee area is part of the comprehensive **Range Mountain Bike Trail System,** with more than 25 miles of trails stretching from Teal Lake to Lake Sally, south of Suicide Bowl. Routes are detailed in the *Marquette Region Hike and Bike Trail Guide.*

◖ Hiawatha Water Trail

One of Lake Superior's greatest kayaking destinations, the Hiawatha Water Trail (www.hiawathawatertrail.org) passes along the shores of Marquette on the way from Big Bay to Grand Marais, for a total of 120 miles. The most beautiful portion of the trail lies to the east, along Pictured Rocks National Lakeshore between Munising and Grand Marais, but getting there will take some hard paddling. Access points and campgrounds are available along the way; get a copy of the official Hiawatha Water Trail Map at **Down Wind Sports** (514 N. 3rd St., 906/226-7112, www.downwindsports.com).

Presque Isle is one of Marquette's most beautiful destinations, and visitors who only see it from land are missing out. This is *the* ultimate kayak trip. The jagged shoreline, more than two miles of it, is dotted with rugged crags, towering sandstone cliffs, rocks, and an undeveloped shore. Put in and take out at the

Presque Isle Marina. For guided tours, contact **Uncle Ducky Outfitters** (434 E. Prospect St., 906/228-5447 or 877/228-5447, www.paddlingmichigan.com, $75 per person, $50 ages 16 and under). Uncle Ducky also offers guided tours of Marquette harbors, Presque Isle to Little Presque Isle, Huron Island, and Big Bay.

Golf

Marquette holds a few surprises for visitors searching out a round of golf. Try a visit to the new Greywalls course at the **Marquette Golf Club** (1075 Grove St., 866/678-7171, www.marquettegolfclub.com, $130 per guest June 1–Sept. 30, discounted rates spring and fall, fees include cart). Greywalls opened in 2005 to wide acclaim, earning it high marks in *Golf Digest* and other golf magazines. The course's 18 holes are complemented by Marquette's natural terrain, featuring views of Lake Superior, rocky crags, and evergreen forests. Another 18 holes at the Heritage Course make the semiprivate Marquette Golf Club the only 36 hole club in the Upper Peninsula. Of course, golfers will want to try the **Chocolay Golf Club** (125 Chocolay Downs Dr., 906/249-3111, www.chocolaydownsgolfcourse.com, $34 with cart), where the 18-hole public course features the world's longest golf hole, a stunning 1,007-yard par 6.

Beaches

Lake Superior isn't exactly made for swimming; it's cold, the shoreline is often rocky, and the water is too deep in many places. Even if you find a few Lake Superior beaches (and in Marquette you can), not many people actually want to dive in. That said, you're still welcome to go for a dip if you're willing to put up with the goose pimples. And of course, there's more to do at a beach than swim: you can grill, sunbathe, play a game of volleyball, or toss a Frisbee. South Beach, just off Lake Street in Marquette, and McCarty's Cove, on Lakeshore Drive, are two of the city's most popular. Both are equipped with playground equipment and restrooms, and each offer

pleasing views and sandy beaches perfect for an afternoon by the lake.

Off-Road Vehicles

For an off-road trail that's part of the state system, head south toward Gwinn. About five miles west of Gwinn, the Bass Lake Motorcycle Trail is open to vehicles less than 50 inches wide. The long loop, just under 25 miles, circles several lakes, including Bass, Crooked, Spring, and Pike. Take M-35 to Crooked Lake Road and head southwest to a parking area, which is near the Pike Lake and Bass Lake Campgrounds. The Porterfield Lake Motorcycle Trail is on the border of Marquette and Dickinson Counties, where more than 20 miles of trail split into several loops. Porterfield Lake Trail is eight miles southwest of Gwinn. Additionally, ORVs are allowed on all trails and forest roads on state land. Contact the **Department of Natural Resources** (DNR, www.michigan.gov/dnr) for more information.

Waterfalls

Among the most scenic of the Marquette region's waterfalls is Warner Falls, a 20-foot drop into the relatively still waters of the Warner Creek, which seems to be more of a pond at this point. Warner Falls is reasonably accessible. About eight miles west of Marquette, take M-35 south past Palmer and pull off less than a mile past the M<!->35/County Road 565 intersection. The falls are on the right and can easily be seen from the road. The Dead River Falls, just west of Marquette, are beautiful but difficult to find and even harder to get to. Take U.S. 41 west of town to Wright Street and head north. Turn left at Forestville Road and drive to a powerhouse about 2.5 miles up. From there, park and take the gravel road to a clear trail on your left. Follow it down a steep hill, then turn right; stay on the path until you reach the falls. For a map of additional falls in the area and detailed instructions on how to get to them, contact the Marquette Country Convention and Visitors Bureau (337 W. Washington St., 906/228-7749 or 800/544-4321, www.marquettecountry.org).

WINTER SPORTS AND RECREATION
Downhill Skiing

Among skiers and snowboarders, **Marquette Mountain** (4501 County Road 553, 906/225-1155, www.marquettemountain.com, lift rates $17–40) gets their nod for its 600-foot vertical drop, one of the highest in the state. The 23 trails may not be exceptionally long, but they offer good variety, including bumps and tree runs. The half-pipe and terrain park grow and improve every year. Located just three miles south of town on County Road 553, it's popular all week long among local residents and college students. Night skiing is offered Tuesday through Sunday in season, which usually runs from about mid-November to early April. Rental equipment is available.

You'd hardly guess that the 300-acre **Al Quaal Recreation Area** (501 Poplar St., 906/486-8301), on the north shore of Ishpeming's Teal Lake, is a city park. To get there, take Deer Lake Road north from U.S. 41. You can make a winter day of it, with a few downhill runs served by a rope tow, a 1.9 mile cross country loop, an outdoor ice rink, and especially the 1,200-foot iced toboggan run where a small hourly fee includes a rental toboggan. The park is open daily, except for the downhill runs, which are open on weekend afternoons only. Call for specific fees and hours.

Ski and Snowshoe Trails

For Nordic skiing, continue heading south on County Road 553 to the **Blueberry Ridge Ski Trails.** Fifteen miles of groomed and tracked trails loop through the Escanaba River State Forest, including one lighted 1.7-mile circuit (free). Another option is the **Anderson Lake Pathway,** five miles south of Gwinn on County Road 557, with four hilly loops ranging from 2 to 4.3 miles in length. Both networks are open to mountain bikes in summer months.

Nordic skiers looking for a challenge should head for the ominous-sounding **Suicide Bowl** trail network between Ishpeming and Negaunee. Groomed for skating and diagonal stride, it offers more than 18 miles of trails and a map dotted with phrases like "hairpin curve," "bad downhill," and "very difficult trail." The parking area is south of Business M-28 (follow it past downtown Ishpeming) on Cliff Drive. This area is also the site of **Suicide Hill,** a ski jump used in international competitions.

Luge

If ski jumping isn't wild enough for you, you might want to try luge. Just south of Negaunee on M-35, **Lucy Hill** meets International Luge Federation standards as an official luge track, dropping 300 feet with 29 turns. It's open to the public most weekend afternoons, with instruction and equipment available. For information, call 765/586-5733.

Dogsledding

If you arrive in winter, try your hand at mushing. **Triple Creek Sled Dog Kennels** (E5372 M-94, 877/275-7533, www.upperpeninsulaonline.com) offers trips ranging from two hours to five days, powered by a team of eager huskies. Owner Bob Johnson was instrumental in bringing dogsled racing to the Upper Peninsula and is one of the most experienced mushers around. Package tours include a stay at Johnson's Buck Sporting Lodge, a solar-powered wilderness lodge north of Rapid River.

Snowmobiling

Marquette County has more land than any other county in Michigan, which means it has a lot of snowmobile trails, too. The main trail in and out of Marquette is Trail 8, pressing west toward Baraga along U.S. 41/M-28 and south to Gwinn. To get to Au Train or Munising, take Trail 417, which more or less follows M-28 east before dipping south a bit and rejoining with Trail 8. If you're heading up to Big Bay, take Trail 310 out of town. For a detailed snowmobile trail map, contact the **Marquette Country Convention and Visitors Bureau** (337 W. Washington St., 906/228-7749 or 800/544-4321, www.marquettecountry.org). Additionally, snowmobiles are allowed to travel with the flow of traffic on the right-hand side of all plowed roads in Marquette County—provided that they stay single-file and travel at a reasonable speed. For everyone's mutual safety, be careful, stop at intersections, and pay attention to all traffic. All snowmobiles are required to be registered and have a state trail permit, available through the DNR (www.michigan.gov/dnr) and at snowmobile shops throughout the state.

ACCOMMODATIONS

The best spot in Marquette is easily the € **Landmark Inn** (230 N. Front St., 888/752-6362, www.thelandmarkinn.com, $100–200). Built in the 1930s as the Northland Hotel, it hosted such luminaries as Amelia Earhart and Abbott and Costello. After falling into disrepair and eventually closing in the 1980s, it has been beautifully restored and reopened as the Landmark. For not much more than you'd pay for a basic chain motel room, you get a taste of history, a touch of elegance, and a primo location, with Lake Superior on one side and downtown Marquette on the other.

South of Marquette, check into € **Blueberry Ridge Bed and Breakfast** (18 Oakridge Dr., 906/249-9246, http://blueberryridgebedandbreakfast.com, $79–119) for a quiet stay in the north woods. Many of the major hotel and motel franchises are represented in Marquette, especially along the U.S. 41/M-28 strip.

Camping

You can't pitch a tent at the **Little Presque Isle State Forest and Campgrounds** (906/228-6561, www.michigan.gov/dnr, $65), but the rustic cabins—no electricity, no running water, no roads all the way in—make for great camping and they're available year-round. A half-mile hike from the parking area will get you to your cabin, and once you're there, it's all hand-pumped water, wood-burning stoves, and those "toilets" that you see at the state's

roadside parks. There are 18 miles of hiking trails here, along with miles of Lake Superior beach, fishing, and other recreational opportunities. Cabins sleep up to six people, and reservations are required.

More traditional camping (either in a tent or at an RV site) can be had at **Marquette Tourist Park** (2145 Sugarloaf Rd., 906/228-0465, www.mqtcty.org/parks.html). The 40-acre in-town park has 10 rustic or tent-only campsites and 15 sites with full hookups. The rest of the more than 100 sites are electric only. You'll find fire rings, picnic tables, bathrooms, and hot showers, as well as a ball field and a playground. There are another 100 or so campsites at **Gitchee Gumee RV Park** (2048 M-28 East, 866/447-8727, www.gg-rv. com), which also features such amenities as more than 70 cable channels, a movie theater, and a fudge factory.

There are four state forest campgrounds in nearby Gwinn: Anderson Lake West (19 sites), Bass Lake (22 sites), North Horseshoe Lake (11 sites), and Pike Lake (10 sites), each accommodating tents and a few small trailers. There are no reservations and a few rustic amenities, including vault toilets and drinking water from a hand pump. For more information, contact the Michigan DNR's Gwinn Field Office (410 West M-35, 906/346-9201, www.michigan. gov/dnr).

FOOD

For a city its size, Marquette has a very good selection of high-quality, locally owned restaurants. The (**Vierling Saloon** (119 S. Front St., 906/228-3533, http://thevierling.com, closed Sun.) stands out for its consistently good food, century old decor, and interesting views of Marquette Harbor ore docks. Ask for a table near the large windows in back. The menu offers lot of variety, including vegetarian and Italian dishes and whitefish served five ways. Excellent breakfasts, soups, and sandwiches are available, too. Dinner entrées start at $15. A few years ago, the owners added a microbrewery downstairs, featuring British-style ales and stouts.

One of Marquette's newer dining additions is (**Upfront and Company** (102 E. Main St., 906/228-5200, www.upfrontandcompany. com). Renovated with wood from the city's old ore dock, it's not only beautiful to look at, it features great wood-fired pizza. Live music every Tuesday through Saturday is turning Upfront into Marquette's most popular nightspot, too. For organic, natural food dishes, you can't do better than the **Sweet Water Cafe** (517 N. 3rd St., 906/226-7009, www.marquettedining.addr.com/Sweet_Water.html, breakfast and lunch daily, dinner Wed.–Sat.). Locals give its tofu scramble and pancakes with whipped maple butter extra-high marks. There are good smoothies, too. Most menu items can be prepared gluten free. Locals will also point you to the no-frills **Border Grill** (180 S. McClellan Ave., 906/228-5228, www.bordergrill.net) for yummy Tex-Mex with fresh salsa.

INFORMATION AND SERVICES

You'll be able to get tourism information from the friendly folks at the **Marquette Country Convention and Visitors Bureau** (337 W. Washington St., 906/228-7749 or 800/544-4321, www.marquettecountry.org).

In an emergency, dial 911. For local medical attention, you'll want to go to **Marquette General Hospital** (580 W. College Ave., 906/228-9440, www.mgh.org), a high-quality hospital, emergency room, and trauma care center located in the neighborhood of Northern Michigan University.

Marquette has plentiful banks and ATMs, too, so you won't have to go too far for easy access to your accounts. Try the various **Wells Fargo** locations (101 W. Washington, 1300 N. 3rd St., 1401 Presque Isle, and 25 Learning Resource Center on the Northern Michigan University campus). Bank by phone at 800/869-3557, www.wellsfargo.com), **River Valley State Bank** (1140 W. Washington St., 906/226-0300, www.rivervalleybank.com), or **Northern Michigan Bank and Trust** (1502 West Washington St., 906/228-7300, www. nmbank.com).

Please note: Marquette and its surrounding areas are in the Eastern Time Zone.

GETTING THERE AND AROUND

Car

Getting to Marquette by car is especially easy: just remember U.S. 41. If you're coming in from the south near Escanaba, take U.S. 41. From the west, take U.S. 41. From the east, you'll want to take either M-28 or U.S. 2 before hooking up with U.S. 41. There are a few smaller roads coming in, of course, M-553 is one of them, but it's best to take the highways. U.S. 41 also runs through Ishpeming and Negaunee just to the west of Marquette. The three cities are beginning to blend into one long stretch of shops and services.

Air

If you're flying into town, **Sawyer International Airport** (MQT, 125 G Ave., Gwinn, 906/346-3308, www.sawyerairport. com), offers regularly scheduled flights to and from Detroit and Chicago. Service is offered by Mesaba Airlines (906/346-6471, www.mesaba. com), which operates as an affiliate of Delta Airlines, and American Eagle (800/433-7300, www.aa.com), an affiliate of American Airlines. You'll likely want to rent a car, and Sawyer offers a bevy of rental services: **Alamo** (800/462-5266, www.alamo.com), **Avis** (800/831-2847, www.avis.com), **Budget** (800/527-7000, www.budget.com), **Dollar** (800/800-3665, www.dollar.com), **National** (800/227-7368, www.nationalcar.com), or **Thrifty** (800/847-4389, www.thrifty.com). Bus service is provided into Marquette (or Gwinn, if you prefer) by **Marq-Tran** (906/225-1112, www.marq-tran.com).

Boat

Marquette has two marinas: the Cinder Pond Marina and Presque Isle Marina. **Cinder Pond Marina** (906/228-0469, www.michigan.gov/dnr) is located near Marquette's distinctive ore dock. There are 91 seasonal slips and 10 transient slips, as well as full amenities like electricity, showers, pump-out, gasoline, and day-use dockage. Cinder Pond Marina is open from early May through late October, can be reached on radio channel 71, and is located at 46° 31.56 N, 87° 22.26 W. The Ellwood Matson Lower Harbor Park stretches out to the west, a 22-acre open space with park benches, picnic tables, and a playground. The **Presque Isle Marina** (906/228-0464, www.michigan.gov/dnr) has 87 seasonal and 10 transient slips and is located at Presque Isle Park. Like Cinder Pond Marina, there are plenty of amenities here. The marina is located at 46° 34.20 N, 87° 22.25 W. It's open from early May through late October and can be reached on channel 9.

Public Transportation

Bus service to Marquette is available through **Indian Trails** (989/725-5105 or 800/292-3831, www.indiantrails.com), on a route that stretches from Chicago to Calumet, passing through Marquette (and Escanaba, Houghton, and Hancock) along the way. Contact Indian Trails for current schedules and rates.

The same public bus that shuttles visitors from Sawyer International Airport to Marquette scoots around the area with regular daily stops at a number of communities: Marquette, Negaunee, Ishpeming, and Gwinn. **Marq-Tran** (906/225-1112, www.marq-tran.com) also offers door-to-door service for a small fee that increases with distance (though it won't jump over $5.60). Contact Marq-Tran for regular schedules and fees. For taxi service, call **Taxi Tycoon** (906/249-4428) or Checker Cab (906/226-7777).

Huron Mountains

Ask 10 people where the Huron Mountains begin and end, and you're likely to get 10 different answers. But everyone will agree that they fall within the vague boundaries of Lake Superior to the north and east and U.S. 41 to the south and west. That's a swath of land of over 1000 square miles, where the terrain rises into rugged hills and, yes, even mountains. Mt. Arvon, about 15 miles due east of L'Anse,

tops out at 1,979 feet, the highest point in the state.

Look at a map, and you'll see it's an intriguing parcel of real estate, virtually devoid of towns and roads. What the Huron Mountains do have, however, is washboard peaks and valleys, white pine forests, hundreds of lakes, the headwaters of a half dozen classic wilderness rivers, dazzling waterfalls, far more wildlife

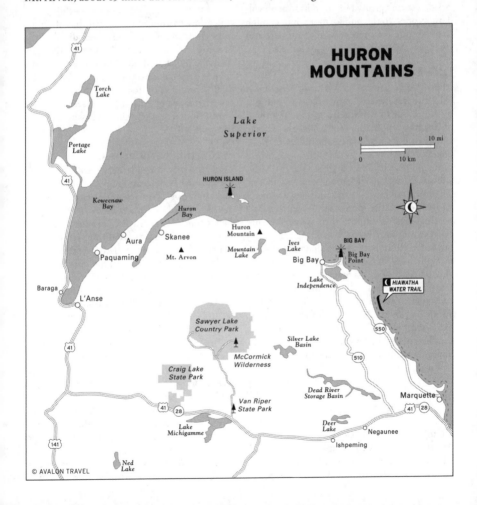

than people, and utter silence. Even by U.P. standards, it's a rugged yet remarkable place. Within its boundaries lie towering virgin pines, blue ribbon trout streams, pristine lakes, and waterfalls that don't even appear on maps. If the Huron Mountain Club should ever come up for sale, government officials would no doubt clamor to turn to it into a state or national park.

In the meantime, the rest of us have to be content simply knowing that such wonderful natural beauty is there, and lovingly protected. Besides, there's plenty of Huron Mountain wilderness open to the public, more than enough to go around for those who are fortunate and smart enough to explore this special place.

BIG BAY AREA

Many people approach the Huron Mountains from the east, where County Road 550 climbs 30 miles out of Marquette to the tiny town of **Big Bay,** population 260. Sited above Lake Independence and within minutes of Lake Superior, Big Bay is a humble little place, where residents take pride in their simple life sandwiched between wilderness and inland sea. The town has swung from prosperity to near-ghost-town status more than once, first as a bustling logging outpost, then as one of Henry Ford's company towns, humming with busy sawmills. More recently residents joke about how the local bank, well aware of the town's volatile economy, was loath to loan money to Big Bay businesses. This staunchly conservative nature proved to be the bank's undoing. While the town's 20 businesses were thriving, the bank closed down. Folks now frequent Big Bay for its Huron Mountains access, Lake Superior harbor, Lake Independence fishing, and unique lodgings.

From Big Bay, your best bets for venturing into the backcountry are County Road 510, which branches off County Road 550 on the southeast edge of town and continues south all the way to U.S. 41 west of Marquette. Another option is the Triple A Truck Trail, which branches off of County Road 510. Both are usually well-maintained dirt/gravel roads,

though wet or snowy weather can quickly render them impassable. Dozens of old logging roads and single tracks branch off of these main routes. To find your way around, you'll either want a topographical or very good local map (sometimes called the "waterfall map") available free from the Marquette Country Convention and Visitors Bureau.

SIGHTS
Craig Lake State Park

Craig Lake is probably unlike any state park you've ever visited. The entrance is nearly seven miles down a rugged truck trail that often requires four wheel drive and is periodically "improved" with sharp old mining rock that can inflict lethal wounds on tires. Once you arrive at the Craig Lake parking area, you access the 7,000-acre park on foot or, with a short portage, by canoe or kayak. No wheeled vehicles or boat motors are permitted anywhere within the park.

McCormick Wilderness

Once the private wilderness retreat of Cyrus McCormick, whose father invented the reaping machine, this 27-square-mile tract of wilderness was willed to the U.S. Forest Service by the McCormick family in 1967. Today it remains in pristine wilderness condition: remote, undeveloped, and largely unused. In other words, perfect for backcountry hiking and camping. No trace camping is permitted throughout the wilderness area. For more information, contact the **Ottawa National Forest Ranger District** (4810 E. M-28, Kenton, 906/852-3500, www. fs.fed.us).

To access the McCormick Tract, follow U.S. 41/M-28 west from Marquette about 50 miles to Champion. Just after you cross the Peshekee River, follow the first paved road north. This is County Road 607, also called the Peshekee Grade or the Huron Bay Grade. In about 10 miles, you'll see a sign for Arfelin Lake; take the next road to your right and watch for a sign and a small parking area.

Once you've arrived, you'll be pretty much on your own to explore this rugged terrain of

high hills, rivers, muskeg, and bedrock outcroppings. Don't expect marked and maintained hiking trails. This tract is wild, so with the exception of a well-worn path to White Deer Lake (where the McCormicks' lodge once stood), you'll mostly be traveling cross-country. A compass and topographical map are absolute necessities. Wildlife sightings can be excellent as the state's largest moose herd roams here, which in turn has attracted predators like the elusive gray wolf. You're not likely to see a wolf, but you may be treated to one's hollow wail at your camp some evening.

Moose

Van Riper State Park is perhaps best known for its Moose Information Center, a kiosk that tells the story of the U.P.'s successful **moose reintroduction program.** Though moose were once common in the U.P., hunting and disease devastated the herd in past decades. Two "moose lifts" in the 1980s transported 59 of the giant mammals from Algonquin Provincial Park in Ontario to the lightly traveled wilderness along the Peshekee Grade near the McCormick Tract. It was quite a project: Wildlife biologists captured each moose, then airlifted them one by one in a sling, dangling beneath a helicopter, to a base camp where they were trucked 600 miles to the Huron Mountains.

Today, the region's moose population has climbed to 200 or 300. You may see them anywhere in this region, but your chances are best at dawn or dusk and in wet, swampy areas. The Marquette Country Convention and Visitors Bureau publishes a *Moose Locator Guide,* detailing six back road tours through areas frequented by moose, including the Peshekee Grade and Wolf Lake Road, east of Champion. For more information, contact **Van Riper State Park** (906/339-4461, www.michigan.gov/dnr).

Mt. Arvon

It's a tough drive to get to Michigan's highest peak, about 12 miles east of L'Anse, and the trip can be disappointing if you're not especially interested in these types of things. It's hard to see the mountain from a distance; and once at the top you won't be rewarded with anything approaching a dramatic view. This is due to the forest at the peak—it's both tall and dense. The only way for a visitor to know she's reached the top is the presence of a small blue sign stating, "You have reached Michigan's Highest Point." The roads are also in rough condition, which makes the 27-mile journey too burdensome for the casual tourist. For a map and directions, contact the Baraga County Convention and Visitors Bureau (755 E. Broad St., L'Anse, 906/524-7444 or 800/743-4908, www.baragacountytourism.org).

Lighthouses

The **Big Bay Point Lighthouse** ranks as an above average light. Located on a cliff at Big Bay Point, the two-story brick building and attached 60-foot-high light have been converted into a charming bed-and-breakfast.

The 1868 **Huron Island Lighthouse,** located northwest of Big Bay and some three miles off the shore, is only accessible by private boat. The island, which is part of the Huron National Wildlife Refuge, is open to the public during the day. You can charter a sightseeing trip to the Huron Islands at Marquette's **Uncle Ducky Charters** (434 E. Prospect St., 877/228-5447, www.uncleducky.com).

SUMMER SPORTS AND RECREATION
Hiking and Biking

Though it's situated right on busy U.S. 41, **Van Riper State Park** is worthy of mention for several reasons. For one, it offers a good, rarely full modern campground on the eastern shore of Lake Michigamme, where you'll find a boat launch, good walleye fishing, and a fine swimming beach with unusually warm water and a sandy bottom. Two, many campers overlook the park property on the north side of the road, its largest and most appealing acreage. It includes a rustic campground on the Peshekee River and four miles of hiking trails. Climb the Overlook Trail, a loop that ascends

a rocky outcrop, for a great view of the rolling forest land and Lake Michigamme. In addition, Van Riper is less than a dozen miles from the gated entrance of the McCormick Tract, so you can take advantage of modern comforts while spending your days in the rugged backcountry that begins just across the highway.

Visitors that make their way into **Craig Lake State Park** will be rewarded with the seclusion and backcountry hiking of Michigan's most remote state park. If you're going to make the journey into the park, you should take a vehicle with a high ground clearance for the seven-mile trek off paved roads, especially after a rainfall when it would be best to have four-wheel drive as well. The park has nearly 7,000 acres and two main trails that total more than 15 miles, half of which is part of the North Country Trail. Trails are rugged and often steep, and are frequently blocked by streams or other obstacles. There are six full lakes, several smaller ponds, and plenty of wildlife, including black bears, moose, and the more common deer. Adequate backcountry practices should be followed; make sure you go in well prepared. Craig Lake State Park is located just north of U.S. 41/M-28 a few miles west of Michigamme. For more information, including backcountry preparation tips, maps, and directions, contact the Michigan DNR (906/339-4461, www.michigan.gov/dnr).

In the town of Big Bay itself, take the Big Bay Pathway, part of the Noquemanon Trail Network. Only one of the loops is for hiking and biking, the four mile relatively flat Hidden Grin Loop. The other three loops, totaling nearly six miles, are more appropriate for cross country skiing in the winter. Take County Road 550 into Big Bay, then turn left on Dump Road and take it less than a mile to the trailhead, which will be on your right.

The Commercial Forest Reserve Act gives property owners a tax break in exchange for allowing others access to their property, so trespassing isn't an issue as you explore the Huron Mountains. In fact, you have nearly limitless possibilities for hiking and mountain biking on old logging roads and various foot trails. Two spots worth exploring are **Gobbler's Knob,** a rock outcrop off County Road 510 that overlooks Lake Independence and Lake Superior and the **Elliott Donnelley Wilderness Area**, off County Road 550, where a four-mile trail winds along the Little Garlic River and past Little Garlic Falls.

Keep in mind that the Huron Mountains can be a confusing place. It can be very frustrating heading down one dead-end logging road after another, or worse, get hopelessly lost on one of hundreds of unmapped, unmarked trails. Before you head off into the woods, make sure you're equipped with a map, compass, and perhaps a handheld GPS unit, and that you're proficient in their use. Otherwise, it's best to hook up with a local guide who can show you around on foot, mountain bike, or snowshoe.

Canoeing and Kayaking

In addition to its backcountry hiking trails, much of **Craig Lake State Park** is accessible by nonmotorized watercraft. There's a quarter mile portage from the parking lot to one of several boat landings on the lakes, though Crooked Lake is perhaps the most appealing, with lots of interesting bays and inlets. To reach it, paddle across the southeastern corner of Craig Lake and follow the half-mile portage east. Be aware that many of the lakes are large enough to cause problems during windy or stormy weather. You'll need a state park pass and a vehicle suitable for rough, unpaved roads. Contact the Michigan DNR (906/339-4461, www.michigan.gov/dnr) for more information.

Other large lakes in the area are suitable for canoeing or kayaking. Check out Lake Independence in Big Bay (try taking the Iron River from the lake to Lake Superior). Closer to Marquette, the Dead River Storage Basin offers some nice paddling opportunities on the long, narrow surface. There are plenty of smaller lakes scattered throughout the Huron Mountains. Ask an outfitter for more information and advice. If you're looking for a

good river, put in the Yellow Dog River at County Road 510 and take out five miles downriver at County Road 550 for an easy-to-middling white-water trip (the section is rated Class II–V).

Of course, experienced kayakers will want to spend some time paddling along the Lake Superior shoreline. Big Bay is the westernmost end of the **Hiawatha Water Trail** (www.hiawathawatertrail.org), more than 120 miles of Lake Superior shoreline that take paddlers all the way to Grand Marais to the east. There are at least 20 public access points and 23 water-accessible campsites along the way. Trail maps for the Hiawatha Water Trail are available for a fee at **Big Bay Outfitters and Anatomy of a Canoe** (308 Bensinger St., 906/345-9399 or 906/250-2457 in winter, www.bigbayoutfitters.com). Big Bay and the shoreline between L'Anse and Marquette aren't as spectacular as Pictured Rocks to the east, but like most of the Great Lakes shoreline, you'd be hard pressed to find a stretch that doesn't make a good place to get your paddle wet. Pay particular attention to the shore on either side of Big Bay Point, and be sure to check the weather reports, as Lake Superior has the tendency to get nasty fast.

Fishing

Big Bay's Lake Independence has the reputation of being a good fishing hole. Anglers can visit the lake for walleye, yellow perch, and smallmouth bass; put in at the boat launch at Perkins Park Campground, just off Big Bay Road/County Road 550. For a more remote, secluded experience, head to Craig Lake, located a little north of U.S. 41/M-28 and a few miles west of Michigamme, where you'll find northern pike, smallmouth bass, and muskie.

As far as rivers go, you'll find them virtually everywhere. There are plenty of suitable rivers and streams in the area, but you'll want to give the Yellow Dog River a shot for some decent trout. Head to the Little Garlic River, about 10 miles northwest of Marquette on Big Bay Road/County Road 550, for steelhead.

Charters on Lake Superior, as well as inland lakes and rivers, can be arranged through a number of area companies, most of them in Marquette. **Uncle Ducky Charters** (434 E. Prospect St., 877/228-5447, www.uncleducky.com) is one of the best all-around charters, while **Rivers North Guide Service** (906/458-8125, www.riversnorth.net) specializes in fly-fishing.

Beaches

Perkins Park Campground on the west side of Lake Independence has a nice, family friendly beach—and the water will be more comfortable than chilly Lake Superior, too. Lake Michigamme, just off U.S. 41, has a pleasant swimming beach along the half-mile frontage of Van Riper State Park. If it's late enough in the season and you don't mind Superior's bite, there's a small beach by the Big Bay Harbor of Refuge.

Off-Road Vehicles

For such a wide expanse of undeveloped land, there are disappointingly few trails marked for off-road vehicles. In fact, one of the only DNR trails for ATVs near the Huron Mountains is the Champion Trail, which ribbons south from Champion on U.S. 41/M-28 to Republic, a seven- or eight-mile ride.

Waterfalls

The waterfall map, which you can get from the Marquette Country Convention and Visitors Bureau (337 W. Washington St., 906/228-7749 or 800/544-4321, www.marquettecountry.org) will indeed point you toward many of the region's wealth of falls. Some of the finest and most accessible include **Little Garlic Falls, Hills Falls,** and **Big Pup Falls.** The latter two are part of the Yellow Dog River, a beautiful river that splashes and tumbles over cliffs and through canyons from the Yellow Dog Plains north to Lake Independence. Pack a fly rod if you enjoy casting for trout; fishing can be great here. As you might have expected, Little Garlic Falls is located on the Little Garlic River, 11 miles northwest of Marquette. Check the waterfall map for more detailed directions.

WINTER SPORTS AND RECREATION
Ski and Snowshoe Trails

The same loops on the Big Bay Pathway that are less suitable for summertime hiking are great for Nordic skiing once the snow is on the ground. Meditation Loop is two miles long and suitable for beginners, while the Hidden Grin Loop, at four miles, is a longer, intermediate loop. The two other paths are more difficult: the three mile Bear Mountain Loop and its mile long Ridgeline Extension Loop.

The Saux Head Trails, which, like Big Bay Pathway, are part of the Noquemanon Trail Network, have about 7.5 miles of two way groomed trails. The loops range from intermediate to advanced. Saux Head Trails are about 11 miles southeast of Big Bay on County Road 550. Take County Road 550 from Marquette, turn right on Saux Head Lake Road, then turn left about a mile later. Parking areas will be on your left. You'll need a trail pass from the **Noquemanon Trail Network** (906/235-6861, www.noquetrails.org) to ski or snowshoe here.

Snowmobiling

Trail 310 winds some 54 miles from Marquette west and north to Big Bay. From the other direction, Trail 14 connects L'Anse and Big Bay over a distance of 56 miles. The two trails merge south of Big Bay via Alternate Trail 310, otherwise they meet up in Big Bay. The Clowry–Big Bay trail (Trail 5) heads north into the Huron Mountains from Clowry, near Champion on U.S. 41/M-23 and joins Trail 14.

Snowmobiles can be ridden on the plowed surface of any of Marquette County's roads, provided you stay on the right-hand side, moving with the flow of traffic and at a reasonable speed. When operating a snowmobile on a public road, be especially careful, stop at all intersections, and watch for traffic. Stay off state highways, and double-check the laws for riding on paved roads within individual towns and cities.

ACCOMMODATIONS

There's a surprisingly good and varied choice of lodgings in tiny Big Bay. Probably the best known is the ❰ **Big Bay Point Lighthouse Bed and Breakfast** (3 Lighthouse Rd., 906/345-9957, www.bigbaylighthouse.com, $150–220). Being a lighthouse, it naturally occupies a dramatic position on a rocky point just a few miles from the town of Big Bay. The red brick lighthouse keeper's home, attached to the 1896 light, has been restored and retrofitted with seven very comfortable guest rooms, all with private baths. Five have Lake Superior views. The inn has extensive grounds, more than 43 acres and a half mile of shoreline, set far back from busy roads and hustle and bustle. Guests are welcome to use the sauna, climb the light tower, or relax in the living room, where owners Linda and Jeff Gamble have collected a storehouse full of lighthouse lore and history. Spa services are also available (details on website). Reserve well in advance.

There are two choices with good locations in Big Bay and rates on the lower end. The **Big Bay Depot** (906/345-9350, 301 Depot Rd. Big Bay, www.exploringthenorth.com/depot/lodge.html, $75–150) occupies an old train depot overlooking Lake Independence. The five refurbished suites include full kitchens, two double beds, and lake views. Pets are welcome. The mom-and-pop **Picture Bay Motel** (348 Country Rd. 550, Big Bay, 906/345-9820, $60–80) is neat as a pin. Two units have basic cooking facilities. Pets are welcome for an additional $5 per night.

A number of houses, cabins, and cottages on Lake Independence are available for rent by the week or day (usually with a minimum stay of at least two nights). Try Henry's Cabin ($65), Mark's Place ($95), or the Dickerson House ($165). Make arrangements with Clarence and Yvonne Stortz at **Alder Bay Lodging** (906/345-9914, www.alderbaylodging.com).

Camping

Backcountry campers will find nearly unlimited options in the **Huron Mountains** and **McCormick Wilderness.** Respect private property rights, observe backcountry camping

principles, and travel with a map, compass, GPS, and other essentials. If you're not experienced in the backcountry, it might be wise to plan your first trip with the company of a local guide like **Huron Mountain Outfitters** (906/345-9265).

Straddling the highway, **Van Riper State Park** (851 County Road AKE, 906/339-4461, www.michigan.gov/dnr) offers easily accessible modern and rustic campsites, although within earshot of U.S. 41. The park also rents out three rustic cabins, two near the modern campground ($60) and one north of the highway on the Peshekee River ($80). Reserve well in advance.

At 7,000-acre **Craig Lake State Park**, you essentially get an organized campsite tucked in the backcountry wilderness. A rough seven-mile drive and a one or two mile hike will bring you to many lovely, and often empty campsites. Choose from sites that sit on beds of pine needles above the east shore of Craig Lake, or follow the portage trail east to sites on a small peninsula sticking out into Crooked Lake. No reservations are needed; pay the $6 nightly fee at the parking area. Reservations (six months in advance is ideal) are necessary for the rustic cabins on the northwestern shore of Craig Lake. Originally built by Frederick Miller of Miller Brewing fame, these bare-bones cabins offer bunks for your sleeping bag, some utilitarian furniture, and protection from the bugs and cold. The larger of the two boasts a huge gathering room with a stone fireplace and sleeps 14 ($80). The other sleeps six ($60). Both have a water pump, firewood, and a rowboat. For maps and information, contact Craig Lake State Park.

FOOD

When Thunder Bay Inn closed its doors in early 2008—citing the declining economy—the community lost more than the iconic hotel where *Anatomy of a Murder* was filmed in the late 1950s; it lost a business that was a true cornerstone of the community. Today, the meager selection of restaurants is a reflection on the poor economy in the Big Bay area.

Lunch and breakfast are served at **Hungry Hollow Café** (County Road 550, 906/345-0075, www.cramsgeneralstore.com/hungry-hollow.html, 7 A.M.–2 P.M. Mon.–Thurs., until 4 P.M. Fri. and Sat., 8 A.M.–4 P.M. Sun.), part of Cram's General Store. Try the homemade pasties and soups. For dinner, you can go to the **Lumberjack Tavern** (202 Bensinger St., 906/345-9912), where you'll find earnest, friendly people, great service, and good food. But people come for the history, not the menu. In 1952 Mike Chenowith was murdered here, and provided the inspiration for Judge John Voelker's bestselling novel *Anatomy of a Murder*, which was later made into the iconic motion picture of the same name.

INFORMATION AND SERVICES

For information about Big Bay and the Huron Mountains, contact the **Marquette Country Convention and Visitors Bureau** (337 W. Washington St., 906/228-7749 or 800/544-4321, www.marquettecountry.org). They'll have plenty of advice, trail maps for hiking and cross-country skiing, and other information.

See **Big Bay Outfitters and Anatomy of a Canoe** (pardon the play on words) (308 Bensinger St., 906/345-9399 or 906/250-2457 in winter, www.bigbayoutfitters.com) for tour and guide services (waterfall, mountain biking, walking, and kayak or canoeing), rentals, and outdoor retail needs.

Although there are no hospitals in Big Bay, there are two located within 30 miles of the city. **Marquette General Hospital** (580 West College Ave., 906/228-9440, www.mgh.org) has a hospital, emergency room, and trauma care center located in Marquette, or you can go to Ishpeming's **Bell Memorial Hospital** (101 South 4th St., 906/486-4431, www.bellmemorial.org), just north of M-28. A third hospital can be found farther away in L'Anse. To get to the **Baraga County Memorial Hospital** (770 N. Main St., 906/524-3300, www.bcmh.org), take Broad Street from U.S. 41 to Main Street and turn right to the hospital.

Likewise, you'll want to do your banking

in the bigger cities outside of Big Bay and the Huron Mountains.

GETTING THERE AND AROUND
Car
The Huron Mountains aren't quite as easily accessible as many of the U.P.'s other areas. In fact, there are only two real roads in. The best of these is Big Bay Road/County Road 550, which heads directly northwest from Marquette towards Big Bay, while County Road 510 is an alternate and slightly more meandering route. If you're planning on getting off the main road, be warned that some of these smaller byways are little more than old logging roads. You'll want to have a vehicle with four-wheel drive or, at the very least, high clearance.

Air
The closest airport is **Sawyer International Airport** (MQT, 125 G Ave., Gwinn, 906/346-3308, www.sawyerairport.com), west of Marquette on U.S. 41/M-28. There

are regular flights to and from Chicago and Detroit via Mesaba Airlines (906/346-6471, www.mesaba.com), which operates as an affiliate of Delta Airlines, and American Eagle (800/433-7300, www.aa.com), an affiliate of American Airlines. You won't have trouble renting a car at the airport (Alamo, Avis, Budget, Dollar, National, and Thrifty are all here), and you can get a bus into Marquette from **Marq-Tran** (906/225-1112, www.marq-tran.com), though you'll have trouble getting to Big Bay from there without your own vehicle.

Boat
If you're boating to Big Bay, you can put in at the **Big Bay Harbor of Refuge** (906/345-9353, www.michigan.gov/dnr). With only six transient and four seasonal slips space is limited, especially for day-use dockage. The Big Bay Harbor has the usual amenities: water, electricity, and gas, as well as bathrooms, showers, and a picnic area. The harbor location is 46° 49.45 N, 87° 43.27 W.

Munising and Grand Island

When it comes to enticing visitors, nature dealt Munising a royal flush. The town of 2,700 curves around the belly of protected Munising Bay. The Grand Island National Recreation Area beckons just offshore. Pictured Rocks National Lakeshore begins at the edge of town and stretches for over 40 miles. The Hiawatha National Forest encompasses the forests to the south and west. If you're looking for outdoor activities, Munising's got all the right cards.

M-28 leads you right to the heart of town, where you'll find most restaurants, mom-and-pop motels, and the ferry dock for cruises to Pictured Rocks.

SIGHTS
◖ Grand Island
Though it's just a 10-minute ferry ride from

Munising, the surrounding Lake Superior waters effectively isolate Grand Island. Owned since 1901 by the Cleveland Cliffs Iron Company, the 13,000-acre, largely wooded island was maintained for decades as a private hunting playground for the firm's executives and stockholders. In 1989, Hiawatha National Forest purchased all but 40 acres of Grand Island and proclaimed it a national recreation area. Except for those few patches of private property, you have the entire island, which is roughly the size of Manhattan, for hiking, beach combing, mountain biking, and camping.

Don't miss the **historic cemetery** near Murray Bay, where you can absorb a little history. You can examine the gravestones of shipwreck victims and the island's first nonnative settlers. Grand Island had long been

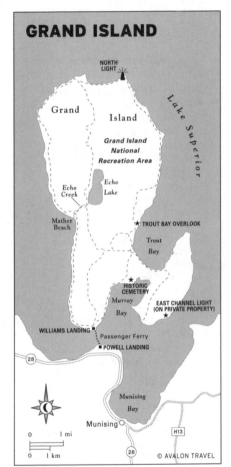

allowed from October 1 to April 15; mountain bikes are permitted anytime on all public-land trails. Dogs are allowed if leashed. Drinking water is not available on the island. The $2 daily user fee is collected by the ferry service. For more information, contact the Hiawatha National Forest, Munising Ranger District (400 E. Munising Ave., 906/387-3700, www. fs.fed.us).

Altran Bus Service offers two to three hour van tours of Grand Island, from June through early October. The tour makes six stops on the southern end of the island, including Echo Lake, the Trout Bay Overlook, and Mather Beach, an excellent swimming beach where Echo Creek empties into Lake Superior. Unless you have limited mobility, however, outdoorsy types likely will grow frustrated with the amount of time spent inside a vehicle. Tours cost $20 for adults, $10 for children, including the ferry fee (but not the $2 recreation-area user fee). For schedule information, contact **Altran Bus Service** (906/387-4845).

◀ Hiawatha National Forest

A huge swath of the massive 860,000-acre Hiawatha National Forest sprawls out to the south of Munising, stretching all the way to Lake Michigan. It offers almost endless opportunities for hiking, mountain biking, and camping. Your best bet for gathering information is the **Hiawatha National Forest Visitors Center** (400 E. Munising Ave., 906/387-3700), which shares a building and staff with the Pictured Rocks National Lakeshore.

Alger County Heritage Center

In Munising, a short way east of downtown on Washington Street, the Alger County Heritage Center (1496 Washington St., 906/387-4308, www.hsmichigan.org, 10 A.M.–9 P.M. Mon.–Fri. and 10 A.M.–2 P.M. Sat. May–Sept., free, donations accepted) keeps a fine collection of local historic artifacts that document the region's past. Visitors can peek at personal objects, Grand Island artifacts (there's even a log cabin from John Jacob Astor's American Fur Company), and Munising Woodenware.

a summering ground for the Ojibwa when Abraham Williams arrived in the 1840s to establish a trading post. He raised a family, and died on the island in 1873 at the then amazing age of 81. Today only the descendants of Williams and their spouses can be buried here.

Autos are not allowed on the island except with special permission or those few owned by island landholders. Van tours now operate under special permit, bumping along a few dirt roads on the island's southern half. ATVs are

HIAWATHA

There he sang of Hiawatha,
Sang the Song of Hiawatha,
Sang his wondrous birth and being,
How he prayed and how he fasted,
How he lived, and toiled, and suffered,
That the tribes of men might prosper,
That he might advance his people!

Henry Wadsworth Longfellow,
"The Song of Hiawatha"

Little is known about the historical figure of Hiawatha, immortalized in the English-speaking world by Longfellow's popular poem. So little, in fact, that some people have questioned whether or not Hiawatha actually existed. The Native American chief is an Ojibwan deity who went by the name of Manabozho, though Longfellow chose his Iroquois name for the simple reason, it would seem, that it sounded better. Some scholars insist, however, that the Iroquois figure of Hiawatha was real and was added to the Iroquois pantheon after his death. According to Dr. Nancy Bonvillain, Professor of anthropology and linguistics at Bard College at Simon's Rock, Hiawatha most likely lived between A.D. 1150 and 1300.

There are several different ideas for the meaning of Hiawatha's name, as well. Dr. Bonvillain explains that the name means "the man who combs" – a reference to a traditional myth about the figure – while it may also refer to "one who seeks something and knows where to find it."

Whether Hiawatha was real or not, the accomplishment attributed to him – the banding together of five separate tribes into the Iroquois Confederacy – was historically real. Interestingly enough, there is almost no similarity between the historical figure who united the tribes and the mythological deity of Longfellow's poem. According to Henry Rowe Schoolcraft, a 19th-century scholar who translated much of the tribes' oral history, the real

Hiawatha's rousing speech went something like this:

Friends and brothers: You are members of many tribes. You have come from a great distance. The voice of war has roused you. You are afraid for your homes, your wives, and your children. You tremble for your safety. Believe me, I am one with you. We have one common object. To oppose these hordes of northern tribes singly and alone would prove certain destruction. We must unite ourselves into one band of brothers. We must have but one voice, one fire, one pipe, and one war club...If we unite in this bond, the Great Spirit will smile upon us and we shall be free, prosperous, and happy; but if we remain as we are, we shall be subject to his frown. We shall be enslaved, ruined, perhaps annihilated forever.

Hiawatha's speech was certainly emphatic. And it worked. The five tribes – the Mohawks, Oneidas, Onondagas, Senecas, and Cayugas – united into this "one band of brothers" known as the Iroquois Confederacy. Later, in the 1720s, the Tuscarora would join them as a sixth tribe. All of the tribes were located in upstate New York. The Confederacy proved so effective that its organization has been cited as influencing the founding documents of the United States, including the Articles of Confederation and the United States Constitution. A Smithsonian Institution specialist on American Indian history says that Benjamin Franklin submitted the constitution of the Iroquois Confederacy as an example of how the burgeoning American nation should be governed. Among the similarities between the Iroquois constitution – known as the Great Law of Peace – and the U.S. Bill of Rights are the freedoms of religion and expression.

Bayshore Park

At Munising's waterfront, the pleasant Bayshore Park provides a place for travelers to stretch their legs, enjoy a relaxing picnic, and admire the marina. In addition to the views of Grand Island just offshore and plenty of picnic tables, take time to visit the lovely Alger County Veterans Memorial Park, where the walkway bricks are engraved with names and messages honoring American soldiers and you can see artillery, a statue, and a monument.

Christmas

If you're driving into Munising from the west, you'll pass through Christmas, a small, fairly hardscrabble town that is most notable its Kewadin Casino and **Santa's Workshop** (E8035 St. Nicholas Ave., 906/387-2929, www.santas-workshop-christmas.com), a gift shop that capitalizes on the town's name by supplying Christmas supplies and decorations throughout the year. On the plus side, it supplies visits with Santa for most of the year as well. Store hours vary by season, so call ahead. You'll also be able to see what's supposedly the world's tallest Santa, the tallest Old Woman in the Shoe, and the largest concrete Frosty the Snowman.

Thankfully, there's more in Christmas than a year-round gift shop and a huge Santa. The **Kewadin Casino** (906/387-5475, www.kewadin.com) is located right on M-28 in Christmas, only a few miles west of Munising. With table games like blackjack, three- and four-card poker, and Let It Ride, in addition to slots, the Kewadin has some of the best U.P. gaming, and only minutes from some of the state's finest natural attractions. While visiting, enjoy a bite to eat at Frosty's Bar and Grill.

Alger Underwater Preserve

When loggers were felling the vast stands of pine across the central Upper Peninsula in the 1800s, Munising grew into a busy port, with schooners carrying loads of timber to the growing cities of the southern Great Lakes and iron ore to an ever-growing number of factories. Yet the narrow and shoaly passage between the mainland and Grand Island and along the Pictured Rocks shoreline was the downfall of many ships; their skeletons litter the lake floor here.

The Alger Underwater Preserve covers 113 square miles, from just west of Grand Island to Au Sable Point near the east end of Pictured Rocks National Lakeshore. Nearly a dozen ships lie here, well preserved in Lake Superior's cold, fresh water. Some wrecks, like the 19th-century *Bermuda* and the 145-foot *Smith Moore,* stand upright and nearly intact. The Alger Underwater Preserve marks many of the dive sites with buoys and helps ensure that they will be protected from poachers. Under Michigan law, it's a felony to remove or disturb artifacts within any Great Lakes underwater preserve.

Lighthouses

Most of Grand Island's private property is on the thumb, including the unique **East Channel Light,** an 1867 wooden lighthouse made of hand-hewn timbers. Sadly, the light is badly deteriorated from vandalism and neglect. Its piecemeal ownership—an amazing 20 landholders each own a piece of the lighthouse—leaves its future uncertain. You can't visit the lighthouse by land, because it's surrounded by private property. You can view it at a distance from Sand Point on the mainland, near the western end of Pictured Rocks National Lakeshore. On North Point, the **North Light** has just a 25-foot tower, but since it rises up from a 175-foot cliff, it earns the honor of being the highest lighthouse above sea level. The 1867 building is now a well cared for private summer residence. Please respect the owner's seclusion and stay off the property. The two **Munising Range Lighthouses** were built in 1908 as a means of helping ships navigate the passage to the east and south of Grand Island. Both are still operating today. The front tower is 58 feet high, while the rear light is 33 feet. The lights and station building are closed to the public. The two **Grand Island Harbor Range**

THE LAKE SUPERIOR SHORE

© HENRYK SADURA/123RF.COM

Grand Island Harbor Range Lighthouse

Lights serve the same purpose for the west passage.

SUMMER SPORTS AND RECREATION
Hiking and Biking Trails

A favorite spot in Hiawatha National Forest is the **Rock River Canyon Wilderness Area.** In this undisturbed corner of the national forest, about 12 miles west of Munising, the Rock River and Silver Creek have carved deep crevices in the sandstone, forming dark and narrow canyons. Adding to the area's wild beauty is **Rock River Falls,** which pours 20 feet over a sandstone ledge. Though there are few developed hiking trails in the area, you can make your way along old logging roads and railroad grades. The canyons themselves require some scrambling for the adventurous. If you plan to explore the area, be sure to bring a compass and topographical map, which are available from the visitors center. To reach the wilderness area, take M-28 west from Munising. About five miles west of Au Train, watch for

Rock River Road on your left (also called County Road H-01). Follow it to Forest Road 2276 and turn right (west). Within four miles, you'll arrive at Forest Road 2293; turn south and travel another three quarters of a mile to a small parking area. A short trail leads down to the canyon and falls.

About 50 miles of trails crisscross Grand Island, mostly old roadbeds. If you're just visiting for a day, a mountain bike is the only way you'll have time to see the entire island: it's about a 23-mile trip around the perimeter. In fact, it's probably one of the best mountain bike routes in the U.P. for the nontechnical rider, with wide grassy paths cutting through hardwood forests, passing under towering pines, snuggling up against Lake Superior shorelines, and rewarding you with spectacular views of wilderness bays and the distant Pictured Rocks.

Both hikers and bikers can reach **Murray Bay,** about two miles from the ferry dock at the southern end of the island. Murray Bay has a nice day-use area and a sand beach nestled in a grove of pines. There also are two campsites here, but the location near the ferry dock will limit your privacy.

North of Murray Bay, the island sprouts a tombolo off its southeastern corner, known as "the thumb." This landmass wraps north and forms **Trout Bay,** a lovely spot ringed with honey hued beaches and sandstone cliffs. Watch for the low profile of loons bobbing in calm waters. Trout Bay is home to the island's four other developed campsites, some of the most attractive you'll find.

Farther north, the island's most interesting trails follow the eastern and western shorelines. The **eastern shore** climbs high above lake level, offering occasional outstanding views of Pictured Rocks and the Grand Sable Dunes. The **western shore** provides ample opportunities to reach the fine sand beaches that line much of this side of the island. The island's interior trails are largely wooded and somewhat less interesting, unless you're hoping to glimpse a black bear. This shouldn't be too difficult; they're quite plentiful here.

Canoeing and Kayaking

Paddlers in particular will enjoy Trout Bay, which features some sea caves along its eastern shore and interesting paddling around the thumb. It's a full two-day journey around the entire island—a trip you'll long remember and an outstanding way to experience this superlative parcel of the Upper Peninsula.

The **Hiawatha Water Trail** (www.hiawathawatertrail.org) is another outstanding way to experience the Lake Superior shoreline in a sea kayak. Bookended by Big Bay to the west and Grand Marais to the east, the water trail stretches in either direction away from Munising and Grand Island. Get a map from **Northern Waters Adventures** (129 E. Munising Ave., 906/387-2323, www.northern-waters.com) in Munising. You can also rent sea or recreational kayaks from Northern Waters, as well as sign up for a guided day or overnight trip.

Fishing

Echo Lake lies near the center of Grand Island. Though it offers great bass and northern pike fishing for anyone with a Michigan fishing license, access can be a little tricky, since it is largely ringed with marshy grasses. You can also fish areas of **Munising Bay** (try Sand Point) and **Anna River.** Ice fishing is particularly good here, too. The more remote northern end of the island is perhaps its most impressive part, with high cliffs, creeks, and untouched beaches. In recent years, peregrine falcons have nested nearby.

Golf

The **Pictured Rocks Golf and Country Club** (10240 County Road H-58, 906/387-3970, www.picturedrocksgolfcourse.com) is an 18-hole, 6,246-yard course in Munising. With the exception of Munising's miniature **Eagle Falls Adventure Golf** (906/387-4653) on M-28 in Munising, Pictured Rocks is the county's only golf course, and it's a good one. The clubhouse has a restaurant and a well stocked pro shop. Take M-28 to East Munising Avenue before continuing on Munising–Van

Meer–Shingleton Road/County Road H-58 to the golf course.

Off-Road Vehicles

Even though there are no state ORV trails near Munising, there's still plenty of opportunity for off-roading, thanks to the vast stretch of **Hiawatha National Forest** (400 E. Munising Ave., 906/387-2512, www.fs.fed.us) that blankets the U.P. all the way down to St. Ignace. You can't ride on any road you choose, however. Contact the U.S. Forest Service for a Motor Vehicle Usage Map, which details mile after mile of forest roads open to ORVs. Bear in mind that there are patches of privately owned land scattered throughout the forest. Respect private property and stay on federal forest roads.

Waterfalls

The Munising area is thick with waterfalls, which run the gambit from easy to difficult to get to. Among the latter, Rock River Falls in the Rock River Canyon Wilderness is especially worthwhile. The **Munising Visitors Bureau** (422 E. Munising Ave., 906/387-2138, www.munising.org) prints a helpful waterfall map that will direct you to most of them. Nearby Pictured Rocks National Lakeshore also contains several notable falls.

The Tannery Creek spills over **Memorial Falls** and **Olson Falls,** just on the northeast edge of town. Follow County Road H-58 (Washington Street), leaving town to the northeast. Watch for a small wooden staircase on the right side of the road, across from the entrance to Sand Point and the National Park Service headquarters. If you've come by car, note that there's no parking alongside the road. Climb the stairs and follow the trail through a small canyon to Tannery Falls. To reach Memorial Falls, it's best to return to County Road H-58, turn right on Nestor Street, and follow the signs.

On the outskirts of town M-28 East leads to **Horseshoe Falls.** Next, turn east on Prospect Street and you'll see **Alger Falls,** which spills down along the highway. The

impressive **Wagner Falls** is in the same area, just off M-94 near the junction with M-28. It's a well-marked spot, operated by the state park system as a scenic site. Though it feels secluded, 20-foot Wagner Falls is just a few minutes' walk from the parking area. Continue up the streamside trail past the main falls to the second cascade. About 20 miles west of Munising, you'll find picturesque **Laughing Whitefish Falls,** which enjoys protection as a state park scenic site. Here, water plunges 30 feet over hard dolomite rock ledges, then continues rolling and frothing at least twice that distance to the bottom of a gorge. To reach Laughing Whitefish Falls, follow M-94 west from Munising to Sundell, then go north on Dorsey Road for 2.5 miles.

Diving

Several factors merge to make the Alger Underwater Preserve one of the finest sport diving locations in the Midwest. There are several wrecks concentrated in one area, and the cold, pristine water keeps them from deteriorating. Many wrecks rest in very shallow water—in as little as 20 feet, where visibility is excellent. Also, Grand Island moderates the cold-water temperatures slightly, making diving a bit more comfortable. "It's one of the best wreck diving sites for beginners that I can imagine," notes Pete Lindquist, who operates a dive charter in Munising.

Just offshore from Munising High School, an **underwater museum** among dock ruins includes subaquatic signs that interpret large maritime artifacts. The Alger Underwater Preserve also attracts divers for its **sea caves** in about 20 feet of water, where sandstone cliffs have been eroded by wave action.

To arrange a dive charter, contact Lindquist's **Shipwreck Dive Tours** (1204 Commercial St., 906/387-4477, www.exploringthenorth.com/scuba/diving.html).

Shipwreck Tours

If you do just one thing in the Munising area, make it this fascinating two-hour tour. Pete Lindquist, an experienced local who also

© TOM BUCHKOE, TRAVEL MICHIGAN

Shipwreck diving provides an underwater glimpse of the past.

operates a dive charter, came up with the idea of installing viewing wells in the hulls of a couple of tour boats, so even nondivers could marvel at the area's shallow-water shipwrecks.

The view through the 8- to 10-foot-long windows is truly remarkable. The boat glides directly over shipwrecks, some in as little as 28 feet of water. They fill the viewing windows like historic paintings, perfectly visible in the clear water and looking close enough to touch. On the *Bermuda,* you can easily make out deck lines, hatches, and even piles of iron ore lying on the deck. Weather permitting, the tour visits three shipwrecks dating from 1860 to 1926. Along the way, Lindquist's knowledgeable crew also shares history and points out features, including the wooden East Channel Light along the shore of Grand Island. Reservations are recommended. Contact **Grand Island Shipwreck Tours** (1204 Commercial St., 906/387-4477, www.shipwrecktours.com) for up-to-date pricing and schedules.

WINTER SPORTS AND RECREATION

Ski and Snowshoe Trails

Four miles south of Munising, in the Hiawatha National Forest, the **Valley Spur** (E8017 M-94, 906/387-4918, www.valleyspur.org) ski trail system has some 27 miles of groomed trails ranging in difficulty from easy to expert. Loops range in length from one to seven miles. The Valley Spur lodge is open most weekends for warmth and a hot beverage. To get to Valley Spur, take M-94 south.

The Munising Ski Trail begins a few miles east of town and skirts close to the Superior shoreline in Pictured Rocks National Lakeshore. Most of the loops on the nearly 12-mile trail are rated for easy to intermediate skiing. Lengths vary from less than 1 mile to 2.5 miles. You'll want to be careful to stay on the trails, too, as many portions are located along the tops of sheer cliffs. These make for beautiful sightseeing, but be sure to exercise caution. For more information, contact the **National Park Service** (906/387-3700, www.nps.gov/piro).

Snowmobiling

Trail 417 leaves Marquette and takes you east to Au Train before hooking south to catch Trail 8 (heading west, 8 will take you to Gwinn). Take Trail 8 east to follow the Pictured Rocks National Lakeshore all the way into Paradise and Whitefish Point. To get to Munising, head north on Trail 7 or 419. If you're interested in heading south, Trails 7 and 41 will take you there, connecting you to the miles upon miles of U.P. snowmobile trails. There are more than 300 miles of trails in Alger County alone, so you won't need to leave the county unless you want to. To get a state trail permit, contact the Michigan DNR (www.michigan.gov/dnr).

Ice Fishing

Many of the locations that provide good summertime fishing do just as well for ice fishing when the water freezes over. Try Anna River and the rest of Munising Bay, where you can break through the ice and angle for whitefish, lake trout, northern pike, and more.

Ice Sports

For winter recreation that's less conventional than skiing or snowmobiling, try **ice climbing** on Grand Island. Ice formations form on the sandstone cliffs on the east side of the island, and once the channel and bay begin to freeze over, ice climbers can tackle the 20- to 90-foot-high ice sheets. The **ice caves** just north of Eben Junction and west of Munising make for tamer recreation, but they're still impressive in their own way. Take snowmobile Trail 8 out of town to the caves that form when water seeping through the walls of Rock River Gorge freezes over.

ACCOMMODATIONS

The **C Sunset Motel on the Bay** (1315 E. Bay St., 906/387-4574, www.sunsetmotelonthebay. com, $100–125) has a great location right on Munising Bay at the east end of town. There are 15 rooms, and the motel's three suites have kitchenettes; each of the rooms faces the bay. It's a great find, with great rates, too. Wireless Internet is free, and pets are welcome. The downtown **Munising Motel** (332 E. Onota St., 906/387-3187 or 906/387-2160, www.munisingmotel.net, $75–140) has 12 rooms within walking distance of the city dock and Pictured Rocks Cruises. Another good option is the **Terrace Motel** (420 Prospect St., 906/387-2735, www.terracemotel.net, $55–65).

Unlike most commercial strips, the one along M-28 on Munising's near east side is still within walking distance of downtown and the waterfront. It has some nice and tidy small motels like the **Superior Motel and Suites** (500 E. M-28, 906/387-1600, $62–125), as well as chain offerings like the **Days Inn** (E. M-28, 906/387-2493, www.daysinnmunising.com, $72–95), the best of the chains with a close-in location and an indoor pool. Two miles east of Munising, the **Alger Falls Motel** (E9427 M-28, 906/387-3536, www.algerfallsmotel. com, $60–70 rooms, $139 cottage) has 16 rooms and a housekeeping cottage.

Camping

There are no reservations, fees, or permits

required for camping on Grand Island. The island has two designated campgrounds, at **Murray Bay** (two sites) and **Trout Bay** (four sites), offering the relative luxury of pit toilets and fire rings. Backcountry camping is permitted throughout the island as long as you stay off the tombolo, off private property, and at least 100 feet away from lakes, streams, cliffs, trails, roads, and natural research areas. No ground fires are permitted. And remember, there is no drinking water anywhere on the island, so come prepared.

For ultimate convenience—and the luxury of seclusion—the Hiawatha National Forest's **Bay Furnace** is a good choice. Just west of Munising, north of M-28, it offers 50 rustic sites with a very nice setting next to Lake Superior and overlooking Grand Island. Some sites almost have their own private stretch of beach, and a short cross-country ski trail at the campground's north end gives campers a little extra breathing room.

Near the day-use area, you can examine the remains of the old charcoal furnace that at one time produced 20 tons of iron a day. During its heyday in the 1870s, as many as eight steamers at a time would line up at docks, bringing in wood to fuel the furnace and hauling away iron. The camping fee is $8, no reservation accepted. Take M-28 west from Munising to Christmas and turn north at the Forest Service campground sign.

The Hiawatha National Forest has several other designated campgrounds nearby. Contact the **Hiawatha Visitors Center** (400 E. Munising Ave., 906/387-3700, www.fs.fed. us) for more information and directions.

Families gravitate to the **Wandering Wheels Campground** (906/387-3315) on M-28, three miles east of Munising, with 89 sites in a nice wooded setting. Rates begin at $24.95. What you lose in wilderness you gain in kid-friendly amenities like an outdoor pool, basketball courts, and a recreation room.

FOOD

For a town on the edge of a national park that presumably gets a fair amount of tourist traffic,

Munising has surprisingly little in the way of dining. Try **Sydney's** (M-28 downtown, 906/387-4067, www.sydneysrestaurant.com, 6 A.M.–11 P.M. Mon.–Thurs., 6 A.M.–2 A.M. Fri.–Sat., 6 A.M.–10 P.M. Sun., $12–23), on M-28 downtown, for fresh whitefish and lake trout, as well as steaks and a Friday seafood buffet, served with an Australian touch. **Muldoon's Pasties** (1246 W. M-28, 906/387-5880, 9 A.M.–9 P.M. daily late June–mid-Oct., off-season hours may vary, $5–7) is the best spot in town for a fresh, authentic taste of this potpie type meal, a true U.P. classic. If you're willing to take a little drive, one of the better restaurants in the Upper Peninsula is about 15 miles west in Au Train. Along the curve of Lake Superior's Au Train Bay on M-28, the ◖ **Brownstone Inn** (906/892-8332, www. brownstoneinn.net, lunch and dinner daily Memorial Day–Labor Day, Tues.–Sun. remainder of the year, $8–10 lunch, $15–20 dinner) serves up original and ever-changing dishes, including delicious versions of the ubiquitous Lake Superior whitefish. Check the menu for Rock Mountain whitefish also. There are good vegetarian options and an excellent Friday night fish fry, too.

INFORMATION AND SERVICES

You can get all of the visitor and tourist information you need by contacting the **Munising Visitors Bureau** (422 E. Munising Ave., 906/387-2138, www.munising.org).

Dial 911 for emergencies, and for immediate medical care, make your way to **Munising Memorial Hospital** (1500 Sand Point Rd., 906/387-4110, www.uphcn.org), a smallish community hospital located a little north and east of town. Take East Munising Avenue where it splits from M-28 and follow it northeast to Washington Street; turn left and follow Washington to the hospital.

There aren't as many banks in Munising as in Marquette, but you shouldn't have trouble finding one if you urgently need cash. There's a **Wells Fargo** on M-28 (419 E. M-28, 906/387-2823, www.wellsfargo.com); more immediately

in town, you'll find the main office of **Peoples State Bank of Munising** (100 E. Superior St., 906/387-2006, www.bankatpsb.com) and a branch of **Citizens Bank** (101 W. Munising Ave., 906/387-2610, www.citizensbanking.com).

GETTING THERE AND AROUND
Car
To get to Munising by car, take M-28 from Marquette and the west. You'll pass through Au Train and Christmas along the way, and you'll be continuously rewarded with views of Lake Superior and Munising Bay, some of the more picturesque locations in the U.P. If you're coming from the east, use M-28, also. It merges with M-94, which heads north from Manistique and the Lake Michigan shore. It's more of a back road, but you can take Forest Highway 13 north from Nahma Junction on U.S. 2.

Air
Munising's closest commercial airport is **Sawyer International Airport** (MQT, 125 G Ave., Gwinn, 906/346-3308, www.sawyerairport.com), just south of Marquette, a little less than an hour away. There's no regularly scheduled public transportation from the airport, so odds are that you'll be renting a car.

Boat
Consider yourself fortunate if you're arriving in Munising by boat. You'll be able to sail past the Pictured Rocks National Lakeshore, an unbelievably scenic stretch of shoreline with plunging cliffs and, in places, very shallow waters. And then you'll sail past beautiful Grand Island into Munising Bay on your way to **Munising-Bayshore Marina** (906/387-3445,

www.michigan.gov/dnr). The marina's slips (9 seasonal and 10 transient) have access to water, electricity, restrooms, and much more. Nearby, there's a pleasant park with picnic tables and benches and plenty of lawn. Contact the harbormaster on channel 16 or 18 from mid-May through mid-October. The marina is located at 46° 24.52 N, 86° 39.06 W.

A **The Grand Island Ferry Service** provides boat transit between Munising and Grand Island daily from Memorial Day to early October. The cost is $15 adults, $10 children, and five and under free. There's a $5 additional charge for bicycles. Call 906/387-3503 for a current schedule. The ferry's departure point is about two miles west of downtown near Powell Point. Follow M-28 west and watch for the signs. Even if you're planning just a day trip, you'd be wise to pack some warm clothing and a method for purifying water. Rough weather can cancel ferry service at any time. It's also easy to lose track of time and missed the last ferry. There is a ship to shore radio at Williams Landing in the event of an emergency. **Private boats** may be pulled ashore at Williams Landing and Trout Bay, and moored offshore in Murray Bay and Trout Bay.

Public Transportation
Although there isn't a major bus company that provides transportation to Munising, you can find regional transportation between Munising and Marquette from **Alger County Transit** (Altran, 906/387-4845, www.altranbus.com) for $6 each way. **Altran** also provides dial-a-ride service for a fee. Call at least 24 hours in advance for reservations. You can also catch an Altran bus tour of Grand Island ($22 adults, $11 children, June 15–Labor Day).

Pictured Rocks and Grand Marais

Lake Superior takes center stage at this national lakeshore, which is a mere 3 miles wide but stretches 40 miles along the magnificent lake from Munising to Grand Marais. Pictured Rocks derives its name from the sandstone bluffs that rise 200 feet directly up from the water's surface, washed in shades of pink, red, and green from the mineral-rich water that seeps from the rock. These picturesque cliffs stretch for more than 15 miles, occasionally forming sculptures of crazy castle like turrets, caves, and arches. The national lakeshore also features a lesser known, but equally spectacular, stretch of shoreline called the Grand Sable Banks, where 200-foot sand dunes are hemmed by a 12-mile ribbon of sand and pebble beach. If that's not enough, you'll also find lakes, forest trails, waterfalls, a lighthouse, and other historic attractions. With all this, you'll want to put Pictured Rocks at the top of your Upper Peninsula list of destinations. For general information, contact Pictured Rocks National Lakeshore (906/387-3700, www.nps.gov/piro).

Pictured Rocks' tourist season is short. Most of the park's 300,000 or so annual visitors come in July and August, when they're most likely to enjoy summerlike weather and daytime temperatures in the 70s. Visit in June and you'll share the park with fewer people, but the black flies and mosquitoes can be onerous. May and September may be the park's finest months.

No matter when you go, pack plenty of warm clothing along with shorts. Even at the height of summer, evenings are almost always cool, dipping into the 50s. And the giant refrigerator of Lake Superior, where the water temperature rarely climbs out of the 40s, can put a chill in the air near the shoreline. In fact, a Lake Superior beach on a sweltering August afternoon may just be the most refreshing place on earth.

The unusal colors at Pictured Rocks make it a favorite for U.P. visitors.

SIGHTS
◖ Pictured Rocks National Lakeshore

To best appreciate the namesake bluffs, you need to get out on the water. **Pictured Rocks Boat Cruises** offers three-hour trips up the shoreline from Munising, sidling up practically close enough to touch the rock formations while giving you the perspective to comprehend the turreted shapes like Miners Castle. Though trips are offered up to seven times a day, plan for either the late afternoon or Sunset Cruises, when the sinking sun shows off the multicolored sandstone in its best light. The boats depart from the Munising City Pier. For more information, contact Pictured Rocks Cruises (906/387-2379, www.picturedrocks.com, Memorial Day–mid-Oct., $35 adults, $10 children 6–12, under 5 free).

Munising Falls Area

The highlight of this spot used to be the trail that led hikers behind the 50-foot Munising Falls, but erosion problems prompted its closure. It's still worth a stop here, though, for the falls and the adjacent **interpretive center,** which offers a glimpse of the history of this peaceful area, home to a belching pig-iron furnace in the 1860s. Munising Falls also marks the west trailhead for the **Lakeshore Trail,** a 43-mile segment of the North Country Trail that spans seven states from New York to North Dakota. The Lakeshore Trail runs the length of the Pictured Rocks National Lakeshore. Predictably, it never strays far from the water's edge. The park's eastern trailhead lies near Sable Falls.

Past Munising Falls, the paved access road ends at **Sand Point,** home of the national lakeshore headquarters. While the headquarters primarily houses offices and not visitor services, it displays some interesting Coast Guard and shipwreck artifacts on its grounds. Sand Point has a small beach and a boat ramp; a good spot to launch a small craft for exploring nearby Grand Island.

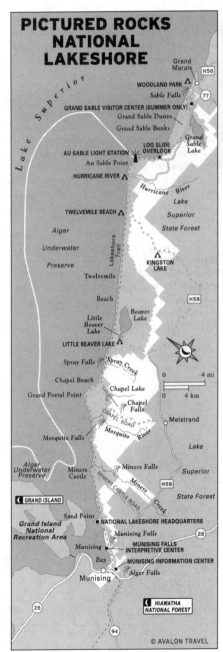

Miners Castle

For whatever reason, most people love to describe natural creations using terms relating to manmade objects. Thus, the sandstone cliffs five miles northeast of Munising Falls are known as Miners Castle, for the turret-like shapes caused by wind and wave erosion. The nine-story high rock formation is most impressive and ranks as one of the park's most popular attractions. Boardwalks and steps lead you to two viewing platforms out on the rock, where you can peer down into the gloriously clear waters of Lake Superior. If that entices you to do a little beach combing and wading, a nearby trail leads down some steps through the pines to the inviting **Miners Beach.**

To reach Miners Castle, follow County Road H-58 east from Munising to the well marked turnoff for Miners Castle Road. Before you reach the Miners Castle formation itself, you'll see another sign on Miners Castle Road directing you to Miners Falls. It's a one-mile walk to these pleasant falls, where Miners Creek tumbles 40 feet over a rocky escarpment.

Chapel Basin Area

Continuing northeast on County Road H-58, the next auto-accessible route into the heart of the park is at Melstrand, where the gravel/dirt Chapel Road bumps six miles toward the shore and another park highlight, the Chapel Basin area. Park your car here and you'll find plenty to entertain you during a long day hike or weekend: three waterfalls, a deep inland lake, Superior beaches, and a good loop hiking trail. **Chapel Falls** is the key attraction, as evidenced by the 1.5 mile paved pathway that leads you there.

If you turn left instead of right at Chapel Beach, you can make a 10-mile loop around Chapel Basin. Along the way, you'll pass **Grand Portal Point,** another significant Pictured Rocks landmark, before returning to the parking area. Don't leave Chapel Basin without a visit to **Mosquito Falls,** which is a bit farther inland off Chapel Road. The Mosquito River spills over a series of ledges, creating an accessible waterfall calm enough for wading and soaking fatigued hiking feet. A trail leads to

Miners Castle, Pictured Rocks National Lakeshore

© HENRYK SADURA/123RF.COM

Chapel Rock at Pictured Rocks is a natural stone formation.

© HENRYK SADURA/123RF.COM

LAKE SUPERIOR

By the shores of Gitche Gumee,
By the shining Big-Sea-Water ...

Henry Wadsworth Longfellow,
"The Song of Hiawatha"

Gitche Gumee is Longfellow's misspelled version of the Ojibwa name for Lake Superior, *Gichigami*, which means "big water." The Ojibwa could be considered guilty of understatement: Lake Superior isn't simply big water – depending on how it's measured, Lake Superior is the largest freshwater lake in the world.

Lake Superior is the largest body of freshwater in the world by surface area. At 31,700 square miles, the lake is about the same size as the state of Maine. The shoreline stretches an amazing 1,826 miles, farther than the distance from Houghton to Miami.

Superior is also the deepest of the Great Lakes (1,332 feet at its deepest point), but if measured by volume there are two lakes that are larger: Lake Tanganyika in East Africa and Lake Baikal in Siberia. However, Lake Superior is large enough to hold each of the other Great Lakes, as well as all the water from Lake Erie, an additional three times. The lake holds 3 quadrillion gallons of water (the numeral 3 followed by fifteen zeros), accounting for a full 10 percent of the world's fresh water. More than half of the water from the Great Lakes is contained in Superior, which is enough to submerge all of North and South America to a depth of one foot.

In addition, the water in Lake Superior is by far the cleanest and clearest water in all the Great Lakes.

Lake Superior was formed in much the same way as the rest of the Great Lakes. Approximately one billion years ago, the Mid-Continent Rift split open and, over a period of several million years, spewed out an enormous amount of volcanic material. This molten basalt eventually formed a heavy rock layer (up to 10 miles thick in places) that sunk as the rift opened, forming the Superior basin. During subsequent ice ages, a succession of glaciers advanced and retreated, continuing to carve the land into the massive basin it is today. As the last of the ice melted, the water was trapped in the lake, which at the time was much deeper than today.

The retreat of the ice was followed by the arrival of humans. A series of native peoples came to the area over the course of at least 10,000 years. These early Native Americans developed different hunting techniques. Some hunted with stone-tipped spears, while others developed new fishing techniques. Eventually Europeans arrived, drawn by the lucrative fur trade. More recently, the lake has drawn several million tourists each year with its reputation as a wild and rugged place, as well as a boater's and angler's paradise.

---

various sections of the falls and links up with the Lakeshore Trail.

Beaver Lake

Located near the center of the park, 800-acre Beaver Lake is the largest inland lake in Pictured Rocks. Anglers are drawn to the lake and the tributaries that feed it, especially for trout. Little Beaver Lake, connected by a small channel, has a boat launch. Boats are limited to 10 horsepower or less, making this a pleasant waterway for paddlers. Little Beaver also has one of the park's three auto-accessible campgrounds, with eight sites available on a first-come, first-served basis. Be aware that wetlands cover much of the terrain between Beaver Lake and Lake Superior, so bugs can be a problem here especially in June and early July.

Lake Superior State Forest

Traveling east from Beaver Basin, several dirt roads spiral south off County Road H-58 into the woods. These lead into the Lake Superior State Forest, part of the buffer zone protecting Pictured Rocks. Here you'll find plenty

of inland lakes, hiking and biking trails, and rustic campgrounds. Many of these are overlooked by the summer visitors to the national lakeshore. For more information on the state forest, contact the Michigan DNR (www.michigan.gov/dnr). Topographical maps ($4) of the area are available at the visitors center in Munising.

Grand Sable Dunes

Just east of Au Sable Point, the **Log Slide Overlook** marks the site of a once busy logging operation. In the late 1800s, loggers used this high point—some 300 feet above Lake Superior—to send freshly cut logs down to the water's edge, where they were loaded on Great Lakes schooners. Today, you can stand on a platform and simply marvel at the view, with the lighthouse to your left, the great dunes to your right, and the brilliant blue of the big lake filling the horizon.

Grand Marais

Though not part of Pictured Rocks National Lakeshore, sweet little Grand Marais marks the park's eastern boundary and is an excellent jumping-off point for a visit to the national lakeshore. This sleepy New England–like village is worth a visit of its own for its simple windswept beauty. With an outstanding natural harbor, rather rare on Lake Superior's southern shore, Grand Marais was originally settled by fishermen. Loggers soon followed, when sawmills were built here in the 1860s and 1870s to handle the logging that went on just south of here.

Commercial fishing remains a key segment of the local economy, but has become an increasingly difficult way to make a living. Today, tourism is what keeps the town slowly ticking along. The downtown huddles around the harbor, which incidentally is a good spot for kayakers to play in the surf on a north to east wind. The few streets here offer some arts and crafts shops and a small number of clean, inexpensive motels and restaurants.

Follow the bay around to its western point to reach the pier. The adjacent Lake Superior shoreline offers a nice sand and pebble beach, which is closed if endangered piping plovers are nesting. Rock hounds should continue west along the beach, past the Woodland Park city campground, to reach a good spot for **hunting agates.**

Lighthouses

It's a 1.5-mile walk along the Lakeshore Trail from the Hurricane River campground to the **Au Sable Light Station** at Au Sable Point. Built in 1874, the 87-foot brick light and its keepers did yeoman's duty for decades—warning ships away from the rock shoals that extend out for nearly a mile and create shallows of just 6 to 30 feet. Nonetheless, at least 10 steamers met their demise here. As you walk the trail from the campground, look for parts of the **shipwrecks** just offshore, which often poke out of the sand bottom and are easily visible in the gin-clear water. The light was automated in 1958.

Several recent restoration projects involved renovating the light keeper's quarters, rehabilitating the landscape and installing a photovoltaic (solar power) system to power the site. Tours are offered for a small fee (noon–5:30 P.M. Wed.–Sun. late June–late Aug., $4 for ages six and older).

SUMMER SPORTS AND RECREATION
Hiking and Biking

Two good hiking trails leave from the campground at Little Beaver Lake. The short and pleasant 0.7-mile **White Pine Trail** is a self-guided nature trail that circles through a 300-year-old pine forest. The five-mile **Beaver Basin Loop Trail** makes a lap around Little Beaver and Big Beaver Lakes, then follows the Lake Superior shore past sea caves cut by the lake's pounding waves. Boardwalks skirt the wetlands before returning you to the trailhead.

If you're in the mood for some exercise, the two-mile stretch of the **North Country Trail** from the Log Slide to the Au Sable Light Station is one of the park's most scenic hikes.

The **Grand Sable Banks and Dunes** (*grand sable* is French for "great sands") stretch for nearly five miles from the overlook, glacial banks of gravel supporting the huge mounds of sand. They are magnificent when viewed from a distance, glowing gold and rising up abruptly from the cobalt waters of Lake Superior. In many areas, especially near the overlook, the dunes are free of grasses and plants, so you can play around on them without fear of damaging fragile plant life or causing erosion.

Most people, however, choose to explore the dunes from the eastern end. Near the Grand Sable Visitors Center, a trail winds across the top of the dunes, where marram grass, beach pea, and sand cherry cling to the sand for dear life. Be careful to stay on the trail here. Interpretive signs discuss the plants' tenuous hold on the environment.

Canoeing and Kayaking

Paddlers can get the best view of Pictured Rock by **sea kayak.** This will allow you to avoid the rather touristy narration of the Pictured Rocks Cruise and really experience the true grandeur of this shoreline. Safety concerns cannot be overemphasized, however. Only experienced paddlers should venture out on their own, only in a closed cockpit (no canoes) and after scrupulously monitoring weather conditions. Paddlers can get themselves into serious trouble at Pictured Rocks, caught in sudden summer squalls along the 15-mile rock wall completely without shelter. Having said that, sea kayaking along Pictured Rocks ranks as one of the finest paddles on all the Great Lakes.

The stretch of Pictured Rocks and Lake Superior shoreline leading into Grand Marais is also the easternmost stretch of the **Hiawatha Water Trail** (www.hiawathawatertrail.org), which ends here, 120 miles from where it began in Big Bay. If you're heading in the opposite direction, it's the beginning of a long and satisfying journey in a sea kayak.

If you're unsure of your abilities, hook up with **Northern Waters** (129 E. Munising Ave., Munising, 906/387-2323, www.northernwaters.com). The company offers outstanding day long guided trips ($125 adults, $85 ages 16 and under), ferrying guests and boats to a departure point at Miners Castle. Beginners are welcome, since the day includes some basic instruction and you'll be traveling with an experienced guide. Kayak rentals (and longer trips to Grand Island and Isle Royale) are also available.

Beaches

An icon near the Twelve Mile Beach campground says it all. In indicating this is a permitted (but discouraged) beach area, it shows a swimmer not in the usual crawl position, but with water lapping at his ankles. In other words, the water here is bone-chilling *cold.* Swim if you dare, but wading is really more realistic...which is what keeps Twelve Mile Beach the pristine, stunning ribbon of sand that it is. After all, if such a perfect beach boasted 75°F water, it would be overrun with Jet skis and zinc oxide. Instead, it's a beach where you can stroll for hours with only the company of peregrine falcons, bald eagles, deer wandering down for a drink, and even the occasional black bear snorting around in the sand.

The **Twelve Mile Beach campground** is easy to reach, just a short drive off County Road H-58 through a pretty birch forest. Many of the 37 campsites string out along a bluff over the beach. Arrive at midweek (or early on Saturday, often a turnover day) for one of the choice spots. Some are larger than the average house lot and undoubtedly have better views. Well-placed stairs allow campers and picnickers to reach lake level. The campground also has a nice **day-use area** at its east end.

Just about five miles farther up the beach (or County Road H-58) lies the auto-accessible **Hurricane River campground,** where the Hurricane River spills into Lake Superior. This is also an exceptionally scenic campground, with 21 sites and a good location near the water and Au Sable Point.

Farther west, across County Road H-58 near the Grand Sable Visitors Center, the sandy shores and often warm waters of **Grand Sable Lake** are a wonderful spot for a swim or picnic.

Fishing

Fishing in the Pictured Rocks National Lakeshore—both in Lake Superior and the inland lakes and rivers—is a bit different from fishing elsewhere in the Upper Peninsula. Specifically, angling has been permitted by Congress for more than 40 years. It's not just an opportunity, it's your right. You'll be able to cast a line for a large selection of game fish, including (but not limited to) walleye, northern pike, whitefish, smelt, smallmouth bass, coho salmon, as well as brook, rainbow, and lake trout. Try Lake Superior, Grand Sable Lake, Beaver Lake, and Little Beaver Lake for the greatest variety of fish. For rivers, it's best to try at Sable Creek, Hurricane River, Beaver Basin Streams, and Miners River, among others. Contact the staff at **Pictured Rocks National Lakeshore** (N8391 Sand Point Rd., 906/387-2607, www.nps.gov/piro) for guidelines, regulations, maps, and tips.

For fishing on state land near Grand Marais, try North and South Gemini Lakes for bass, bluegill, perch, and walleye. Ross Lake, two miles east, is a source for bass, bluegill, perch, and pike. Canoe Lake, two-and-a-half miles south, offers perch and pike. Contact the Michigan DNR (906/452-6227, www.michigan.gov/dnr) for more info.

Off-Road Vehicles

East of Grand Marais, near Lake Superior between Blind Sucker Flooding and Muskalonge Lake, the first of two DNR ATV trails has an impressive 46 miles in three large loops. Pine Ridge Trail has parking at the intersection of County Road 416 and County Road 407; there's also access from Holland Lake Campground if you continue west on County Road 416. The Two Heart Trail actually connects to the Pine Ridge Trail, adding almost 34 miles, for a total of some 80 miles. Use the same trailhead parking as Pine Ridge, or you can get access to Two-Heart from the Mouth of Two-Hearted River Campground (there's gas here, too) or Pike Lake Campground. The DNR (906/452-6227, www.michigan.gov/dnr) has more information and maps.

Waterfalls

Just inside the park's western boundary, a short trail leads to 50-foot **Munising Falls,** which spills into a narrow gorge before emptying into Lake Superior's Munising Bay. Head east to the Chapel Basin Area where, amid a pale birch forest some 1.5 miles from the parking area, a stream of frothing water drops like a horsetail 90 feet into a deep gorge and Chapel Lake below. Continue past the falls another 1.75 miles to reach Chapel Beach, where you'll find a backcountry campground. From here, you can turn right to Chapel Rock and follow the Lakeshore Trail 1.5 miles to **Spray Falls,** one of the least visited and loveliest waterfalls in the park, where Spray Creek drops over the sandstone cliffs right into Lake Superior.

The trail to **Sable Falls** leaves from the Grand Sable Visitors Center, a half-mile walk largely composed of steps. As you work your way downhill, you'll be treated to several views of this exceptionally pretty falls, which drops in tiers through a narrow canyon and out to a rocky Lake Superior beach.

WINTER SPORTS AND RECREATION
Ski and Snowshoe Trails

The **Grand Marais Ski Trail** has several loops on the extreme east end of Pictured Rocks National Lakeshore, where County Road H-58/Au Sable Point Trail passes near Sable Falls and the Lake Superior shoreline. In fact, one of the trails (E) loops close to the shore on an intermediate, two-mile journey out and back. All of the loops here range from easy to intermediate, and vary in distance from less than a mile to nearly 2.5 miles, for a total of 10.4 miles altogether. Parking is on either side of County Road H-58, just west of William Hill Road. Be sure to watch for both car and snowmobile traffic when crossing the highway. For trail maps and additional information, the staff at **Pictured Rocks National Lakeshore** (N8391 Sand Point Rd., 906/387-2607, www.nps.gov/piro) would be more than happy to help. You can jump on the North Country Trail as well.

Snowmobiling

There are more than enough snowmobile trails in the Pictured Rocks/Grand Marais region. The most important one is Trail 8, which cuts east–west from Munising to Sault Ste. Marie. At Pictured Rocks National Lakeshore, Trail 89 bends away from 8 and takes you north to the Superior shoreline. South of town, Trails 443 and 43 connect to the rest of the U.P.'s snowmobile trails—south to St. Ignace, west to Escanaba, Ironwood, and the Keweenaw Peninsula. There's also a web of smaller trails that weaves around the city: Trails 88, 888, 9, and 492 will take you between the main trails and to other places in the region. Contact **Grand Marais Sno-Trails** (800/831-7292, www.sno-trails.net) for more information and a detailed map. And remember: According to the state, snowmobiles are allowed on the shoulders of plowed roads, and on any unplowed road. Follow the speed limits and drive with care.

ACCOMMODATIONS

The **Beach Park Motel** (21795 Randolph St., 906/494-2681, www.beachparkmotel.grandmaraismichigan.com, $75 d, pets welcome for an additional $10) has large rooms, each with a view of the water. A block east of County Road H-77 on Randolph, it's within walking distance to everything in town. East of County Road H-77 on Wilson Street, **Voyageur's Motel** (21906 Wilson St., 906/494-2389, www.voyageursmotel.grandmaraismichigan.com, $95–125) sits atop a ridge overlooking Grand Marais Harbor. Nice newer rooms, each with two queen sized beds, mini-fridge and coffee maker, plus a sauna/whirlpool facility make this a good choice. Other affordable options include **Dunes Motel** (906/494-2324, www.voyageursmotel.grandmaraismichigan.com) on the corner of West Wilson and M-77, **North Shore Lodge** (22020 Coast Guard Point, 906/494-2361, www.northshorelodgemi.net), and the historic ◖ **Superior Hotel** (14245 Lake Ave., 906/494-2539, www.superiorhotel.grandmaraismichigan.com).

Still affordable, **Hilltop Cabins** (14176 Ellen St., 906/494-2331, www.hilltopcabins.net, $75–175) rents one-, two-, and three-bedroom cabins, each furnished with a full living room, kitchen, and bathroom. Motel rooms with views of the bay are available, but the cozy cabins are much more desirable. For more information and other lodging options, contact the Grand Marais Chamber of Commerce (906/494-2447, www.grandmaraismichigan.com).

Camping

Pictured Rocks has three auto-accessible campgrounds: Beaver Lake, Twelve Mile Beach, and Hurricane River. Each is equipped with water and pit toilets. No reservations are accepted, and fees are $10 per night. **Backcountry camping** is permitted only at designated hike-in sites, mostly along the Lakeshore Trail. A $15 permit, good for one to six campers and for any number of nights, is required. Most sites do not have water or toilets. Camping is also available in Munising, Grand Marais, and in Lake Superior State Forest, which borders Pictured Rocks to the south.

With an excellent location just outside the national lakeshore boundary, **Woodland Park** has more than 100 sites. Opt for the more secluded ones that require you to get some exercise and walk up the beach a bit. It's open May 15–October 15.

FOOD

Grand Marais has a few good dining spots, both right downtown on County Road H-77. The ◖ **Sportsman's Restaurant** (N14260 Lake Ave., 906/494-2800) is more distinctive than its name suggests, with good fish dishes, salads, and homemade soups, as well as plenty of burgers and steaks. This is a good place for breakfast; how many places have "two eggs and pan fried whitefish" on the menu? Down the street, ◖ **Lake Superior Brewing Company** (N14283 Lake Ave., 906/494-2337, noon–9 P.M. Mon.–Wed., 11 A.M.–midnight Thurs.–Fri., 11 A.M.–2 A.M. Sun., 1–10 P.M. Sun.) does the microbrewery tradition proud, with homemade beers like Sandstone Pale Ale and Granite

Brown, as well as sandwiches, soups, and great homemade pizzas. For a summer treat, stop in the retro-style **Superior Hotel** on the corner of Lake Avenue and Randolph Street, where a soda fountain still sells phosphates and penny candy. Hours vary.

INFORMATION AND SERVICES

You'll find visitors centers at both ends of the national lakeshore. One is in Munising, the other is located inside the park at the Grand Sable Dunes, just a few miles from Grand Marais. Be sure to stop at one of these centers before beginning your visit. They have rangers on duty and excellent maps, displays, and historical information that will enhance your visit. Both also offer small but comprehensive bookstores. The **Munising Information Center** (400 E. Munising Ave., 906/387-3700, www.nps.gov/piro, 9 A.M.–4:30 P.M.), serving both the Pictured Rocks National Lakeshore and Hiawatha National Forest, is open year-round, daily during "peak season" (which does vary slightly from year to year), and is closed Sundays and holidays from mid-September through Memorial Day. The **Grand Sable Visitors Center** (E21090 County Road H-58, 906/494-2660, www.nps.gov/piro, 9 A.M.–5 P.M.) is open from late May to Labor Day only.

The two closest hospitals are **Helen Newberry Joy Hospital** (502 W. Harrie St., Newberry, 906/293-9200 or 800/743-3093, www.hnjh.org) and **Munising Memorial Hospital** (1500 Sand Point Rd., Munising, 906/387-4110, www.munisingmemorial.org). To access either hospital, head south on M-77 until you get to M-28. For Helen Newberry Joy Hospital, turn left and follow M-28 to M-123; turn left again and travel north on M-123 to Harrie Street, then turn left to the hospital. For Munising Memorial Hospital, turn right onto M-28 from M-77, then turn right on Connors Road. Make a left at Munising/Shingleton Road, then another right at Washington Street to the hospital.

In Grand Marais, you can do banking at the **Peoples State Bank of Munising** (N14264 Lake St., 906/494-2265, www.bankatpsb.com). There's another branch of the Peoples State Bank on M-28 in Seney (906/499-3306). You'll find more choices in Newberry and Munising.

GETTING THERE AND AROUND
Car

The easiest route between Munising and Grand Marais will bring you well south of Pictured Rocks. Take M-28 east from Munising, then M-77 north to Grand Marais.

County Road H-58 offers closer access the area around the national lakeshore. From the Grand Marais end, you'll be able to get as far as the Kingston Lake Campground. From Munising and the west, you can get to the Little Beaver Lake Campground.

As a linear park, Pictured Rocks perennially struggles with auto accessibility versus invasiveness. There have been sporadic discussions for decades about a "Beaver Basin Rim Road" that would weave through the park nearer Lake Superior, offering easier auto access to park attractions but undeniably changing the spirit and peacefulness of the largely road-free preserve.

Air

The closest commercial airport is **Chippewa County International Airport** (CIU, 5019 Airport Dr., Kincheloe, 906/495-2522, www.airciu.com), nearly 80 miles away, south of Sault Ste. Marie. Mesaba Airlines (in cooperation with Delta) offers regularly scheduled flights to and from Detroit; car rentals are available from **Avis** (906/495-5900, www.avis.com) and **Thrifty** (906/495-8000, www.thrifty.com). If you're traveling from other major cities, you may need to fly into **Sawyer International Airport** (MQT, 125 G Ave., Gwinn, 906/346-3308, www.sawyerairport.com) instead, though Marquette is much more distant than Sault Ste. Marie.

Boat

The **Burt Township Marina** (906/494-2613 or 906/494-2381 off-season, www.michigan.gov/

dnr) in Grand Marais is the only natural harbor of refuge between Munising and Whitefish Point. You'll find a boat launch, fuel, electricity, water hookups, a pump-out station, and transient dockage. The marina is open seasonally from May 1 to October 15 and is located at 46° 41.05 N, 85° 58.15 W.

Public Transportation

For now, consider a superb compromise: the **Altran Shuttle,** a county bus that makes regular runs (three times a week during the high season) to Munising Falls and Grand Marais and will drop off hikers at any point along County Road H-58. It's the perfect way for backpackers to enjoy the park without contributing to the growing vehicle problem. Call Altran (906/387-4845) for updated schedules and rates or to make a reservation (at least one day in advance).

Seney and Vicinity

The train went up the track and out of sight, around one of the hills of burnt timber. Nick sat down on the bundle of canvas and bedding the baggage man had pitched out of the door of the baggage car. There was no town, nothing but the rails and the burnt-over country. The thirteen saloons that had once lined the one street of Seney had not left a trace.

– Ernest Hemingway,
Big Two-Hearted River

Applied to the small town of Seney, Hemingway's quote may be a bit of an exaggeration. Seney is still there; a small dot on the map at the crossroads of M-77 and M-28. But by the time Hemingway's protagonist Nick Adams was exploring the central U.P., the town of Seney was indeed just a shadow of its former self.

"Hell town in the Pine!" loggers once called it, the new center of a logging trade that had crept northward into the U.P. after depleting the lucrative stands of red and white pine in the northern Lower Peninsula. Seney was the center of the action in the 1880s, both in and out of the woods. Situated along a railroad siding and the shores of the Fox River—used to transport the logs—the city became an important transit point. Besides logging, the local economy thrived on drinking, gambling, and womanizing. Seney didn't lack for local color:

legendary characters included P. K. "Snap Jaw" Small, who entertained barroom crowds by biting the heads off live toads and birds, and "Protestant" Bob McGuire, who sharpened his thumbnails into miniature bowie knives. Seney was sensationalized in the national press, right along with Tombstone, Arizona, and other towns of the Wild West.

Seney never had the huge fertile forests so common elsewhere in Michigan. Glaciers scrubbed this swath of the central U.P. flat, creating a patchwork of rivers, wetlands, and rocky, sandy soil. The red and white pines that did grow here were leveled in just a few short years. Soon loggers were settling for the less valuable hardwoods and small conifers, burning the scrub as they went. Shortly after the turn of the century they moved on, leaving behind barren land and vast "stump prairies."

Optimistic farmers followed the quickly departed loggers. They burned the brush and went to great lengths to drain the wetlands, digging miles of 20-foot ditches. Yet their hopes were quickly dashed by the area's poor soil and short growing season. Soon, they too departed almost as quickly as they came. But the fires had a more lasting effect, scarring the fragile soil deeply.

These days humans are finally trying to help instead of harm this beleaguered land. The immense Seney National Wildlife Refuge now manages and protects 150 square miles

immediately west of M-77, restoring the wetlands with an intricate series of dikes and control ponds that began as a 1930s Civilian Conservation Corps project. Today the refuge is an important sanctuary and nesting place for a rich variety of waterfowl.

The area's rivers remain a wonderful resource as well. The Fox, Manistique, and Driggs all snake through this area, along with countless creeks and lesser branches. Henry Ford, Calvin Coolidge, and Ernest Hemingway all fished these legendary trout waters, as anglers continue to do today. Here, too, Hemingway used a little literary license: It was really the Fox that he so eloquently chronicled in his Nick Adams stories. He merely borrowed the more romantic sounding name of the Big Two-Hearted River, which in fact flows just east of here.

SIGHTS
◖ Iverson Snowshoe Company
Aluminum snowshoes now dominate the sport, but for beauty and tradition, they simply can't match white ash and rawhide snowshoes. In Shingleton, 25 miles west of Seney on M-28, Anita Hulse and her two sons operate this wonderful factory, where workers hand-shape strips of local ash into classic snowshoe frames.

Visitors are welcome to visit Iverson Snowshoe (E12559 Mill St., 906/452-6370, www.iversons-snowshoes.com, 8 A.M.–4 P.M. Mon.–Fri.), one of just two wooden snowshoe manufacturers left in the country. You can watch workers shave and saw strips of ash, steam them, bend them around a form, and send them to a drying kiln overnight. Finished frames are laced with gummy strips of rawhide or newer-style neoprene. All of this happens in a small building, where visitors can practically lean over the shoulders of the workers.

Iverson manufactures about 11,000 snowshoes a year, about a third of which go to L.L.Bean. Other customers include REI, the Norwegian army, park rangers, and utility workers. Iverson also makes rustic chairs and tables, by order only. It's best to call ahead if you're interested in a tour. (Groups of more than five or six should definitely call.) To find Iverson, turn north on Maple Street (just west of the stoplight) in Shingleton.

Seney National Wildlife Refuge
The Seney National Wildlife Refuge occupies a huge swath of land west of M-77 and south of M-28. It is an intensely managed 95,000-acre parcel, with dikes and control structures used to artificially raise and lower the water levels in 21 major pools, simulating a natural wetlands cycle.

The system impounds more than 7,000 acres of water in these pools, and natural wetlands sprawl beyond that. While humans on foot or bicycle can access much of this preserve via an extensive network of maintenance roads, the refuge offers plenty of seclusion for its inhabitants. More than 200 species of birds and nearly 50 species of mammals have been recorded here, including bald eagles, trumpeter swans, loons, and even on rare occasions, moose or wolf. Whether you're an experienced bird watcher or just a casual observer, Seney is a wonderful place to get in among a fascinating array of wildlife.

Start your visit at the excellent **National Wildlife Refuge Visitors Center** (9 A.M.–5 P.M. daily May 15–Oct. 15), five miles south of the town of Seney on M-77. A 15-minute audiovisual program, informative displays, and printed materials will provide a good overview of what you can expect to see in the refuge. Some of the handouts will increase your chances of spotting bird life, pinpointing things like eagle nests and ponds frequented by loons. Sightings are often best in early morning and evening.

The **Pine Ridge Nature Trail** departs from the visitors center and allows for a quick 1.4-mile foray into wetland habitat. The self-guided trail circles a pool, and a stretch of boardwalk spans a marshy area.

The one-way **Marshland Wildlife Drive** also departs from the visitors center and makes a seven-mile auto-accessible loop through the refuge, with several interpretive signs placed along the way. The route includes three observation decks equipped with spotting scopes.

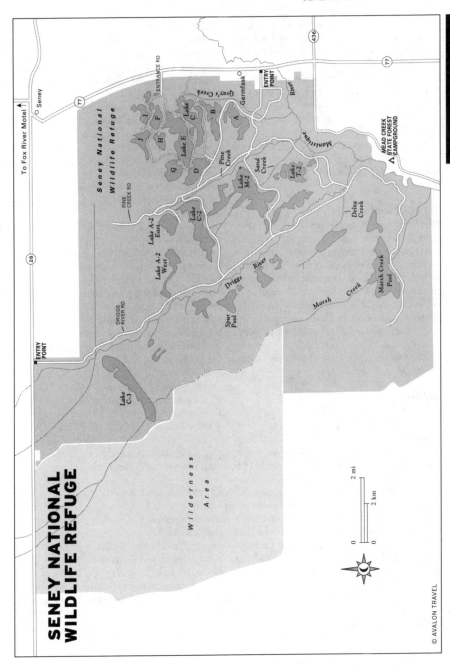

SENEY NATIONAL
WILDLIFE REFUGE

© AVALON TRAVEL

You can borrow binoculars from the visitors center. An eagle's nest is visible from the road, as are several pools frequented by herons and swans. Trumpeter swans were hand-raised and released here, and are now seen regularly. Tundra swans also migrate through in spring and fall. An adjacent three-mile **fishing loop** accesses a fishing platform and is also open to autos.

For information, contact Seney National Wildlife Refuge (1674 Refuge Entrance Rd., 906/586-9851, www.fws.gov/midwest/ Seney).

Strangmoor Bog

One of Seney's most unusual features, Strangmoor Bog lies deep in the wetlands near the refuge's western boundary, and is unfortunately not too accessible to visitors. Strangmoors, or string bogs, are fingerlike bogs alternating with sand ridges that are relics from ancient beaches. They are typically found only in arctic and subarctic regions, and Seney's bog is one of the southernmost examples in North America. The bogs are accessible only on foot. Consult refuge officials at the visitors center for details.

SUMMER SPORTS AND RECREATION
Hiking and Biking

Many visitors to Seney never get out of their cars and beyond the Marshland Drive, which is a shame. A bicycle is really the way to experience Seney. Bikes are welcome on more than 100 miles of gravel and dirt maintenance roads, which are closed to all motorized traffic except refuge vehicles. Though you won't find any exciting or technical rides (the land is *flat*) a bicycle allows you to cover far more ground than by hiking and is quiet enough not to frighten the wildlife. There's also something magical about spinning down a gravel road amid all the chirping, twittering, and honking sounds of wildlife, with nothing but waving grasses and glinting ponds surrounding you for miles.

Easy terrain, easy access, and well-marked trails make Seney a great choice for families or novice cyclists. You will want a mountain bike or hybrid bike, since the gravel can be tough on skinny tires. No off-road riding is permitted in the refuge.

There are three main access points for the refuge. One is at the visitors center on M-77, where trails sprout off Marshland Drive. This area is the most heavily visited, but trails here weave between many different pools, so the ride is interesting, and waterfowl sightings can be particularly good. Note that Loops 1 and 2 are part of Marshland Drive and are open to motor vehicles.

A second access point is about three miles south of the visitors center, near Grace Lutheran Church. Turn west at the sign for the Northern Hardwoods cross-country ski area, referred to as Smith Farm by locals. You'll soon reach a small parking area and a gate across the road. The trail begins just a few hundred yards west. This is a more lightly visited area of the refuge. From here, Loop 5 makes a 12.2-mile circle, including a stretch that runs parallel to the Driggs River.

If you stay on the trail that follows the Driggs, rather than swinging back east to complete Loop 5, you'll emerge onto M-28 after about nine miles, or eight miles west of the town of Seney. This is the third access point, called Driggs River Road. It's a well defined road for the first mile and a half south of M-28 until it arrives at the refuge boundary.

Canoeing and Kayaking

Paddling is an excellent way to explore the western reaches of the refuge, and it happens that the Manistique is an easily navigable canoeing river, with a sand bottom and just enough twists and turns to keep things interesting. It can be popular at the height of summer, so it's best to go off season or early in the day for optimal solitude and wildlife watching. Put in at the roadside park on M-77, a mile south of Germfask, or arrange a trip through Northland Outfitters. If you have your own

boat, you can opt for the lightly traveled Driggs or Creighton Rivers. Both cross M-28 west of Seney. Paddling is not permitted on any refuge pools or marshes.

Northland Outfitters (906/586-9801, www.northoutfitters.com) is located on M-77 in Germfask, just south of the refuge entrance. The company rents mountain bikes, camping gear, canoes, and kayaks, and offers paddling trips on the Manistique.

Fishing

The refuge allows some fishing within its boundaries. Pick up information on its special regulations at the visitors center. Perch and northern pike are most common. Fishing can be quite good on area rivers, especially for bass, northerns, and walleye. You'll need to move to the upper reaches if you're after trout.

The Fox River

In 1919, Ernest Hemingway stepped off a train in Seney, asked for directions to a good trout stream, and was directed up an old railroad grade to the east branch of the Fox. Where truth meets fiction we'll never know, but Hemingway's U.P. travels resulted in "Big Two-Hearted River," his Nick Adams tale about fishing on the Fox. Consequently, the Fox has always carried a special cachet in the U.P. and among trout fishermen.

Of course, Michigan has dozens of superb **trout fishing** streams, but most anglers seem to agree that the Fox belongs on the A-list. According to Jerry Dennis, author of several Michigan fishing books, it has produced some gargantuan brookies: "The Fox even today has a reputation for brook trout of a size rarely encountered elsewhere in the United States. Fish fifteen to twenty inches long are taken with fair regularity," he writes. The east branch is still considered the river's prime stretch, partly because it's more difficult to reach. To get there, you can hike in from M-77 north of Seney where it flows just west of the road. A state forest campground eight miles up M-77 from Seney offers public access. Many locals simply

cast near the bridge at Seney, where the main river flows under M-28. Because of the Fox's allure, the DNR is considering instituting special fishing regulations. Check with authorities before heading out.

The establishment of the **Fox River Pathway** was no doubt prompted by perennial interest in Hemingway's narrative. The route stretches 27 miles north from Seney, to just shy of Pictured Rocks National Lakeshore, and by U.P. standards, it's somewhat bland. Its most appealing stretch—especially for anglers looking for fishing access—is the southern end, where the trail parallels the main river for 10 miles. Farther north, it follows the Little Fox and the west branch. Heading north, the trail traverses the Kingston Plains, where loggers left behind "stump prairies." Markers along this route offer information about the area's logging history.

Because it passes through a good deal of cut-over land, the trail can be extremely hot and dry. If you plan to hike it, be sure to carry a water purification system. You'll find rustic campgrounds at both trailheads, and just one along the route, about six miles from the southern end.

For hikers, another option (albeit much shorter) is the trail that heads north from the Fox River Pathway's northern terminus at the Kingston Lake Campground. Not considered part of the pathway, this trail winds through pines and hardwoods in the Lake Superior State Forest for four miles before spilling out onto a particularly deserted and delightful stretch of Twelve Mile Beach on Lake Superior, inside Pictured Rocks National Lakeshore.

WINTER SPORTS AND RECREATION
Ski and Snowshoe Trails

It seems that as soon as the snow falls, the wildlife refuge is open for cross country skiing and snowshoeing. The largely flat trails are groomed from the mid December through mid March and make for a pleasant way to pass an afternoon. The trailhead for six different skiing

loops is located just off Robinson Road west of M-77. Stop by the visitors center for maps and more information. Half of the trails are easy and suitable for beginners. The others will present a bit of a challenge, but given the relatively flat terrain experienced skiers shouldn't experience any problems. Loops range from less than one mile to two miles in length. You can snowshoe anywhere in the refuge except on the groomed ski trails.

Snowmobiling

The best part about snowmobiling in Seney is its proximity to the trails that spread across the Grand Marais region north of town. The Seney Trail (Trail 43) cuts diagonally through Seney before connecting to the remaining miles of the Upper Peninsula's trails. Unplowed roads and the shoulders of plowed roads are open to snowmobiles as well.

ACCOMMODATIONS AND FOOD

There is lodging in Seney, but you'll find better choices elsewhere. Newberry, Manistique, Munising, and Grand Marais are all within a half an hour drive or less. If you'd like to stay in town, try a room at the affordable **Fox River Motel** (906/499-3332, www.foxrivermotel.com, $40–60 in summer, $50–75 in winter) on the corner of M-77 and M-28 downtown. Free wireless Internet is now offered.

If you're hungry, stop at any of the smattering of restaurants that have gathered along M-28 as you approach town from either direction.

Camping

There are plenty of campgrounds to choose from, even if none of them are in the refuge, where no overnight camping allowed. Still, there are a few places to go nearby. The **East Branch Fox River State Forest Campground** (906/452-6227, www.michigan.gov/dnr, $15) has 19 sites for tents or small trailers that work on a first come, first served basis. Take M-77 north of Seney about seven miles. To get to

the **Fox River State Forest Campground** (906/452-6227, www.michigan.gov/dnr, $15), take County Road 450 northwest of Seney to the seven rustic campsites for tents and small trailers only. This campground is first come, first served also. For more camping options, ask at the wildlife refuge visitors center.

INFORMATION AND SERVICES

Tourist information for the Seney National Wildlife Refuge can be obtained from the **U.S. Fish and Wildlife Service** (1674 Refuge Entrance Rd., 906/586-9851, www.fws.gov/midwest/Seney). When you first arrive, stop by the visitors center to view an orientation slide show, exhibits, and obtain information. The center is located on M-77 a few miles north of Germfask.

For medical care or the hospital, head east along M-28 to Newberry and the **Helen Newberry Joy Hospital** (502 W. Harrie St., 906/293-9200 or 800/743-3093, www.hnjh.org). Take M-28 to M-123 and turn left; take another left on Harrie Street to the hospital. You can do your banking at the **Peoples State Bank of Munising's** Seney branch (906/499-3306, www.bankatpsb.com) on M-28. For more banks and other services, drive to one of the larger towns nearby.

GETTING THERE AND AROUND
Car

Getting to Seney by car is simple. The town is at the intersection of M-77, the north–south highway that runs between U.S. 2 and Grand Marais, and M-28, the main artery that cuts east–west through the middle of the peninsula. Seney is 40 miles from Manistique; 35 miles from Munising; and 25 miles from Grand Marais.

Air

Unfortunately, Seney is a fairly long drive from either **Chippewa County International Airport** (CIU, 5019 Airport Dr., Kincheloe,

906/495-2522, www.airciu.com), south of Sault Ste. Marie, or **Sawyer International Airport** (MQT, 125 G Ave., Gwinn, 906/346-3308, www.sawyerairport.com), near Marquette. Both airports have plenty of car rental options, and it's easy to get to Seney: just get on M-28 and drive. Driving time from either airport is about one and a half hours.

Public Transportation

Currently there is no public transportation serving Seney.

WHITEFISH BAY TO THE LAKE HURON SHORE

On the western end of the bay, Whitefish Point boasts the oldest active lighthouse on Lake Superior, but it is probably better known for its proximity to Tahquamenon Falls, the largest waterfall in the U.P. Whitefish Bay is the place to go for Lake Superior swimming, since the water tends to be warmer here than in Marquette. Paradise is going to be your destination and base of operations for visits to Whitefish Point and Tahquamenon Falls State Park, a must-see for all visitors to the U.P.

The quickest way to Sault Ste. Marie from the west is to take M-28 to I-75, but then you'll miss out on the drive along Whitefish Bay, where Lake Superior narrows to become the St. Mary's River. To enjoy this beautiful scenery, take a leisurely ride along the Lake Shore Drive/Whitefish Bay Scenic Byway instead.

You'll want to spend time at Sault Ste. Marie, watching the big ships make their way through the locks or strolling along quaint Portage Avenue. Don't forget to cross into Canada and visit the other Sault Ste. Marie. You'll love what America's friendly northern neighbor has to offer.

Les Cheneaux and Drummond Island are perfect for pure relaxation. These quiet isles are close to both Sault Ste. Marie and busy Mackinac Island, but you'd never know it. Here you can get out on the water and explore the channels and islands. And when you discover how much you love the area, remember to keep it a secret.

© SVETLANA FOOTE/123RF.COM

HIGHLIGHTS

◖ **Lake Superior Nature Sanctuary:** Located on a remote portion of Lake Superior's shore, the sanctuary is home to several endangered and rare species (page 224).

◖ **Great Lakes Shipwreck Museum:** An informative, if slightly somber museum that commemorates ships that succumbed to the lakes and honors those who were lost while sailing them. An important link to upper Michigan's nautical past (page 224).

◖ **Tahquamenon Falls State Park:** The *grand dame* of Upper Peninsula waterfalls, Tahquamenon is unquestionably one of the most photographed and widely loved landmarks in the entire state (page 226).

◖ **Soo Locks:** It may sound boring, but watching giant freighters navigate the locks is an engaging way to spend a few hours (page 235).

◖ **Drummond Island:** Snowmobile trails, hiking paths, and unmatched golf courses are only a few reasons to head to this relaxing, out-of-the-way destination (page 246).

◖ **Les Cheneaux:** Although the 36 islands are located only 30 miles from the Bridge, the Les Cheneaux is often overlooked by tourists and is worth a visit for its sightseeing and seclusion (page 248).

THE LAKE HURON SHORE

LOOK FOR ◖ TO FIND RECOMMENDED SIGHTS, ACTIVITIES, DINING, AND LODGING.

PLANNING YOUR TIME

Sault Ste. Marie is the largest city in the eastern U.P. It's certainly worth a day or two of your time (you could easily spend an entire afternoon at the locks). Work in a trip to Tahquamenon Falls and a visit to Les Cheneaux, and most visitors will want to be here for about three days. Serious hikers, bikers, or boaters should plan on a longer stay, since there are plenty of outdoor attractions—state parks galore, Hiawatha National Forest,

and the placid waters of Lake Huron. Head out to Drummond Island for some fairly secluded hiking if you have time.

HISTORY

The Ojibwa were the first settlers of the area, migrating here in the 1500s. They discovered a rich supply of whitefish in the area's turbulent waters, and established a permanent settlement at the edge of the rapids, making this one of the oldest continuously settled areas

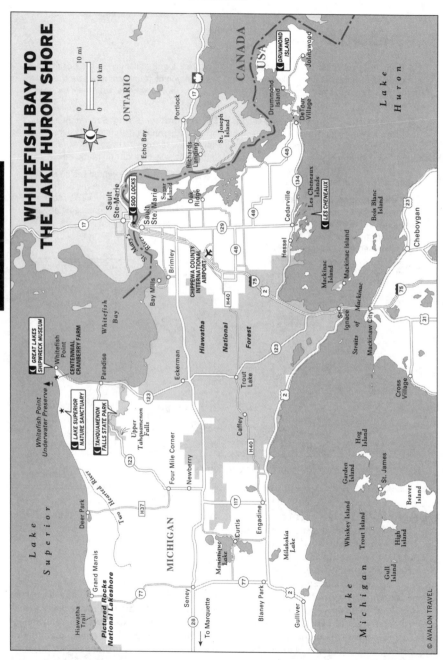

WHITEFISH BAY TO
THE LAKE HURON SHORE

© AVALON TRAVEL

in the Midwest. *Addik-kim-maig,* the Ojibwa name for whitefish, means "deer of the waters," a reference to the fish's importance as a food source. The Ojibwa lived off the river's riches here for more than 300 years. But in a sad and repetitive tale, Europeans put an end to the Ojibwa way of life and took away this important fishing ground. The combination of warring Iroquois—forced west by immigrants taking over their homelands—and new European settlement at the Soo eventually drove the Ojibwa out of the region.

The French also lived off the area's riches for many years, establishing a major fur-trading post here in the mid-1600s, then a Jesuit mission. By the early 1800s, Michigan's northern reaches were thoroughly settled, and people were discovering the bounty of the area's natural resources: copper, iron, lumber, and grain, all ringing the shores of Lake Superior.

The only problem was the rapids. For decades, ship cargo had to be unloaded by hand, portaged around the rapids by horses and mules pulling carts, then reloaded onto another boat. In 1839, the American Fur Company built a short railroad line, which eased the job, but transport remained backbreaking and exceedingly slow. While Great Lakes shipping was booming on the lower Great Lakes, Lake Superior remained largely isolated, its cargo backed up by the rapids.

Eastern industrialists began lobbying for government-funded locks. But the portaging business had become the lifeblood of Sault Ste. Marie's economy, and the community opposed such a project. Locals managed to stave off the inevitable until 1852, when President Millard Fillmore signed a bill authorizing the first lock at Sault Ste. Marie.

In 1855, the State Lock opened, which was actually a system of two locks, each 350 feet long. They were an instant success. In the first year, nearly 12,000 tons of iron ore passed through the locks. Within a decade, that figure soared to more than 120,000 tons per year. By World War I, the nation's hunger for iron and copper, coupled with the opening of vast iron mines in Minnesota's Mesabi Range, made the Soo Locks the busiest shipping canal in the world. Even today, the freight transported across Lake Superior and through the Soo Locks exceeds that of the Panama and Suez Canals combined.

Soon after the completion of the State Lock, the burgeoning commercial traffic made it clear that more locks were needed. The 515-foot Weitzel Lock opened in 1881. Since then, several additional locks have been built, to handle both the increased traffic and the ever-expanding size of Great Lakes ships. Today, one Canadian and three American locks are in operation, including the 1,200-foot Poe Lock, built in 1968 to accommodate the huge lakers now common on the Great Lakes.

The oldest city in Michigan, Sault Ste. Marie is inseparable from the locks that shaped its past and continue to define it today. The linchpin of Great Lakes commerce, the city's own economy has remained rather stagnant. The Ojibwa-owned Kewadin Casino and a prison complex south of town rank as the area's largest employers. Some state government administrative jobs and the small Lake Superior State University also help. But tourism remains the lifeblood of the local economy, with many of those visitors coming specifically to see the parade of goods that passes continually through town.

Paradise and Vicinity

"The searchers all say they'd have made Whitefish Bay if they put 15 more miles behind her. . . ." Singer-songwriter Gordon Lightfoot immortalized the ill-fated ore carrier *Edmund Fitzgerald* for the masses, but locals here need no reminders. Less than 20 miles from Whitefish Point and the safety of Whitefish Bay, the huge laker and all 29 hands on board perished in mere minutes during a fierce November squall in 1975.

On Lake Superior, the largest and fiercest of the Great Lakes, northwest storms can build over 200 miles of cold, open water. They unleash their full fury on an 80-mile stretch of water from Grand Marais to Whitefish Point and earn the area its nickname "Graveyard of the Great Lakes." Whitefish Point has long served as a beacon for mariners, a narrow finger of land reaching toward Canada and forming the protected waters of Whitefish Bay, one of the few safe havens on this unpredictable inland sea.

SIGHTS
◖ Lake Superior Nature Sanctuary

The Lake Superior Nature Sanctuary is wild and undeveloped by even Upper Peninsula standards. The 369-acre plot of land, right on the Lake Superior shoreline, is filled with endangered, threatened, and rare plant species, in addition to common Upper Peninsula wildlife: bears, deer, and coyotes. The land is preserved by the Michigan Nature Association (517/655-5655, www.michigannature.org), which recommends guided visits and organizes field trips to the sanctuary. It's difficult to get to, and only foot traffic is allowed within the sanctuary. Plan on it being a full day trip if you decide to go. Contact the MNA to inquire about visiting.

Centennial Cranberry Farm

Wisconsin and Massachusetts are usually thought of first when thinking about cranberries. Yet Michigan also claims this heritage, and Whitefish Point is known as cranberry country. In fact, the Michigan House of Representatives in 2008 passed a resolution making it official. Centennial Cranberry Farm (30957 W. Wildcat Rd., Paradise, 906/492-3314 or 877/333-1822, www.centennialcranberry.com) was established back in 1876. The gift shop sells fine cranberry-related products and fresh cranberries at harvest time, which is the best time to visit. You'll find more hustle and bustle in the flooded cranberry fields. Centennial Cranberry Farm is open from Memorial Day through the end of October.

◖ Great Lakes Shipwreck Museum

To commemorate the many ships that failed to round that point of safety, Whitefish Point is now the appropriate home of the Great Lakes Shipwreck Museum (18335 N. Whitefish Point Rd., 888/492-3747, www.shipwreckmuseum.com, 10 A.M.–6 P.M. daily May 1–Oct. 31, $13 adults, $9 children and students, 5 and under free, $35 families). With dim lighting and appropriately haunting music, this fine, compact museum traces the history of Great Lakes commerce and the disasters that sometimes accompanied it. Several shipwrecks are chronicled here, each with a scale model, photos or drawings, artifacts from the wreck, and a description of how and why the ship went down. Most compelling is the *Edmund Fitzgerald* display, complete with a life preserver and the ship's huge bell, recovered in a 1995 expedition led by museum founder Tom Farnquist, an accomplished diver and underwater photographer.

Housed in the former Coast Guard station, the museum also includes the restored light keeper's home, a theater showing an excellent short film about the *Fitzgerald* dive, and an interesting gift shop with nautical charts, prints, books, and more. To reach the museum, take M-123 to Paradise and follow Whitefish Point Road 11 miles north. This absorbing museum

THE MEMORY AND THE MYSTERY OF THE *EDMUND FITZGERALD*

Superior they said never gives up her dead when the gales of November come early...

Gordon Lightfoot,
"The Wreck of the Edmund Fitzgerald"

In early November 1975, the 729-foot lake carrier *Edmund Fitzgerald* departed Superior, Wisconsin, loaded with 26,000 tons of taconite pellets, bound for the port of Detroit and area steel mills. Launched in 1958, the *Fitzgerald* had a long and profitable record for the Columbia Line, the ship's Milwaukee-based owner. This was to be one of the last trips across Lake Superior before the shipping lanes and Soo Locks shut down for the season.

The *Fitzgerald* had rounded the Keweenaw Peninsula when, at dusk on November 10, one of the worst storms in 30 years screamed across Lake Superior. Winds howled at 90 miles an hour, whipping the immense lake into 30-foot seas. The *Fitzgerald* was prepared for bad weather from the northeast, as Superior was notorious for its November gales. Like the captain of the 767-foot *Arthur M. Anderson* traveling nearby, the captain of the *Fitzgerald* had chosen to follow a more protected route across the lake, some 20 to 40 miles farther north than usual.

Just 10 miles apart, the two captains had been in intermittent visual and radio contact, discussing the perilous weather, which had dangerously shifted from northeast to northwest. At 7:10 P.M., the *Fitzgerald* captain radioed, "We are holding our own." Then abruptly at 7:15, radio contact was lost. Turning to his radar, the captain of the *Anderson* was shocked to see the *Fitzgerald* completely vanished from the screen. The 729-foot lake carrier and all 29 hands disappeared without transmitting a distress call.

When the storm cleared, the *Edmund Fitzgerald* was found in 530 feet of water, just 17 miles from the shelter of Whitefish Bay. The wreck lay at the bottom severed in two pieces some 170 feet apart. Debris was scattered over three acres, evidence of the force with which the massive hull hit bottom. Many believe the *Fitzgerald* torpedoed bow first, which would have meant nearly 200 feet of the ship was towering over the water's surface at impact.

But after more than 35 years, an exhaustive Coast Guard investigation, and several dives to the site, crucial questions about the incident will most likely never be answered. Of the many theories put forth, the Coast Guard postulates that the ship took on water through leaking hatches, then developed a list and was swamped by the storm's huge waves. Others believe that, outside the normal shipping lane, the vessel scraped bottom on uncharted shoals. Still others believe the warm taconite pellets weakened the structure of the ship, causing it to snap in two when caught between two particularly enormous waves. It's also possible that elements from each of these theories contributed to the ship's demise.

Each November the victims of the disaster, along with those of other maritime tragedies, are remembered at Mariners Church in Detroit during the Great Lakes Memorial Service. Mariners is referenced by Lightfoot in his iconic song, which he refers to as "the Maritime Sailors Cathedral."

The ship was named after the Chairman of Northwest Mutual Life Insurance Co., which commissioned the ship as an investment in 1957. At its 1958 christening, Fitzgerald's wife experienced difficulty breaking the champagne bottle, ultimately having to make three attempts – considered a harbinger of bad luck in nautical lore.

THE LAKE HURON SHORE

makes Whitefish Point a most worthwhile destination.

Whitefish Point Underwater Preserve

For experienced divers, this preserve (www. whitefishpoint.net) offers a fantastic array of wrecks—18 steamers and schooners are littered all around the point. (The *Edmund Fitzgerald* is not among them.) Good visibility is a hallmark of this 376-acre preserve. Most wrecks lie in water between 40 to 270 feet deep, and are located in areas unprotected by harbors. Only very experienced divers and boaters should dive here. Contact the **Paradise Area Tourism Council** (P.O. Box 64, 906/492-3927, www. paradisemi.org) for information on area dive services.

◖ Tahquamenon Falls State Park

West of Newberry, the headwaters of the Tahquamenon bubble up from underground and begin a gentle roll through stands of pine and vast wetlands. Rambling and twisting

northeast through Luce County, the river grows wide and majestic by the time it enters its namesake state park. Then, with the roar of a freight train and the power of a fire hose, it suddenly plummets over a 50-foot drop, creating a golden fountain of water 200 feet wide.

As many as 50,000 gallons of water per second gush over the Upper Tahquamenon, making it the second largest falls (by volume) east of the Mississippi, exceeded only by Niagara. Adding to Tahquamenon's majesty are its distinctive colors: bronze headwaters from the tannic acid of decaying cedars and hemlocks that line its banks, and bright white foam from the water's high salt content.

Accessing Tahquamenon Falls is easy, since both the Upper Falls and Lower Falls lie within Tahquamenon Falls State Park (41382 West M-123, 906/492-3415, www.michigan.gov/ dnr), which provides short, well-marked paths to prime viewing sites. At the Upper Falls, follow the trail to the right and down the 74 steps to an observation deck, which will bring you so close you'll feel the fall's thundering power

Tahquamenon Falls, both picturesque and powerful, is a must see.

© SVETLANA FOOTE123RF.COM

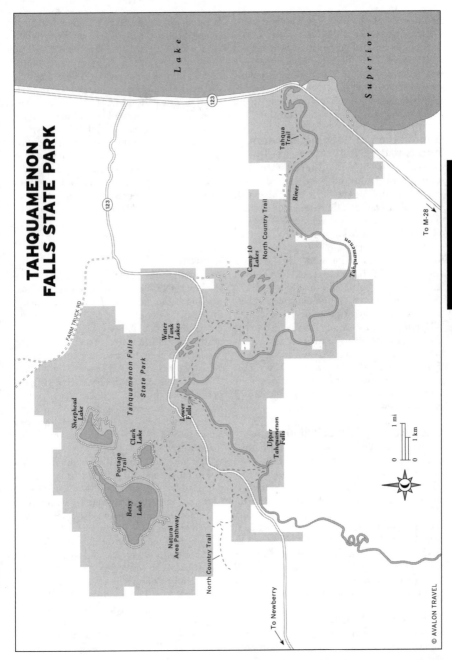

THE LAKE HURON SHORE

© AVALON TRAVEL

and its cool mist on your face. The view offers a stunning glimpse of both the placid waters above and the furious frothing below. Four miles downstream, the Lower Falls plunge over a series of cascades. The best vantage point is from a small island in mid river. A state park concessionaire obliges visitors by renting canoes and rowboats to make the short crossing.

Tahquamenon Logging Museum and Nature Study Area

Just north of Newberry, the Tahquamenon Logging Museum and Nature Study Area (906/293-3700, 10 A.M.–5 P.M. daily Memorial Day–Labor Day, $5 adults, $2 children ages 6–12, ages 5 and under free) presents an overview of the region's logging history. Antique mining equipment, old logs of impressive size, and photos, maps, and other artifacts are all housed in original, rustic Civilian Conservation Corps buildings. Stop by the Cook Shack Kitchen for an old-time lumberjack meal in an old-time lumberjack setting. The phrase "Nature Study Area" added to the museum's name refers to the trail and boardwalk that can take you into the Tahquamenon Forest and along the Tahquamenon River. This walk offers an exceptional opportunity to view nature in its most pristine form. Take M-123 north of Newberry to the museum.

Luce County Historical Museum

Another of Newberry's history museums, the Luce County Historical Museum (411 W Harrie St., 906/293-5709, 1 P.M.–4 P.M. Tues.–Thurs. mid-June–late September or by appointment through the fall season, free) doesn't just retell area history—it *is* history. The 1894 building is listed on the National Register of Historic Places, and has served as both the jail and the sheriff's home. Today, it houses historic artifacts, an original jail cell, and an old-fashioned schoolroom, courtroom, and scores of other items of interest.

Oswald's Bear Ranch

It's true: There are bears in the Upper Peninsula. Wild black bears. Bumping into them on a camping excursion can be a frightening experience. Seeing them at Oswald's Bear Ranch (13814 County Road 407, 906/293-3147, www.oswaldsbearranch.com, $15 per car or motorcycle, $10 for an individual) is anything but. Thirty live black bears roam the habitats here, safe for visitors to observe in a natural setting. This is one of the United States' largest bear ranches, and once held the largest captive black bear in the world. Tyson Bear, who died in 2000, weighed 880 pounds. You won't see Tyson Bear anymore, but you can observe the rest on a walking tour from the Friday prior to Memorial Day through the end of September (tours offered 9:30 A.M.–5 P.M.). North of Newberry, take M-123 to M-407/County Road H-37 and head west to the ranch.

Lighthouses

Whitefish Point Light first beamed a warning light in 1849, and has done so ever since, making it the oldest operating light station on all of Lake Superior. Marking the bay's entry, the Whitefish Point Light is a utilitarian-looking 80-foot steel structure. Though it looks relatively modern, the current tower actually dates to 1902. The beefy design was considered an extraordinary engineering experiment at the time, but one deemed necessary to withstand the gales that frequently batter this exposed landscape. The light was automated in 1970 and continues to do yeoman's duty.

If you're an especially passionate lighthouse buff, here you'll find a truly obscure one to add to the list. The 58-foot **Crisp Point Light** sits on a tiny arc of land 14 miles west of Whitefish Point, on an isolated, unbroken stretch of Lake Superior shoreline. Though an automated light took over duty decades ago, the handsome 1904 tower and adjacent home still stand. The tower was recently painted, the beginning of some much needed preservation work. You'll need a map or the *DeLorme Gazetteer* to find the light. A four-wheel-drive vehicle will also be helpful. Don't attempt the last couple of miles if the ground is wet and muddy. The light is about nine miles east of

the mouth of the Two Hearted River. Reach it from the west on County Road 412, or from the east via the Farm Truck Road truck trail off M-123.

SUMMER SPORTS AND RECREATION
Hiking and Biking

Wedged on a quarter mile strip of land between Lake Superior and Muskallonge Lake, **Muskallonge Lake State Park** (906/658-3338, www.michigan.gov/dnr) occupies the site of the old Deer Park township. It was once home to a sawmill, a hotel, and no doubt a saloon or two. Today, a couple of fishing resorts represent the only commerce in this remote area, about 18 miles east of Grand Marais. The North Country National Scenic Trail passes through here, and there are a few feeder trails letting you hook up and hike a section of the historic path.

The trails at **Pretty Lakes Quiet Area** (906/293-3293) connect to the North Country Trail, too. The five beautiful lakes are connected by a short trail. Take M-123 to County Road 407 north of Newberry and go left on County Road 416 to the campground. There's another short trail (1.25 miles) at nearby **Bodi Lake State Forest Campground** (906/293-3293). M-123 connects with County Road 500 near Tahquamenon Falls State Park. Take County Road 550 north to County Road 437 and follow it to Bodi Lake.

The dominance of Tahquamenon Falls makes it easy to overlook the rest of 40,000 acre Tahquamenon Falls State Park, Michigan's second largest. In sharp contrast to the often frenzied crowds at the falls (over half a million visitors per year, the most of any U.P. state park), the vast majority of the park remains peaceful, etched with 25 miles of little used **hiking trails.** From the Upper Falls, the Giant Pines Loop passes through a stand of white pines before crossing M-123. Once on the north side of the highway, you can link up with the Clark Lake Loop, a 5.6-mile hike that traces the southern shoreline of the shallow lake.

Canoeing and Kayaking

The Two Hearted River is well suited for canoeing; clean and clear and usually quite mellow. In spring, however, rapid snowmelt can cause it to produce a serious amount of white water. A state designated wilderness river, the Two-Hearted winds through pine and hardwood forest; the only signs of civilization you're likely to see are a handful of cottages at the river's mouth. There are several low banks and sandbars, so picnic spots are easy to find. The Two Hearted is also a widely regarded blue-ribbon trout stream, so be prepared for plenty of anglers when the season opens in April.

Put in at the High Bridge State Forest Campground on County Road 407 for a 23-mile trip to the mouth. You'll find two state forest campgrounds and other camping sites along the route. As an alternative, you can hook up with **Two Hearted Canoe Trips** (32752 County Road 423, 906/658-3357, www.exploringthenorth.com/twoheart/rainbow.html), a livery based out of the Rainbow Lodge at the river's mouth. It operates trips ranging from a few hours to three days. A popular half-day trip departs from the Reed and Green Bridge (east of Muskallonge Lake State Park on County Road 410) and takes out at Lake Superior.

It's possible to **paddle** nearly all 94 miles of the Tahquamenon. A popular put in is off County Road 415 north of McMillan, but you'll start off through several bug-infested miles of wetlands. A better choice is about 10 miles downstream, off County Road 405 at Dollarville, where you'll also avoid portaging around the Dollarville Dam. Beyond Newberry, you'll be treated to a trip with nice natural feel, since no roads come anywhere near the river. Watch the banks for bears, deer, and other wildlife. Naturally, you'll have to portage around the falls, but then you can follow the river to its mouth without any other interruptions.

Fishing

Water is the draw at **Muskallonge Lake State Park** (30042 County Road 407, 906/658-3338,

www.michigan.gov/dnr). The park's two miles of Lake Superior frontage are wonderfully secluded, with low, grass-covered dunes stretching off to the east and west and no visible development in either direction. Muskallonge Lake is stocked by the DNR and produces good fishing opportunities for northern pike, walleye, smallmouth bass, and perch. Because the lake is relatively shallow, it warms up enough for comfortable swimming—a rarity in the U.P. that explains this park's somewhat surprising popularity in summer. A modern campground offers several sites overlooking the water. Sites are usually available even in summer, but you can always reserve one by phone or online.

The final 16 miles of the Tahquamenon River wind through the park, spilling into Lake Superior's Whitefish Bay at its eastern end. Fishing for muskie and walleye is usually quite good in the pools below the Lower Falls. Also consider joining the fleet of runabouts and anglers in waders near the mouth of the river, where trout often school.

Bird-Watching

A vital resting spot for birds migrating across Lake Superior, Whitefish Point is a birdwatcher's dream. Beginning with the hawk migration in April, and continuing through late fall, the point attracts an amazing variety of birds. Eagles, loons (by the *thousands!*), songbirds, waterbirds, owls, unusual arctic species like arctic loons and arctic terns, and more all pass through, some 300 species in all. Even if you're not a birder, plan to spend some time at this remarkable point, where you can wander the sand beaches, watch the birds, and keep an eye out for the big lakers that pass quite close to shore as they round the point. Bring along binoculars and an extra jacket. Contact the **Whitefish Point Bird Observatory** (6914 N. Whitefish Point Rd., 906/492-3596, www.wpbo.org) with any questions or for more information.

Golf

For golfing in the area, head to **Newberry Country Club** (5073 M-123, 906/293-8422,

www.golfnewberry.com, $23 for 9 holes with cart, $39 for 18 holes with cart), a challenging, 18-hole championship course on the corner of M-28 and M-123. The Newberry Country Club has been around for more than 80 years—not as long as some clubs up here, but it's not exactly short in the tooth, either—and provides a driving range, a pro shop, and a refreshment bar. Contact the country club to ask about packages, special rates, and events.

Off-Road Vehicles

Choices are limited for off-road vehicle trails in the Whitefish Point area. Some DNR trails aren't too far away, of course, but you'll need to head west or south to find them. You can, however, ride on any state forest road that hasn't been specifically marked otherwise, so you'll find a few trails nearby. Try Lake Superior State Park or many of the roads in the nearby Hiawatha National Forest. Contact the Sault Ste. Marie Ranger District (4000 I-75 Business Spur, 906/635-5311, www.fs.fed.us) for more information and motor vehicle usage maps.

Waterfalls

For another look at Tahquamenon River and Falls, you may want to plan a day for the **Toonerville Trolley and Riverboat** (906/876-2311 or 888/778-7246, www.exploringthe-north.com/toonerville/trolley.html, hours vary, mid-June–Labor Day, $45 adults, $29 youth 9–15, $20 children 4–8, 3 and under free). It's much more appealing than its saccharine name suggests and a good way to experience a remote stretch of the river. Departing from Soo Junction near Newberry (watch for a sign on M-28), a narrow-gauge train crawls its way five miles along an old logging route, through a roadless spruce and maple forest, tamarack lowlands and peat bogs. In about half an hour, the train sighs to a stop deep in the woods at the Tahquamenon's banks. Here you'll transfer to a large tour boat and cruise downstream nearly two hours toward the falls. Just as the river begins roil and boil, the boat docks on the river's south shore, and guests walk the last half mile to the falls. It's an entertaining 6.5-hour

trip, one that has been in operation since long before a state park provided easy access to the falls. Originally, the tour operator (the grandfather of present day owner Kris Stewart) used a Model T truck with train wheels to reach the river. You can choose just the train trip to the riverbank and back, a 1.75-hour trip ($15 adults, $9 youth 9–15, $7 children 4–8, 3 and under free). Show up by 10 A.M.; reservations are recommended.

WINTER SPORTS AND RECREATION
Ski and Snowshoe Trails
The exciting thing about Paradise is that it really is a paradise, even when it's buried under several feet of snow. Nordic skiers will find a couple of well-groomed loops just off M-123 about a mile west of town. Paradise Pathway's loops range between 1.5 and 3 miles long. Contact the **Paradise Area Tourism Council** (P.O. Box 64, 906/492-3927, www.paradisemi. org) for more information.

Nearby, **Tahquamenon Falls State Park**

(41382 West M-123, 906/492-3415, www. michigan.gov/dnr) has several miles of groomed ski trails, and countless more if you're interested in backcountry skiing. The River Trail leaves the parking area and runs about four miles to the ranger station. This trail isn't a loop, so you'll have to double back. There's also the mile-long Nature Trail, too. The Giant Pines Loop is 3.5 miles and closest to the parking area; farther away are the Wilderness Loop at 7.4 miles and the 5.6-mile Clark Lake Loop. A number of these loops and trails connect to the North Country Trail, so you potentially have an additional 4,400 miles available!

In Newberry, try the **Canada Lake Pathway** (906/293-3293) for 14 miles of groomed ski trails near Natalie State Forest Campground, southeast of Newberry.

Snowmobiling
If you want to snowmobile up to the very end of Whitefish Point, take Trail 453 which will eventually gets you there, although there's a network of trails that you'll need to navigate

Grand Marais and Paradise are linked by snowmobile trail.

© VITO PALMISANO, TRAVEL MICHIGAN

first. If you're heading east from Grand Marais, Trail 8 will get you to Paradise before it curves south and east to Sault Ste. Marie. Several miles before Paradise, however, Trail 8 intersects with Trails 452 and 451, which head north and hit 453 and continue to the tip of Whitefish Point. Heading down to Newberry, take Trail 49.

ACCOMMODATIONS

There are some nice hotels in and around Paradise and Newberry, but for more selection (including plenty of chains), it's worth the drive into Sault Ste. Marie. One of the best hotels up here, though, is the **Paradise Inn** (906/492-3940, www.exploringthenorth.com/paradiseinn/motel.html, $75–125), located at the junction of M-123 and Whitefish Point Road. Two of the 36 rooms at this modest but well kept motel have hot tubs. Continental breakfast and guest laundry are available as well. If you're more comfortable with the familiar, there's a **Best Western** (8112 North M-123, 906/492-3770, www.bestwestern.com, $130–175) on M-123.

There are more options in Newberry than up in Paradise. The **Bear Den Motel** (20906 M-28, McMillan, 906/293-8023, $50–100) is located several miles west of Newberry on M-28, owner Linda Pease has done a fine job with the place. It's clean and affordable, and comes with Wi-Fi. Be warned, though, that the beds are doubles, not the more typical queens. Pets are welcome for an extra $5.

At the historic **〔 Falls Hotel** (301 Newberry Ave., 906/293-8621, www.thefallshotel.com, $60–100), you'll find some of the town's more exceptional lodging, and still at an incredibly affordable rate. The 1915 hotel has plenty of options to choose from (standard rooms, two-bedroom suites, and a corner suite with a sitting area). For another vintage option, try an elegant, intimate bed-and-breakfast, **The MacLeod House** (6211 County Road 441, 906/293-3841, www.superiorsights.com/macleodhouse/page2.html, $75–105). Chain hotels include America's Best Value Inn, Comfort Inn, and Super 8.

Camping

There are several campgrounds in the area, offering primitive or rustic camping (with vault toilets and hand-pumped water). The fee for each of these campground listings is a flat $15 per night.

About 11 miles east of Grand Marais on County Road H-58, you'll reach the **Blind Sucker River** campground, a deceptively terrible name for such an appealing place to camp. There are three state forest campgrounds in this area: along the Blind Sucker River, along the Blind Sucker Flooding, and near Lake Superior. Remember, if you choose to camp along the Superior shore, be prepared for cold nights, even in August.

Even more attractive may be the state forest's **Pretty Lakes Quiet Area,** about eight miles to the southeast. Here you'll find five small and clear lakes, ringed with sand and linked together by short portages. There are canoe campsites on Beaverhouse, Camp Eight, and Long Lakes, along with an 18 unit rustic campground near the approach road at Pretty Lake. No motors are allowed on Pretty, Brush, Beaverhouse, or Long Lakes. This is indeed a pretty, secluded spot where you'll listen to loons and other wildlife rather than the whine of powerboats and automobiles. To reach it, it's easiest to stay on County Road H-58, which becomes County Road H-37/County Road 407 when it swings south at Muskallonge Lake State Park. About five miles south, turn west on County Road 416 and follow it 2.5 miles to the campground. If you have a good map, you can also follow County Road 416 from the Blind Sucker area.

There are dozens of other lakes and campsites in the Lake Superior State Forest. Pick up a good topographical map and contact the state forest office (906/293-5131) for more information.

FOOD

In addition to being one of Newberry's nicest hotels, the **Falls Hotel** (301 Newberry Ave., 906/293-8621, www.thefallshotel.com) also has a casual, tasty restaurant and lounge. There's

nothing fancy here, but the menu's large selection of appetizers and entrées and the full bar in the lounge make this a great place to stop for a quick bite, or to wind down before turning in for the night. If you want to cut loose, head to **Timber Charlies** (110 Newberry Ave., 906/293-3363, www.timbercharlies.com, 7 A.M.–7 P.M. daily), a family-friendly place that serves your basic restaurant fare and a little something special: the five-pound Ox Burger. That's right. Five pounds of ground beef on a massive bun. It puts that 72-ounce steak place in Texas to shame. And no, you can't eat it by yourself; you'll want to split this one with your friends. For a normal-sized meal, try selections of Mexican, Italian, seafood, steak, ordinary-sized burgers, and more. There's also a full bar.

In Paradise, you can't do much better than the **Tahquamenon Falls Brewery and Pub** (906/492-3300, www.superiorsights. com/tahqfallsbrew/), a microbrewery and restaurant with great food and a relaxed brew pub atmosphere. Selections of steak, fresh fish, hefty burgers, and other sandwiches give way to that Yooper classic, the pasty. If you haven't stopped for one at a roadside diner, you'll want to get one here.

INFORMATION AND SERVICES

For tourism and visitor information for the area, contact the friendly people at the **Newberry Area Tourism Association** (P.O. Box 308, 906/293-5562 or 800/831-7292, www.newberrytourism.com) or the **Paradise Area Tourism Council** (P.O. Box 64, 906/492-3927, www.paradisemi.org).

Since the stretch of land between Grand Marais and Sault Ste. Marie is relatively secluded, most (but not all) essential services (airports, hospitals, and the like) are located in the bigger cities to the west and east of Whitefish Point. Although Newberry is small (1,550 people), there's a good community hospital here. The **Helen Newberry Joy Hospital** (502 W. Harrie St., 906/293-9200 or 800/743-3093, www.hnjh.org) provides health care services to Newberry and the surrounding communities.

You can get there by taking M-123 into Newberry and continuing west on Harris Street to the hospital. The hospital also offers weekly clinic services in Paradise, with a physician or nurse practitioner visiting the **Paradise Community Health Center** (906/492-3881) on M-123 each Thursday.

Most of the area's easily accessible banks are located in Newberry. The **Tahquamenon Area Credit Union** (www.tacumi.com) has a branch in Paradise (7960 N. M-123, 906/492-3555) as well as in Newberry (7693 M-123, 906/293-5117 or 800/575-5117) and a few other locations: Engadine, Rudyard, and Pickford. Other branches in Newberry include **mBank** (414 Newberry Ave., 906/293-5165, www.bankmbank.com) and **First National Bank of St. Ignace** (1014 S. Newberry Ave., 906/293-5160, www.fnbsi.com).

GETTING THERE AND AROUND
Car

If you're driving in from Grand Marais, you'll have two choices. The quickest and easiest is to head south on M-77 to M-28 and turn left, then take M-28 east until you reach M-123. Another left onto M-123 and take it through Tahquamenon Falls State Park into Paradise. The trip should take 1.5 hours, maybe a bit more. The other option will take longer. The first stretch stays close to Lake Superior, and is more scenic than M-28's stretches of pavement and flat, uninspired scenery. It's about a two hour drive if you head east out of Grand Marais on the Grand Marais Truck Trail, which bends south after Muskallonge Lake State Park as M-407. Continue on the road south, follow the leftward bend to the east, then turn left on M-123 and follow it into Paradise. After Paradise, M-123 continues south until it reconnects with M-28 east of Newberry.

From Sault Ste. Marie, take I-75 south to M-28 and head west until you come to M-123; take it north.

Air

The closest airport to Paradise, Tahquamenon Falls, and the rest of Whitefish Point is

Chippewa County International Airport (CIU, 5019 Airport Dr., 906/495-5631 or 800/225-2525, www.airciu.com), south of Sault Ste. Marie. The airport offers two flights daily to and from Detroit on Mesaba Airlines (an affiliate of Delta). You'll need to rent a car if you fly in, since there's no regular public transportation to Paradise. The airport has both **Avis** (906/495-5900, www.avis.com) and **Thrifty** (906/635-0800, www.thrifty.com) car rental offices. The drive to Paradise will take you a little more than an hour if you follow M-80 toward I-75 (follow the signs), and take the interstate north to M-28. Take M-28 west for 30 miles before you hit M-123, which will take you north to Whitefish Point.

Boat

There's a small state dock located near the tip of Whitefish Point, with only a handful of slips and limited amenities. But **Whitefish Point State Dock** (906/492-3415, www.michigan.gov/dnr) is passable, and it's one of only a couple harbors between Grand Marais and Sault Ste. Marie. The other is **Little Lake State Dock** (906/658-3372, www.michigan.gov/dnr), which pretty much splits the difference between Grand Marais and Paradise. Little Lake has even fewer amenities than Whitefish Point State Dock. Whitefish Point is located at 46° 45.32 N, 84° 57.52 W; coordinates for Little Lake are 46° 43.06 N, 85° 21.48 W.

Sault Ste. Marie

At the foot of Whitefish Bay, grand Lake Superior narrows to a close at the St. Mary's River, the waterway that links it to Lakes Huron, Michigan and their counterparts to the south. With Superior 21 feet higher than the other lakes, the St. Mary's naturally erupted in a series of falls and rapids near Sault Ste. Marie. "Sault," pronounced SOO (and often used as a nickname for the city), means "Falling Water," a name bestowed by early French explorers.

Compared to much of the eastern U.P., Sault Ste. Marie is urban. It's the U.P.'s second-largest city, with a population of 14,000. This historic city is well worth a visit, especially to view the boat traffic through the famous Soo Locks, which link Lakes Superior and Huron. But don't overlook the area to the south and east, where the lovely blue-green waters of Lake Huron wrap around the end of the peninsula, a scalloped shoreline of quiet bays and a scattering of isolated islands.

SIGHTS
Curtis Lewis Memorial Highway
The twisting, scenic Curtis Lewis Memorial Highway (also called Lake Shore Drive) follows the curve of Lake Superior's Whitefish Bay from M-123 east 20 miles or so to Sault Ste. Marie. It's almost an attraction in itself, passing through the Hiawatha National Forest and offering views of Lake Superior's eastern end and a handful of worthwhile stops.

Mission Hill Overlook is the kind of road where every view is better than the last. As the highway curves south, watch for the turnoff to the west marking this terrific overlook. Drive up the sand and gravel road for grand, sweeping views of the river and bay, Ontario's Laurentian Mountains, the cityscape of Sault Ste. Marie, freighters that look like toy ships, the Point Iroquois light, and, just below, Spectacle Lake.

Four miles west of tiny Dollar Settlement, the federally run **Pendills Creek National Fish Hatchery** (21990 W. Trout Lane, 906/437-5231, www.fws.gov) raises thousands of lake trout that grow up to tempt anglers in Lakes Superior, Michigan, and Huron. Visitors can wander around the tanks to peer down at the hundreds of wriggling trout fry and the breeder trout that weigh in at 15 pounds or more. The raceways are covered to keep birds and other predators at bay. The hatchery is free and open

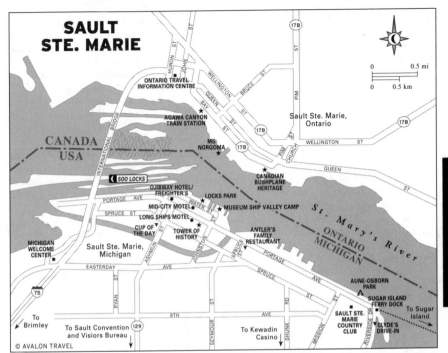

THE LAKE HURON SHORE

weekdays. Call for current hours. Outdoor areas are also accessible on weekends.

Just beyond the Bay View campground, the **Big Pine Picnic Grounds,** a day use area in the Hiawatha National Forest, is a wonderful spot to take a break. It offers a pleasant shaded area under a canopy of huge white pines, and a pretty sand and pebble beach along Whitefish Bay.

Continuing east, don't miss a chance to climb the tower at the **Point Iroquois Light** (www.exploringthenorth.com/ptiroquois/iroquois.html), where Whitefish Bay narrows into the St. Mary's River. Since 1855, a beacon here has helped guide ships through this extremely difficult passage, where reefs lurk near the Canadian shore and the rock walls of Point Iroquois threaten on the American side. In 1870, the original wooden light tower was replaced with the present one, a classic white painted brick structure. A keeper's home was added in 1902.

With fewer and fewer lighthouses open to the public, it's fun to climb the iron spiral staircase for a freighter captain's view of the river, the bay, and the continuous shipping traffic. Stop in the adjacent light keeper's home, where the local historical society has restored some rooms to illustrate the life of a light keeper; other rooms feature displays and old photos. The lighthouse and adjacent beach are now part of the Hiawatha National Forest, which should help ensure continued protection. The complex is open 9 A.M.–5 P.M. daily, May 15–October 15. Hours may vary, however. Call 906/437-5272 for more information.

❰ Soo Locks

Nearly every visitor to the Soo makes a pilgrimage to the locks, right in the heart of downtown at the end of Ashmun Street (Business I-75). The city has smartly dressed up this area, with lovely **Locks Park.** Blue

freighter signs mark the **Locks Park Walkway,** which wanders along Water Street and is dotted with interpretive plaques that share the city's history.

In the heart of the rather formal park, the U.S. Army Corps of Engineers manages the locks and a **visitors center** (906/632-7020, www.saultstemarie.com/soo-locks-46/, 9 A.M.–9 P.M. mid-May–mid-Oct.) next to a raised **viewing platform** that lets you see the locks in action. Start at the visitors center to get some background on how the locks work. A moving model shows how the locks raise and lower ships by opening and closing the gates of a lock chamber and allowing water to rush in or rush out. No pumps are required; the water simply seeks its own level. Other displays explain the construction of the locks. A knowledgeable staff with a P.A. system, along with video cameras upriver, notify you about approaching vessels. In summer months, you can usually count on a ship coming through about once an hour. You can also call the visitors center to get the day's shipping schedule,

but times can change depending on weather conditions and other factors.

It's easy to while away an hour or two watching the ships as they crawl through the locks with seemingly just inches to spare. Summer evenings are especially pleasant, when you'll likely have the platform to yourself to watch the illuminated ships. If you're lucky, you might see a "saltie," an ocean-going vessel that's likely hauling grain to foreign ports. Overall, the three most plentiful Great Lakes shipments are iron ore (for steelmaking), limestone (a purifying agent for steelmaking, also used in construction and papermaking), and coal (for power plants).

The locks and viewing platform are open throughout the Great Lakes shipping season, which runs from March 25 to January 15. Those are the official dates when the locks terminate operations for winter maintenance. Ice buildup on Superior sometimes affects the length of the shipping season, too.

After viewing the locks, you can "lock through" yourself on an extremely popular

The Soo Locks allow ships to cross from Lake Superior to Lake Huron.

© TRAVEL MICHIGAN

THE HISTORY OF THE SOO LOCKS

The St. Mary's Rapids have been causing problems for as long as people have lived in the area. Faced with an over-20-foot drop on the way from Lake Superior to Lake Huron, the native Ojibwa would take their canoes out of the water and portage around the rapids before continuing their journey. Early European settlers did the same thing, which proved adequate until the fur trade and an increased European presence demanded larger ships too large to portage. So they solved the problem by having two sets of ships, one on the Lake Superior side, and one on the Lake Huron side. After reaching the Lake Superior Rapids, good would be unloaded and transported to ships waiting on the Lake Huron side. This proved to be a workable but inefficient solution.

The Northwest Fur Company built the first locks in the 1790s on the Canadian side of the river. Though small (38 feet), and they remained in use until being destroyed in the War of 1812, forcing a return to the old system.

The next locks weren't built until 1853-1855, when the Fairbanks Scale Company agreed to construct two locks in exchange for a quarter million acres of public land, which the company hoped to exploit by mining. The two 350-foot locks were turned over to state control upon completion. In 1881 demand for newer and larger facilities prompted a transfer to the United States Army Corps of Engineers,

which continues to operate and maintain the locks today.

The locks are an amazing feat of engineering, consuming an enormous amount of power and requiring regular maintenance. To meet the challenge, the U.S. Hydroelectric Power Plant just north of the locks is part of the overall facility. The plant generates more than 150 million kilowatt-hours of electricity each year, with the locks receiving first priority. Any remaining power is distributed to Sault Ste. Marie, Michigan, and surrounding eastern U.P. communities.

Of the four locks — the Davis Lock, Sabin Lock, MacArthur Lock, and Poe Lock — the Poe Lock is the largest and one of two (along with the MacArthur Lock) that see regular use. Each is capable of handling large ships (the Poe Lock is 1,200 feet long and can take ships with up to 72,000 tons of cargo) and are capable of quick operation, each able to drain and fill in a matter of minutes. Some 10,000 ships pass through the locks each year, despite their annual winter closing. During this time the Corps of Engineers works on maintenance and repairs.

You can watch the daily operations of the Soo Locks from the visitors center. The center lets you get up close (but not too close) to the massive freighters as they make their way along the St. Mary's River. You'll also find several informative displays about the history and operation of the locks. Try a trip through the locks with Soo Locks Boat Tours.

Soo Locks Boat Tour (800/432-6301, www. soolocks.com, early May–mid-Oct., $22 adults, $10.50 children 5–12). The two-hour trip takes you through both the American and Canadian locks and travels along both cities' waterfronts. Also offered are lunch, dinner and, lighthouse cruises. At busy times, you'll be in the midst of freighter traffic, dwarfed by their enormous steel hulls. The large passenger boats have both heated and open deck areas. Boats depart as early as 9 A.M., from two docks on Portage Avenue.

Museums

After you've watched the big Great Lakes boats, the **Museum Ship Valley Camp** (501 Water St., 906/632-3658 or 888/744-7867, www.thevalleycamp.com, 10 A.M.–6 P.M. May 10–mid-Oct., longer hours in July and Aug., $12 adults, $6 children 6–16) gives you a chance to see what it was like to live and work aboard a giant steamer. This 550-foot steamship logged more than a million miles on the Great Lakes, hauling ore, coal, and stone from 1907 to the mid-1970s. Now it's permanently docked five blocks east of the Soo

Locks. Visitors can tour the pilothouse, engine room, main deck, crew quarters, coal bunker, and more. Throughout, the ship has a number of aquariums and maritime displays, some better than others. The most popular is a display on the sinking of the *Edmund Fitzgerald,* including two tattered lifeboats found empty and drifting on the lake. All in all, it's well worth a couple of hours. Make sure to stop at the museum shop, housed in a separate building next to the parking lot. It has an excellent selection of maritime books and videos.

Like most observation towers, the **Tower of History** (326 Portage Ave., 906/632-3658, www.thevalleycamp.com, 10 A.M.–5 P.M. daily mid-May–mid-Oct., $6.50 adults, $3.25 children 6–16), four blocks east of the Soo Locks, is an ugly blight on the landscape: a 21-story stark concrete monolith, but with a wonderful 360-degree view of the twin Soos, the St. Mary's River, Lake Superior, and forests rolling off in the distance. Rather than being stuck behind windows, you get to enjoy the views from an open-air deck. Bring a jacket, as it can get chilly! The tower also includes a few small exhibit areas and a theater showing documentary videos. There is an elevator to the top. Interestingly, the tower was originally built as a bell tower for the neighboring church. Intended as part of a larger church complex, financial difficulties caused the project to be abandoned. In 1980 the tower was donated to Sault Historic Sites.

The **River of History Museum** (209 E. Portage Ave., 906/632-3658, www.thevalleycamp.com, 10 A.M.–5 P.M. Mon.–Sat. and noon–5 P.M. Sun. mid-May–mid-Oct., $6.50 adults, $3.25 children 6–16) uses the St. Mary's River as the framework for telling the story of the region's history. Life-size dioramas depict things like Native Americans spear fishing in the rapids and a French fur trapper's cabin (the French were the first European settlers in the region). The museum incorporates lots of sound in its displays: dripping ice from melting glaciers, roaring rapids, Ojibwa elders passing down legends. One hopes this relatively new museum (founded in 1992) will keep building on this idea.

Lighthouses

Soo Locks Boat Tours (1157 E. Portage Ave. and 515 E. Portage Ave., 906/632-6301 or 800/432-6301, www.soolocks.com, $49 adults, $35 children, free for children age 3 and under) offers the option of extending their popular locks tour with the **St. Mary's River Lighthouse Cruise.** After riding through the Soo Locks, you'll get a short tour of the St. Mary's River and a float past a number of picturesque lighthouses. See the unoccupied but intact keeper's residence at **Cedar Point** and the remains of the original light on **Round Island.** You'll cross into Canadian waters (there's no need for a passport) and see the **Gros Cap Reefs Lighthouse** and the **Point Louise Range Lights.** Morning departures include a continental breakfast and coffee, and box lunches are available with advance reservations. During the trip, you'll be able to see the **Point Iroquois Lighthouse** from the boat, but this one is worth going out of your way to visit on land.

Sault Ste. Marie, Ontario

Just across the International Bridge lies the Soo's sister city in Ontario, also named Sault Ste. Marie. With a population of 75,000, it's the larger of the two cities and home to a huge steel plant and paper company. Aside from these industries, Sault Ste. Marie, Ontario, also has a great deal to offer visitors. Downtown, a lovely **boardwalk** rambles along the river for about a mile, beginning at the bridge and extending east past fishing platforms, shops, and the MS *Norgoma,* the last passenger cruise ship built for the Great Lakes, now a museum. On Wednesday and Saturday, there's a farmers market near the tented pavilion.

One of the most advertised and popular visitor attractions is the **Agawa Canyon Train Tour** (129 Bay St., 705/946-7300 or 800/242-9287, www.agawacanyontourtrain.com, once daily early June–mid-Oct. and weekends Jan.–Mar., C$79 for adults, C$35 children five and older, C$20 children under five), a seven-hour round-trip through the scenic wooded gorge of the Agawa Canyon. The daylong tour includes a two-hour stopover in the canyon, where you

THE OTHER CITY

Sault Ste. Marie, Ontario, is located just across the St. Mary's River from its sister community, Sault Ste. Marie, Michigan. The Michigan city is the oldest in both the state and the Midwest, founded by Jesuit missionaries in 1688. Sent to establish a mission at the mouth of Lake Superior, the Jesuits first called the area Sault du Gaston before renaming Sault Ste. Marie to honor the mother of Christ. Although a number of the Jesuits gradually moved on from the mission, the French settlement remained for much longer, before splitting in the late 1700s into two separate cities sharing a common name. Translated from the French, the cities' name reads "The Saint Mary Rapids."

Today, the cities are bound together by the International Bridge, which stretches nearly two miles and carries 7,000-10,000 cars on a busy day. The sister cities are also joined by the Soo Locks. Essential to the Great Lakes shipping industry, the locks are a critical link in the Great Lakes Waterway and the St. Lawrence Seaway.

But despite their similarities, the two cities do have some unique characteristics. Sault Ste. Marie, Michigan, has a population of only 14,000, with an economy based largely on tourism. Its Canadian counterpart is home to some 75,000 and its economy is based on the forestry and steel industries.

But Sault Ste. Marie, Ontario, welcomes tourists also. If you've brought your passport, you'll find it worthwhile to cross the river for an evening, day, or weekend. Popular attractions include the Agawa Canyon Train Tour, the Canadian Bushplane Heritage Centre, the Sault Ste. Marie Museum, the Prince Township Museum, and the Casino Sault Ste. Marie. Its close proximity and easy accessibility make Sault Ste. Marie, Ontario, a perfect place to experience America's friendly neighbor to the north.

can hike to lookouts, visit waterfalls, wander along the river, or just enjoy the grassy picnic area. The train trip is even more popular (and more expensive) in the fall color season, which usually runs from mid-September to mid-October, and in winter, when it is known as the "Snow Train." (The two-hour layover is eliminated during the winter trip.) Tours depart at 8 A.M. from the station. Reservations are recommended.

As in Alaska, bush planes are an integral part of life in the wilds of the Canadian interior. A small plane with pontoons can get you where no auto can, since almost any remote lake can serve as a landing strip. The **Canadian Bushplane Heritage Centre** (50 Pim St., 705/945-6242 or 877/287-4752, www.bushplane.com, open daily year-round, C$10.50 adults, C$2 children), near Pim and Bay Streets on the waterfront, chronicles the history of Canada's bush planes, which began with the Ontario Air Service in the 1920s and was established to fight forest fires. Others besides aviation buffs will enjoy this unique museum, housed in the Air Service's old waterfront hangar.

You can reach Ontario via the three-mile-long **International Bridge** (934 Bridge Plaza, 906/635-5255 U.S., 705/942-4345 Canada, $2 toll one-way). You can exchange money and pick up maps and other useful area information at the **Ontario Travel Information Centre** (705/945-6941) at the foot of the bridge. Either a valid U.S. passport or a Michigan enhanced driver's license is necessary for entry into Canada.

ENTERTAINMENT AND EVENTS
Bay Mills Resort and Casino

Bay Mills Casino (11386 W. Lakeshore Dr., 888/422-9645 or 877/229-6455, www.4baymills.com) in Brimley offers the usual gaming standbys—blackjack, roulette, craps, three-card poker, Texas Hold 'Em, and more. It also has something that few other

U.P. casinos provide: complimentary drinks while actively gaming. If that's not enough to bring you to their doors, there are more than 1,000 slot and video poker machines and Royal Ascot video horse racing. You'll also find several varied dining options. Black Bay Grille and Games is located right on the waterfront, Sacy's Restaurant offers a fine dining environment, and there are also two lounges and a café. Bring your clubs for a round of golf (you can also rent some from the pro shop), or stay the night in the hotel with 140-plus rooms.

Brimley's other casino, **Kings Club Casino** (12140 W. Lakeshore Dr.), is actually part of the Bay Mills Resort. Shuttle service is offered between the two casinos. Kings Club is one story, and has more than 250 slot and video poker machines. That's a far cry from the casino's beginning, when Kings Club was the first tribally operated blackjack casino in the States and the first in Michigan to offer slots and keno.

Events

The **International 500 Snowmobile Race** has been held in Sault Ste. Marie since 1969. At its inception, the I-500 was conceived as a snowmobiling version of the Indianapolis 500. The 500 miles are handled by a team of drivers (although someone will occasionally go it alone) on a one-mile iced track, while Sno-Cross races are held at the same time and venue. Races are usually held in February.

The **International Bridge Walk,** is held each summer on the last Saturday of June as a symbol of friendship between two cities and two nations. It's similar to the annual bridge walk across the Mackinac Bridge, except that the 2.8-mile walk is about half the distance and you actually get to stroll into Canada. Be sure to bring your passport or enhanced driver's license.

SUMMER SPORTS AND RECREATION
Hiking and Biking

West of town, the **Algonquin Pathway** has more than nine miles of trails for hiking and biking and, in the winter, cross-country skiing.

Two miles of the path are lighted. Take I-75 to 3 Mile Road and head west, turn right on 20th Street and left on 16th Avenue to the trailhead. Another good spot is the **Pine Bowl Pathway,** 19 miles southwest of Sault Ste. Marie. Pine Bowl has nearly eight miles of trails and rolling terrain. To get there, take I-75 south to the Kinross/Tone Road exit and head east on Tone Road, then turn right onto Wilson Road.

You'll be able to find some good trails at a number of area campgrounds, as well. **Monocle Lake Campground** (Forest Road 3699, Hiawatha National Forest, 906/635-5311), 21 miles west of Sault Ste. Marie, near the Point Iroquois Light, has an inviting two-mile loop accessible from its day-use parking lot. A viewing platform overlooks an active beaver pond before the trail heads uphill to another overlook, which will let you peer out to the St. Mary's River and beyond before returning to the parking lot. At **Soldier Lake Campground** (Forest Road 3138, Hiawatha National Forest, 906/635-5311), some 30 miles west of the city, there's a footpath that winds its way around the 15-acre lake and a spur that connects to the North Country Trail. Slightly farther out, 38 miles west of Sault Ste. Marie and a few miles south of M-28, **Three Lakes Campground** (Forest Road 3142, Hiawatha National Forest) has an easy one-mile loop around Walker Lake.

Fishing

Sault Ste. Marie is uniquely positioned for some of the Upper Peninsula's finest fishing. With Lake Superior above and Huron below, the Sault sits on the wide ribbon of St. Mary's River that links the two, and offers you the chance to snag some walleye, perch, pike, trout, salmon, and of course, whitefish. Contact the Sault Ste. Marie Convention and Visitors Bureau (536 Ashmun St., 906/632-3366 or 800/647-2858, www.saultstemarie.com) for more detailed information and a peak fishing guide. What follows is more general information.

For inland lake fishing, try a visit to Monocle Lake, a 172-acre inland lake with walleye, smallmouth bass, pike, and perch. The

lake is 40–45 feet deep and has two reefs near **Monocle Lake Campground** (Forest Road 3699, Hiawatha National Forest, 906/635-5311). There's a boat launch between the campground and the day use area. **Soldier Lake Campground** (Forest Road 3138, Hiawatha National Forest, 906/635-5311) is on the shores of a much smaller lake (15 acres) with bass and perch for the catching. Consider **Lake George** and **Munuscong Lake** as well.

, Captain Harold Bailey runs **Blue Heron Fishing Charters** (11589 E. Village Rd., 906/635-5134 or 906/632-1775, www.blue-heronfishingcharters.com, $300 day trip, $55 each additional person) from April through November. His qualifications are stellar: he's a local fisherman with more than 40 years of experience on the St. Mary's River and the surrounding waters. Captain Bailey will provide you with all the equipment you need (you can bring your own if you prefer), but you'll be responsible for bringing along a lunch and, more importantly, a Michigan fishing license. An Ontario license, although not totally necessary, would be a good idea. **River Cove Fishing Charters** (2841 Riverside Dr., 906/632-7710, www.rivercove.com, $280 half day, $390 full day, $250 night) offers half- and full-day charters, as well as night fishing for walleye. Although not local, **RiverQuest Charters** (616/837-0440 or 866/837-0440, www.riverquestcharters.com), located in the Lower Peninsula, offers seasonal charters for St. Mary's Atlantic salmon.

Boating

In addition to fishing charters, **River Cove** (2841 Riverside Dr., 906/632-7075, www. rivercove.com) can take up to five passengers on a scenic boat cruise. Choose from Soo Harbor and the north end of Sugar Island ($250), Neebish Island Cut/St. Joseph Island iron bridge ($275), and a sunset Soo Harbor cruise ($225). Rates may vary depending on fuel costs. You can get scenic dinner cruises from **Soo Locks Boat Tours** (1157 E. Portage Ave. and 515 E. Portage Ave., 906/632-6301 or 800/432-6301, www.soolocks.com, $43 adults,

$30 children 3–12). After the dinner buffet and dessert, you'll experience what it's like to travel through the impressive Soo Locks.

Golf

The 18 holes at the **Sault Ste. Marie Country Club** (1520 Riverside Dr., 906/632-7812, www.saultgolfing.com, $22 for 9 holes with cart, $38 for 18 holes with cart) are among the choicest of the Upper Peninsula, and some of the oldest as well. The course opened more than 100 years ago, and was expanded into an 18-hole course in the 1980s. Visit the pro shop or have an evening dinner at the clubhouse restaurant. Take Portage Avenue east out of the city to the country club. There are another 18 holes at **Tanglewood Marsh** (2600 W. 16th Ave., 906/635-0617 or 906/635-7651, www. tanglewoodmarsh.com, $19 for 9 holes with cart, $34 for 18 holes with cart). Take I-75 to exit 392 and head west on 3 Mile Road. Turn right on 20th Street and left on Oak Street, then curve right on 16th Avenue to the clubhouse.

Brimley has one of the U.P.'s top-rated golf courses at Brimley's **Wild Bluff Golf Course** (11335 W. Lakeshore Dr., 906/248-5860 or 888/422-9645, www.wildbluff.com, $34 for 9 holes with cart, $62 for 18 holes with cart), which is part of the Bay Mills Resort. The 18-hole championship course received an impressive 4.5 stars from *Golf Digest,* and it's easy to see why. A fine pro shop and an elegant player's lounge complete the golf experience. Don't forget the casino across the street.

Bird-Watching

Like Whitefish Point, the Sault Ste. Marie area is a popular spot for bird watching. Among the best places to scout for avian life is **Sugar Island,** the large island east of Sault Ste. Marie between Michigan and Ontario. Fifteen-mile-long Sugar Island and the St. Mary's River both attract migratory birds, particularly snowy and great gray owls. Both the Little Traverse Conservatory and the Osburn Preserve, which is owned by the University of Michigan Biological Station, help conserve and preserve

the island's wildlife and make the southern part of the island a great place for bird watching. Look for spruce grouse, black terns, sedge wrens, and long eared owls.

Beaches

One of the finest beaches in the area is on the edge of **Monocle Lake** (906/635-5311, www.fs.fed.us) in Hiawatha National Forest, some 20 miles west of Sault Ste. Marie on Lake Shore Drive. The large lake makes for some great swimming, certainly better than chilly Lake Superior nearby. This swimming area is easily accessible from the day-use parking area and is equipped with grills and picnic tables. To get there, take the Whitefish Bay National Scenic Byway (Lake Shore Drive) as it follows the shoreline west of St. Ignace to Forest Road 3699. If you're determined to swim in Lake Superior, head over to **Brimley State Park** (9200 W. 6 Mile Rd., 906/248-3422, www.michigan.gov/dnr) on the shores of Whitefish Bay. The water here tends to be among Lake Superior's warmest, relatively speaking.

Off-Road Vehicles

Off-road trails are scarce in this area. The only one in Chippewa County is the **Kinross Motorcycle Trail,** a nearly 29-mile trail about 20 miles south of Sault Ste. Marie, near Kinross and the Chippewa County International Airport. As its name implies, the trail is open only to motorcycles. The trail's three main loops all extend from a central parking area. Take Tone Road east from I-75 to Wilson Road and turn right to parking. Although there are no other designated trails in the county, all state forest roads are open to off-road vehicles unless specifically marked otherwise. Many roads in the Hiawatha National Forest are open to ATV/ORV use—more than 2,000 miles worth. For motor vehicle usage maps and more information, contact the Sault Ste. Marie Ranger District (4000 I-75 Business Spur, 906/635-5311, www.fs.fed.us).

WINTER SPORTS AND RECREATION
Ski and Snowshoe Trails

On the west side of the city, the trails at the **Algonquin Pathway** offer cross country skiers a series of loops that total some nine miles, with the longest two-mile loop illuminated for night skiing. To get there, take I-75 to 3 Mile Road, then head west to 20th Street and turn right. Take 20th Street to the intersection with 16th Avenue. The Pine Bowl Pathway is about 20 miles southwest of the city, and has nearly eight miles of groomed trails. To get to Pine Bowl from Sault Ste. Marie, head south on I-75 to the Kinross/Tone Road exit (exit 378) and take Tone Road east to Wilson Road; turn right on Wilson to the pathway.

Downhill Skiing

You could go to **Sault Seal Recreation Area** (2601 Minneapolis St., 906/635-6961, www.sault-sainte-marie.mi.us) for some downhill skiing, but the big draw here is tubing, with seven downhill runs. If you're looking for better skiing, you'll be better off heading elsewhere in the U.P., or consider crossing the border into Canada for the **Searchmont Resort** (103 Searchmont Resort Rd., Searchmont, 705/781-2340 or 800/663-2546, www.searchmont.com) in northern Ontario. Either option will require several hours of driving time.

Snowmobiling

The main drags into and out of Sault Ste. Marie by snowmobile are Trail 8, which heads west and north to Whitefish Point, Manistique, and Marquette, and Trail 49, which drops south toward Les Cheneaux before connecting to the rest of the Upper Peninsula's network of trails. In the city itself, Trails 8, 49, and others (449 and 497) run parallel to many of the streets. After crossing Power Canal near the Soo Locks, you must stay on the trail or risk a fine.

ACCOMMODATIONS

Now part of the Ramada chain, the rather plush ◖ **Ojibway Hotel** (240 W. Portage

Ave., 906/632-4100 or 800/654-2929, www.ramada.com, $95–240) has the nicest accommodations in town, and the best location, too, overlooking the St. Mary's River and the locks. For the very best view, ask for an upper-level room facing north. The elegant 1928 building has been beautifully restored, with large rooms, an indoor pool, a whirlpool, and the enjoyable Freighters restaurant. Ask about packages for a better deal.

For the same good location but for less money, try the (**Long Ships Motel** (427 W. Portage Ave., 906/632-2422 or 888/690-2422, www.longshipsmotel.net, $50–100), a clean and comfortable mom and pop style motel with a fine spot across from Locks Park. A little farther east, but still within walking distance of the river and downtown is the **Mid City Motel** (304 E. Portage Ave., 906/632-6832, $40–60).

Much of the Soo's lodging is sadly giving way to chain motels, which tend to boost the number of available beds (good for tourism), but lose the charm and surprise of the old mom and pops. The Sault Ste, Marie area has the highest concentration of chains in the eastern U.P., as it's the region's largest city and most popular tourist draw. Most are not within walking distance of the Locks, however.

Camping

Right in Sault Ste. Marie, there's a modern, 65-site **municipal campground** at Aune-Osborn Park, on the St. Mary's River near the Sugar Island ferry dock. Just east of Brimley, **Brimley State Park** (906/248-3422, www.michigan.gov/dnr) offers about a mile of sandy Lake Superior beach, a large modern campground. It's a good choice for anyone looking for an easy place to set up camp to enjoy the Soo and other nearby attractions. Although it's just a campground, Brimley is a popular park, so consider making reservations if you're aiming for a summer weekend. For a little more seclusion, head farther west to the **Hiawatha National Forest** (906/635-5311, www.fs.fed.us). Within a half-hour drive of the Soo, you

can find pretty and private tent sites next to the Lake Superior shore at Bay View, or near the great fishing point at Monocle Lake. No reservations are taken.

FOOD

Start your day at **Cup of the Day** (406 Ashmun St., 906/635-7272, www.cupoftheday.com, 7:15 A.M.– 6 P.M., closed Sun., coffee drinks $2–5, food $8–12) for good coffee drinks, a juice bar, and sandwiches and salads at lunchtime. In the Ojibway Hotel, (**Freighters** (240 Portage Ave., 906/632-4211, 6 A.M.–10 P.M. daily, $5–25) offers a wall of windows overlooking the locks and a very nice menu featuring steaks and seafood, with an emphasis on local fish. This is a great spot for a good breakfast, too. For an old-fashioned "service at your car" burger place, cruise on over to (**Clyde's Drive In** (1425 Riverside Dr., 906/632-2581, 9 A.M.–9 P.M. daily, $7–10), at the Sugar Island ferry dock, for the great grilled hamburgers they've been making since 1949. Inside seating and a menu of other fried items are available also. **Antler's Family Restaurant** (804 E. Portage Ave., 906/632-3571, www.antlersgiftshop.com, 9 A.M.–midnight Mon.–Wed., 9 A.M.–2 A.M. Thurs.–Sat., 9 A.M.–10 P.M. Sun., $10–30) serves up burgers, ribs, fresh fish, and Mexican-style dishes, amidst a setting with more than 300 game head mounts. Don't go when you have a headache—they have a strange habit of setting off sirens and whistles for no particular reason. Kids love this place, naturally.

INFORMATION AND SERVICES

For more information on the Sault Ste. Marie area, contact the **Sault Ste. Marie Convention and Visitors Bureau** (536 Ashmun St., 906/632-3366 or 800/647-2858, www.saultstemarie.com). For regional information and maps, stop by the **Michigan Welcome Center** (1001 Eureka St., 906/632-8242) near the International Bridge.

LAKE SUPERIOR STATE UNIVERSITY

Perhaps the least known of the Upper Peninsula's three state institutions of higher learning, Lake Superior State University, while with just 3,000 enrolled students, proudly maintains its heritage as a rugged, if slightly quirky northern Michigan institution.

The campus of LSSU is on land deeded to the State of Michigan in 1946 after having served as Fort Brady, a sporadically used military facility dating from the early 19th century. The facility was part of a network of forts along the Great Lakes constructed by the War Department to discourage a possible British invasion. Fort Brady was used up until World War II by the military as a marshalling area for troops.

After the war, the state used the land to construct a new college to serve residents of the eastern U.P., mostly returning veterans. Since the original curriculum was similar to that taught at Michigan Technological University, the school was initially set up a satellite campus of the Michigan College of Mining and Technology (now Michigan Technological University). The Sault Ste. Marie facility was informally known as Soo Tech, and eventually as Lake Superior State College of Michigan

Technological University. In 1970 the school became independent as Lake Superior State College, achieving university status in 1987.

Over the years LSSU has developed some of the finest programs in the nation in robotic technology, as well as computer, mechanical, and electrical engineering. LSSU also boasts highly regarded liberal arts programs.

But perhaps the school's greatest claim to fame lies in some of the peculiar customs that have become part of the institution's DNA. One campus organization is known as the Unicorn Hunters, which holds stone-skipping contests and paper snowman burnings in early spring to celebrate the end of winter. Since 1976 the Hunters have published an annual "List of Words and Phrases Banished from the Queen's English for Misuse, Overuse and General Uselessness." Released each year on New Year's Day, the list is chosen by the Hunters from nominations submitted by the general public. Additions for 2011 include "wow Factor," "a-ha moment," "backstory," "BFF," and "man up." The complete list (going all the way back to 1976) can be read at http://lssu.edu/banished/.

When you plan to **cross the border** (either entering or leaving the United States), you'll need to make sure you have a passport, a passport card, or another travel document that's compatible with the Western Hemisphere Travel Initiative (this can include a Michigan enhanced driver's license, U.S. military ID with military travel orders, Native American Tribal Photo ID, or a trusted traveler card, such as NEXUS). For a complete list of acceptable documents, visit the U.S. Department of State's travel website (http://travel.state.gov), but for most visitors it's as simple as a passport and, for foreign visitors, a passport from your country of citizenship along with a travel visa. You'll be stopped at the border crossing, asked to show your documents, and be asked a few simple questions. Make sure you're prepared and truthfully answer all of the questions. Also, refrain

from making ANY kind of humorous remark to the customs agents. They're instructed to take everything a traveler says seriously.

There are a few situations when things can get a bit more complicated. Be prepared to declare all goods, particularly items purchased or left abroad (gifts) and firearms. You'll have to pay duty on larger amounts of certain items: wine and liquor (more than 40 ounces), beer (more than 23 12-ounce cans or bottles), and cigarettes (more than 200). If you're traveling with children and you're not their parent or legal guardian, you need to have a letter from their parents or legal guardians giving them permission to leave the United States and enter Canada. Make certain a contact phone number is included. For more information, you can get contact the **United States Customs and Border Patrol** (906/632-2631, www.cbp.

gov) or **Canada Border Services Agency** (204/983-3500, www.cbsa.gc.ca).

What about medical care in Sault Ste. Marie? In case of emergency, call 911. And for hospitals, Sault Ste. Marie's got one of the best. For more than a century, **War Memorial Hospital** (500 Osborn Blvd., 906/635-4460, www.warmemorialhospital.org) has been providing the eastern Upper Peninsula with quality health care. To get there, take Ashmun Street to Spruce Street and head west to the hospital.

You won't have a problem finding banks or ATMs in Sault Ste. Marie. Two large national institutions are located on Ashmun Street, just south of Portage Avenue: **Huntington Bank** (511 Ashmun St., 906/635-5251, www.huntington.com) and **PNC Bank** (320 Ashmun St., 906/635-4300, www.pnc.com). There are several other banks near the Soo's waterfront. These include **Citizens Bank** (501 Court St., 906/632-6888, www.citizensbanking.com) or **Central Savings Bank** (3501 I-75 Business Spur, 906/635-8320, www.centralsavingsbank.com), plus others.

GETTING THERE AND AROUND
Car
If you're coming north over the Mackinac Bridge from the Lower Peninsula, Sault Ste. Marie is a short (45 min.), easy drive along I-75. If you're going to Portage Avenue and downtown, get off at exit 394 and turn left onto Easterday Avenue. Take the next right, onto Eureka Street, which quickly becomes Portage Avenue and takes you along the riverfront to the locks. There's a very helpful visitor information center as soon as you turn onto Eureka Street. Stop here for maps, brochures, and additional information.

If you decide not to get off at exit 394, you'll soon find yourself at the International Bridge and a border crossing into Canada. In this event, make sure you have your passport and/or other travel documents. And if you're entering the United States from across the border, Highway 17 (the Trans-Canada Highway) will get you to the International Bridge.

If you're arriving from elsewhere in the Upper Peninsula you'll want to get on M-28 anywhere west of I-75 and take it east to the interstate, then north to Sault Ste. Marie.

Air
The closest commercial airport is **Chippewa County International Airport** (CIU, 5019 Airport Dr., 906/495-5631 or 800/225-2525, www.airciu.com) in Kinross, about 20 miles south of Sault Ste. Marie. Daily flights are scheduled to and from Detroit by Mesaba Airlines (an affiliate of Delta Airlines) and car rentals are available from **Avis** (906/495-5900, www.avis.com) and **Thrifty** (906/635-0800 www.thrifty.com).

Boat
There are two marinas in Sault Ste. Marie: the **Charles T. Harvey Marina** (2442 Riverside Dr., 906/632-6741, www.michigan.gov/dnr) and the **George Kemp Marina** (485 E. Water St., 906/635-7670, www.michigan.gov/dnr). The Charles T. Harvey Marina is located on the lower St. Mary's River and has more than 30 boat slips and the usual amenities: electricity, water, shower, pump-out, and more. Charles T. Harvey Marina is located at 46° 28.15 N, 84° 18.00 W and can be reached on channel 9. The George Kemp Marina, meanwhile, is in downtown Sault Ste. Marie. It has more than 50 slips with the same basic amenities as the Harvey Marina. Kemp Marina is located at 46° 29.57 N, 84° 20.21 W. Use radio channel 9.

Public Transportation
If you're trying to get to Sault Ste. Marie by public transportation from elsewhere in the United States, your best option is **Indian Trails** (989/725-5105 or 800/292-3831, www.indiantrails.com). The bus line has regular service to the Sault. Call for current schedules and rates, or use the convenient quote finder tool on their website. You can also access the **Mackinaw Shuttle** (888/349-8294, www.mackinawshuttle.com) if you're already in northern Michigan.

The Huron Shore

East of I-75, the Upper Peninsula narrows and dribbles off into a series of smaller peninsulas, points, and Lake Huron islands. The area has a simple, pretty, and tranquil feel, the kind of place where casual cycling, beach combing, and picnicking set the pace for a summer day. While there's plenty to explore for the casual, unhurried visitor, there are few true "destinations." In fact, the whole area is often overlooked by guidebooks, which suits the locals and summer cottage owners just fine. So don't get too excited about sightseeing. Just pack a lunch, put on a pair of comfortable shoes, and while away the day along a rocky shoreline.

SIGHTS
DeTour Village

DeTour Village marks the end of the road and the end of the Upper Peninsula mainland. This small village has long served an important navigational role for ships heading up and down the St. Mary's River. Many ships squeeze through DeTour Passage here; the narrow waterway between the point and Drummond Island. They make a turn, or detour, to chart a course from the St. Mary's River to the Straits of Mackinac. DeTour Village is a *very* old community, which has guided ships with its navigational light since 1848. It remains a pleasant place to watch the ship traffic from public parks and gardens along M-134.

Nearby Lime Island marks the centerpiece of the **Island Explorer Water Trail,** a boater's route that travels from Lime to Mackinac Island along a linked network of islands. For more information, contact the **DeTour Area Chamber of Commerce** (906/297-5987, www.detourvillage.com). You can also stay at cabins and cottages on state forest land on Lime Island. For more information on rates and availability, contact the Sault Ste. Marie Forest Management Unit (906/635-5281, www.michigan.gov/dnr).

◖ Drummond Island

Here's a trivia question: What's the largest U.S. island in the Great Lakes? Probably few would guess Drummond, a quiet, low-key type of place. Some 65 percent of Drummond Island is state-owned land. The rest is owned mostly by summer residents, who swell the island's population to about 5,000 in July and August. You'd never know it, however. Life on this idyllic island is geared towards fishing, so most residents cluster along the shorelines. These cloistered places can rarely be seen from the island's few roads.

With rocky shorelines, inland lakes, marshy lowlands, hardwood forests, and open meadows, Drummond Island boasts remarkably diverse animal and plant habitats. More than 24 different kinds of orchids grow wild on the island. Loons, bobcats, moose, and a pack of wolves all roam here along with more common species.

Drummond and its neighboring islands are humps of limestone, part of the Niagara escarpment that stretches from Door County, Wisconsin, and across northern Lake Michigan. In an area called the Maxton Plains at the island's north end, this slab of limestone bedrock lies near the surface, covered by just a thin layer of alkaline soil. This unusual combination supports one of the world's foremost examples of alvar grassland, a rare mix of Arctic tundra and Great Plains plants, including Hill's thistle, false pennyroyal, and prairie dropseed. The Nature Conservancy owns more than 800 acres of the Maxton Plains. The preserve is open to the public, so you can explore this lunar-like landscape where large boulders of conglomerate flecked with red jasper, called "puddingstone" punctuate the barren expanses of limestone bedrock.

For more information on Drummond Island, call the **Drummond Island Tourism Association** (906/493-5245 or 800/737-8666, www.drummondislandchamber.com).

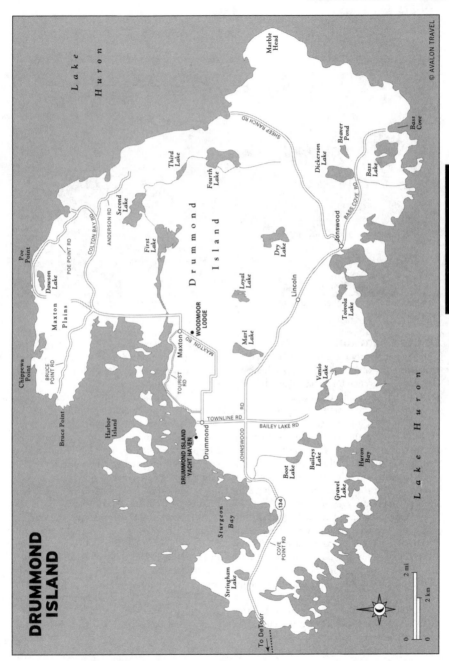

THE LAKE HURON SHORE

© JACK KUNEN/123RF.COM

The Maxton Plains Preserve, one of the rarest habitats in the world, is located on Drummond Island.

🅲 Les Cheneaux

"The Snows," everyone calls them, though the real name for these islands is Les Cheneaux (lay shen-O), French for "The Channels." And there are channels aplenty. Like shards of glass, 36 long and narrow islands lie splintered just off the U.P.'s southeastern shore, forming a maze of calm channels and protected bays in northern Lake Huron. Not surprisingly, it's a delight for boaters. Tall sailboats, small runabouts, classic cabin cruisers, and simple canoes all share these waters, as they have for more than a century.

Les Cheneaux first attracted boaters in the 1880s for the area's renowned fishing. Early enthusiasts came here from nearby Mackinac Island, already a popular vacation getaway for the wealthy. At first, these resorters from Mackinac came on daylong excursions. Before long, they were building their own cottages, reveling in the solitude not found in the other established Great Lakes resort areas. Though its summer guests were predominantly wealthy industrialists from southern Michigan, Indiana, Illinois, and Iowa, Les Cheneaux maintained a tactful, understated style. Cottages were elegant, but not ostentatious. Boats were sleek, but not showy.

Les Cheneaux still maintains that genteel, yet simple air. If you're the kind of person who doesn't need (or even like) to "be entertained," then you'll enjoy this charming area, free of crass tourism. Boating remains king here and in proper Les Cheneaux style, it is rarely expressed in macho powerboat posturing or screaming Jet skis. Boating here is best exemplified by the amazing array of classic wooden craft you'll see puttering and purring through the channels. The nation's first (and now, oldest) Criss Craft franchise was founded in Hessel in 1926. Many of those early boats survive today; thanks to the area's clean freshwater, short boating season, and locals' careful maintenance, which all help preserve the somewhat tender wooden hulls.

Les Cheneaux's love affair with classic boats is put on parade each summer at the annual **Les Cheneaux Antique Boat Festival** at the

Hessel docks. Held the second Saturday in August, it is believed to be the largest such show in the country, featuring more than a hundred wooden hulled vessels. For information, contact the **Les Cheneaux Historical Association** (906/484-2821, www.lchistorical.org).

For information on the Les Cheneaux area, contact the **Les Cheneaux Islands Area Tourist Association** (670 W. M-134, Cedarville, 888/364-7526, www.lescheneaux.org).

Harbor Island National Wildlife Refuge

About 1.5 miles off the shore of Drummond Island, the comparatively small Harbor Island National Wildlife Refuge is far enough to be remote, but still close enough that it isn't hard to get to. You can access the 695-acre island by private boat. Some popular recreational activities include offshore fishing and hunting. There's also a small swimming beach. Wildlife includes foxes, snowshoe hares, grouse, and sparrows. During the winter the refuge has been known to welcome timber wolves from Ontario's nearby St. Joseph Island. The refuge is managed by **Seney National Wildlife Refuge** (1674 Refuge Entrance Rd., 906/586-9851, www.fws.gov).

Lighthouses

Lighthouse lovers won't want to miss a tour of **DeTour Reef Light Station,** a more than 80-foot-tall light that's listed on the National Register of Historic Places. Stationed between Drummond Island and the village of DeTour, the 1931 light underwent an extensive restoration project and reopened for tours in 2005. It's a bold, boxy lighthouse, with sharp lines that seem suited to its job of warning ships of the dangerous reef below the surface. The DeTour Reef Light Preservation Society (906/493-5648 June–Aug., 616/874-9458 Jan.–May, www.drlps.com, $95 nonmembers, $75 members) arranges tours of the lighthouse Saturdays and Sundays during the summer. The two-hour tour, which is limited to six people, begins with a boat ride to the light to the light, up a 20-

foot ladder, through the house, and to the top of the watch room.

ENTERTAINMENT AND EVENTS

The eastern U.P. seems to be pretty heavy on the casino count. There are gaming parlors in St. Ignace, Sault Ste. Marie, Christmas, Brimley, and more, all within a couple of hours of Les Cheneaux and Drummond Island. But that hasn't stopped Kewadin from opening a small **Kewadin Casino** (3395 N. 3 Mile Road, 906/484-2903) in Hessel. Gaming is limited to slots and some blackjack. There are no hotel rooms here, and a deli is first among the casino's few amenities.

Every August, Hessel is home to the **Les Cheneaux Islands Antique Wooden Boat Show,** the largest show of its kind in the Midwest. Wooden boat owners and aficionados from around the country show up in the small U.P. town to celebrate wooden boats of all types. **The Festival of Arts** goes on at the same time, so even if you're not interested in wooden boats, there's plenty for you to do. Browse the vendor booths in search of handmade crafts and artwork.

SUMMER SPORTS AND RECREATION
Hiking and Biking

A mountain bike is a fun way to explore Drummond Island, since M-134 dissolves into a variety of double tracks and, eventually, single-track roads. Don't expect technical riding as the island is quite flat. When you venture into state land, you'll likely end up sharing some of the designated DNR trails with ATVs, which can be both irritating and potentially dangerous. But with 76 miles of trail, you're sure to find stretches with little or no traffic. For specific trails, ask about **Marble Head View Point,** and **Warners Cove** and **Gravel Lake** on the south shore. Trail information is available from the **Drummond Island Tourism Association** (906/493-5245 or 800/737-8666, www.drummondislandchamber.com).

An eastern Upper Peninsula road biking map

LAKE HURON

When thinking about the inland seas that border Michigan's Upper Peninsula, Lake Huron may occur as an afterthought. It tends to be overlooked for Lake Superior's rugged shorelines and Lake Michigan's reputation as a pleasure seeker's destination. But Lake Huron's shallow sandy shores are immensely popular for summer cottages and vacation homes, particularly in the Lower Peninsula and Canada. In the Upper Peninsula, the Huron shoreline is home to the boating paradise of Les Cheneaux. Just offshore, Drummond Island, a secluded recreational paradise, beckons.

Lake Huron is the third largest of the Great Lakes by volume, holding some 849 cubic miles of water, but the second largest by surface area (23,010 square miles).

The competition is largely irrelevant, since the two lakes are hydrologically one. This is a scientific way of explaining that they have the same surface elevation and are connected by the Straits of Mackinac, which has a depth of 295 feet. Since the flow occasionally reverses direction, the straits can't be considered a river. In fact, the United States Army Corps of Engineers considers the two lakes to be one, called Lake Michigan-Huron. Amazingly, due to its incredible depth, Lake Superior's water volume is still far larger than the two lakes combined.

That said, there are some other remarkable facts about Lake Huron. Manitoulin Island is the largest island in a freshwater lake in the world, with an area of more than 1,000 square miles. The island also has more than 100 lakes of its own, including the world's largest lake on an island in a lake. And if the collective perimeters of the lake's some 30,000 islands were added to its mainland coastline, Lake Huron can suddenly boast the longest shoreline of any of the Great Lakes.

Lake Huron was the first of the Great Lakes to be discovered by Europeans and its initial name was "The Freshwater Sea" prior to the discovery of the other lakes.

is available from the Michigan Department of Transportation or from the **Les Cheneaux Tourist Association** (670 W. M-134, Cedarville, 888/364-7526, www.lescheneaux. org). The map highlights major biking roads in the area, including Hessel, Cedarville, DeTour, and other cities. It also offers advice on traffic levels, shoulder width, and other issues of concern to bikers. For mountain bikers, there are plenty of two tracks, trails, and back roads. You can get detailed information from the visitors center on the island, located at the corner of M-134 and Townline Road.

Canoeing and Kayaking

A canoe or kayak is a great way to explore the waters of Les Cheneaux. The fjord-like bays and 150 miles of ragged shoreline make this a magical place to paddle. One of the best routes to take is the **North Lake Huron Paddle Trail,** which extends for some 75 miles from DeTour nearly to St. Ignace, passing among the islands of Les Cheneaux on the way. It's best to get a guide while paddling the islands, since the ins and outs of the waterways make it easy to lose yourself. For kayak tours, rentals, and advice pay a visit to **Woods and Waters Ecotours** (20 Pickford Ave., 906/484-4157, www.woodswaterecotours.com), an outfitter and guide company in Hessel. Multi-day guided tours of the North Lake Huron Paddle Trail are offered, as well as half- and full-day kayak trips. Custom tours can be arranged.

Fishing

Anglers aren't going to spend much time in Les Cheneaux before the channels start calling. It's easy to see why. This is a place unlike any other. Book a fishing charter with specifically and lengthily named **Les Cheneaux Islands Water Tours and Charter Services** (117 N. Greenwood Dr., Cedarville, 906/484-3776 or

866/322-3776, www.fishingwithnorm.com, $375 half day, $700 full day) for a full- or half-day trip. You can also arrange for a tour with **Dream Seaker Charters and Tours** (888/634-3419, www.dreamseaker.com, $695 full day, $495 half day).

One of the popular spots for inland fishing is **Munuscong River State Forest** (906/635-5281, www.michigan.gov/dnr), where you can cast at the river for walleye, pike, bass, perch, and more, or head a mile east to Lake Munuscong for more fishing. For additional fishing spots and information about fishing seasons, contact the Les Cheneaux Islands Tourist Association (670 W. M-134, Cedarville, 888/364-7526, www.lescheneaux.org).

Boating

The best way to see Les Cheneaux, of course, is to get out on the water. Aside from the pretty wooded islands themselves, part of the fun is eyeing the beautiful old boathouses that dot the shorelines, especially on Marquette Island. If you have your own craft, you'll find launches in Hessel and Cedarville, the only two towns in the area. Though the waters are protected and normally quite safe, be sure to bring a chart, or at least a map provided by local businesses. The various bays, channels, and points can be rather confusing to a newcomer. Many cottages rent boats or include them in their rates.

Golf

For such a mellow place as Drummond Island, you might be surprised to run across **The Rock** (33494 S. Maxton Rd., 906/493-1000 or 800/999-6343, www.drummondisland.com, $49–59 for 18 holes, depending on season), a spectacular "designer" golf course completed in 1990. The first rate course makes fine use of the natural environment, its holes weaving through woods and limestone outcroppings. In 2008, The Rock earned a four-star rating from *Golf Digest* as part of the magazine's "Best Places to Play." Contact The Rock for specials and packages.

The nine-hole **Les Cheneaux Club Golf Club** (1407 Golf Links Rd., 906/484-3606,

© CARL TER HAAR, TRAVEL MICHIGAN

A vintage wooden boat show in Hessel attracts tourists and locals.

www.lescheneauxgolfclub.com, $15 for 9 holes, $21 for 18 holes, $12–24 for a cart, per person) in Cedarville is the oldest still playable and continuously played links in Michigan. It was first played more than 110 years ago, in May 1898 on grounds dictated by the land: forest, sand, water, and rock. In Hessel, try the **Hessel Ridge Golf Course** (2061 N. 3 Mile Rd., 888/660-9166, www.hesselridge.com, $20 for 9 holes with cart, $36 for 18 holes with cart, reduced rates after 3 P.M. and on weekdays). The 18-hole, 6,415-yard course is located on a ridge overlooking Hessel, with tree-lined boundaries, well-manicured greens, and beautiful views.

Off-Road Vehicles

Three off-road trails are maintained within the Les Cheneaux area. The farthest west is Bay City Lake Trail, a short distance north of Hessel. The 50-inch trails here consist of three loops that total nearly eight miles around Bay City Lake. To get there, take 3 Mile Road north of Hessel to Bay City Lake Road, just past Hessel Ridge Golf Course and turn left to parking. The 8.4-mile Birch Hill Trail is for motorcycle use only, and is located east of Cedarville. Take M-134 to Prentiss Bay Road and continue north to parking. Nearby, the Foreman Lake Trail has several additional miles of trails. Continue north on Prentiss Bay Road, turn right on Traynor Road, and then right again on Springer Road. Closer to DeTour, Cranberry Lake Trail runs for eight miles from M-48 to Caribou Lake. This trail is for vehicles less than 50 inches in width, and there's parking at the trailheads on M-48, just north of M-134, and on M-134 itself, near the turnoff for DeTour Campground.

Drummond Island, with its vast stretches of state-owned land, is an ideal place to take your ATVs. There are more than 65 miles of trails, many of them looped and much of them through old-growth boreal forests. Pay special attention to the island's northern shore, which has plenty of stunning Lake Huron views. Also, with the exception of M-134 between the ferry

and Channel Road, all of Drummond Island's roads (paved and unpaved) are ATV friendly. Ask for a full color map from the **Drummond Island Tourism Association** (906/493-5245 or 800/737-8666, www.drummondisland-chamber.com) or local businesses. But it doesn't stop there. Drummond Island is also home to **Turtle Ridge Off-Road Terrain Challenge Park** (www.turtleridgeorv.com, $25 per day, multiple day discounts), which has rock crawls, hill climbs, mud, and more.

WINTER SPORTS AND RECREATION
Ski and Snowshoe Trails

On Drummond Island, cross-country ski trails include 4.5 miles at the Rainbow Trail, a groomed, mostly flat trail on Maxton Cross Road. No snowshoeing is allowed at the Rainbow Trail. The Drummond Island Resort and Conference Center has 15 miles of groomed trails for Nordic skiing. Rental skis are available to resort guests for free.

Visitors interested in snowshoeing can head to a section of trails specifically set aside by Drummond Island Resort, and there are two miles of snowshoe trails available on the Island Heritage Trail at Drummond Island Township Park. Additionally, all 76 miles of the island's designated DNR trails are accessible by snowshoe. The Drummond Island Tourism Association (906/493-5245 or 800/737-8666, www.drummondislandchamber.com) will have more information for you.

Back on the mainland, skiers can try the five groomed miles at the **Peek-A-Boo Hill Cross Country Ski Trail,** maintained by the Les Cheneaux Nordic Ski Club. To get to the trail, take Blindline Road north of M-129, then go west on State Avenue to the Les Cheneaux Community Schools' running track, where you'll find the trailhead. The Search Bay Back Country Ski Trail is a good option, located five miles west of Hessel. The two 1.5-mile loops make a figure eight. They're groomed and easy to ski, taking you out onto the small peninsula of St. Martin's Point. The trailhead is accessible south of M-134.

Snowmobiling

Drummond Island Resort and Convention Center is a good place to start when snowmobiling on the island. From here you can gain access to Drummond Island's astonishing 100 miles of groomed snowmobile trails. As for rentals: Drummond Island Resort rents snowmobiles for $199–225 per day, along with a required $500 damage deposit. Free snowmobile maps are available from local businesses and the tourism association.

The trails in Les Cheneaux connect with the hundreds of miles of trails that crisscross the Upper Peninsula. Trail 47 extends from DeTour and will take you to Trail 2 near St. Ignace, making stops in Cedarville and Hessel along the way. Trail 491 splits north from 47, taking you to Pickford, while Trail 49 will take you north to Kinross and Sault Ste. Marie. Additionally, you can operate your snowmobile on all unplowed roads in Mackinac County, as well as on the far right side of paved roads and the unpaved portions of highways. Obey traffic laws and speed limits, and be careful.

ACCOMMODATIONS

On Drummond Island, stay in luxury at **Ⅽ Woodmoor Lodge** (33494 S. Maxton Rd., 906/493-1000 or 800/999-6343, www.drummondisland.com, $119–155), a grandiose retreat with a handsome log lodge. Guests have access to all Drummond Island Resort facilities, including an outdoor pool, tennis courts, bowling, and even sporting clays. You can also rent some Frank Lloyd Wright–style cottages, many overlooking Potagannissing Bay, for varying rates. Another good lodging choice is **Ⅽ Drummond Island Yacht Haven** (33185 S. Water St., 906/493-5232, www.diyachthaven.com, $105–400 per night, $675–1,975 per week), with large cabins overlooking island-studded Potagannissing Bay. The larger three-bedroom cabins have limestone fireplaces. The property also offers sandy beaches, boat rentals, and other amenities. Contact the Drummond Island Tourism Association (906/493-5245 or 800/737-8666, www.drummondislandchamber.com) for more choices.

Along the Lake Huron shore near Cedarville, the **Spring Lodge Cottages** (916 Park Ave., 906/484-2282 or 800/480-2282, www.springlodge.com, $100–150) have a wonderful location in the heart of Les Cheneaux, right on the Snows Channel. Large and well-kept grounds house cottages, most overlooking the water. Boat rentals are available on site. For nicer-than-average motel rooms and an indoor pool, try the **Cedarville Inn** on M-134 in Cedarville (906/484-2266, $100–150). **Islands Inn Motel** (90 E. M-134, 906/484-2293, www.islandsinnmotel.com, $75 and up) and **Les Cheneaux Motel** (769 E. M-134, 906/484-2581, http://lescheneaux.com, $59 and up) are other good, affordable choices.

Camping

Drummond Island's best camping is at **Township Park,** just north of M-134, not far from the ferry dock. This rustic campground (no showers) has pretty sites tucked in the woods on Potagannissing Bay. There's a sand beach and a boat launch. No reservations; $8 for sites without electricity; $9.25 for sites with electricity.

Camp along the Lake Huron shore and under the pines in a former state park now managed by the **Lake Superior State Forest** (906/293-5131, www.michigan.gov/dnr). The marked beach/picnic area is on M-134, six miles west of DeTour Village. For more seclusion, boaters should head for **Government Island,** the only publicly owned island in Les Cheneaux. Once a Coast Guard station, it's now part of the **Hiawatha National Forest** (906/643-7900, www.fs.fed.us). Outhouses and picnic tables are available at a couple of primitive sites on the northeastern and southern ends of the small island; no trace camping is permitted anywhere on the island.

FOOD

One of the local standbys, where the home cooked food is always good, is **Hessel Bay Inn** (186 Pickford Ave., 906/484-3203). Open for breakfast, lunch, and dinner, Hessel Bay Inn has a wide selection of menu options,

including fish, pasta, corned beef, steaks, and more. Make sure you try the all-you-can-eat whitefish, or stop by for the Sunday buffet. If the weather's nice, ask for a seat on the deck, which has an attractive view of Hessel Bay and the marina.

For such a small town, Cedarville actually has a nice selection of restaurants. **◖ Cattail Cove Restaurant and Lounge** (22 Hodeck St., 906/484-2995) is a good example. It's no surprise to see fresh, local fish on the menu here; and you really should try a Great Lakes catch while you're in the area! You can get a good char-grilled prime rib, too. The outdoor deck overlooks Cedarville Bay, making it the perfect place for a fair-weather cocktail or two. If you're in the mood for some Italian, head over to **Ang-Gio's** (232 W. M-134, 906/484-3301) for some tasty pizza.

In DeTour, stop by **Fisher's Restaurant** (168 Ontario St., 906/297-2801, www.fishersrestaurant.net, 9 A.M.–4 P.M. Tues.–Thurs., 9 A.M.–7 P.M. Fri.–Sun., closed Mon.) for good food, great service, and a worthwhile lunch buffet. Another favorite is **◖ Mainsail Restaurant and Saloon** (410 N. Ontario St., 906/297-2141, www.mainsailrestaurant.com), a casual restaurant that serves three hearty meals daily. Offerings include steak, shrimp, fresh fish, salads, and burgers—solid American food plus a few burritos. Stop by the saloon for draft beer and mixed drinks. As an added bonus, Mainsail is home to the original blueprints for the *Edmund Fitzgerald,* the tragic freighter made famous by Gordon Lightfoot's song.

Drummond Island has a fair handful of restaurants, too. The **Port of Call Restaurant** (30420 E. Johnswood Rd./M-134, 906/493-5507, www.drummondislandfudge.com) is a high-end establishment which prides itself in offering a selection of international items that aren't usually found in U.P. restaurants. Traditional breakfast items like eggs Benedict and bagel sandwiches give way to Belgian waffles, Greek gyro omelets, and European bake house breads like Russian pumpernickel and Jewish rye. Lunch and dinner menus feature Oriental vegetable noodle soup, Greek gyros, English fish and chips, pierogi with Polish sausage. You'll find plenty of traditional, Midwestern American food, too. Port of Call features an impressive wine selection. **◖ Bayside Dining** (33494 S. Maxton Rd., 906/493-1000 or 800/999-6343, www.drummondisland.com) is another higher end restaurant located at Drummond Island Resort and Conference Center. There aren't many restaurants in the Upper Peninsula where entrees top $30, and this is one of them. Here's where you'll find shrimp and lobster crusted whitefish, buffalo strip loin, duck, and braised lamb. For the resort's more humble fare, try **Pins** (33494 S. Maxton Rd., 906/493-1000 or 800/999-6343, www.drummondisland.com), where you'll find burgers, pizza, wings—and bowling.

INFORMATION AND SERVICES

There are a few sources for helpful visitor information. Among the finest are **Les Cheneaux Islands Tourist Association** (670 W. M-134, Cedarville, 888/364-7526, www.lescheneaux. org) and the **Drummond Island Tourism Association** (906/493-5245 or 800/737-8666, www.drummondislandchamber.com).

The nearest hospital is St. Ignace's **Mackinac Straits Hospital** (220 Burdette St., 906/643-8585, www.mshosp.org), about a half-hour drive from Cedarville and an hour from DeTour. Take M-134 to I-75, then head south until you hit U.S. 2, just before the Bridge; turn left on U.S. 2, then right on Burdette Street to the hospital. Another option is **War Memorial Hospital** (500 Osborn Blvd., 906/635-4460, www.warmemorialhospital.org) in Sault Ste. Marie, although it's a bit farther away. Dial 911 for emergencies.

Most of the area's banks are in Cedarville. Here you'll find a **Central Savings Bank** (143 W. M-134, 906/484-2036, www.centralsavingsbank.com) on M-134 as you pass through town; **First National Bank of St. Ignace** (192 S. Meridian St., 906/484-2262, www. fnbsi.com) has a branch; and the **Soo Co-Op Credit Union** (90 Beach St., 906/484-2073,

www.soocoop.com) is downtown. In DeTour, go to the **Central Savings Bank** (109 Elizabeth St., 906/297-3061, www.centralsavingsbank.com) near the Drummond Island Ferry dock. While on the island itself, go to **Detour Drummond Community Credit Union** (34857 S. Townline Rd., 906/493-5721, www.ddccu.com).

GETTING THERE AND AROUND
Car
One of the Huron Shore's draws is its convenient accessibility. If you're taking the Bridge up from the Lower Peninsula, then Cedarville is a short half hour drive up I-75 and along M-134. It's another half hour along M-134 to DeTour and Drummond Island. From Sault Ste. Marie, you can head south on I-75 and catch M-134 or take M-129 straight down. M-129 is a shorter distance, but the interstate is fast and convenient and won't add much time to your drive.

The one-mile-long auto crossing is managed by the **Drummond Island Ferry** (906/235-3170, $12 per vehicle, plus an additional $2 per passenger) for a 10-minute trip across the St. Mary's River. Ferry service is offered year round. For current schedules and additional pricing for trailers, snowmobiles, camper units, and other details, contact the Drummond Island Tourism Association (906/493-5245 or 800/737-8666, www.drummondislandchamber.com).

Air
As with most air passengers to the eastern U.P., you'll likely be flying into **Chippewa County International Airport** (CIU, 5019 Airport Dr., 906/495-5631 or 800/225-2525, www.airciu.com). Daily flights are offered to and from Detroit by Mesaba Airlines (an affiliate of Delta Airlines), and rental cars from two companies: **Avis** (906/495-5900, www.avis.com) and **Thrifty** (906/495-8000, www.thrifty.

com). Driving time to DeTour from Chippewa County Airport should be between one and one and a half hours. **Pellston Airport** (231/539-8423), south of Mackinaw City in the Lower Peninsula, is about 80 miles away. There's a small airport on Drummond Island, too, but no commercial service is offered there.

Boat
Les Cheneaux's 36 islands, sheltered channels, and bays make it a boater's dream. If you're one of the fortunate ones boating here, you'll want to head to the **Hessel/Clark Township Marina** (906/484-3917 or 906/484-2672, www.michigan.gov/dnr), which has 30 transient slips and a boatload of amenities. Along with the expected water, electricity, pumpout, showers, and the like, Hessel Marina is close to marine repair supplies, a fish cleaning station, laundry, and more. The marina is open from late May through early September and is located at 46° 00.05 N, 84° 25.30 W. Use radio channel 9. Farther east, you can go to **DeTour State Dock** (906/297-5947, www.michigan.gov/dnr). Another marina with basic amenities, DeTour has a harbormaster on duty from mid-May through late September. Use radio channel 16, then switch to 9. It's located at 45° 59.43 N, 83° 53.50 W. For other marinas, consider **Cedarville Marine** (906/484-2815) in Cedarville or Hessel's E.J. **Mertaugh Boat Works** (906/484-2434, www.ejmertaughboatworks.com). Additionally, there are a number of private marinas on Drummond Island. Contact the Drummond Island Tourism Association (906/493-5245 or 800/737-8666, www.drummondislandchamber.com) for more information.

Public Transportation
There is no regularly scheduled public transportation to take you into Les Cheneaux, so you'll want to make sure you've got your own mode of transport lined up ahead of time.

BACKGROUND

The Land

GEOLOGY AND GEOGRAPHY

Michigan is easily one of America's most geographically peculiar states. Split in two, it consists of two enormous peninsulas, each surrounded on three sides by the Great Lakes. Many people immediately associate the state with its mitten shaped Lower Peninsula. The Upper Peninsula, however, looms quite large—big enough to hold the combined states of New Jersey, Connecticut, Rhode Island, and Delaware all within its scalloped borders.

A combination of cataclysmic volcanic eruptions and soupy tropical seas initially formed what we know now as Michigan. In the northeastern part of the state, near Lake Superior and northern Lake Huron, volcanoes erupting billions of years ago laid down thick layers of basalt, which later tilted and faulted, forming the area's rugged, rocky topography of ancient mountain ranges and steep, saw-toothed shorelines.

Much later, powerful glaciers added their indelible touch to the Michigan landscape, the most recent just 12,000 years ago. Four separate ice sheets scraped across the region, scouring out depressions that became lakes, lowlands, and ragged shorelines. When the ice melted and the glaciers retreated, the meltwater filled the vast basins and created the modern-day Great Lakes.

© PAUL VACHON

Michigan's Upper Peninsula comprises two distinct land regions, the Superior Uplands and the Northern Highlands. The Superior Uplands spans the western two-thirds of the Upper Peninsula, the region formed by the ancient volcanic activity. It is a landscape of dramatic beauty, characterized by rugged basalt cliffs and thick boreal forests of fir, spruce, and birch, all of it part of the vast Canadian Shield that dips down from the Canadian arctic, across portions of the northern Great Lakes region, and back up the west side of Hudson Bay in a giant horseshoe. Much of the region rises more than 1,000 feet above sea level, including the state's highest point, Mt. Arvon, which tops out at 1,979 feet. The Superior Uplands also harbor some of the nation's richest sources of minerals, most notably copper and iron ore deposits.

South and east of the Superior Uplands lies the Northern Highlands, covering the eastern Upper Peninsula and extending down into the northern half of the Lower Peninsula. Here basalt bedrock gives way to sandstone and limestone, and boreal forests segue into pine and hardwoods. Once heavily logged for its vast, valuable stands of white and red pine, the Northern Highlands area today is prized largely for the recreation provided by its woods, water, and wildlife.

Geographically, no other state displays such a striking dichotomy; the Upper Peninsula is largely circled by Lakes Michigan, Superior, and Huron, and is connected to the Lower Peninsula solely by the Mackinac Bridge. Unless they arrive by boat or drive through Wisconsin, everyone traveling between the peninsulas gets there by the same 54-foot-wide roadway.

The Upper Peninsula shares a border with northeastern Wisconsin, then stretches east for 334 miles between Lakes Superior and Michigan. It reaches a third Great Lake, Huron, where it terminates at Drummond Island. Also considered part of the U.P. is the 45-mile-long archipelago Isle Royale, the largest land mass in Lake Superior, and Michigan's only national park, one of the most remote and least visited in the national park system.

Collectively, the U.P.'s landmass covers more than 16,000 square miles, but it is water that principally defines the peninsula. Of Michigan's 3,288 miles of shoreline (second only to Alaska), the U.P. accounts for more than half of them: 1,700 miles on the shores of the three largest Great Lakes. The inland U.P. incorporates more than 4,000 lakes, 12,000 miles of rivers, and over 300 named waterfalls. It boasts 11 federally designated Wild and Scenic Rivers and is home to America's first national lakeshore, Pictured Rocks.

The Great Lakes State, Water Wonderland, Land of Hiawatha…many of Michigan's nicknames accurately describe the Upper Peninsula, but up here you're more likely to hear that you're in God's Country.

CLIMATE

Weather patterns in the Upper Peninsula vary widely, since the Great Lakes tend to complicate a great deal. Temperatures in the U.P. can be unexpectedly moderate, since the lakes tend to cool the hot air of summer and warm the cold winds of winter. There are four distinct seasons. Average July and August temperatures are in the 70s (except near the shorelines). From December through February, they drop to the 20s, and they often get much, much colder. Temperatures listed in the book are in degrees Fahrenheit.

But don't let this deter you. You can enjoy spring-like skiing conditions in February or find yourself in the single digits at Thanksgiving. You may swelter on a summer hike through the woods, and then later feel compelled to put on a jacket while visiting a Great Lakes beach.

The Lake Effect

The Great Lakes act as large insulators—slow to warm up, slow to cool down—and have a dramatic effect on snowfall. Dry winter air travels over the Great Lakes on the prevailing western winds, absorbing moisture. When this air hits land, it dumps its precipitation in the form of snow. Meteorologists and locals alike refer to this phenomenon as **lake effect snow.** These snows can be surprisingly

© JASON ROSS/123RF.COM

Lake of the Clouds at Porcupine Mountains State Park

from land to several miles out. The commercial shipping season shuts down from January 15 to March 25, but bad weather often hampers it for much longer. Commercial ships regularly cut through ice up to a foot thick. Ice more massive requires them to rely on the Coast Guard's *Mackinaw*, a 240-foot heavily reinforced ship specifically designed for ramming a passage through ice. The *Mackinaw* can "back and ram" its way through walls of ice as high as 10 feet.

A Few Words about Winter

The Upper Peninsula's winter is long and cold. Snow and cold temperatures are virtually constant from Thanksgiving to Easter. In an average season, the U.P. gets covered with some 160 inches.

This represents an average. U.P. snows are legendary, especially in the Keweenaw Peninsula, where 300-inch winters are not unusual. In summer, curious pier-like devices can be seen sprouting from front doors and leading to sidewalks on Keweenaw homes, usually a few feet off the ground. These serve as a guide to show shoveling. The accepted standard is not to do so until at least 24 inches are on the ground. Ladders nailed to roofs are there for a specific reason as well. When accumulated snows threaten to collapse the roofs, the ladders provide a foothold from which to clear it.

It's important to be aware of the **wind chill factor,** the threat that comes when cold temperatures are coupled with biting winds. When it's 5°F outside, a 15-mph wind will make it feel like -25°. Not only is this exceedingly uncomfortable, it also elevates the risk for frostbite or hypothermia. Weather forecasts usually warn about the wind chill factor, but not always. Remember to take into consideration both the temperature and the wind speed when dressing for the outdoors.

Despite this, many people welcome the Upper Peninsula's winter, as it's a huge part of the state's tourism revenue. Few other areas in the Midwest can offer as reliable a season for skiing, snowboarding, snowmobiling, ice fishing, and snowshoeing.

localized, which is one reason why most of the U.P.'s successful ski resorts are clustered near Iron Mountain along the western edge of the peninsula.

The prevailing western breezes also affect Great Lakes water temperatures, most noticeably on Lake Michigan. In summer, the warm surface waters tend to blow into the eastern Lake Michigan beaches along the Lower Peninsula. While Lake Michigan is rarely warm enough for much swimming on the Wisconsin side, it can be exceedingly pleasant in the Lower Peninsula and at least tolerable in the Upper, as evidenced by the hundreds of popular swimming beaches lining the west side of the state.

Lake Superior is altogether different. Water temperatures in this northern lake rarely climb out of the 40s, save for the occasional shallow bay. "No one's ever drowned in Lake Superior," the saying goes. "They all die of hypothermia first."

Freshwater freezes more quickly than saltwater, and the Great Lakes will often ice over

When to Go

When to visit Michigan's Upper Peninsula depends on your interests. For traditional warm-weather pursuits, count on summer arriving sometime in early June and lasting until early September. July is the warmest month, but in the U.P., it is also the most bug infested. Try to time a camping trip before the mosquitoes and black flies hatch, which *usually* means by mid-June or after mid-August.

Autumn may be the best time to visit, when days are warm, nights are cool, the bugs are gone, and Upper Michigan's hardwoods put on a color show to rival Vermont's. September and October are fine months in the U.P., although late October can be somewhat cold. Predicting the period of peak color is an inexact science, but the first or second week of September is generally a safe bet.

Winter hits around early December and usually lingers through March. For snow sports, February is your best choice to ensure good cover.

If you can, avoid November and April, both of which are characterized by unpleasant gray skies and rain/snow/sleet mixtures. Spring usually doesn't begin until about mid-May, and the shady pine forests of the U.P. can easily hold snow until Memorial Day. Like autumn, spring in Michigan can be wonderful, with moderate temperatures and blossoming trees.

ENVIRONMENTAL ISSUES

The Upper Peninsula's primary environmental concern is the safeguarding of the area's prized natural resources. Thankfully, citizens have traditionally been more than willing to step in and oppose those who would abuse the land. Over the years, various threats to the region's ecosystem have occurred. These began with the fur trade, followed by mining and logging and more recently by asbestos dumping, nuclear waste, and water use issues. Currently there's a debate over metallic sulfide mining, which has the potential to cause devastating environmental damage. Whether or it goes forward or not is still undetermined.

In sum, the fact that the Upper Peninsula is a relatively wild place does not mean that it will

© PAUL VACHON

In the U.P., streams and lakes blend beautifully with the land.

necessarily stay that way. The Upper Peninsula Environmental Coalition and similar organizations work diligently to keep this land the outdoorsy paradise it is today.

PRESERVATION

Beginning in the 1920s, as the mining and timber industries began their declines, modern concepts of land and resource preservation became a priority, beginning with the establishment of the Ottawa and Hiawatha National Forests in the late 1920s. In 1931, Isle Royale became part of the National Park System. The 1940s saw the addition of the Porcupine Mountain and Tahquamenon Falls State Parks. Still more designations would follow, including the Pictured Rocks National Lakeshore in 1966. The recent history of the Upper Peninsula tells the story of a region that had once been exploited for its resources gradually becoming a region that stresses the importance of preservation.

Flora and Fauna

Though it's called the Wolverine State, only meager evidence exists of wolverines ever having lived in Michigan, even in the Upper Peninsula. One possible explanation as to how the state obtained its name can be attributed to early fur traders, who may have brought wolverine pelts to the numerous trading posts in Upper Michigan. It is worth noting, however, that in early 2004 a wolverine was sighted and photographed in Huron County, located at the tip of the thumb in the Lower Peninsula. It was the first confirmed sighting in some 200 years and shocked state DNR biologists.

With an estimated 85 percent of the peninsula forested, the U.P. harbors a considerable number of gray and red foxes, skunks, squirrels, beaver, minks, muskrats, and other small **mammals.** All of Michigan has a huge, and often problematic, population of white-tailed deer, with the Upper Peninsula being no different. Of all the large mammals, this is the one you'll see more often than any other—often not until one of them leaps out in front of your car. The U.P. has some more uncommon mammals as well: a very healthy number of black bears, between 200 and 300 wolves, moose, bobcats, and cougars.

Some 300 varieties of **birds** live in the state, including such notable species as bald eagles, peregrine falcons, loons, swans, herons, and dozens of songbirds. Hunting for game birds such as ducks, geese, grouse, and pheasant is popular. Michigan lies on a major migratory pathway, offering excellent bird-watching in both spring and fall. Of special note is the hawk migration, as thousands fly between the southern Lower Peninsula and Canada.

With an abundance of water, **fish** thrive in both the Great Lakes and inland waters. Though commercial fishing has decreased dramatically in the last few decades (the result of overfishing and the accidental introduction of the lamprey eel and zebra mussel), sport fishing remains popular on the Great Lakes, especially for Chinook salmon, coho, steelhead, lake trout, and brown trout. On inland waters, walleye and yellow perch are prized for flavor, while the muskie and northern pike are considered a top sport fish. Bass, trout, and pan fish can also be found in inland waters. Michigan has several blue-ribbon streams, especially in the eastern U.P.

INSECTS

Michigan's Upper Peninsula certainly has its share of insects. The first hatch of mosquitoes usually occurs in early June, depending on local weather conditions. Their bite causes little or no pain, but will leave a small lump and an itchy reaction. Be aware also that some mosquitoes can carry communicable diseases. Malaria is nonexistent this far north, but infections such as West Nile virus have made national headlines in the past, so it'd be best to

take measures against bites. Mosquitoes can persist all summer, but tend to be less of a problem as the season wears on, especially if conditions are dry. Mosquitoes are most populous in low-lying wet areas and woods. Unfortunately, this accounts for a vast portion of the U.P. They tend to be most active at dusk. The best way to avoid them is to stay in a breeze and wear long pants and long sleeves. While many people will endorse repellent as an effective measure (with those containing DEET as the best), studies have linked it to several health risks. If you choose to use repellent, be sure to read the label warnings, wash your hands carefully before eating, and exercise particular care before applying it to small children.

Black flies can be an equally bothersome travel companion. They pose less of a health risk than mosquitoes but have a far more painful bite—somewhere between a mosquito bite and a bee sting on the pain scale. Black flies resemble houseflies, only larger. They tend to be worst in the deep woods and in early summer. U.P. black flies can be the stuff of legend;

anyone planning time in the backcountry would be wise to carry the strongest repellent available and to pack a head net. Even if you're not in the backcountry, black flies can make their presence known. If you come prepared, they're more irritating than problematic.

REINTRODUCTION AND MANAGEMENT PROGRAMS

Two of the Upper Peninsula's mammals are testimonies to the effectiveness of reintroduction and management programs. The **gray wolf** is believed to have been present in each of Michigan's counties at some point, but by 1910 they were relegated to just the Upper Peninsula. Before their reappearance in the 1990s, Michigan's last wolf pups were born in the mid-1950s, in the area of today's Pictured Rocks. Wolves were first protected in 1965, and were listed as endangered in 1973. Four of the animals were relocated to the U.P. from Minnesota in 1974, but none survived. However, in 1991 a pair of wolves produced the first pups born in the state's mainland in more

© JACK DEO, TRAVEL MICHIGAN

Thanks to preservation efforts, moose are once again flourishing in the U.P.

MICHIGAN STATE SYMBOLS

- State tree – white pine
- State bird – American robin
- State fish – brook trout
- State flower – apple blossom
- State gem – Isle Royale greenstone
- State stone – Petoskey stone
- State reptile – painted turtle
- State fossil – mastodon
- State soil – Kalkaska Sand
- State wildflower – dwarf lake iris
- State game mammal – white-tailed deer

than four decades. That population (estimated at about 20 animals in 1992) is believed to have descended from animals that wandered to the U.P. from Minnesota, Wisconsin, or Ontario. Although the wolf remains on the state's list of threatened species, there was a healthy population of more than 557 as of 2010, most of which inhabit the Upper Peninsula.

In the 1980s, **moose** were reintroduced to a remote area south of the U.P.'s Huron Mountains, with officials releasing a total of 61 moose from Ontario in two separate operations. Most interesting was the method of reintroduction: Wildlife biologists airlifted the moose one by one in a sling dangling beneath a helicopter to a base camp, from where they were trucked 600 miles to the Huron Mountains. Van Riper State Park in Michigamme has an interesting display with photos of the famous "moose lifts." The reintroduction worked, though not as well as hoped for. The moose population failed to meet the project goal of 1,000 animals by the year 2000. Today, several hundred moose roam the western U.P., and the population continues to grow.

The programs of wolf and moose management in the Upper Peninsula don't involve Isle Royale, where there are healthy, dynamic natural populations of both animals. A separate and ongoing study of the predator–prey relationship between the species on the island has been conducted for more than 50 years, the longest continuous study of its kind anywhere. Island populations rise and fall from year to year: At last count, the moose population was around 450, while the wolf population hovered at around 30.

TREES

There's a reason the **white pine** is the state tree. Vast stands of the magnificent trees once covered the northern portions of the state, making Michigan the nation's leading lumber center. Pines from Michigan rebuilt much of Chicago after the Great Fire and supplied a hungry nation as it expanded westward across the treeless plains.

Today, a few tracts of virgin white pine, red pine, hemlock, and cedar remain in the Upper Peninsula; magnificent species scraping the sky several stories above. Much of the U.P.'s original prime logging land is now second-growth pines, many growing tall again. Today's logging operations still clear cut, but in much smaller sections, and are increasingly shifting to selective cutting methods.

History

MICHIGAN'S NATIVE PEOPLES

Buried under layers of glacial ice until about 10,000 years ago, the land that is now Michigan was inhospitable to many of the native cultures that thrived in much of the Midwest, such as the Paleo and Archaic Indians. Some of the first signs of human civilization in Michigan can be found in the Upper Peninsula's Keweenaw Peninsula, where the Copper Culture Indians of about 5000–500 B.C. left evidence of their skill as prehistoric miners, devising ways to extract copper from bedrock and fashioning it into tools. Some archaeologists believe these people may have been the earliest toolmakers anywhere.

The **Algonquin** people migrated to the Great Lakes region from the banks of the St. Lawrence Seaway later, most likely after 1000 A.D. The Algonquin were divided into three tribes: the **Ottawa** (or Odawa), the **Ojibwa** (or Chippewa), and the **Potawatomi.** Together, they called themselves the **Anishinabe,** or "First People." They named their new land "Michi Gami," meaning "Large Lake." In and around that lake they found the state's abundant wildlife, including white-tailed deer, abundant schools of fish, moose, elk, and black bears, as well as rich natural resources that nourished the tribes for centuries before the arrival of Europeans.

The three tribes coexisted peacefully, each moving to a different area. The Ottawa settled around the Straits of Mackinac, Sault Ste. Marie, and the Leelanau Peninsula; the Ojibwa moved west, along the shores of Lake Superior; and the Potawatomi headed south, to the southern half of the Lower Peninsula. They communicated regularly, and their peaceable relationship proved valuable when invaders came to their lands. Together, they successfully fought off the warring Iroquois who came from the east in the 1600s, and they presented themselves as a strong, unified people when Europeans arrived.

THE FRENCH

Étienne Brûlé, the first European to arrive on the state's soil (in 1615), was more interested in exploiting the land than conserving it. Brûlé was sent by Samuel de Champlain, lieutenant governor of New France, who hoped to find copper and a shortcut to the Far East. Brûlé sent back reports recounting the land's untamed beauty and strange new flora and fauna.

Other opportunists soon followed. Some were after Michigan's rich supply of furs, others after the souls of what they saw as a godless land. Among the most famous of these early explorers was Father Jacques Marquette, who established the state's first permanent settlement, at Sault Ste. Marie in 1668, and a second outpost at the straits of Michilimackinac in 1671. The arrival of the French *coureurs de bois,* a loose term referring to unlicensed traders, provided a sharp contrast to the priests and nobility. Rugged individualists, they lived among the Native Americans, respected their customs, and hunted and trapped the region's rich stores of game.

Marquette's 17th century writings attracted even more settlers, mostly fur traders including John Jacob Astor. By the early 1800s, Astor's American Fur Company, headquartered on Mackinac Island, had made him the wealthiest man in the United States.

THE BRITISH

The area did not remain peaceful for long. As the fur trade became more lucrative, the British decided they wanted a larger share. The late 1600s saw British traders traveling from New York and across Lake Huron, finally arriving in St. Ignace. They began bartering their goods for pelts and, from the French point of view, interfering with the fur trade and threatening the alliances made with local tribes. Before too long, the intensity of the British and French animosity reached its peak, resulting in the French and Indian Wars in the mid-1700s. The

war effectively ended the 150-year French era, and in 1759 ushered in British rule. Occasional skirmishes between the French, British, and natives continued, especially around the Straits of Mackinac. In one of history's more exciting moments, a group of Ojibwa successfully raided the British-run Fort Michilimackinac in 1763 as part of Pontiac's Rebellion. Today, museums and historic state parks in the area chronicle the events.

The British ruled the colony with an iron fist. While the French had treated the Native Americans with a certain amount of respect, the British allied themselves with tribes that were traditional enemies of those native to the area. After Pontiac's Rebellion, the natives negotiated slightly better terms for their relationships with the ruling British, who made peaceable and necessary changes to some of their policies. The British actively discouraged settlement of the state's interior to protect their rich fur empire. In 1783, the Treaty of Paris gave the lands to the newly independent United States.

ON TO STATEHOOD

In 1825 New York's Erie Canal opened, which connected Albany on the Hudson River to Buffalo on Lake Erie. This new water route enabled more and more people to move westward and settle in the Michigan Territory. From 1820 to 1830, the population more than tripled to just over 31,000. In 1837, the burgeoning territory was awarded statehood, making Michigan the 26th state admitted to the Union.

However, most of the Upper Peninsula was nearly left out. Due to poor surveying at the time, the state of Ohio and up-and-coming Michigan were feuding over a 468-square-mile section of land known as the Toledo Strip. The Toledo War (a bit of a misnomer, as there was no physical fighting) ensued, and the dispute wasn't resolved until U.S. Congress awarded the strip to Ohio and gave Michigan the western three quarters of the Upper Peninsula in compensation, which otherwise would have likely gone to Wisconsin. It seemed like little consolation for Michigan, until the seemingly worthless frontier of the Upper Peninsula began to yield its mother lode of minerals during the subsequent copper and iron booms.

By 1840 more than 200,000 people had moved to Michigan. Early industries revolved around farming and agriculture, with lumber becoming a hugely successful enterprise by the later part of the century. Altogether, more than 160 billion board feet of pine were cut and hauled from Michigan's north woods by the 1890s—enough to build some 10 million six-room houses. While the southern part of the state grew increasingly civilized, the north woods and the Upper Peninsula became filled with wild and rollicking logging camps.

INDIAN REMOVAL ACT

In one of the saddest chapters in American history, President Andrew Jackson signed the Indian Removal Act in 1830, giving the U.S. government permission to "trade" Native American lands east of the Mississippi for unspecified lands out west. The federal government claimed it was for the tribes' own protection, correctly predicting that settlers would continue to surge into their homelands in the name of frontier expansion.

The Native Americans obviously had no interest in leaving areas that had been their homelands for centuries. For unknown reasons, tribes in northern Michigan and Wisconsin were largely ignored by the federal Indian Bureau at first. Most likely, it was because the federal government found their lands undesirable at the time. The Potawatomi, who lived on choice farmland in southern Michigan, were forcibly removed.

Unfortunately, the federal government didn't leave Michigan's Native Americans alone permanently. By the mid-1800s, treaties had "legally" confiscated much of the tribes' land in both the Upper and Lower Peninsulas and established many of the reservations that exist today.

The government of the new State of Michigan, however, did treat the tribes with a modicum of decency. In 1850, Native Americans were given the right to vote and even to run for office in counties where the

TWO STATES IN ONE

Is it a case of simple sibling rivalry or a marriage of irreconcilable differences? The relationship between the Upper and Lower Peninsulas of Michigan represents a true paradox. While the two Michigans are physically linked by a five-mile-long bridge, they remain a world apart culturally. Many Lower Peninsula residents dismiss the Upper Peninsula as a bug-infested backwoods filled with yokels. U.P. residents (who proudly call themselves "Yoopers") find the generalizations insulting, especially when those same Lower Peninsula people seem to enjoy the U.P.'s woods, wildlife, and beaches while on vacation.

The fact the two are joined as a single state is a historical curiosity to begin with. The Michigan Territory actually wound up with the Upper Peninsula as compensation pursuant to an agreement struck with Ohio in 1837. Both Michigan and Ohio had fought over the "Toledo Strip," a valuable port on Lake Erie. For Michigan to earn admission to the Union, Congress demanded that the Michigan Territory relinquish all rights to the Toledo Strip in exchange

for the "barren wasteland" of the Upper Peninsula. What seemed at first unfortunate for Michigan, however, proved to be a boon when priceless quantities of iron ore and copper were discovered just a few years later.

Much of the rivalry is good natured. U.P. residents like to joke about blowing up the Mackinac Bridge and are given to displaying bumper stickers portraying a giant U.P. with a tiny Lower Peninsula dangling from its eastern end. Yet there is a kernel of seriousness to the squabble. Upper Peninsula residents feel they pay state taxes to a distant state capital and receive very little in return, save for government-protected land and wildlife programs. From time to time, residents launch pseudo-serious drives to declare sovereignty from the rest of Michigan and create the state of Superior. As a musical group from Ishpeming, "Da Yoopers," satirically sings, "Dear Mr. Governor, you better turn us loose/ We asked you for some rest stops, instead you sent us moose/The honeymoon is over, the declaration's written/We'll take what's above the bridge, and you can keep the mitten."

population was predominantly native, a concession unheard of elsewhere at the time.

THE COPPER RUSH

In 1840, state geologist Douglass Houghton confirmed the presence of copper in the Upper Peninsula's Keweenaw Peninsula. These were vast deposits of pure, native copper, much of it right near or at the surface. The federal government acquired the western half of the U.P.—along with its mineral rights—from the Ojibwa in 1842, just as prospectors began flooding toward the wild and remote Keweenaw. The young United States had an insatiable appetite for the metal, first for new industrial machinery and later for Civil War hardware, plus electrical wiring and other innovations. Houghton's discovery was of virtually incalculable value.

The Copper Rush began almost overnight, first with prospectors, then with large mining

enterprises swarming the Keweenaw. Lucky prospectors secured deck space on Great Lakes vessels, sailing up Lakes Huron and Michigan, then along the southern shore of Superior. At the same time, hundreds of others straggled through the roadless wilderness, trudging overland through northern Wisconsin by snowshoe, or following rivers through thick forests to reach the fabled riches. It was the nation's first mineral rush. Copper employed thousands of immigrant laborers, built cities, made millionaires, and made possible extravagant luxuries like opera houses and "copper baron" mansions. Before it was over, King Copper had generated more than $9.6 billion in wealth—some 10 times more than the California Gold Rush.

The entire nation turned to the Keweenaw for its copper. From 1845 to 1895, the Keweenaw Peninsula produced 75 percent of U.S. copper; during the Civil War, it produced 90 percent. More than 400 mining companies

operated in the Keweenaw over the course of the 19th century. The resulting demand for labor drew immigrants from more than 30 countries, most notably the British Isles and Scandinavia. With multiple cultures sharing the same mine shafts and communities, Copper Country served as perhaps the nation's first display of ethnic diversity.

But virtually all the big mines closed by the mid-1900s, caused by depletion and poor economic conditions, leaving behind tattered houses and empty streets. They had extracted the most accessible copper. Soon after, newer mines in the southwestern United States and South America proved more productive and cost effective.

Economy and Government

ECONOMY

For almost two centuries, Michigan has been a microcosm of the country's great industrial transition. As the state's economy evolved from agriculture and fur trading to metals, logging, and, in the Lower Peninsula, automobile manufacturing, the state has ridden a rocky road of economic instability that shows no signs of ending.

Unfortunately, the severity of this downturn in the Upper Peninsula is much more pronounced. When the mines closed, many U.P. communities were left without a new source of jobs and income, leaving them a shell of what they once were. Driving through Escanaba's historic downtown, for example, it's almost impossible to ignore that the city is a just shadow of what it once was, and that its streets are an echo of more prosperous times.

Many of the small former mining towns are beginning to show significant wear around the edges, which contributes to their unassuming, small-town charm. At the same time, residents of the U.P. are not the sort of people to surrender during tough times, whether it's a particularly bitter winter or a persistently rough economy. In any case, the reason most people come to the U.P. is precisely because it's decidedly rustic. Don't let a few shabby downtowns distract you from the Upper Peninsula's remarkable beauty.

INDUSTRY
Logging and Mining

The Upper Peninsula's economy was long based on logging and mining. Great fortunes were made in logging in the late 1800s, as Michigan's vast stands of virgin timber produced enough wood to lay an inch-thick plank across the state with enough left over to cover Rhode Island as well. It can be difficult to gain an appreciation of the riches harvested from Michigan's copper and iron mines, each of which dwarfed the Gold Rush in California. Michigan produced more than $9.6 billion worth of **copper** and a staggering $48 billion worth of **iron,** in contrast to just $955 million produced from the Gold Rush. The riches and the miners disappeared as the most accessible deposits were exhausted and global economics began to play a role. Nearly all of the U.P.'s mines shut down by the mid-1900s.

Tourism

As the mines became less productive and more costly to operate, and as the U.P.'s lucrative timber began to thin, those industries gave way to tourism, which emerged as the U.P.'s most prolific industry, and its economic salvation. Mackinac Island already had a reputation as one of America's prime vacation spots, even before the iconic Grand Hotel was built. Today, the entire U.P. is capitalizing on tourism, successfully marketing its natural resources and recreational opportunities as its most attractive assets. *Midwest Living* magazine describes the Upper Peninsula perfectly, noting that "Deep woods laced with streams and waterfalls sweep across 300-plus miles of mostly wilderness, Michigan's northernmost

© PAUL VACHON

flags at the Governor's Residence on Mackinac Island

territory, and three of the Great Lakes almost surround it, inspiring four seasons of compelling outdoor activities."

Shipping

Just as tractor-trailers rumble down the interstate, commercial ships transport commodities across the Great Lakes. Officially designated as the nation's "Fourth Seacoast" by Congress in 1970, the Great Lakes serve as a vital transportation artery for much of the nation's commerce.

With its hundreds of miles of Great Lakes shoreline and deepwater ports, Michigan's Upper Peninsula is a key player in the Great Lakes transportation network. In addition, the Soo Locks which link Lakes Superior and Huron at Sault Ste. Marie rank as the largest and busiest lock system in the world.

Iron ore forms the foundation of the Great Lakes trade. In Upper Peninsula ports like Escanaba and Marquette, huge lake carriers (as long as 1,000 feet) load iron ore from nearby mines, then transport it to steelmaking

centers in the southern Great Lakes, which supply industrial manufacturers including the nation's auto industry. The Great Lakes fleet hauls up to 125 million tons of cargo each year, including more than 58 million tons of iron ore—nearly twice the "float" of any other commodity. Shipping is a highly economical method of transporting heavy and bulky commodities such as ore.

Great Lakes shipping is affected by global competition. Durable goods ranging from refrigerators to automobiles regularly arrive from overseas, which translates to a decrease in domestic steel production, which in turn reduces the need for iron ore shipments. Second, other transportation networks, such as trains and trucks, compete with shipping for certain commodities. Overall, however, shipping has proven to be a stable industry, with total cargo shipments remaining even over the last decade.

GOVERNMENT

During the early 20th century, Michigan was traditionally a stronghold of the Republican party. Beginning with the Great Depression, however, a competitive two-party political system emerged, as the Democratic Party made major inroads throughout the state.

Since then, parts of Michigan—particularly the Detroit area and most of the Upper Peninsula—have proven influential in determining the direction of presidential elections. Democratic candidates have carried Michigan during presidential elections since 1992 and have dominated the state's two U.S. Senate seats over the past 40 years.

But all this talk of Republicans and Democrats seems rather passé when compared to the Upper Peninsula's relatively recent and occasionally serious talks of seceding from Michigan to form its own autonomous state. It would be called Superior, clearly a reference to Lake Superior. Little has come from these efforts and it's likely nothing ever will. The movement was most popular back in the 1960s and 1970s, and occasionally lives on today in half-joking comments and a few satirical bumper stickers.

People and Culture

The residents of Michigan's Upper Peninsula today reflect a diverse background. The French "empire builders" were the first Europeans to arrive, and in due time the British replaced the French. Early American settlers included large and varied groups from western New York and New England. During the 19th century, immigrants from Europe came seeking a better life, particularly Finns, Swedes, Italians, and Cornish natives who worked in the Upper Peninsula mines and lumber camps. Many of today's residents are directly descended from those pioneers.

Today, Upper Peninsula residents number around 312,000, comprising about three percent of Michigan's more than 9.8 million citizens, making Michigan the eighth most populous state. According to the U.S. Census Bureau, the U.P.'s five largest cities contain about 20 percent of its people: Marquette's population is 20,780, Sault Ste. Marie's 14,000, Escanaba's 12,300, Menominee's 8,400, and Iron Mountain's 7,800.

NATIVE AMERICANS

In most books of Michigan history, the land's first inhabitants are given little more than a cursory nod, a line or two that identifies the approximately 100,000 early Native Americans as belonging to the tribes of the "Three Fires," the **Ojibwa, Ottawa,** and **Potawatomi.** The three tribes collectively called themselves the *Anishinabe,* or "First People." Another tribe with a significant presence in the Upper Peninsula during the 1700s was the **Menominee,** who lived in northern Wisconsin and parts of the U.P.

Today, Michigan is home to one of the largest Native American populations in the country, estimated at 50,000, many of them in the Upper Peninsula. Arriving at a precise figure is impossible, since the label of "Native American" or "Indian" can be defined in one of several ways: politically (tribal membership), ethnically (genealogy), or culturally (personal identification). Depending on the method used, Michigan may have the largest Native American population east of the Mississippi. Today, only a small percentage of these people live on reservations.

There are a number of reservations scattered throughout the peninsula, including federally recognized tribes in Brimley, Wilson, Baraga, Watersmeet, Manistee, L'Anse, Ontonagon, and Sault Ste. Marie, home of the Sault Ste. Marie Tribe of Chippewa Indians, the largest federally recognized tribe in the Great Lakes area. Of these, five are authorized to operate their own tribal courts, which exercise exclusive jurisdiction over certain laws involving Native Americans and events that occur on their reservations. Tribal courts have broad powers in matters involving child welfare and in a variety of civil matters involving tribe members and nonmembers when the activities in question occur within their reservations. In addition, Native American tribal councils throughout the state provide a variety of outreach services, economic development initiatives, and cultural activities.

Most reservations have cultural centers with museums or displays open to the public. Many tribes also host powwows (native dance ceremonies) and festivals. Check with local convention and visitors bureaus, or inquire at tribal headquarters, which are prominent and well-marked buildings on most reservations.

THE IMMIGRANTS

French fur traders, missionaries, and voyageurs were the area's first European settlers; they traveled Michigan's numerous rivers as early as the 1600s and established posts in far-flung areas across the state. Most of the area's European immigrants, however, didn't arrive until more than a century later, traveling from abroad in great waves during the early 1800s. Still more settlers came in the 1830s and over the proceeding two decades, in response to widespread famines in Europe.

The Lower Peninsula is home to descendents of immigrants from many foreign lands, including Holland, Germany, various African nations, India, the Middle East, and more. By contrast, the ethnic heritage of Upper Peninsula residents is considerably different. The iron and copper mines lured immigrants from Sweden, Finland, Italy, and Cornwall, England, with promises of steady work and decent wages. **Swedes** and **Finns** in particular took to the U.P., possibly due to the area's resemblance to their native Scandinavia.

There are still significant Finnish and Swedish influences in the U.P., including active Finnish- and Swedish-speaking communities. Finnish names, foods, and the ubiquitous sauna can be found throughout the Keweenaw Peninsula. The community of Hancock remains largely Finnish, reflected even in its street names. Some 16 percent of the Upper Peninsula population is Finnish, while the northwest Upper Peninsula represents the largest population of Finnish descent in the United States. Finnish influences can also be found in Marquette, while Escanaba reflects a noticeable Swedish character.

Arts and Entertainment

HISTORICAL MUSEUMS

Not surprisingly, many of the peninsula's museums cover the lore and legends of the Great Lakes and the state's maritime industry. Paradise, located near the eastern U.P.'s Whitefish Point, is home to the **Great Lakes Shipwreck Museum,** which includes artifacts from 13 shipwrecks, including an exhibit that features the bell from the *Edmund Fitzgerald,* the Great Lakes ship that sank mysteriously in 1975 and later became the subject of a hit song by folk singer Gordon Lightfoot. The museum does an excellent job of telling the haunting tale of the hundreds of ships that met their demise in the area's frigid, turbulent waters. Also in the U.P., the **National Ski Hall of Fame** in Ishpeming chronicles the downhill and cross-country versions of the sport, while neighboring Negaunee is home to the **Michigan Iron Industry Museum,** an excellent state-run facility on the site of one of the state's first iron forges.

ENTERTAINMENT

Due at least in part to its rural character, the Upper Peninsula lacks much of the cultural entertainment common in more populated areas: theater, music, dance, nightlife, and so on. However, several towns host summertime music festivals (the largest of which is the Pine Mountain Music Festival) featuring opera, symphony, and chamber music. These can be found at various locations across the peninsula each summer. You'll be able to find theatrical production and musical performances in the peninsula's college towns, particularly at Northern Michigan University in Marquette.

Native American Gaming

Gaming is a form of entertainment the U.P. excels in. As sovereign lands, reservations often are able to offer high-stakes gambling that isn't legal elsewhere in the state. Michigan's first Native American casino opened near Sault Ste. Marie in 1984. The Bay Mills Blackjack Casino originally had just 15 blackjack tables and one dice table in a 2,400-square-foot room located in the tribal center. Visitors promptly displayed their love of gambling, pouring tens of millions of dollars into casino coffers, initiating a gambling tradition that has escalated ever since.

There are several Native American casinos in Michigan, many of them in the Upper Peninsula. They range from small, simple gambling halls to sumptuous showplaces; many are open seven days a week, 24 hours a day, and have become enormous tourism draws. The Vegas Kewadin complex in Sault Ste. Marie

has added an interesting art gallery, which displays paintings, jewelry, and crafts by Native American artists. Not surprisingly, more and more tribes, many of whom live at or near the poverty level, are seeking to open their own casinos.

By the early 1990s, the state government decided to enter the picture. In September 1993, the state legislature passed and Governor John Engler signed the Tribal–State Gaming Compact, giving the state eight percent of net win income derived from games of chance. Contributions total hundreds of millions of dollars. While providing the state government with an easy source of funds, the success of Native American gaming has also given new power and influence to tribal governments.

While the pros and cons of gambling remain a matter of political and ethical debate, there's no arguing the positive effect gaming has on the reservations' economies. Within the tribal community, gambling provides jobs and funds schools, health care facilities, cultural centers, and other essential resources. Many overlook the significant economic benefits gaming provides to those outside the Native American community, as well; creating jobs for the building trades and the tourism industry. By all appearances, Michigan residents and visitors will never lose their determination in pursuing Lady Luck.

ESSENTIALS

Getting There

BY CAR

The only route to the Upper Peninsula from the Lower Peninsula by car is via the Mackinac Bridge on I-75, which is an exhilarating experience for most but a frightening experience for some. Tolls are $4 per passenger car in 2012, although tolls are slated to gradually increase until 2014. From Wisconsin, U.S. 41 will take you north of Green Bay into Menominee, while U.S. 141/U.S. 8 enters Michigan near Norway and Iron Mountain. Moving west, U.S. 45 connects with U.S. 2 at Watersmeet, and both U.S. 51 from the south and U.S. 2 from the west meet in Ironwood.

Visitors from Canada may take Highway 17 (the Trans-Canada Highway) to Sault Ste. Marie, Ontario, and cross the St. Mary's River via the International Bridge into the U.S. Passenger cars are currently charged a $3 (USD) toll. Please visit www.michigan.gov/iba for the latest information. Current international exchange rates are available at www.xe.com/ucc/.

BY BUS

Indian Trails (800/292-3831, www.indiantrails.com) is a Michigan-based company that provides regularly scheduled routes throughout the Upper Peninsula. Main routes go between Calumet and Milwaukee, Wisconsin, via Marquette and to St. Ignace and Ironwood

© PAUL VACHON

via Escanaba. Contact Indian Trails for current rates and schedules.

BY PLANE

Detroit Metropolitan Airport (DTW) (800/642-1978) is the state's hub for **Delta Airlines** (888/750-3284, www.delta.com), allowing you to fly to Detroit from virtually anywhere in the United States and connect to most of the Upper Peninsula's commercial airports, including Escanaba, Marquette, Pellston/Mackinac Island, and Sault Ste. Marie. Houghton is only accessible by way of Chicago.

Flights from Detroit are rather limited. Most airports have only one or two arrivals and departures per day. Contact your arriving airport to double-check flight availability and schedules. The major airports for U.P. destinations are:

- **Pellston Regional Airport (PLN)**
  U.S. 31
  Pellston, MI 49769
  231/539-8441
  www.pellstonairport.com

- **Chippewa County International Airport (CIU)**
  119 Airport Dr.
  Kincheloe, MI 48471
  906/495-2522
  www.airciu.com

- **Delta County Airport (ESC)**
  3300 Airport Rd.
  Escanaba, MI 49829

906/786-4902
www.deltacountymi.org

- **Sawyer International Airport (MQT)**
  225 Airport Ave.
  Gwinn, MI 49841
  906/346-3308
  www.sawyerairport.com

- **Houghton County Memorial Airport (CMX)**
  23810 Airpark Blvd.
  Calumet, MI 49913
  906/482-3970
  www.houghtoncounty.org

BY BOAT

Surrounded by hundreds of miles of shoreline, Michigan's Upper Peninsula is easy to enter via the Great Lakes, and visitors who do will find a high concentration of marinas. The Parks and Recreation Division of the state DNR has established a network of protected **public mooring facilities** along the Great Lakes, a "marine highway" which ensures that boaters are never far from a safe harbor. More facilities are being added every year, with the ultimate goal of assuring that a boater is never more than 15 shoreline miles away from a protected public mooring. Mooring fees vary. For more information or a free *Michigan Harbors Guide,* contact the Department of Natural Resources (DNR), Parks and Recreation Division (P.O. Box 30257, Lansing, MI 48909, 517/373-9900, www.michigan.gov/dnr).

Getting Around

BY CAR

Roads in the Upper Peninsula are plentiful, with most major arteries in good condition. Along with interstates and federal highways, the state is honeycombed with numerous state highways, marked on road maps by a number surrounded by a circle or oval. On road signs, however, state highways are identified by their official insignia, which is the number of the road centered within a white diamond.

In conversation, they are often preceded by an "M," as in, "Follow M-28 west to Marquette." County roads are marked with squares on most road maps, and may be designated "CR."

Two routes traverse the peninsula from east to west: M-28 is the northern route, passing through Marquette; U.S. 2 is the southern route, passing through Escanaba. If you're traveling from the eastern end of the U.P. all the way to Ironwood, M-28 is usually faster.

MACKINAC BRIDGE TOLLS

	2012	2013	2014
Auto/Passenge rVehicle	$4	$4	$4.50
Vehicles with trailers (per axle)	$2	$2	$2.25
Commuter	$2	$2.10	$2.20
Motor home (per axle)	$5	$5	$6
Truck (per axle)	$5	$5	$6

In 2013, the governing board of the Mackinac Bridge Authority will determine any possible toll increases beyond 2014.

Several state (and some federal) highways running north–south link M-28 and U.S. 2. These include, from east to west, I-75, M-123, M-77, U.S. 41, U.S. 145, and U.S. 45, among others.

When planning a route to or in the Upper Peninsula, consult your map legend regarding road surfaces. Roads you might assume are paved may be gravel or dirt, which can make for very slow going. All state and federal highways are paved and well-maintained,

as are most county and secondary roads. For construction updates, please visit www.michigan.gov/roadwork, or call the Michigan Department of Transportation's road construction hotline (800/641-6368).

Interstate speed limits in Michigan are 70 mph, unless otherwise posted. Most four-lane highways, and many two-lanes, now have limits of 65 mph.

For first-time visitors to the Michigan,

© PAUL VACHON

Cars are certainly the most flexible way to get around the U.P.

one of the most confusing aspects of driving the state's major roads is a type of turn only found here: the Michigan left. Ordinarily, no left turn is allowed at an intersection where a Michigan left is in place. Instead, to turn left onto an intersecting road, it's necessary to continue past the intersection and make a U-turn at the median crossover, double back to your intended street, and finally turn right. To turn left onto a major cross road, turn right, then make a U-turn at the median and continue on your way. According to the Department of Transportation, these turns serve to relieve congestion and reduce both the number and the severity of crashes. Crashes at intersections with a Michigan left have dropped 30 to 60 percent overall, enough to make one wonder why other states haven't adopted the the idea. Since these turns are usually installed at high-traffic intersections (and can only be used when at least one of the roads is a divided highway), there are relatively few in the Upper Peninsula, but they are present in some of the larger cities, particularly along U.S. 41/M-28 near Marquette.

There's a long-standing joke about Michigan roads that goes: "Michigan has four seasons: winter, winter, winter, and road construction." While certainly an exaggeration, the quip does refer to a perennial problem caused by the state's weather: temperatures swing from frozen to thaw and back to frozen, and the snows bring with them heavy snowplows, sand, and salt. These road surfaces go through quite a bit and deteriorate quickly, forcing the Michigan Department of Transportation works all the way from Easter through Thanksgiving to correct the problem.

Winter Driving

Michigan roads are generally very well-maintained in winter, plowed free of snow, then salted or sanded. While salt is more effective at melting, sand is less destructive to the pavement and to the environment. During or immediately after a storm, however, difficult or even dangerous conditions can occur, as road crews strive to keep up with conditions. County and city crews have a well-established protocol which prioritizes their attention. First preference goes to federal and state highways, major thoroughfares, and roads to schools and hospitals, followed by less vital routes. Minor roads are handled a bit differently, especially in the Upper Peninsula. A sign reading "Seasonal Road: Not Maintained in Winter" indicates the route is neither plowed nor patrolled. To check winter driving conditions before you travel, please call the AAA road conditions number, 800/337-1334.

If you're unfamiliar with driving in snow, drive with special caution; allow ample extra room between you and the car in front, and remember that stopping distances can be considerably longer. If you don't have antilock brakes, tap your brakes lightly in rapid succession to come to a stop. Do not stomp on them, or you'll lose control of your vehicle. If your car is equipped with ABS antilock brakes, apply steady pressure, and the system's computer will do the work. A four-wheel-drive vehicle will provide better traction, but not greater stopping ability.

Chains and studded snow tires are not permitted on Michigan roads. Many residents do switch to snow tires, which have a heavier tread. If you have a rear-wheel-drive car, adding weight to the back end can greatly improve traction. Bags of sand or water softener salt work well, with sand also being useful in getting a vehicle unstuck.

Bear in mind that ice is considerably more dangerous than snow, since it limits traction and stopping ability even more. Be especially aware of "black ice," pavement that looks wet, but is actually covered with glare ice. Watch for icy roads as rain turns to snow (called "freezing rain"), especially on bridges, which freeze first due to cold air circulating above and below the road. Ice also forms after a number of cars travel over a snowy surface, compressing it into an especially slick hard pack. This often happens on heavily traveled federal and state highways. On four-lane roads, the little-used left

HOW FAR IS IT?

For some unknown reason, visitors often think the Upper Peninsula is a small place. The reality is quite different. The long, narrow stretch of land is approximately 320 miles across and 125 miles between its northern and southern shores, which makes the drives between cities considerably longer than you might expect. Here's a handy guide giving distances between points within the U.P. and elsewhere.

Distance from St. Ignace to:

- Escanaba: 140 miles
- Ironwood: 320 miles
- Copper Harbor: 320 miles
- Marquette: 175 miles
- Sault Ste. Marie: 45 miles
- Detroit: 300 miles
- Chicago: 400 miles
- Toronto: 475 miles

Distance from Marquette to:

- Escanaba: 65 miles
- Ironwood: 145 miles
- Copper Harbor: 145 miles
- St. Ignace: 175 miles
- Sault Ste. Marie: 160 miles
- Detroit: 470 miles
- Chicago: 390 miles
- Toronto: 600 miles

lane usually looks snowier but may actually be less icy and less slippery.

Equip your vehicle with a shovel, sand (kitty litter works even better), and boots in case you get stuck. Throw the sand or kitty litter under the front tires for a front wheel drive car, the rear tires on a rear wheel drive. Keep the tires straight and *slowly* apply the gas—doing so excessively will only make the problem worse. Gently rocking the car forward and back, es-

pecially if you have someone who can push, works best.

Keep a flashlight, flares, blankets, and extra clothing in your vehicle in case you have to spend the night in your car. It could save your life. In rural areas, help may not always be at the ready. If you see a car stuck on a snowbank or in a ditch, be a Good Samaritan by offering a push or a ride to town.

Driving and Deer

Several million deer inhabit Michigan, posing a significant threat to drivers. Several thousand collisions between deer and motor vehicles occur each year, some of them fatal. In the U.P. alone, between 5,000 and 8,000 deer–vehicle accidents are reported annually, while many more go unreported. Deer behave erratically and will dart in front of your car with absolutely no warning, suddenly emerging from the woods or a roadside ditch. Be particularly alert at dawn and dusk, when they tend to be most active, and especially during firearm hunting season in November. Yellow and black "leaping deer" signs warn motorists of roadways where crossings are common, but they can appear absolutely anywhere.

If you see deer by the side of the road, slow down and prepare to stop. If you see a deer cross ahead of you, be especially cautious. Where there's one deer, there are usually several. If you do hit a deer, notify the nearest law enforcement office immediately.

Car Rentals

Rental cars are available at most commercial airports around the peninsula. Even in the U.P.'s larger cities, you'll generally be limited to the major companies like **National** (800/227-7368), **Budget** (800/527-0700), **Hertz** (800/654-3131), **Dollar** (800/800-3665), and **Avis** (800/831-2847). It is highly recommended you reserve a car in advance, as small locales have a very limited inventory. If you plan to do any exploration in the Upper Peninsula, ask about the rental company's policies regarding off-road driving. Some forbid

you to leave pavement, which can curtail your access to many U.P. sights.

ENTERING CANADA

U.S. citizens entering Canada are usually given little more than a perfunctory glance. Due to heightened national security, however, the traditionally lax rules at the Canadian border crossing have become significantly stricter. As of June 2009, a passport or an equivalent travel document is required (visit the U.S. Department of State's travel website at http:// travel.state.gov for a complete list of acceptable documents). You'll also be questioned briefly about the reason for your visit. Pets require proof of proper vaccinations; any plants will be confiscated.

Canadians will need a passport to enter the United States. For all other travelers, security can be surprisingly tight. Visit www.usa.gov/ visitors/arriving.shtml or www.dhs.gov/xtrvlsec for current information and requirements.

Unless you travel from Michigan to Canada by boat, you'll do so by road bridge. The toll bridge connecting Michigan's Upper Peninsula and Ontario is the International Bridge from Sault Ste. Marie to Sault Ste. Marie ($3). If you arrive by boat, you're required to check in at the nearest customs station immediately upon arrival.

Recreation

NATIONAL PARKS AND FORESTS

Michigan's Upper Peninsula is home to two national forests and a national lakeshore: the **Ottawa National Forest** in the western Upper Peninsula covers 982,895 acres; the **Hiawatha National Forest** in the eastern U.P. adds another 860,000 acres; and **Pictured Rocks National Lakeshore** extends along 42 miles of Lake Superior shore. **Seney National Wildlife Refuge** occupies 95,000 acres of cutover logging land in the eastern Upper Peninsula, while **Isle Royale National Park** is virtually a world of its own, a 45-mile-long wilderness surrounded by the waters of Lake Superior.

Even in the Upper Peninsula, where national land is highly valued, you'll find most parks (save for a few key attractions such as noteworthy waterfalls or beaches) are still notably secluded visitor destinations, yet they offer a remarkable quantity and quality of activities for anyone interested in the outdoors. **Hiking** trails tend to be little used. **Campsites** are more secluded, more rustic, and also lightly used. **Mountain biking** is permitted in most federal forest land, although forbidden in state or national parks. Inland lakes can be a little difficult to reach with a boat trailer, so they tend to be ideal for those looking for a quiet **paddling** experience.

Contact the national forest headquarters to receive information on hiking, camping, paddling, and other activities: **Ottawa National Forest,** Ironwood (E6248 U.S. 2, Ironwood, MI 49938, 906/932-1330, www.fs.fed.us/ r9/ottawa/); **Hiawatha National Forest,** Escanaba (2727 North Lincoln Rd., Escanaba, MI 49829, 906/786-4062, www.fs.fed.us/r9/ forests/hiawatha/).

STATE FORESTS

Like national forests, state forests are a hidden gem for anyone seeking a quiet corner of woods or water. Much of the state's forest land was actually acquired by default, picked up during the Depression when property owners were unable to pay the taxes. Their loss was certainly the public's gain. Much of the property is exceptional, consisting of rivers, waterfalls, lakes, beaches, and forest. Collectively, state forest land in the U.P. amounts to 3.9 million acres, the largest such holding in any state east of the Rocky Mountains.

Visit the **Department of Natural Resources (DNR)** website (www.michigan.gov/dnr) or contact the following offices to receive maps and

Conservation is the responsibility of every U.P. visitor.

information on Upper Peninsula state forest camping, hiking, and more: Copper Country State Forest, Baraga (906/353-6651); Escanaba River State Forest, Escanaba (906/786-2351); Lake Superior State Forest, Newberry (906/293-5131).

STATE PARKS

You'll see it written scores of times in this book: Michigan's Upper Peninsula has an outstanding state park system. They're well planned and well maintained, and showcase some of the state's most diverse and beautiful land. Some state parks were clearly set aside for public access—the state park beaches along the Lake Michigan shore come to mind—while others preserve historic sites and state jewels like the Porcupine Mountains and Mackinac Island.

The U.P. has 21 state parks and nearly 60 state forest campgrounds. **The Michigan DNR Parks and Recreation Division** (517/373-9900, www.michigan.gov/dnr) publishes a handy *State Parks Guide* that includes a map, a short profile of each park, and a chart listing each park's amenities. You can get much of the same information from the DNR website, www.michigan.gov/dnr.

As of October 2010, Michigan no longer charges daily entry fees for state parks. In their place the state has introduced the Passport Perks program. Under the new program, any driver with a car licensed in Michigan can purchase an annual pass for $10 ($29 for nonresidents), regardless of the number of passengers in the vehicle. The annual pass (issued in the form of a sticker placed either on the license plate or on the inside passenger side windshield) is valid for all Michigan state parks. Senior citizens can obtain an annual pass for $6, but only with a vehicle registered in Michigan. Participation in Passport Perks also allows the user to access discounts at businesses located near the parks. For more information, please visit www.michigan.gov/passport perks.

There is an additional fee for **camping,** which costs $6–9 per night for rustic campsites and $15–20 per night for modern campsites (with flush toilets, showers, and electricity),

depending on location. Some parks also rent "mini cabins," tiny shelters that offer you a roof and walls to protect you from the elements, but little more, for around $40 a night. These book up fast, so reserve yours well ahead of time. A few parks, including Porcupine Mountain Wilderness State Park and Craig Lake State Park, rent rustic cabins, equipped with bunks and a stove or other cooking facility, for $25–65 per night. They're great if you have a group or if you're visiting when bugs are particularly fierce. These are *extremely* popular; calling as early as January is advised.

For a $2 fee, you can make a camping reservation at any park in advance by calling 800/447-2757 or reserving online at www.midnrreservations.com. You can request a specific site, but it is not guaranteed. Camping reservations are highly recommended in summer months at many state parks. This book indicates if a park is particularly popular.

HIKING

With its bevy of national and state parks, national and state forests, national lakeshores, and private land accessible for public use, Michigan's Upper Peninsula has almost unlimited offerings for hikers. Where you go depends certainly on your taste. This book will give you numerous ideas.

For backpackers, Isle Royale National Park in Lake Superior is an outstanding choice, free of roads and other development. Rustic campsites along the way allow you to walk your way across the 45-mile-long island and water taxi services can get you back to your starting point. Slightly less remote, Porcupine Mountains Wilderness State Park in the western Upper Peninsula also offers great backpacking in a rugged backcountry environment not normally seen in state parks.

Michigan also has hundreds of miles of linear hiking trails, such as the Bay de Noc to Grand Island Trail, which bisects the U.P. And for those really looking for an adventure, the North Country National Scenic Trail traverses the Upper Peninsula as part of a national trail that, when complete, will stretch from North Dakota to New York. Many long segments of the trail crossing national forest land are already open to hikers in Michigan. Check with national forest officials for more information.

BICYCLING

With its rolling topography, shorelines, and ample country roads, Michigan's Upper Peninsula makes for a great bicycling destination. Some favorite areas for road riding include the quiet roads near Les Cheneaux and through the temperate Garden Peninsula. Check with local visitors bureaus for suggested routes.

Michigan leads the nation in its number of rails-to-trails, with 55 old railroad beds converted into multi-use trails. Some, like the Bill Nichols trail in the Keweenaw Peninsula, are very rough. Basically the rails were removed while everything else was left in place, including railroad ties and sharp old mining rock. Some of these more primitive trails are appropriate only for snowmobiles and all-terrain vehicles, although most are great for mountain bikes passing through wonderful wilderness terrain—especially the Bill Nichols venue.

Unlike much of the Midwest, Michigan is kind to mountain bikers. Good technical mountain biking can be found in many state and national forests. In fact, you'll probably find more miles than you could ever ride. Off-road riding in places like the Keweenaw and the Huron Mountains is the best between the Rockies and the Appalachians, and Michigan adds an extra perk—some stunning Great Lakes views.

SKIING

The Great Lakes churn out plentiful lake effect snows, which drop onto some of the Midwest's hilliest terrain. That convenient marriage has made the Upper Peninsula the top ski destination in the Midwest. While the area can't be considered truly mountainous, the resorts do an admirable job of working creatively with the terrain, carving out 600-foot vertical drops and runs that wind through the pines or offer spectacular views of the Great Lakes.

Though downhill ski areas can be found

throughout the peninsula, most are concentrated in the western U.P. from Ironwood to the Porcupine Mountains.

Cross-country skiers have even more to choose from. Though they don't all offer lodging, several privately run Nordic trail systems call the U.P. home. Many of the downhill resorts, such as Big Powderhorn Mountain in Bessemer, also have notable Nordic trails. The national lakeshores and many state parks groom trails for skiing, and the state and national forests offer virtually limitless opportunity for backcountry skiing.

For information on both downhill and cross-country skiing, contact **Pure Michigan** (800/644-2489, www.michigan.org/skiing).

GOLFING

The U.P. has plenty of top-tier courses, many which feature a diverse terrain of hills and water views that make for an extraordinary golfing experience. Drummond Island, Mackinac Island, and Marquette are home to some of the U.P.'s finest golf courses. Here, you'll find award-winners like The Rock at the Drummond Island Resort and Conference Center, The Jewel at the Grand Hotel on Mackinac Island, and Greywalls at the Marquette Golf Club. You'll find plenty of well-kept and challenging courses elsewhere in the peninsula as well. For more information, contact **Pure Michigan** (800/644-2489, www.michigan.org/golf).

BOATING AND FISHING

With an astonishing figure of 940,000, Michigan leads the nation in boat registrations. There are also an estimated 200,000–300,000 legally unregistered boats in the state, adding up to well over one million watercraft in the state. Michigan boaters cruise from port to port on the Great Lakes, sail along scenic shoreline like Pictured Rocks and along island chains, water ski on thousands of inland lakes, paddle white water rivers and quiet waters, and fish just about everywhere.

Small watercraft like day sailors, fishing boats, and canoes are readily available in many U.P. communities. Contact the local chamber of commerce or visitors bureau in the area you plan to visit for more information. For larger sailboats or powerboats, contact the **Michigan Charter Boat Association** (800/622-2971, www.micharterboats.com). The Pure Michigan website (www.michigan.org) also has an interactive travel planner that can provide you with a list of charter operations in a given region.

If you'll be hauling your own boat by trailer, the **Department of Natural Resources** (DNR, 517/373-9900, www.michigan.gov/dnr) publishes a list of public launch sites. A Coast Guard–approved lifejacket—known as a PFD, or personal flotation device—is required for each person on any kind of boat.

Michigan's Upper Peninsula is truly a paddler's dream. You can **canoe** down several national Wild and Scenic Rivers, **surf** waves along Lake Michigan's shoreline, **sea kayak** along Pictured Rocks or Isle Royale National Park or run white water. For mellow paddling, the Sturgeon River is a favorite. The U.P. also has several notable white water rivers, including the beautiful Presque Isle River and the Ontonagon. For more information on paddling destinations and liveries, contact the **Michigan Association of Paddle Sports Providers** (www.michigancanoe.com).

Fishing is extremely popular in Michigan, deeply embedded in the state's psyche. It comes in all seasons and styles, from fly-fishing along a pristine stream to relaxing in an ice-fishing shanty while watching a football game. The quantity of blue-ribbon trout streams is unrivaled this side of Montana. The Fox, the Chocolay, the Carp...you'll find most of the best ones in the eastern U.P.

"Deep-sea" charters on the Great Lakes go after the big Chinook salmon, coho, and lake trout. Lake Michigan's Bay de Noc arguably offers the finest walleye fishing in the state, if not all the Great Lakes. Inland, literally thousands of lakes harbor walleye, northern pike, muskie, bass, and pan fish. Some of the most popular spots are the Manistique Lakes chain and huge Lake Gogebic.

But the optimal level of solitude can be

boats in a small lake near Tahquamenon Falls

© SNEHIT/123RF.COM

found in the dozens of small lakes in the Ottawa and Hiawatha National Forests, which are peaceful, harder to get to, and lightly used. As a result, these waterways teem with fish. Some, like the Sylvania Wilderness, have special fishing regulations, so check with authorities. All Michigan waters require a valid Michigan fishing license. For specific fishing information, contact the **DNR Fisheries Division** (517/373-1204) or visit the DNR website (www.michigan.gov/dnr).

HUNTING

With its abundance of wildlife, forests, and undeveloped land, Michigan's long history of hunting continues as strongly today as it ever has. And when most people think about hunting in Michigan, the white-tailed deer tends to be the first creature that comes to mind. There are some 325,000 deer in the Upper Peninsula. Of these, hunters take tens of thousands each year. In 2010, hunters killed some 42,000 deer.

While the sentiment and sympathies of many people tend toward the deer, this annual culling of the herd helps prevent much larger problems, chief among them being deer–vehicle accidents and fatalities. When the statewide deer population peaked in the 1980s at about 2 million animals, signs of distress were seen in the herd. Animals were perilously underweight and in some places as many as 6 out of 10 fawns died. Some 125,000 animals starved to death during a single hard winter. Deer–vehicle accidents increased to 40,000 each year, killing an average of five people and injuring an additional 1,500 annually. Crop damage appeared and threatened significant economic damage as the urban and suburban deer population grew. Fencing, trapping, and birth control have proven far less effective in controlling the population than recreational hunting, which is the most efficient means of balancing the population and encouraging healthy cohabitation with human interests and the economy.

The DNR has spent many years trying to strike a balance between scientific herd management and other considerations to maintain

a healthy population, working with hunters and members of the agricultural industry to develop a mutually beneficial situation. The ideal herd size is around 1.5 million animals, with a buck population of approximately 35 percent. Hunting rules and regulations change frequently as management needs vary. Special hunting seasons are declared and cancelled as needed, and specific rules balance the number of antlerless and antlered (see below) deer that can be taken by each hunter. There are a number of general regulations, in addition to season-specific rules, which often change from season to season and year to year.

Hunting Licenses

No one can hunt in Michigan without the proper license. For state residents, this is a fairly easy and inexpensive process, costing $15 each for a firearm or archery license (allowing one buck during each season) and $10 for an antlerless license. Nonresidents will have to pay considerably more, at $138 each for firearm and archery seasons, and $100 for antlerless deer. It's a much steeper price, but given the abundance of deer and the quality of Michigan hunting, it's worth it. To apply for a license, residents need a valid driver's license or a State of Michigan ID card. Nonresidents need to obtain a MDNR Sport card, a type of Michigan ID allowing you to hunt, fish, and trap in the state. The cost is only $1 and can be ordered online (www.mdnr-elicense.com). Both residents and nonresidents born on or after January 1, 1960, must either present a hunter safety certificate or a previous hunting license, or must sign their license in the presence of a license agent. Hunters are required to carry the signed license and I.D. whenever hunting or trapping.

What type of license you get depends on how you like to hunt, and when or where you'd like to do it. Buck hunting regulations are different in the U.P. than in the rest of the state and vary depending upon the type of license purchased, so take your time and make sure you're buying exactly what you intend. Please note that any deer that has at least one antler

extending three or more inches above its skull is considered *antlered*. Any deer without antlers or with the longest antler extending less than three inches above the skull is considered *antlerless*.

You can buy a separate license for both archery and firearm season, which will limit you to only one antlered deer in the U.P. for all seasons combined. You can also use the archery license to tag an antlerless deer during archery season. The Michigan DNR also sells combination deer hunting licenses, which consist of a regular and a restricted license. In the Upper Peninsula, both the restricted and regular licenses have antler point restrictions. With the restricted license, hunters can take a deer that has at least one antler with four or more antler points, each at least one inch in length. The regular license can be used on deer with at least one antler with three or more antler points, each at least one inch in length. Both the regular and combination license can be used for antlerless deer in the U.P.

Deer are not the only animals hunted in the Upper Peninsula. Hunters can go after both black bear and elk, although there is a lottery system and drawing for each of these animals. There are also drawing systems for wild turkey, antlerless deer, reserved waterfowl, and special deer hunts. Rabbit and hare, crow, pheasant, quail, grouse, and squirrel can also be hunted in Michigan. Fur harvesters and trappers can hunt fox, coyote, badger, beavers, bobcat, muskrat, mink, and more.

Public and Private Land

The Upper Peninsula has seemingly endless acres of public land accessible to hunters. Contact the Michigan DNR for a comprehensive list of locations. In addition to public land, the state has purchased public hunting rights to select privately owned land, as well more than 2 million acres statewide of commercial forests. Hunters can also ask permission to hunt on private land. A verbal agreement from the landowner is all that's necessary. A few tips for asking: Get permission well in advance, and approach the door with only yourself or one

other person. Be certain to leave your firearm behind. If you can't visit the landowner, write a letter or email asking to meet in person or make arrangements by phone. Provide your name and contact information, the dates and times you'd like to hunt, and exactly where on the land you prefer to hunt. Ask if there are any prohibited areas, and respect any additional requests from the landowner, including party size limits, ORV limits, safety zones, etc. Leave the property exactly as you found it, or better. And always thank the landowner when finished.

Hunting Safety

It goes without saying that firearms and bows are deadly, so carry and use them with utmost care. The state has a strictly-enforced clothing requirement as a means of reducing hunting accidents: "You may not hunt with any device or trap with any firearm, on any lands during daylight hunting hours from August 15–April 30 unless you wear a hat, cap, vest, jacket or rain gear of highly visible orange color, commonly referred to as Hunter Orange." The Hunter Orange garment must be the outermost garment and visible from all sides. Camouflage items that have at least 50 percent or more of the surface in Hunter Orange are legal. There are a few exceptions. The requirements don't apply to archery deer hunters *except* when hunting during the youth firearm season and the November firearm deer season. Waterfowl, crow, wild turkey, and archery bear hunters are also exempt.

This information explains only the highlights of Michigan's complex hunting regulations. For complete information, please consult www.michigan.gov/dnr and choose "Hunting and Trapping." From this resource you can also request a print copy of all Michigan Hunting and Trapping guidelines.

BEACHES

The beaches of the Upper Peninsula have a completely different mood than most of the Lower Peninsula's sandy destinations. Often wild and windswept, rocky and remote, these coastlines remind visitors that they are definitely in "the Other Michigan." Striped cliffs rise directly from Lake Superior at **Pictured Rocks National Lakeshore;** nearby, the **Grand Sable Dunes** and **Twelve Mile Beach** provide enough sand to thrill even the most devoted beachcomber. You probably won't see many people along Twelve Mile Beach, but you may catch a glimpse of a deer, or even a black bear, headed to the water's edge for a drink. While perfect for long, sandy walks, only a hardy few actually swim in Lake Superior, as the water temperatures rarely climb out of the 40s.

The U.P. shares its southern shore with Lake Michigan, a winding border filled with secluded bays and inlets. A favorite of anglers, it also offers some good beaches—if you know where to look. Public access is a bit more difficult here. The best spots are along U.S. 2 from Naubinway to the Straits of Mackinac, where rest stops and county parks point you toward nice sandy beaches hidden behind the pines. You'll find another good sandy stretch along Green Bay between Menominee and Escanaba, where **J. W. Wells State Park** and several county parks offer several inviting beaches.

DIVING

A century ago, the Great Lakes were the highways of their era—the fastest and most efficient mode of transport. Commodities like lumber and iron ore were hauled from the forests and mines to Great Lakes ports; passengers traveled on steamships from urban areas around the southern Great Lakes to imbibe the fresh, cool air of northern resorts.

Of course, the Great Lakes also were known for shallow reefs and violent storms, which led to hundreds of shipwrecks. Additionally, the fresh, cold, barnacle- and worm-free waters prevented those shipwrecks from decaying. Today many sit on the lake floor, undisturbed and almost unchanged.

A century later, these freshwater time capsules are an unending source of delight for divers. Michigan has set aside nine areas where shipwrecks were particularly prevalent as **underwater preserves,** protecting their

historic significance and mapping and marking them for divers. Together, they cover 1,900 square miles of Great Lakes bottomland—an area roughly the size of Delaware. Off the shores of the Upper Peninsula, underwater preserves are located off the Keweenaw Peninsula, and at Marquette, Munising, and Whitefish Point on Lake Superior, as well as around the Straits of Mackinac in Lake Huron.

Most of the popular dive sites are marked with buoys in summer by volunteers of the Michigan Underwater Preserve Council. All the preserves are served by dive charters. For more information, request the booklet that describes each preserve and provides a list of dive charters and other services from the **Michigan Underwater Preserve Council** (560 N. State St., St. Ignace, MI 49781, 800/970-8717, www.michiganpreserves.org). You can also contact the chamber of commerce or visitors bureau near the preserve you wish to visit and consult the appropriate chapters in this book.

Accommodations and Food

LODGING OPTIONS

Michigan's Upper Peninsula is well served by most of the moderately priced national chains, but lacks the higher-end hotel groups such as Hilton or Westin. If you prefer staying in a chain establishment, pick up a copy of its national directory or consult its website to find current locations, rates, and services for its properties in Michigan. There's nothing inherently wrong with chains, but there are plenty of alternatives. All Michigan lodgings charge a 6 percent "use tax," similar to a sales tax. Many counties also have additional room taxes, ranging from 2 to 5 percent, to fund their visitors bureaus and other tourism related services.

Camping

Camping in Michigan's Upper Peninsula can run a very wide gamut. You can park an RV next to a pool with a waterslide, or you can pitch a tent in backcountry so remote you could go weeks without seeing another soul. Most of us would tend to seek out something in between. With tens of thousands of campsites in the state, you'll have no problem finding the option best for you.

This book lists many campgrounds, though it admittedly does shy away from highly developed RV-type properties. Many of the state park campgrounds are included, since they are almost universally good and often the best in a particular area. Some can get busy in summer

months, though. You can reserve one ahead of time (and even request a specific site, although it's not guaranteed) by calling 800/447-2757 or visiting www.midnrreservations.com.

State and national forests also tend to have excellent camping facilities; generally more rustic but located in appealing, isolated places. A directory of Upper Peninsula campgrounds is available from the **Michigan DNR** (517/373-9900, www.michigan.gov/dnr). Backcountry camping is also permitted in many forests and commercial lands owned by paper and mining companies.

For a complete list of private campgrounds, view a free *Michigan Campground Directory* at the Association of RV Parks and Campgrounds of Michigan website (9700 M-37 South, Buckley, MI 49620, 231/269-CAMP, www.michcampgrounds.com) or order a print copy for $3. You can also order a free *RV and Campsite Guide* from the **Michigan Association of Recreational Vehicles and Campgrounds** (2222 Association Dr., Okemos, MI 48864, 517/349-8881, www.marvac.org).

For help in selecting public or private campgrounds geared to your tastes and destination, check out the interactive Travel Planner on the Pure Michigan website, www.michigan.org.

Independent Motels

The combination of interstate highways and chain motels proved fatal to hundreds of

independently owned motels in the last few decades, as Americans proved their love for efficiency and predictability. Recently, however, the pendulum seems to be swinging the other way—interesting inns and distinctive lodges seem to be cropping up in the most unlikely places.

Many of these are traditional old mom-and-pop motels reminiscent of the 1960s—places with a neon vacancy sign and lawn chairs out front, the kind of places now romanticized along Route 66.

The good news is that they never really left the Upper Peninsula. Too out-of-the-way to attract the big chains, many U.P. towns still have several independent motels. They're still not fancy, and in some cases *can* appear tired and unappealing. But on the other hand, many mom-and-pop motels are clean, tidy, and remarkably inexpensive, and sometimes offer perks most national chains don't—allowing pets, for example. Additionally, they're often pedestrian-friendly, located in town or along a waterfront, rather than stranded out along a highway. Be aware that some do not accept credit cards, but if they don't, they will almost always take a personal check. Many are listed in this book, and you may discover many more. Don't be afraid to try.

Bed-and-Breakfasts

The Upper Peninsula has dozens of bed-and-breakfast inns. Some are the traditional, old-fashioned variety—a spare room or two in someone's quaint old farmhouse, but those have become the exception rather than the norm. Today's B&Bs run the gamut from large inns with amenities like pools and tennis courts to renovated lighthouses and other quaint historic buildings. For a Michigan bed-and-breakfast directory, contact the **Michigan Lake to Lake Bed and Breakfast Association** (888/575-1610, www.laketolake.com).

Ski and Golf Resorts

Several of the U.P.'s ski resorts double as golf resorts in summer, ringed with lodging that ranges from motel-style rooms to condo units and townhouses with kitchens, which allow you to save money by eating in. Many also offer a number of other amenities, such as pools, game rooms, and fitness centers, so they can be a particularly good choice for families with active kids. While golf resorts tend to be pricey, ski resorts that *don't* have the summer golf draw can be great bargains. For information on golf resorts and ski resorts with lodging open in the off-season, consult **Pure Michigan** (800/644-2489, www.michigan.org).

FOOD AND DRINK

Throughout the Upper Peninsula, many Main Street cafés and bakeries serve up the pasty, a potpie creation of beef, potatoes, onions, rutabagas, and other vegetables. (Pronounce it PASS-tee, not PACE-tee.) Brought to the U.P. by Cornish miners, the pasty made for a hearty and filling meal, one that was easy to transport deep into the mine and warm up later with their candles. The same concept works well today if you're headed from town to your campfire.

Another Michigan food well worth tasting

PASTIES

Prepare your favorite pie-crust recipe, making enough for four nine-inch pans. Then mix together:

- 2 pounds cooked pork and/or beef, cut into half-inch cubes
- 2 cups onion, diced
- 1 cup rutabaga, diced
- 1 cup potatoes, diced
- Salt and pepper to taste

Roll pastry out and cut four circles, using a nine-inch plate as a pattern. On one half of dough, layer meat, then onion, rutabaga, potatoes, and more meat. Fold pastry in half, then roll and crimp edges tightly together. Prick with a fork three times. Bake on a cookie sheet for one hour at 400°F. Makes four large pasties.

is its abundant fresh fish, from brook trout to Great Lakes whitefish. In Great Lakes ports, you'll often be able to find a commercial fishery operating a small retail store, usually down by the docks. They often sell both fresh catch and smoked fish. The latter is absolutely superb with a bottle of wine and a Great Lakes sunset.

Wine and Beer
There are relatively few wineries in the Upper Peninsula. **Threefold Vine Winery** (5856 NN Road, Garden, 906/644-7089, www.exploringthenorth.com/threefold/vine.html) in the Garden Peninsula is a noteworthy exception, due to its fortuitous location offering mild winters and temperate weather, excellent for grape growing. Instead, beer is the craft beverage of choice, at which a number of microbreweries across the peninsula excel. Among the best are the **Keweenaw Brewing Company** (408 Shelden Ave., 906/482-5596, www.keweenawbrewing.com) and the **Library Bar and Restaurant** (62 N. Isle Royale St., 906/487-5882) in Houghton, and **Hereford and Hops Steakhouse and Brewpub** (624 Ludington St., 906/789-1945, www.herefordandhops.com) in Escanaba.

Health and Safety

Every major city in the sparsely populated Upper Peninsula has a hospital, so you likely won't be too far away from quality medical care, unless you're deep in the woods.

CONTAMINATED WATER
There are a few hazards worth mentioning here. Even many of the most pristine Michigan waters may be tainted with *Giardia lamblia,* a microscopic organism most commonly transmitted in the feces of beavers, moose, and other mammals. It is present in many lakes and streams in the Upper Peninsula. **Giardiasis** can result in severe stomach cramps, vomiting, and diarrhea. As one Isle Royale ranger says, "It won't kill you, but it may make you wish you were dead." Neither chemical treatment with Halizone nor a water filter will make water safe from giardia. The safe alternative is a water purifier capable of filtering down to 0.4 microns or less. Boiling is also effective, but make certain to get the water to a full, rolling boil for five minutes. Isle Royale waters also may be infected with the **hydatid tapeworm,** also requiring purifying or boiling.

TICKS
Wood ticks and **deer ticks** are found in U.P. woods and grasslands. The larger wood tick, which is about a quarter-inch long, can attach itself to the skin and suck the blood of its victim. Despite this ominous-sounding fact, the insect is relatively harmless. If you find a wood tick on yourself, your companion, or your pet, grasp it as close to the head as possible and yank. Don't leave a piece of the animal embedded, as this can lead to infection. Ticks prefer warm areas of the body (human or canine)— the scalp, neck, armpits, or genitals. Check under your dog's collar and around its ears.

Deer ticks are considerably more dangerous. They may transmit **Lyme disease,** a potentially debilitating condition. Lyme disease shows up as a temporary red rash that often resembles a ring, which slowly expands outward. Other symptoms as the disease progresses include sore joints, fatigue, and nausea. If left untreated, it can lead to arthritis and severe neurological and cardiac problems. Caught early, antibiotics can treat it effectively.

Additionally, deer ticks are tiny—often hardly larger than the head of a pin. Like wood ticks, they burrow into the skin, especially in warm places. After hiking, check yourself and your hiking partners carefully. If it's large enough, grasp the tick and pull it like you would a wood tick, or use tweezers. If you've been in a tick-infested area, watch for a

rash within the next week and have anything suspicious looked at by a doctor promptly. Your best defense against ticks is to wear long pants and long sleeves and to spray yourself liberally with an effective repellent, such as those containing DEET.

Dogs are also highly susceptible to Lyme disease. Check your dog carefully and thoroughly for deer ticks by slowly running your fingers or a comb through her coat to get a look at the skin—a task that requires considerable patience from both you and your dog. Again, ears, necks, bellies, and genitals are areas most preferred by ticks. Signs that your dog may have acquired Lyme disease include nausea, fatigue, and lameness that may come and go from different joints. If you see potential symptoms, take your pet to a veterinarian immediately. Like humans, dogs respond well to antibiotics if the disease is caught early enough.

There is a canine vaccine for Lyme disease, but veterinarians are divided on how effective it is. There are some very good tick repellent sprays on the market intended for dogs.

BLACK BEARS

When it comes to bigger animals, deer are by far your biggest danger, as they cause thousands of accidents a year on Michigan roads. But black bears certainly seem more frightening, especially when you're deep in the woods. Black bears are found throughout northern Michigan, with the Upper Peninsula having an especially large population. They usually live in areas of heavy forest, but will routinely wander into open spaces, especially for berries and other food sources. They're beautiful animals, and you should consider yourself lucky if you observe one.

Black bears are generally shy creatures that would prefer to have nothing to do with you. If they hear you coming down the trail, they'll likely run the other way. If you happen to see one before it sees you, make sure you've left it an escape route, then clap, yell, or bang pans. Give especially wide berth to a mother with cubs. There are very, very few documented cases of black bear aggression against humans, and theories vary on what to do if you should ever find yourself in such a situation. Most behaviorists believe that, unlike grizzlies, black bears will be intimidated by dominant behavior such as shouting and waving your arms.

The worst problems occur when bears are lured into populated areas by human carelessness. It's always sad to see a bear relocated away from its home territory, but it happens frequently in campgrounds when humans don't properly store food or dispose of garbage. If you're car camping, keep all foodstuffs in your car (with the doors and windows closed and locked!). If you're tent camping, keep everything in airtight storage containers if possible, and suspend the containers on a line between two trees, high enough off the ground and far enough apart to be out of a bear's reach. Latched coolers placed under a picnic table are insufficient to keep bears out.

Clean pans and utensils right away, dumping the water well away from camp, and store them with the food. Never, ever keep any food (even gum) in your tent. Bears have an extremely good sense of smell and may be tempted to join you. Some say cosmetics also can attract them, so play it safe and store your soap and toothpaste with the food. You might want to leave your tent unzipped during the day while you're gone. Bears are curious, and if they want to look inside your tent, they'll make their own entrance if they can't find one.

If you're at a campground, deposit garbage in the animal-proof refuse containers provided. If you're backcountry camping, pack it out. Never, ever attempt to feed a bear, no matter how "tame" it may seem.

Information and Services

TOURIST INFORMATION

For general information on traveling in Michigan, your best source is the state-run **Pure Michigan** travel and tourism service (800/644-2489, www.michigan.org, 9 A.M.–5 P.M. Mon.–Fri.). Your call is answered by a real person who can send or fax brochures and consult a vast database to field your questions about events, lodgings, and a myriad of other topics. It's a much more helpful service than many tourism hotlines.

You may find it even more convenient to visit the state tourism database yourself, at **www.michigan.org.** This is a very comprehensive website, with an interactive menu that gives you specific information tailored to the parameters you set. Tell it you want to go charter fishing on Lake Superior in fall, and it will display a list of appropriate charters; click on each for a detailed description, rates, directions, and more. Currently, the site has categories for accommodations, attractions, camping, charter boats, communities, events, golf, restaurants, shopping, and skiing.

For information specific to the Upper Peninsula, contact the **Upper Peninsula Travel and Recreation Association** (P.O. Box 400, Iron Mountain, 906/774-5480 or 800/562-7134, www.uptravel.com).

The Michigan Department of Transportation operates seven **Welcome Centers** throughout the entire state. These facilities are stocked with travel literature and staffed with "travel counselors" who are quite knowledgeable about the state in general and their region in particular. The Welcome Centers are open year round.

You'll find Welcome Centers at major gateways to the peninsula and at a couple other "interior" locations. They're marked on the state highway map and with signs on the nearest highway. Hours vary.

BORDER CROSSINGS

You'll find this information elsewhere in the book, but it's important enough to bear repeating. Since 9/11, border procedures for traveling to and from Canada have become much stricter. The easiest approach is to make sure you have a passport. There are other acceptable forms of ID—a passport card, Michigan enhanced driver's license, NEXUS or other trusted traveler card, military ID, etc.—but it's best to simply pack your passport. Each vehicle is stopped at the border, where all of the passengers will have to present proper ID and answer a few questions. If you're traveling with a minor for whom you aren't the parent or legal guardian, you'll need a signed letter from the parent or legal guardian that grants permission for the child to leave the country and that includes a contact phone number. Travelers who aren't residents of Canada or the United States should have the proper travel visa and other documentation and be prepared for more extensive questioning.

You'll need to declare any goods purchased abroad, and you'll have to pay a duty on certain items (alcohol and cigarettes beyond those for personal use). If you're bringing firearms across the border for lawful sporting purposes such as hunting, make certain you have the proper paperwork and declare your weapon at the border. Failure to do so may result in your arrest.

MAPS

Michigan's official state road map is one of the few maps of the state that doesn't parcel the Upper Peninsula into frustrating and impossible-to-follow pieces. You can pick one up at a Michigan Welcome Center or request one from Pure Michigan.

For more detail, the DeLorme *Michigan Atlas and Gazetteer* portrays the state in 102 large-scale maps. Though the 15-inch-long format is unwieldy for hikers, it's a great resource for trip planning, and even identifies lighthouses, historic sites, waterfalls, industrial tours, and other points of interest. You can find it at many Midwestern bookstores for $19.95, or contact **DeLorme** (800/561-5105, www.delorme.com).

If you'll be exploring the backcountry; you're best off with an official topographical map produced by the U.S. Geological Survey. Michigan's national forests and lakeshores have topographical maps for sale at their visitors centers and ranger stations. Outside federal lands, you may find them (or other good detailed maps) in local outfitter shops, but don't assume it will. If you can, buy one ahead of time at an outfitter or map specialty store that carries topographical maps. If they don't have the one you need, they can help you look up its number and should be able to order it for you. You also can contact the U.S. Geological Survey (800/872-6277) for a free map index and order form.

TIME AND MONEY

The Upper Peninsula is located in the Eastern Time Zone, with the exception of the four Upper Peninsula counties that border Wisconsin. Gogebic, Iron, Dickinson, and Menominee Counties are in the Central Time Zone.

Visa and MasterCard are accepted throughout the peninsula, except for in some of the smallest towns. ATMs also are becoming more and more prevalent, tied into the national Cirrus network. That being said, there still are a number of mom-and-pop motels that accept only cash or checks. You might be surprised at how many small establishments are willing to take an out-of-town check, which they may prefer over credit cards. Cash is needed at self-registration campgrounds. As any wise traveler knows, never count on getting by with only plastic.

If you're traveling to or from Canada, you'll find currency exchanges at the border and at nearby banks in both countries. In the past Canadian and U.S. money was accepted interchangeably border areas, especially coins. In recent years, however, exchange rates have fluctuated dramatically. Plan to exchange currencies when traveling in either direction.

If you're a U.S. resident with Canadian currency left over at the end of a trip, it's best to have bills, not coins. Many banks (especially away from border areas) will exchange only paper money.

EMERGENCIES

All of Michigan's Upper Peninsula is tied into the 911 emergency system. Dial 911 for free from any telephone (including pay phones) to reach an operator who can quickly dispatch local police, fire, or ambulance services. This service also works from cellular phones. Be aware, however, that cell towers can be few and far between in rural areas. Much of the Upper Peninsula remains without reliable cellular or digital wireless service, but this can vary from carrier to carrier.

Hospitals

In case you need it, here's a listing of a few of the region's major hospitals: **Mackinac Straits Hospital** (220 Burdette St., St. Ignace, MI 49781, 906/643-8585, www.mshosp.org), **Marquette General Health System** (580 W. College Ave., Marquette, MI 49855, 906/228-9440, www.mgh.org), and **War Memorial Hospital** (500 Osborn Blvd., Sault St. Marie, MI 49783, 906/635-4460, www.warmemorialhospital.org). Most of the Upper Peninsula's larger cities have hospitals and emergency medical care.

RESOURCES

Suggested Reading

ATLASES

DeLorme. *Michigan Atlas and Gazetteer.* Yarmouth, ME: DeLorme, 2006. Covering everything from major highways and byways to the back roads, this is one of the most detailed atlases you can find. Topographical maps and GPS grids are included.

Sportsman's Connection. *Northern Michigan All-Outdoors Atlas and Field Guide.* Superior, WI: Sportsman's Connection, 2008. Detailed maps, supplemental information, and helpful advice make this a must-have atlas for anyone who wants to spend any amount of time in Michigan's outdoors.

FICTION

Harrison, Jim. *True North.* New York: Grove, 2004. Best known as the author of *Legends of the Fall,* Michigan native Harrison tells the story of a wealthy, dysfunctional family with the Upper Peninsula's harsh landscape as the backdrop. A tragedy, the book can be shocking and dark, but filled with beauty.

Hemingway, Ernest. *The Nick Adams Stories.* New York: Scribner, 1972. Hemingway's semiautobiographical account tells the story of Nick Adams as his life progresses from soldier to veteran, writer, and parent.

Monson, Ander. *Other Electricities.* Louisville, KY: Sarabande, 2005. Raised in the U.P., Monson presents a melancholic vision of his native peninsula through this critically acclaimed collection of stories and lists. Highly recommended.

Traver, Robert. *Anatomy of a Murder.* New York: St. Martin's Press, 1983. This immensely popular novel was penned by author Robert Traver (a.k.a. state Supreme Court Justice John Voelker), about an actual love triangle murder that took place in Big Bay. The gripping novel was made into a feature-length film by legendary director Otto Preminger in 1959.

GENERAL INTEREST

Emerick, Lon L. *The Superior Peninsula: Seasons in the Upper Peninsula of Michigan.* Skandia, MI: North Country, 1996. A collection of essays about and "love letters" to the big lake and its peninsula, categorized by season.

Peterson, Carolyn C., *A View From the Wolf's Eye.* Calumet, MI: Copper Island Printing Co., 2008. The personal account of a woman who with her husband worked on Isle Royale for 37 summers conducting the ongoing study of the moose–wolf relationship while raising a family at the same time. An intimate account of nature from the perspective of one of its custodians.

Peterson, Rolf O. *The Wolves of Isle Royale: A Broken Balance.* Ann Arbor, MI: University of Michigan, 2007. Internationally known wolf researcher Peterson has compiled a first-hand account of Isle Royale National Park's

ongoing wolf study. A delightful, informative book, it's filled with personal stories and powerful images.

Stonehouse, Frederick. *The Wreck of the Edmund Fitzgerald.* Marquette, MI: Lake Superior Press, 1997. A thorough and thoughtful analysis of one of the most tragic disasters to occur on the Great Lakes. While offering no firm opinions, the author discusses the events leading up to this famous shipwreck and the various theories of what caused its demise.

Traver, Robert. *Trout Magic.* New York: Simon and Schuster, 1989. Personal reflections on the pleasures and solitude of trout fishing from accomplished author Robert Traver, better known as Justice John Voelker.

NATURAL HISTORY

Acorn, John, and Gregory Kennedy. *Birds of Michigan.* Auburn, WA: Lone Pine, 2003. More than 300 of the state's birds are identified in this color-coded, well-organized book that's immediately accessible to casual and passionate birders alike. Filled with beautiful, clear, color illustrations.

Grady, Wayne. *The Great Lakes: The Natural History of a Changing Region.* Vancouver: Greystone, 2007. A wonderfully illustrated natural history of the lakes, the author shares fascinating information on the formation of the lakes as well as their ecology and biology in the present era. Part written history, part photographic record, this book would be a beautiful and informative addition to any coffee table in the Great Lakes region.

Isle Royale Natural History Association. *Island Life: An Isle Royale Nature Guide.* Hancock, MI: Book Concern Printers, 2007. A comprehensive reference to the flora and fauna of Isle Royale in small paperback form. Excellent companion for a fishing or camping trip.

Kershaw, Linda. *Trees of Michigan.* Auburn, WA: Lone Pine, 2006. This is *the* guide for tree identification in Michigan. Nearly 300 species of trees referenced here, with color photographs and illustrations of the bark, leaves, flowers, and overall shape of each tree. Tips are included for distinguishing between similar species.

OUTDOOR RECREATION

DuFresne, Jim. *Isle Royale National Park: Foot Trails and Water Routes.* MichiganTrailMaps. com, 2011 (fourth ed.). The definitive guide to Isle Royale, filled with practical information about campsites, portages, fishing spots, and more. Small enough to carry along, as you should.

DuFresne, Jim. *Michigan State Parks: A Complete Recreation Guide.* Seattle: The Mountaineers, 1998. Michigan outdoor writer DuFresne worked with the Michigan Department of Natural Resources to compile this handy guide, which devotes a couple pages to each of Michigan's state parks.

DuFresne, Jim. *Porcupine Mountains Wilderness State Park: A Backcountry Guide for Hikers, Backpackers, Campers, and Winter Visitors.* San Diego: Thunder Bay Press, 2009. An indispensable guide to this mammoth, beautiful park, DuFresne offer extensive coverage to the park's trail system, for both day hikers and backpackers.

Hansen, Eric. *Hiking Michigan's Upper Peninsula.* Guilford, CT: Falcon, 2005. Hansen set out to hike and map 50 of the Upper Peninsula's finest trails, many of them little-known gems. His work is magnificently displayed in this book.

Hillstrom, Kevin and Laurie Collier Hillstrom. *Paddling Michigan.* Guilford, CT: Falcon, 2001. This extensive paddling guide predominantly covers routes and rivers in the Upper Peninsula but also includes some Lower Peninsula waterways.

Suggested Viewing and Listening

SUGGESTED VIEWING

Anatomy of a Murder, 1959. Based on the novel by local state Supreme Court Justice John Voelker, this film starring Jimmy Stewart and George C. Scott was inspired by real events and was filmed in Big Bay and Marquette.

Escanaba in da Moonlight, 2001. Starring, written by, and directed by Jeff Daniels, this offbeat comedy has taken some heat for its portrayal of the residents of Escanaba. Some people claim it's spot on. With a strange plot and a good deal of off-color humor, this film isn't for everyone, but many find it enjoyable.

Somewhere in Time, 1980. While not a classic, this film has acquired a cult following and a reputation as a timeless love story. Its stars, Jane Seymour and Christopher Reeve, are overshadowed only by the Grand Hotel and the Mackinac Island setting.

SUGGESTED LISTENING

Stevens, Sufjan. *Greetings From Michigan: The Great Lakes State,* 2003. When Michigan native Sufjan Stevens released his indie ode to Michigan, people everywhere began to pay attention to Michigan's geography and history. Pay special attention to songs set in the Upper Peninsula, including "For the Widows in Paradise, For the Fatherless in Ypsilanti," "The Upper Peninsula," "Tahquamenon Falls," "Sleeping Bear, Sault Saint Marie," and "Oh God, Where Are You Now? (In Pickerel Lake? Pigeon? Marquette? Mackinaw?)."

Lightfoot, Gordon. "The Wreck of the *Edmund Fitzgerald,*" 1976. From the album Summertime Dream, Gordon Lightfoot's folk retelling of the tragic sinking of the *Edmund Fitzgerald* during a Lake Superior storm immortalized the accident in popular memory.

Internet Resources

STATEWIDE INFORMATION
Travel Michigan
www.michigan.org
Michigan's official travel website is an integral part of the state's Pure Michigan tourism campaign. It's the most visited state tourism site in the United States.

Upper Peninsula Travel and Recreation Association
www.uptravel.com
Upper Peninsula–specific tourism information and numerous helpful links. Request the free (and indispensable) travel planner.

OUTDOOR RECREATION AND CAMPING
Michigan Department of Natural Resources
www.michigan.gov/dnr
The site for state park info, campground reservations, and information on all sorts of outdoor recreation, including fishing, hunting, and snowmobile registration.

Michigan Interactive
www.fishweb.com
A great resource for all sorts of outdoor activities in Michigan, including interactive maps for fishing, hiking, and snowmobile and off-road vehicle trails.

National Park Service
www.nps.gov
Official one-stop shopping for all of the national parks in the U.P.: Isle Royale, Keweenaw, and Pictured Rocks—plus the North Country National Scenic Trail.

U.S. Forest Service
www.fs.fed.us
Go here for information about both the Hiawatha and Ottawa National Forests.

TRANSPORTATION
Michigan Department of Transportation
www.michigan.gov/mdot
The best, most up-to-date source for information on tolls, Michigan lefts, lane closures, and various public transportation options.

WEATHER
Weather Michigan
www.weathermichigan.com
An easy-to-use collection of Michigan-related weather links, all in one place.

Tourist Information

Bays de Noc Convention and Visitors Bureau
230 Ludington Street
Escanaba, MI 49829
906/789-7862
800/533-4386
www.travelbaysdenoc.com

Delta County Area Chamber of Commerce
230 Ludington Street
Escanaba, MI 49829
906/786-2192
888/335-8264
www.deltami.org

Drummond Island Tourism Association
P.O. Box 200
Drummond Island, MI 49726
906/493-5245
800/737-8666
www.drummondislandchamber.com

Ironwood Chamber of Commerce
150 North Lowell Street
Ironwood, MI 49938
906/932-1122
www.ironwoodmi.org

Keweenaw Convention and Visitors Bureau
56638 Calumet Avenue
Calumet, MI 49913
906/337-4579
800/338-7982
www.keweenaw.info

Les Cheneaux Tourist Association
P.O. Box 10
670 West M-134
Cedarville, MI 49719
888/364-7526
www.lescheneaux.org

Mackinac Island Tourism Bureau
P.O. Box 451
Mackinac Island, MI 49757
877/847-0086
www.mackinacisland.org

Mackinaw Area Visitors Bureau
10800 West U.S. 23
Mackinaw City, MI 49701
231/436-5664
800/666-0160
www.mackinawcity.com

Manistique Tourism Council
800/342-4282
www.visitmanistique.com

**Marinette/Menominee Area
Chamber of Commerce**
601 Marinette Avenue
Marinette, WI 54143
Menominee, MI 49858
906/863-2679
715/735-6681
www.marinettechamber.com

**Marquette Country Convention
and Visitors Bureau**
337 West Washington Street
Marquette, MI 49855
906/228-7749
800/544-4321
www.marquettecountry.org

Newberry Area Tourism Association
P.O. Box 308
Newberry, MI 49868
906/293-5562
800/831-7292
www.newberrytourism.com

**Paradise, Michigan,
Chamber of Commerce**
P.O. Box 82
Paradise, MI 49768

906/492-3219
www.paradisemichigan.org

**Sault Ste. Marie Convention
and Visitors Bureau**
536 Ashmun Street
Sault Ste. Marie, MI 49783
906/632-3366
800/647-2858
www.saultstemarie.com

St. Ignace Visitors Bureau
6 Spring Street, Suite 100
St. Ignace, MI 49781
800/338-6660
www.stignace.com

**Tourism Association of the
Dickinson County Area**
600 South Stephenson Avenue
Iron Mountain, MI 49801
800/236-2447
www.ironmountain.org

**Western U.P. Convention
and Visitors Bureau**
P.O. Box 706
Ironwood, MI 49938
906/932-4850
800/522-5657
www.westernup.info

Index

List of Maps

Acknowledgments

Capturing the splendor of Michigan's Upper Peninsula was made easier by the invaluable assistance of the staff at Avalon. Despite being three times zones away, their cheerful attitude and quick responsiveness made me feel like they were just down the street! I want to express my sincere gratitude to Jamie Andrade, Kat Bennett, Lucie Ericksen, Kathryn Ettinger, and Kevin McLain for their high level of professionalism. My thanks also to Acquisitions Director Grace Fujimoto and Publishing Assistant Sierra Machado.

www.moon.com

DESTINATIONS | ACTIVITIES | BLOGS | MAPS | BOOKS

MOON.COM is ready to help plan your next trip! Filled with fresh trip ideas and strategies, author interviews, informative travel blogs, a detailed map library, and descriptions of all the Moon guidebooks, Moon.com is all you need to get out and explore the world—or even places in your own backyard. While at Moon.com, sign up for our monthly e-newsletter for updates on new releases, travel tips, and expert advice from our on-the-go Moon authors. As always, when you travel with Moon, expect an experience that is uncommon and truly unique.

KEEP UP WITH MOON ON FACEBOOK AND TWITTER
JOIN THE MOON PHOTO GROUP ON FLICKR

MAP SYMBOLS

▦ Expressway	◖ Highlight	✕ Airfield	⚲ Golf Course
▦ Primary Road	○ City/Town	✈ Airport	▯ Parking Area
▦ Secondary Road	◉ State Capital	▲ Mountain	⛏ Archaeological Site
- - - - Unpaved Road	⊛ National Capital	✚ Unique Natural Feature	⛪ Church
------ Trail	★ Point of Interest		
·········· Ferry	• Accommodation	≈ Waterfall	⛽ Gas Station
▦ Railroad	▼ Restaurant/Bar	▲ Park	⬭ Glacier
▦ Pedestrian Walkway	■ Other Location	⬒ Trailhead	▨ Mangrove
▥ Stairs	Δ Campground	⛷ Skiing Area	▨ Reef
			▨ Swamp

CONVERSION TABLES

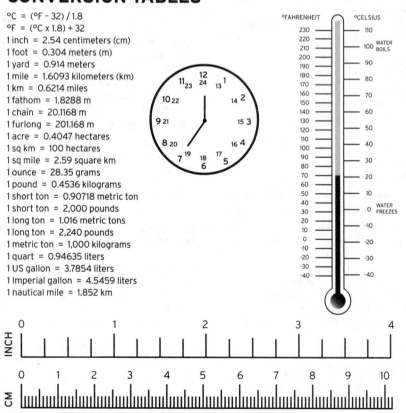

°C = (°F - 32) / 1.8
°F = (°C x 1.8) + 32
1 inch = 2.54 centimeters (cm)
1 foot = 0.304 meters (m)
1 yard = 0.914 meters
1 mile = 1.6093 kilometers (km)
1 km = 0.6214 miles
1 fathom = 1.8288 m
1 chain = 20.1168 m
1 furlong = 201.168 m
1 acre = 0.4047 hectares
1 sq km = 100 hectares
1 sq mile = 2.59 square km
1 ounce = 28.35 grams
1 pound = 0.4536 kilograms
1 short ton = 0.90718 metric ton
1 short ton = 2,000 pounds
1 long ton = 1.016 metric tons
1 long ton = 2,240 pounds
1 metric ton = 1,000 kilograms
1 quart = 0.94635 liters
1 US gallon = 3.7854 liters
1 Imperial gallon = 4.5459 liters
1 nautical mile = 1.852 km

MOON MICHIGAN'S UPPER PENINSULA

Avalon Travel
a member of the Perseus Books Group
1700 Fourth Street
Berkeley, CA 94710, USA
www.moon.com

Editors: Kathryn Ettinger, Jamie Andrade,
  Kevin McLain
Series Manager: Kathryn Ettinger
Copy Editor: Maura Brown
Graphics Coordinator: Kathryn Osgood
Production Coordinators: Lucie Ericksen,
  Apollo Publishing Services
Cover Designer: Lucie Ericksen
Map Editor: Kat Bennett
Cartographers: Chris Hendrick, Kaitlin Jaffe,
  Heather Sparks
Proofreaders: Jessica Garcia, Sabrina Young
Indexer: Rachel Kuhn

ISBN-13: 978-1-61238-136-7
ISSN: 1946-312X

Printing History
1st Edition – 2009
2nd Edition – June 2012
5 4 3 2 1

Text © 2012 by Avalon Travel.
Maps © 2012 by Avalon Travel.
All rights reserved.

Some photos and illustrations are used by permission and are the property of the original copyright owners.

Front cover photo: small waterfall along the edge of Lake Superior, Pictured Rocks National Seashore, Michigan's Upper Peninsula © Stephen Matera/DanitaDelimont.com
Title page photo: Sunset at Pictured Rock National Lakeshore © Rudolf Balasko/123rf.com
Interior color photos: pgs. 4, 7 top left & right, 14 top, 15, 16, 19, 21 top: © Paul Vachon; pg. 5 left: 123rf.com; pg. 5 middle: © Vito Palmisano, Travel Michigan; pg. 6 small: © Maciej Maksymowicz/123rf.com; pg. 6 bottom: © Michigannut/Dreamstime.com, pg. 7 bottom left: © Dean Pennala/Dreamstime.com, pg. 7 bottom right © James Phelps/123rf.com; pgs. 8, 10, 18 top: © Jason Ross/123rf.com; pg. 9: © snehit/123rf.com; pg. 11: © Jeffrey Foltice, Travel Michigan; pg. 12: © Bonita Cheshier/Dreamstime.com; pg. 14 bottom: © bigstock.com; pg. 17: © Michael Thompson/dreamstime.com; pg. 18 bottom: © John Shibley, Lake Superior State University; pg. 20: © Mark G. Mittlestat; pg. 21 bottom: © Paul Lemke/Dreamstime.com; pg. 22: © Angela Nebel, Summit Public Relations Strategies; pg. 23 top © Michael G Smith/123rf.com; pg. 23 bottom: © Sault Ste. Marie Convention & Visitors Bureau; pg. 24: © Tom Buchkoe, Travel Michigan

Printed in Canada by Friesens

KEEPING CURRENT

If you have a favorite gem you'd like to see included in the next edition, or see anything that needs updating, clarification, or correction, please drop us a line. Send your comments via email to feedback@moon.com, or use the address above.